A Longman Cultural Edition

PERCY BYSSHE SHELLEY

Edited by

Stephen C. Behrendt
University of Nebraska

Longman
New York   San Francisco   Boston
London   Toronto   Sydney   Tokyo   Singapore   Madrid
Mexico City   Munich   Paris   Cape Town   Hong Kong   Montreal

Senior Sponsoring Editor: Virginia L. Blanford
Editorial Assistant: Rosie Ellis
Executive Marketing Manager: Joyce Nilsen
Production Coordinator: Scarlett Lindsay
Project Coordination, Text Design, and Electronic Page Makeup: Grapevine
   Publishing Services, Inc.
Senior Cover Designer/Manager: Nancy Danahy
Cover Art: © Walker Art Gallery, National Museums, Liverpool
Senior Manufacturing Buyer: Roy L. Pickering, Jr.
Photo Researcher: Ilene Bellovin
Printer and Binder: Courier Corporation / Westford
Cover Printer: The Lehigh Press, Inc. / Hagerstown

Library of Congress Cataloging-in-Publication Data

Shelley, Percy Bysshe, 1792–1822.
   [Selections. 2009]
   Percy Bysshe Shelley / edited by Stephen C. Behrendt.
      p. cm. — (A Longman cultural edition)
   Includes bibliographical references.
   ISBN-13: 978-0-321-20210-9
   ISBN-10: 0-321-20210-4
   I. Behrendt, Stephen C., 1947. II. Title.

PR5403.B44 2009
821'.7—dc22

                                                                    2008043344

1 2 3 4 5 6 7 8 9 10—CRW—12 11 10 09

Longman
is an imprint of

ISBN 13: 978-0-321-20210-9
ISBN 10:   0-321-20210-4

www.pearsonhighered.com

Contents

List of Illustrations

Cover. Louis Edouard Fournier, *The Funeral of Shelley*, 1889 (oil on canvas), © Walker Art Gallery, National Museums, Liverpool.

p. xxviii. Percy B. Shelley. From an original picture in the possession of Mrs. Shelley. Engraved William Finden, 1787–1852 from a painting by Amelia Curran. Humanities and Social Sciences Library / Henry W. and Albert A. Berg Collection of English and American Literature, New York Public Library.

p. 60. Page from *The Examiner*, 1818; University of Iowa Libraries.

p. 76. *The Massacre of Peterloo*, political cartoon about public demonstration agitating for parliamentary reform at St Peter's Fields, Manchester, on August 16, 1819. The authorities panicked and in an attempt to arrest organizer Henry Hunt, 11 were killed and over 400 injured. The Art Archive. Ref: AA349928.

p. 112–13. *The political house that Jack built: with thirteen cuts*, by Hone, William, 1780–1842, Cruikshank, George, 1792–1878. Printed by and for William Hone, 1819. New York Public Library.

p. 114–15. *The Queen's matrimonial ladder, a national toy, with fourteen step scenes; and illustrations in verse, with eighteen other cuts.* By Hone, William, 1780–1842, Cruikshank, George, 1792–1878. Printed by and for William Hone, 1820. p. 114. New York Public Library. p. 115. The Art Archive/ British Museum/Eileen Tweedy.

About Longman Cultural Editions

Inspired by the innovative *Longman Anthology of British Literature*, the Longman Cultural Editions are designed to illuminate the lively, ever variable intersections of literature, tradition, and culture. In each volume, a work or works of literary imagination gather new dimensions from materials that relate to informing traditions and debates, to contemporary conversations and controversies, and to later eras of reading and reaction. While the nature of the contexts vary from volume to volume, the reliable constants (in addition to handsome production and affordable pricing) are expert editing and helpful annotation throughout; a stimulating introduction; a table of dates to track composition, publication, and reception in relation to biographical, cultural, and historical events; illustrations guaranteed to spark conversation; and a guide for further browsing and study. Whether you are reading this volume along with the *Anthology*, or in a different or more specialized kind of course, or reading independently of any coursework, we hope you'll encounter much to stimulate your attention, curiosity, and pleasure.

SUSAN J. WOLFSON
General Editor, Longman Cultural Editions
Professor of English, Princeton University

About This Edition

This Longman Cultural Edition reflects Shelley's passionate conviction that he was a political writer, not just a visionary poet. He saw himself as a social, political, intellectual, and artistic activist who could help to shape events and attitudes in Britain. Sharply critical of the conservative values of much of British society during the Napoleonic wars and afterward, Shelley witnessed Britain's uneasy transition from an agrarian and mercantile trading nation to an economic, industrial, and imperialist power. After Napoleon was defeated at Waterloo (18 June 1815), England emerged as a premier world power. But at home the economy was in crisis, and the government's ineffective leadership provoked radical dissent. One issue was the Corn Laws, passed in 1815 to protect the inflated wartime prices commanded by all grains ("corn"). The great landowners reaped the benefit while the poor and working classes faced starvation. Parliament's Six Acts (1819) enforced social control by regulating everything from public meetings to public speech. Shelley joined contemporary activists in advocating reform of government and its institutions. Even poems that may seem visionary and highly esoteric to us—for example, "Ode to the West Wind" or the great lyrical drama *Prometheus Unbound*—would strike Shelley's contemporaries as political: a vision of society founded upon liberty, love, and universal benevolence.

Shelley's esoteric poems addressed the cultural elite that Shelley believed would lead the reform movement, but he also wrote for the masses. As early as 1812, Shelley distributed in Ireland poems and pamphlets he wrote on behalf of Irish nationalism; in 1817, his powerful *Address to the People on the Death of the Princess Charlotte* raised political questions about the conduct of the royal family; and in 1819, his angry "exoteric" poems, calculated to motivate both the working classes and the reformist organizers, proved too hot for his usual publishers to publish in an atmosphere of official, militant suppression. Even his youthful, gothic prose romances, *Zastrozzi* (1810) and *St. Irvyne* (1810–11) bristle with political themes: the duty to resist oppression; the rejection of revenge; and an embrace of selfless, self-sacrificing *love* as a moral *and political* efficacy.

Mainstream Victorian-era editors cleansed Shelley of his oppositional politics, setting the pattern for most of the twentieth century. But poetry participated in a public discourse, often appearing in the press side by side with war dispatches, accounts of political events, and reports of sensational domestic crimes. Books of poetry were reviewed as seriously as books on philosophy, religion, economics, history, science, and technology. To be a poet was to take part in a public conversation whose local and national stakes were high. And the reviews were often vicious and personal. Revolutionary, visionary Shelley was a poet of great skill, and reactionary reviewers aimed to "contain" his literary force by stigmatizing him personally. In an age preoccupied with disease and epidemics (Edward Jenner had just developed a smallpox vaccine), critics frequently branded their targets as "contagion" and set out to inoculate their readers—not only against Shelley but also Leigh Hunt (radical journalist) and fellow poets Lord Byron and John Keats. Shelley never surrendered to the efforts to silence him, addressing his arguments to later generations with more enlightened minds and hearts. By the 1840s, Shelley was a hero to Chartist reformers. Friedrich Engels saw the political force of his arguments, and later in the century, George Bernard Shaw and the Fabian socialists called fresh notice to his poetry. "Red Shelley" remains a favorite among the British political left.

Two detailed scholarly editions of Shelley's poetry now exist. One, edited for Pearson Longman by Kelvin Everest, will command three full volumes, with detailed notes and commentary. Another, edited by Donald H. Reiman and Neil Fraistat, will fill seven volumes, with even more extensive annotation and scholarly apparatus. There is no comparable edition of Shelley's prose, though there is an initial venture by E. B. Murray (1993), and I have edited a volume of Shelley's prose fiction (2002), including his two teenage gothic romances, *Zastrozzi* and *St. Irvyne*.

Like all modern editors of Shelley, I am indebted to my predecessors: the complete works edited by Harry Buxton Forman (1876) and the ten-volume "Julian Edition" edited by Roger Ingpen and Walter E. Peck (1926–30). Shelley's first comprehensive editor was his widow, Mary Shelley, who prepared editions of the poetry in 1824 and 1839, and letters and prose (1840), from a combination of (sometimes flawed) printed volumes and manuscripts in often deplorable condition. Although her editions were important, historically and critically, and set the standard until Forman's edition, I use Forman's work as my basis because it marks Shelley's emergence into modern scholarship. My annotations reflect my work as a scholar and teacher, and my appreciation for the work of fellow editors, especially Donald Reiman and Neil Fraistat (1977, 2002) and Timothy Webb (1977). My desire has been to make Shelley's work more accessible, by clarifying its relationship to the concerns of an activist poet and thinker, and to the cultural milieu that formed him and that he in turn sought to reform.

I want to thank Susan Wolfson for inviting me to prepare this edition and for her invaluable editorial expertise and unfailing patience, and Dianne Hall for her brilliant preparation of the texts. This pleasurable task has reinforced my admiration for Shelley's artistry even as it has reminded me of how much we all benefit from our contemporaries and from the thought, work, conversation, and sentiment through which we share our commitment to the culture of Romanticism.

STEPHEN C. BEHRENDT
University of Nebraska

Abbreviations used in this edition:

1824	*Posthumous Poems of Percy Bysshe Shelley*, ed. Mary Shelley (1824)
1839	*The Poetical Works of Percy Bysshe Shelley*, ed. Mary Shelley, 4 vols. (1839)
1840	*Essays, Letters from Abroad, Translations and Fragments*, ed. Mary Shelley (1840)
PU	*Prometheus Unbound*, Shelley
Defence	*A Defence of Poetry*, Shelley
PL	*Paradise Lost*, John Milton
⁓	introduces a contextual item

Introduction

Percy Bysshe Shelley was born on 4 August 1792, three years after the French Revolution, and came of age in an era of war not concluded until 1815 at Waterloo. In this climate of international war and domestic unrest, the forces of liberty and oppression, and even their very definition, were in an intense struggle. As the eldest son of a conservative country gentry family whose wealth was relatively new and whose rise would culminate in his father's baronetcy, Percy Shelley was the focus of high expectations. At their large country house, Field Place, near the village of Horsham in Sussex, Shelley spent a comfortable childhood until he was sent, at the age of 10 years, to Syon House Academy in London, then Eton in 1804. At both schools Shelley was bullied and sought refuge in literature, imaginative, philosophical, and political, developing an acute sense of tyranny and oppression. He began writing verse, and by the time his father enrolled him in 1810 at University College, Oxford, he already considered himself an author, having written a number of shorter poems and a long one, *The Wandering Jew*. The injustice suffered by outcast figures would pervade all his writings.

At Oxford Shelley published two prose gothic romances, *Zastrozzi* (1810) and *St. Irvyne; or, The Rosicrucian* (1810–11), as well as *Original Poetry of Victor and Cazire* (an immature and heavily plagiarized collection coauthored with his sister Elizabeth, 1810) and another volume of verse, *The Posthumous Fragments of Margaret Nicholson* (purporting to be by the mad woman who had attempted to assassinate George III in 1786). With his Oxford friend Thomas Jefferson Hogg, Shelley also wrote *The Necessity of Atheism*, a short pamphlet of "rationalist" polemic, which they published and circulated widely, hoping to spark philosophical dialogue. Shelley's father, Sir Timothy Shelley, scrawled "Impious" across the top of a copy he received. Shelley and Hogg were expelled from Oxford, and though Hogg soon reconciled with his father, the break between Percy and Sir Timothy was never repaired. This early adventure characterizes Shelley's extremism: on one hand, the intellectual, scientific rationalist undaunted by complex abstract subjects; on the other, the idealist, heedless of practical constraints or terrible consequences.

Freshly expelled from Oxford, Shelley's next adventure involved a young woman, Harriet Westbrook, whom he had met in London through his sister. Convinced that she was being mistreated because of her acquaintance with him, Shelley talked her into eloping. In August 1811 they fled to Scotland for a clandestine marriage, then on to Ireland, where Shelley campaigned for Irish independence and Catholic emancipation. He distributed political poems and other radical documents and apparently delivered a public speech that was published as *An Address to the Irish People*. Although Shelley was bitterly disappointed at his lack of impact, he was energized by his experience.

He was soon corresponding with William Godwin, an influential political theorist in the 1790s. Shelley was among the ardent fans of his *Enquiry Concerning the Principles of Political Justice* (1793), an "anarchist" treatise on the evils of government and institutions coupled to an argument for rational individual judgment, acting in the best interest of the community. Godwin's writings seemed to embody a philosophy already taking shape in Shelley's mind, and he embraced Godwin's ideas with an enthusiasm that never waned. One of the institutions Godwin rejected was monogamous marriage. When Percy and Harriet settled in Wales in 1812, where Percy hoped to form an association of philanthropists, he invited a young woman with whom he had been corresponding, Elizabeth Hitchener, to join them as a sort of protegée and resource for intellectual and emotional enrichment. The arrangement proved unworkable, and Elizabeth Hitchener soon moved on. It would not be his last attempt.

In September 1812, Shelley went to London, where he visited Godwin frequently during a stay of some six weeks. He met Thomas Hookham, the liberal publisher who subsequently issued several of Shelley's works, and the satirical essayist and novelist Thomas Love Peacock. The next February, the Shelleys left Wales, perhaps to avoid debts, and after a brief visit to Ireland settled in

London. There Shelley oversaw the publication of his most radical work to date, the long poem *Queen Mab*, which assaulted Christianity (and Jesus Christ), the King and his ministers and government, the clergy, and social institutions such as marriage. So inflammatory did it prove that Shelley himself tried to suppress it almost immediately, but the copies that stayed in circulation were pirated by the radical press, feeding Shelley's growing reputation as a political, spiritual, and social apostate. Cast in the form of a Godwinian dream vision, *Queen Mab* argues that a glorious future awaits if only mankind will abandon self-interest and live according to love, reason, and the common good. Though much of this wild and extravagant poem and its long and detailed notes reflect immature enthusiasm, its ideas and positions would inform Shelley's writing for the rest of his life.

On one of his visits to Godwin in the fall of 1812, Shelley met Godwin's daughter, Mary, whose mother, pioneering feminist Mary Wollstonecraft, had died shortly after giving birth to her in 1797. They fell in love, notwithstanding the fact that Shelley and Harriet had already had a daughter, Ianthe, in 1813 and that Harriet was pregnant again; in July 1814, Percy and Mary eloped for the Continent, taking with them Mary's stepsister Mary Jane (Claire) Clairmont. They traveled about, living in relative squalor; their first child was born prematurely in February 1815 and died within days. (Meanwhile, Harriet bore Shelley's son back in England in November 1814.) Lack of funds finally forced the lovers' return to England, where the death in June 1815 of Shelley's grandfather, Sir Bysshe Shelley, left him an annuity of £1000 (£200 designated for Harriet). In January 1816, Mary bore another child, William, whose death in 1819 in Italy, from malaria, devastated his parents.

Shelley's new collection of poems, *Alastor; and Other Poems*, the first volume to bear his full name, appeared in February 1816. Later in the year he, Mary, and Claire went back to the Continent, Napoleon's defeat at Waterloo in June 1815 having made international travel easier for everyone. They took up residence on Lake Geneva, where the famous Lord Byron was their neighbor for the summer. Suffering bitterly cold weather (the result of the largest volcanic eruption ever recorded, at Mount Tambora in Indonesia on 5 April 1815), the group spent countless days and nights together, reading, talking, and writing. Mary began *Frankenstein*, and Shelley and Byron became fast friends. Convinced of Byron's superior poetic talents and popular appeal, Shelley urged Byron to advocate political and philanthropic causes. The Shelleys returned to England at the end of the year. In despair, Harriet Shelley drowned herself. Percy and Mary married soon after and settled in the village of Marlow, Buckinghamshire, so that Shelley could devote himself to writing, even as he kept abreast of British politics.

In the wake of Waterloo and two years of weather-related bad harvests (1815–16), there was considerable unrest: prices for bread and other essentials were high, as was unemployment; discontent over government was growing; calls increased for parliamentary reform to provide proper representation for the burgeoning working-class populations of Birmingham, Nottingham, and Manchester. The government, under the Liverpool ministry that served the unpopular Prince Regent, responded with a series of increasingly harsh measures to stifle dissent and frustrate the reformers. By 1817 armed bands of dissidents, many of them former soldiers, appeared throughout the nation. The government, fearing a revolution, reacted with extensive surveillance, spies, *agents provocateurs*, and informants.

One notorious machination was the Pentrich rebellion in Derbyshire. A government *agent provocateur* goaded a group of radicals into a demonstration and march on London, gathering strength along the way, to support a (nonexistent) uprising of reformers there. Local authorities broke up the rebellion and arrested its leaders, who were tried, convicted, and executed on 7 November 1817. Though meant to suppress further uprisings, the government's severity itself became a scandal, undercutting its authority and fueling dissent. Its waning prestige was worsened in November with the sudden death in childbirth of the Prince Regent's only child, the Princess Charlotte Augusta of Wales, together with her infant son. Not only was this the end of the Prince Regent's line of succession (he was long estranged from his wife, Princess Caroline of Brunswick), but it was the death knell for the affection of the British public, for whom this generation promised a new era of domestic respectability. Immediately grasping the political capital of this tragedy, Shelley issued *An Address to the People on the Death of the Princess Charlotte*, a pamphlet that weighed the royal losses against the executed Derbyshire rebels: the death to mourn, he proposed, was not Princess Charlotte but Liberty.

Earlier in 1817 Shelley had been writing a plan for reform by popular vote. He had also completed *Laon and Cythna; or, The Revolution of the Golden City: A Vision of the Nineteenth Century*, a semiepic poetic vision of what the French Revolution could have been, had it not led to the Terror and then Napoleonic imperialism—events that dismayed its most ardent sympathizers. The poem presents a despotic king invoking fellow monarchs to help crush a popular uprising. Among his victims are the young childhood lovers (who *may* be brother and sister) Laon and Cythna. Their self-sacrifice for the good of others turns the poem's final section into an inspirational vision of human dignity. When the printer objected to the apparent incest, the publisher refused to proceed. Shelley then revised the poem to weaken this suggestion and reissued it as *The Revolt of Islam*. But its revolutionary themes still drew the reviewers' fire. The press could be highly partisan, and literary criticism often consisted of scurrilous *ad hominem* attacks upon authors of objectionable political views. Although friends such as Leigh Hunt (who with his brother published the dissenting weekly *The Examiner*) stood by Shelley steadfastly, it was no help that the Hunts, too, were targets. Yet amidst all the political warfare, admiration for Shelley's skill as a poet was widely voiced.

Sometime during 1817 Shelley seems to have drafted a fragmentary essay on Christianity, one more nuanced than the outraged reviews would make it seem. The essay makes clear that Shelley respected Jesus as a humanitarian thinker and social activist. His quarrel is with the reactionary institution of orthodox Christianity that distorted and perverted Jesus's teachings, especially in its ideology of a "God" of inflexible, absolute *justice*. To Shelley, Jesus was a *man* whose divinity was shown in his love, forgiveness, and extraordinary self-sacrifice. Shelley links this humanitarian Jesus to other self-sacrificing reformers, most notably Socrates and Cicero, and he is not shy about listing himself among these martyred reformers: prophets whose clarity of vision and benevolence of purpose went unappreciated by their self-interested contemporaries.

Shelley's sense of martyrdom was aggravated by chronic financial distress. To escape their unpaid bills, the Shelleys left for Italy in the spring of 1818. They went first to Leghorn (Livorno) in May, where they presented a letter of introduction from Godwin to John and Maria Gisborne, English citizens who with Henry Reveley (Maria's son from a prior marriage) lived there. All soon became good friends and would remain so. Shelley returned to writing by translating Plato's *Symposium* and working on prose essays, including the platonic-themed "On Love," and a poem begun in Marlow the year before, *Rosalind and Helen: A Modern Eclogue.* Two friends, meeting in Italy after a long estrangement, share stories of misfortune and disappointed love and discover the restorative powers of friendship.

Shelley was experiencing many of these feelings himself. During the summer he again spent time with Byron, primarily to help with arrangements for the care of Byron's daughter by Claire Clairmont, Allegra, who had been conceived in Switzerland in 1816 and born in 1817 (she would die of typhoid in a convent at age 4). One result of their time together was "Julian and Maddalo," a coded Byron-Shelley conversation in verse not published until 1824, after Shelley's death. Shelley soon turned to one of his most ambitious projects, his great lyrical drama *Prometheus Unbound,* which takes up the agon of this Titan god from the point at which Aeschylus had left it at the conclusion of *Prometheus Bound.* Shelley once again imagines a successful revolution. Refusing revenge, the tortured Prometheus repudiates his curse on Jupiter, his tormentor, setting in motion a bloodless revolution that strips Jupiter of monarchal power and redefines true power as a liberty—and hence a moral authority—of individual minds, which can never be wholly crushed by oppression.

In a remarkable burst of creative activity, Shelley worked on several projects more or less simultaneously in 1819, drafting the second and third acts of *Prometheus Unbound,* which he had begun in late 1818, and finishing "Julian and Maddalo" and numerous shorter poems and essays, including *A Philosophical View of Reform.* He also composed his stunning political-gothic stage drama, *The Cenci,* then more political poems and the fourth act of *Prometheus Unbound.* At the end of August, about a month after he had finished *The Cenci,* Shelley heard about the government's violent suppression of a peaceful mass meeting of reformers in Manchester. He responded with a barrage of livid poems, hoping to activate the long-suffering British into necessary but nonviolent rebellion—a passive resistance that would shame the oppressors. Even so, when he sent his poems to Hunt in England for publication, some in *The Examiner* and some in book form, Hunt demurred. To publish such works would have put Hunt in jeopardy—and probably in prison—while Shelley was safe in Italy.

As Shelley was imagining a political transformation back home in 1819, he was struggling with a poet whose works he had admired early in his life and whose influence was now considerable: William Wordsworth. Shelley adored his early poetry, but by 1819 Wordsworth had become an Establishment poet, accepting a government sinecure in 1813 and then in 1814 publishing a long didactic poem, *The Excursion*, widely ridiculed as a decline in power. A new edition of his poems in 1815 was better received, and in 1819 Wordsworth decided to publish a poem written much earlier, *Peter Bell*. But this hectoring poem, graced with a self-promoting prose preface at a time when the nation seemed on the verge of wholesale rebellion, struck Shelley and many contemporaries as self-infatuated, arrogant, and irrelevant. Before the poem had even appeared, John Hamilton Reynolds (1796–1852) rushed into print a parody called *Peter Bell, a Lyrical Ballad*, which his friend John Keats reviewed. In an *Examiner* of December 1816, Hunt had heralded Shelley, Reynolds, and Keats as the new generation of note. He quickly sent the Reynolds-Keats dossier to Shelley, who added his own parody, *Peter Bell the Third*. Shelley saw a failed modern prophet in this sorry Wordsworth. For Shelley, there could be no separation of poetry, politics, and morals: this would be the heart of his *Defence of Poetry* (written in 1821). The poet was bound to his nation's welfare: the greater a poet's powers, the greater his obligations.

But before drafting this *Defence*, Shelley was negotiating the cause of justice amid the seductive compulsion to revenge in *The Cenci*. Written in 1819, it is related to *Prometheus Unbound* in portraying a revolution. Its factual basis is a sixteenth-century Roman family dominated by the brutal Count Cenci, who orchestrates the deaths of two of his sons and then celebrates their deaths with a grand banquet. His daughter, Beatrice, who is herself a victim of abuse (and will soon be raped and perhaps sodomized by her father), tries to enlist the aid of both the government and the Pope in bringing her father to justice. But these patriarchal authorities refuse to intervene. Thus thwarted, Beatrice plots to have her father killed by two assassins. Immediately after they dispatch him comes the knock on the door: the Pope's emissaries have arrived to arrest Cenci. Beatrice is subsequently tried, together with her mother and brother, and the play concludes with their impending execution. What makes the play so affecting is Shelley's portrayal of Beatrice

Cenci as a paragon of physical beauty and moral virtue subjected to despicable violence and who, when all courses of redress have been closed to her, takes matters into her own hands. Her plight resonates with the recent course of the French Revolution, a principled rebellion against atrocious tyranny that descended into a vengeful Terror. Shelley sent *The Cenci* to his English publisher with instructions to issue it anonymously and then arrange for a performance in London. Certain of the play's dramatic power, he hoped that a stage success would let him name his authorship and accept the public praise—mindful of his caution against revenge in the climate of political unrest in England in 1819.

The Cenci was not staged and was harshly reviewed when published; by 1820 Shelley was losing faith in his ability to promote immediate social and political reform. He turned his hopes to succeeding generations. When in 1820 *Prometheus Unbound, and Other Poems* appeared, Shelley had already suggested to his publisher, Charles Ollier, that the volume (one of the most brilliant in all of English literature) might find no more than twenty or so readers. If Ollier was taken aback by this pessimism, Shelley meant to address a *cognoscenti*, an elite of knowing readers. The Preface stated his desire "to familiarise the highly refined imagination of the more select classes of poetical readers with beautiful idealisms of moral excellence." If in 1820 his "reasoned principles of moral conduct" seem mere "seeds cast upon the highway of life which the unconscious passenger tramples into dust, although they would bear the harvest of his happiness," he meant the metaphor of "seeds": these will "quicken a new birth" in future generations (in the phrasing of Shelley's most famous poem, "Ode to the West Wind").

Events in England in 1820 and 1821 were producing rapid changes. "Mad" King George III died on 29 January 1820; the Prince Regent assumed the throne as George IV, although the formal coronation did not occur until July 1821. Meanwhile, the Prince Regent's estranged wife, Caroline of Brunswick, attempted to assume her status as queen. Her return to England in July 1820 was championed by liberals, in no small part to embarrass the new king. When George IV's government launched a "trial" for adultery by the House of Lords to discredit her (it failed), the partisan politics erupted into street theater. When Caroline finally appeared at Westminster Cathedral on the day of the coronation, she was turned away by a group of prize fighters hired by the king and disguised as pages. She left in disgrace and died less than three weeks later, very likely from cancer. These events unfolded in the wake of the Cato Street Conspiracy, a failed plot in February 1820 to assassinate the ministry. Things were roiling abroad, too. In March, the Spanish army staged a revolt and established a constitutional monarchy. The summer brought a constitutional revolution in Naples and new uprisings in Greece against Turkish occupation. The events of 1820–21 energized Shelley with new hope.

Now in Pisa, Shelley continued to write works both in elevated style ("Ode to Liberty") and in the more rough-and-tumble satirical style he called "exoteric" (the dramatic *Swellfoot the Tyrant*, also suppressed until after his death). Fresh from reading Thomas Love Peacock's satire on modern poetry, *The Four Ages of Poetry*, which appeared in *Ollier's Literary Miscellany* (November 1820), Shelley drafted a detailed response. When Ollier announced that there would be no further issues, Shelley suggested that he publish the essay as a pamphlet, but Ollier, whose publishing and bookselling business was failing, apparently declined. Shelley abandoned the essay after its first section, which would not see print until Mary Shelley published it in 1840, under the title of *A Defence of Poetry*, with its famous closing assertion, "Poets are the unacknowledged legislators of the World."

In November 1820 the Shelleys met Teresa ("Emilia") Viviani, the young woman who became the subject of Shelley's *Epipsychidion* (1821). The circle was further enhanced by the arrival of Edward and Jane Williams early in 1821. In this year Shelley composed his aesthetically elaborate political elegy on the death of John Keats, *Adonais*. Having heard of Keats's fragile health (he was terminally ill with tuberculosis), Shelley wrote to him in July 1820, inviting him to join Shelley in Italy. Keats and his friend Joseph Severn arrived in Naples in October 1820 and went to Rome for medical care, where Keats died on 23 February 1821. A story had been circulating that Keats's collapse had been precipitated by a cruel review of *Endymion* in the *Quarterly Review*. Shelley took the occasion to meditate on the fate of visionary genius in a benighted and hostile world. Shelley's ringing assertion of the visionary poet's ultimate victory over the limitations of mortal experience was a vindication of himself no less than of Keats.

After finishing another drama on liberty, "Hellas," toward the end of 1821, Shelley turned in 1822 to several shorter works and then, in May, he began what would be his last major poetic project, "The Triumph of Life," left unfinished at his death. Other friends and acquaintances joined them in Italy, including Edward John Trelawny (1792–1881). In May Shelley's new boat, the *Don Juan* (named in honor of Byron's sensational poem), was delivered to him at San Terenzo, on the Bay of Lerici. Leigh Hunt and his large family were soon to join them, and in July Shelley sailed with Edward Williams on the *Don Juan* to meet them. On their return, Shelley and Williams drowned in a severe storm and after a few days of anxious waiting at home, their widows and friends heard that their bodies had been found on the coast. Following temporary burials, they were cremated on successive days, 13 and 14 August, the proceedings supervised by Trelawny.

The "Pisan circle" soon dispersed. Jane Williams returned to England, where she married Shelley's old college friend Thomas Jefferson Hogg. With Byron at hand, Leigh Hunt tried to make a success of his new journal, *The Liberal*, that had been envisioned as a collective project involving himself, Shelley, and Byron; but it soon failed, and Hunt's own financial difficulties forced him and his family to return to England. Mary Shelley worked for a while transcribing manuscripts for Byron, but in 1823 she returned to England with her only surviving child, Percy Florence, and began editing Shelley's works for publication. *Posthumous Poems of Percy Bysshe Shelley* was published in 1824 by John and Leigh Hunt. Still stinging from scandal, Sir Timothy Shelley threatened to cut Mary and Percy Florence off financially if she published any more of his son's writings. Only in 1839 did he finally relent and give permission for a new edition of the poetry, and for another of the prose in the following year, on the condition that Mary Shelley not write Shelley's biography. She did manage to write some biographical notes for the editions. When Sir Timothy died in 1844 all remaining restrictions disappeared, and Percy Florence succeeded to the baronetcy. Always famous for *Frankenstein* (1818, 1831), Mary Shelley became a successful novelist, biographer, and essayist, and this development, together with Percy Florence's marriage to Jane St. John in 1848, brought her comfort during the final years of her life (she died in 1851) and the assurance that Percy Shelley's reputation would be left in good hands.

While Shelley's views of the "real world" were inextricably involved with his writing, his participation was selective. He held a sharp focus on domestic politics but had relatively little to say about the war with Napoleonic France, beyond its impact on the economy and a distaste for Napoleon himself. Shelley's early devotion to Irish causes ceased when he moved to London. And although he followed politics and the careers of liberal and radical politicians, read *The Examiner* and William Cobbett's newspapers, he was more of an abstract thinker or philosopher than a political activist, and his residence abroad attenuated his engagement. This distance gave him a long view on political history and culture. Always and foremost a poet, Shelley cared for socially committed art: to whom am I addressing myself, why am I doing so, and in what form(s) do I need to frame my discourse? Writing in a wide range of genres—prose, verse, and drama—and testing stylistic registers from the dauntingly esoteric to the frankly earthy, Shelley was always experimenting with ways to engage an audience. The medium could very much be the message: the duty of the poet to serve and to save, to teach and to love.

In this devotion, Shelley took extravagant risks in poetic style. Readers may occasionally complain of Wordsworth's "wordiness," Coleridge's "obtuseness," Byron's apparent "carelessness," or Keats's "lushness." With Shelley, the problem was often sheer obscurity or unintelligibility. Feeling the limitations of language (even poetic language) when it came to conveying the complexity of his ideas and passions, Shelley catalogs images, piles up grammatical modifiers, and mixes sensory data to produce events that transcend conventional language with new forms of vital communication. The *interaction* among all these elements in the reader's mind yields a meaning that transcends the limitations of ordinary language.

Shelley's first reviewers found the poetry mystifying and called it nonsense. But even Wordsworth admired his fine style and craftsmanship, and by the end of the twentieth century, Shelley's challenge seems to have found his able and appreciative readers. Shelley's prose essays are philosophical in nature but no less attentive to language. The prose style is often slow paced, highly detailed, poised between the abstract and the particular. Shelley's writings—poetry and prose—are not only subjects for reading but also training exercises in new ways to read. We need to open ourselves, imaginatively and intellectually, not just to the words but also to their extraordinary combinations.

Table of Dates

1789   French Revolution, launched 14 July.

1792   French Republic proclaimed; royal family imprisoned. France declares war on Austria, Prussia, and Sardinia. September Massacres of royalist sympathizers in France.

        Shelley born, 4 August, at Field Place, Horsham, Sussex, first of seven children of Sir Timothy Shelley and Elizabeth Pilfold Shelley.

1793   Execution of Louis XVI (January) and Marie Antoinette (October). "Reign of Terror" begins. Britain enters the war against France. William Godwin's *Political Justice* published.

1797   Mary Wollstonecraft Godwin born, 30 August.

1798   Irish rebellion suppressed. Wordsworth and Coleridge publish *Lyrical Ballads* anonymously.

1802–04 Peace of Amiens between Britain and France (1802–03). Napoleon crowned Emperor (1804).

        Shelley at Syon House Academy, a boarding school.

1804–10 Shelley attends Eton, studies science and gothic literature.

1807   Shelley begins writing poetry.

1810   Shelley's first long poem, *The Wandering Jew*, unpublished. Publishes gothic romances, *Zastrozzi* (Spring) and *St. Irvyne* (December), and *Original Poetry by Victor and Cazire* (September), written with his sister Elizabeth. Moves to University College, Oxford, becomes friends with Thomas Jefferson Hogg. Publishes *Posthumous Fragments of Margaret Nicholson* (November).

1811 George III declared insane; the Prince of Wales assumes rule as Prince Regent.

Shelley meets Harriet Westbrook (January). Expelled with Hogg from Oxford (25 March) for coauthored pamphlet, *The Necessity of Atheism*. Elopes with Harriet to Edinburgh (29 August). Estrangement from Hogg, who tried to seduce Harriet. The Shelleys meet Robert Southey (Poet Laureate from 1813), who tries to assist them financially and in reconciling with Shelley's family.

1812 Napoleon's defeat in Russia. British Prime Minister Spencer Perceval assassinated in the House of Commons (11 May). U.S. declares war on Britain.

Shelley abandons a political novel, *Hubert Cauvin* (January); campaigns for reform in Ireland; publishes two political pamphlets and *Declaration of Rights* (February–March). Disillusioned, the Shelleys move to Wales, then to Devon, then back to Wales, where he is politically active. Meets William Godwin (October), with whom he had been corresponding, and Thomas Love Peacock (November).

1813 Napoleon defeated at Leipzig, and then by Wellington at Vitoria; Wellington enters France.

The Shelleys flee Wales (27 February), revisit Ireland (March), and relocate to London (5 April). Shelley publishes *Queen Mab* privately, at his own expense (May). His and Harriet's daughter, Ianthe, born 23 June.

1814 Napoleon abdicates and is banished to Elba. Louis XVIII restores Bourbon monarchy. Congress of Vienna begins. British forces burn Washington, D.C. Treaty of Ghent ends the War of 1812 (24 December).

Shelley publishes *A Refutation of Deism* (winter). Visits Godwin in London (May–June) and secretly leaves for Europe with Mary Godwin, 27 July; Percy, Mary, and her stepsister Claire Clairmont travel to Switzerland. Returns to England 13 September, ill and heavily in debt. Charles Shelley born to Harriet (30 November).

1815 Napoleon returns to France, resumes power (the "Hundred Days"), is defeated at Waterloo (18 June), and is banished to St. Helena. Corn Laws passed in Britain.

Sir Bysshe Shelley, the poet's grandfather, dies (5 January); Sir Timothy allots Shelley £1000 per year (£200 for Harriet and the children). Mary's first child born (22 February), dies (6 March). Shelley makes loans to Godwin. Percy and Mary move to Windsor Park (August). Shelley writes *Alastor*.

1816   The Prince Regent's only child, Princess Charlotte Augusta of Wales, marries, focusing new national hopes.

William Shelley born to Mary (24 January). Shelley publishes *Alastor and Other Poems* (February). Travels to Switzerland with Mary and Claire. The Shelleys and Byron become neighbors and friends at Geneva during summer. Shelley writes "Hymn to Intellectual Beauty" (June) and "Mont Blanc" (July). The Shelleys return to England (8 September); suicide of Mary's half-sister Fanny Imlay; suicide by drowning of Harriet Shelley (9 November). Shelley meets John Keats and Horace Smith and begins friendship with liberal publisher and writer Leigh Hunt (December). Marries Mary Godwin (30 December).

1817   Attempt on the life of the Prince Regent after opening of Parliament. Habeas corpus suspended. Seditious Meetings Act passed. Arrest (May), trial and acquittal (June) of Thomas Wooler for seditious libel for attacks on the government in his radical journal, *Black Dwarf*. Childbed death of Princess Charlotte Augusta (November). Execution of Derbyshire insurgents (November).

The Shelleys settle at Marlow, near London. Shelley publishes *A Proposal for Putting Reform to the Vote throughout the Kingdom* (March). Lord Eldon, the Lord Chancellor, denies Shelley custody of his children by Harriet (27 March). Shelley writes *Laon and Cythna* (April–September); printed in late October and suppressed, then revised and republished as *The Revolt of Islam* (December; dated 1818). Begins *Rosalind and Helen* (September). Clara Shelley born (2 September). *History of a Six Weeks' Tour*, coauthored with Mary, published anonymously (November). Writes *An Address to the People on the Death of the Princess Charlotte* (November). Writes "Ozymandias" (December; published in *The Examiner*, January 1818). Mary Shelley's *Frankenstein* published anonymously (December; dated 1818).

1818   The Shelleys (with Claire Clairmont) leave England for Italy (11 March); meet John and Maria Gisborne and Maria's son Henry

Reveley in Leghorn (Livorno) (May); move to Bagni da Lucca, where Shelley translates Plato's *Symposium* and completes *Rosalind and Helen*. Shelley and Claire meet Byron in Venice (August); Mary and William Shelley join them at Este (September). Shelley begins *Prometheus Unbound* (September). Clara Shelley dies (24 September); Shelley's depression recorded in "Lines Written among the Euganean Hills." Begins "Julian and Maddalo" (late September). The Shelleys travel to Rome and on to Naples, where they settle until late February 1819.

1819   Queen Victoria and Prince Albert born.

The Shelleys move to Rome (March). Shelley composes *Prometheus Unbound*, Acts 2 and 3 (March–April); finishes "Julian and Maddalo" (May); publishes *Rosalind and Helen, with Other Poems* (Spring). William Shelley dies at age 3 (7 June), is buried in Rome. The Shelleys move to Leghorn (17 June). Shelley completes *The Cenci* (8 August). Learns of Peterloo Massacre (5 September), writes political poems, including *The Mask of Anarchy* (unpublished until 1832). The Shelleys move to Florence (October), where Percy Florence Shelley is born (2 November). Shelley writes "Ode to the West Wind," *Peter Bell the Third* (October–November), *A Philosophical View of Reform* (November–December), "England in 1819" (December); completes *Prometheus Unbound*, Act 4 (December).

1820   George III dies; Prince Regent becomes George IV. Cato Street Conspiracy foiled and leaders executed (February). Spain establishes constitutional monarchy (March).

The Shelleys move to Pisa (29 January). *The Cenci* published (spring). Shelley writes "The Sensitive-Plant" (March) and "Ode to Liberty." Shelleys return to Leghorn to live in the Gisbornes' house (June–August). Shelley writes "Letter to Maria Gisborne," "To a Sky-Lark." Shelley writes "The Witch of Atlas," "Ode to Naples," "Oedipus Tyrannus (Swellfoot the Tyrant)." Publishes *Prometheus Unbound, with Other Poems* (September). Shelleys return to Pisa (late October), meet Emilia Viviani (December). Shelley invites Keats to join them in Italy (November).

1821   Austria crushes fledgling republics in Italy; Greeks rise against Turkish occupiers in war for independence (March). Napoleon dies on St. Helena.

Edward and Jane Williams arrive in Pisa and become friends with the Shelleys (January). Shelley writes *Epipsychidion* (January–February), *A Defence of Poetry* (February–March). The first pirated editions of *Queen Mab* appear in England. Shelley learns of Keats's death (11 April; Keats died in Rome on 23 February), and writes *Adonais* (May–June). Meets Byron at Ravenna (August). Writes "Hellas" (October). Byron moves to Pisa (1 November).

1822   Greeks adopt republican constitution, declare independence. Turks seize island of Chios, massacre Greek inhabitants, invade Greece. Byron joins the Greek cause. British Foreign Secretary Lord Castlereagh commits suicide.

Shelley begins *Charles the First* (January). E. J. Trelawny arrives in Pisa (14 January). The Shelleys and Williamses move to the Bay of Lerici for the summer (30 April). Shelley begins "The Triumph of Life" (late May). Mary miscarries (16 June). Leigh Hunt and his family arrive in Italy to join Shelley and Byron in founding a new journal, *The Liberal*. Shelley and Edward Williams sail to Leghorn to meet them (1 July) and drown in a storm while returning (8 July). Their bodies are washed up separately on the shore near Viareggio and are cremated there on 13 and 14 August, in the presence of Byron, Hunt, and Trelawny (see cover illustration). Mary and the Hunts return to Genoa with Byron and live together until July 1823.

1823   Shelley's ashes interred in the Protestant Cemetery in Rome (21 January).

1824   Mary Shelley publishes her edition of *Posthumous Poems* (June), which is suppressed in September at Sir Timothy Shelley's insistence. Death of Byron.

1832   *The Masque of Anarchy* published.

1839   Mary Shelley's annotated, four-volume edition of Shelley's poetry published.

1840   Mary Shelley's edition of Shelley's prose and letters from abroad published.

1851   Death of Mary Shelley.

1880   H. Buxton Forman's 10-volume edition of the *Poetic Works*.

1886   *The Cenci* first staged, privately, through the Shelley Society.

Engraved portrait of Shelley, after an original by Amelia Curran (mid 19th century).

Percy Bysshe Shelley

Shelley's Works

Alastor

Alastor, written in 1815 and published in 1816 as the first poem in a volume bearing the same title, marks Shelley's swerve from the overt political and philosophical radicalism of Queen Mab (1812) and his early prose pamphlets and treatises. The new poetry was influenced by William Wordsworth. For a poet not yet 24 years old to confront this influential, and by then established, predecessor was a considerable risk. But Shelley's generation had grown weary of Wordsworth, who, for all the power of his early verse, a modernist break with the eighteenth century, seemed by 1815 to have settled into political conservatism. Shelley's sonnet, "To Wordsworth" (included in this volume), is a virtual elegy on the death of Wordsworth's youthful self. The echoes of Wordsworth in Alastor mark out Shelley's visionary orientation against Wordsworth's still abiding faith in "natural piety."

The structure of Alastor reflects one of Shelley's favorite modes: an implicit debate, in which opposing arguments engage our attention. Shelley presents a young poet who, finding the mortal, social world insufficient to his aspirations, wanders the world in search of his ideal, which shimmers in an erotic dream of a female poet. But when at its climax the dream collapses, the poet is devastated, unable to see in the waking world anything but desolation and vacancy. This tale of visionary desire and frustration is rendered by a frame-narrator whose view is very different—very Wordsworthian. From the start, this narrator states his faith in the restorative beauty of the natural world. Does he pity or does he obliquely admire this radical visionary?

Shelley's friend, Thomas Love Peacock, took credit for the title. According to him, "Alastor" means "the spirit of evil"; it is not the young poet's name, Peacock emphasized, but a judgment on his otherworldly, fatal idealism. Alastor has affinities with "Hymn to Intellectual Beauty," composed in the summer of 1816 and likewise negotiating social affiliation against isolated selfhood.

3

Shelley's Preface to Alastor *is part of the debate. The rhetoric appears disinterested and impartial at the beginning, but by the end it seems to chastise those who turn from social obligations. At the same time, the second paragraph seems also to judge those who reject visionary aspirations. The dilemma is not solved by the Preface's enigmatic conclusion, which quotes Wordsworth's* The Excursion *(1814). The lines are spoken by another frame-narrator whose epithet, the Wanderer, might have suggested an affinity with Shelley's questing hero. But Wordsworth's Wanderer survives in the world, determined to be detached from human sympathy, but also prone to real grief for the hard lives he encounters. The lines Shelley quotes are fraught with sorrow for a woman named Margaret, the former inhabitant of a ruined cottage that the Wanderer visits with a young poet to whom he tells her story.*

Alastor; or, The Spirit of Solitude

Preface.

The poem entitled "ALASTOR" may be considered as allegorical of one of the most interesting situations of the human mind. It represents a youth of uncorrupted feelings and adventurous genius led forth by an imagination inflamed and purified through familiarity with all that is excellent and majestic, to the contemplation of the universe. He drinks deep of the fountains of knowledge, and is still insatiate. The magnificence and beauty of the external world sinks profoundly into the frame of his conceptions, and affords to their modifications a variety not to be exhausted. So long as it is possible for his desires to point towards objects thus infinite and unmeasured, he is joyous, and tranquil, and self-possessed. But the period arrives when these objects cease to suffice. His mind is at length suddenly awakened and thirsts for intercourse with an intelligence similar to itself. He images to himself the Being whom he loves. Conversant with speculations of the sublimest and most perfect natures, the vision in which he embodies his own imaginations unites all of wonderful, or wise, or beautiful, which the poet, the philosopher, or the lover could depicture. The intellectual faculties, the imagination, the functions of sense, have their respective requisitions on the sympathy of corresponding powers in other human beings. The Poet is represented as uniting these requisitions, and attaching them to a single image. He seeks in vain for a prototype of his conception. Blasted by his disappointment, he descends to an untimely grave.

The picture is not barren of instruction to actual men. The Poet's self-centred seclusion was avenged by the furies of an irresistible passion pursuing him to speedy ruin. But that Power which strikes the luminaries of the world with sudden darkness and extinction, by awakening them to too exquisite a perception of its influences, dooms to a slow and poisonous decay those manner spirits that dare to abjure its dominion. Their destiny is more abject and inglorious as their delinquency is more contemptible and pernicious. They who, deluded by no generous error, instigated by no sacred thirst of doubtful knowledge, duped by no illustrious superstition, loving nothing on this earth, and cherishing no hopes beyond, yet keep aloof from sympathies with their kind, rejoicing neither in human joy nor mourning with human grief; these, and such as they, have their apportioned curse. They languish, because none feel with them their common nature. They are morally dead. They are neither friends, nor lovers, nor fathers, nor citizens of the world, nor benefactors of their country. Among those who attempt to exist without human sympathy, the pure and tender-hearted perish through the intensity and passion of their search after its communities, when the vacancy of their spirit suddenly makes itself felt. All else, selfish, blind, and torpid, are those unforeseeing multitudes who constitute, together with their own, the lasting misery and loneliness of the world. Those who love not their fellow-beings live unfruitful lives, and prepare for their old age a miserable grave.

> "The good die first,
> And those whose hearts are dry as summer dust,
> Burn to the socket!"[1]

December 14, 1815.

Alastor; or, The Spirit of Solitude

Nondum amabam, et amare amabam, quærebam quid amarem, amans amare.[2]
—*Confessions of St. Augustine.*

Earth, ocean, air, belovèd brotherhood!
If our great Mother has imbued my soul
With aught of natural piety[3] to feel

[1]William Wordsworth, *The Excursion* (1814), 1.531–33.

[2]From St. Augustine's *Confessions* (c. 400), book 3, ch. 1, describing sexual lust, a misplaced desire to be fulfilled only by a love of God: "I did not love and yet I was in love with loving. . . . I sought after what I might love, being in love with loving."

[3]See Wordsworth's "My Heart Leaps Up": "And I could wish my days to be / Bound each to each by natural piety" (8–9). Natural piety is a faith grounded in Nature.

Your love, and recompense the boon[4] with mine;
If dewy morn, and odorous noon, and even,   5
With sunset and its gorgeous ministers,
And solemn midnight's tingling silentness;
If autumn's hollow sighs in the sere wood,
And winter robing with pure snow and crowns
Of starry ice the grey grass and bare boughs;   10
If spring's voluptuous pantings when she breathes
Her first sweet kisses, have been dear to me;
If no bright bird, insect, or gentle beast
I consciously have injured, but still loved
And cherished these my kindred; then forgive   15
This boast, belovèd brethren, and withdraw
No portion of your wonted favour now!

     Mother of this unfathomable world!
Favour my solemn song, for I have loved
Thee ever, and thee only; I have watched   20
Thy shadow, and the darkness of thy steps,
And my heart over gazes on the depth
Of thy deep mysteries. I have made my bed
In charnels and on coffins, where black death
Keeps record of the trophies won from thee,   25
Hoping to still these obstinate questionings[5]
Of thee and thine, by forcing some lone ghost
Thy messenger, to render up the tale
Of what we are. In lone and silent hours,
When night makes a weird sound of its own stillness,   30
Like an inspired and desperate alchymist
Staking his very life on some dark hope,
Have I mixed awful talk and asking looks
With my most innocent love, until strange tears
Uniting with those breathless kisses, made   35
Such magic as compels the charmèd night
To render up thy charge: . . . and, though ne'er yet
Thou hast unveiled thy inmost sanctuary,
Enough from incommunicable dream,

[4]Repay the gift.
[5]In the visionary desire of "Ode: Intimations of Immortality," Wordsworth is compelled by "obstinate questionings / Of sense and outward things" (142–43).

And twilight phantasms,[6] and deep noon-day thought,   40
Has shone within me, that serenely now
And moveless, as a long-forgotten lyre[7]
Suspended in the solitary dome
Of some mysterious and deserted fane,
I wait thy breath, Great Parent, that my strain   45
May modulate with murmurs of the air,
And motions of the forests and the sea,
And voice of living beings, and woven hymns
Of night and day, and the deep heart of man.

   There was a Poet whose untimely tomb   50
No human hands with pious reverence reared,
But the charmed eddies of autumnal winds
Built o'er his mouldering bones a pyramid
Of mouldering leaves in the waste wilderness:—
A lovely youth,—no mourning maiden decked   55
With weeping flowers, or votive cypress wreath,[8]
The lone couch of his everlasting sleep:—
Gentle, and brave, and generous,—no lorn bard
Breathed o'er his dark fate one melodious sigh:
He lived, he died, he sung, in solitude.   60
Strangers have wept to hear his passionate notes,
And virgins, as unknown he passed, have pined
And wasted for fond love of his wild eyes.
The fire of those soft orbs has ceased to burn,
And Silence, too enamoured of that voice,   65
Locks its mute music in her rugged cell.

   By solemn vision, and bright silver dream,
His infancy was nurtured. Every sight
And sound from the vast earth and ambient air,
Sent to his heart its choicest impulses.   70
The fountains of divine philosophy
Fled not his thirsting lips, and all of great,
Or good, or lovely, which the sacred past

[6]In his youth, Shelley experimented with ways to communicate with the spirit world; see "Hymn to Intellectual Beauty."

[7]The strings of the Aeolian harp produce sounds when the wind blows over them. For Shelley and others, this is a metaphor for poetic imagination.

[8]Emblems of death and mourning.

In truth or fable consecrates, he felt
And knew. When early youth had passed, he left   75
His cold fireside and alienated home
To seek strange truths in undiscovered lands.
Many a wide waste and tangled wilderness
Has lured his fearless steps; and he has bought
With his sweet voice and eyes, from savage men,   80
His rest and food. Nature's most secret steps
He like her shadow has pursued, where'er
The red volcano overcanopies
Its fields of snow and pinnacles of ice
With burning smoke, or where bitumen lakes   85
On black bare pointed islets ever beat
With sluggish surge, or where the secret caves
Rugged and dark, winding among the springs
Of fire and poison, inaccessible
To avarice or pride, their starry domes   90
Of diamond and of gold expand above
Numberless and immeasurable halls,
Frequent with crystal column, and clear shrines
Of pearl, and thrones radiant with chrysolite.
Nor had that scene of ampler majesty   95
Than gems or gold, the varying roof of heaven
And the green earth lost in his heart its claims
To love and wonder; he would linger long
In lonesome vales, making the wild his home,
Until the doves and squirrels would partake   100
From his innocuous hand his bloodless food.⁹
Lured by the gentle meaning of his looks,
And the wild antelope, that starts whene'er
The dry leaf rustles in the brake,¹⁰ suspend
Her timid steps to gaze upon a form   105
More graceful than her own.

                      His wandering step
Obedient to high thoughts, has visited

---

⁹Shelley advocated vegetarianism in a long note to *Queen Mab* (1812), later expanded and published as a pamphlet, *A Vindication of Natural Diet* (1813).
¹⁰Brush or shrubbery.

The awful ruins of the days of old:[11]
Athens, and Tyre, and Balbec, and the waste
Where stood Jerusalem, the fallen towers   110
Of Babylon, the eternal pyramids,
Memphis and Thebes, and whatsoe'er of strange
Sculptured on alabaster obelisk,
Or jasper tomb, or mutilated sphynx,
Dark Æthiopia in her desert hills   115
Conceals. Among the ruined temples there,
Stupendous columns, and wild images
Of more than man, where marble dæmons[12] watch
The Zodiac's brazen mystery, and dead men
Hang their mute thoughts on the mute walls around,   120
He lingered, poring on memorials
Of the world's youth, through the long burning day
Gazed on those speechless shapes, nor, when the moon
Filled the mysterious halls with floating shades
Suspended he that task, but ever gazed   125
And gazed, till meaning on his vacant mind
Flashed like strong inspiration, and he saw
The thrilling secrets of the birth of time.

Meanwhile an Arab maiden brought his food,
Her daily portion, from her father's tent,   130
And spread her matting for his couch, and stole
From duties and repose to tend his steps:—
Enamoured, yet not daring for deep awe
To speak her love:—and watched his nightly sleep,
Sleepless herself, to gaze upon his lips   135
Parted in slumber, whence the regular breath
Of innocent dreams arose: then, when red morn
Made paler the pale moon, to her cold home
Wildered, and wan, and panting, she returned.

[11]Most of the places named in this paragraph (ll. 106–28) can be found in Count Volney's *Ruins of Empire* (1791), a meditation on the title subject and a case for the ideals of the French Revolution. *Ruins* was translated into English in 1795.

[12]In Greek mythology, supernatural beings (halfway between human and divine), sometimes benevolent but often malignant.

The Poet wandering on, through Arabie[13]   140
And Persia, and the wild Carmanian waste,
And o'er the aërial mountains which pour down
Indus and Oxus from their icy caves,
In joy and exultation held his way;
Till in the vale of Cashmire, far within   145
Its loneliest dell, where odorous plants entwine
Beneath the hollow rocks a natural bower,
Beside a sparkling rivulet he stretched
His languid limbs. A vision on his sleep
There came, a dream of hopes that never yet   150
Had flushed his cheek. He dreamed a veilèd maid
Sate near him, talking in low solemn tones.
Her voice was like the voice of his own soul
Heard in the calm of thought; its music long,
Like woven sounds of streams and breezes, held   155
His inmost sense suspended in its web
Of many-coloured woof and shifting hues.
Knowledge and truth and virtue were her theme,
And lofty hopes of divine liberty,
Thoughts the most dear to him, and poesy,   160
Herself a poet. Soon the solemn mood
Of her pure mind kindled through all her frame
A permeating fire: wild numbers then
She raised, with voice stifled in tremulous sobs
Subdued by its own pathos: her fair hands   165
Were bare alone, sweeping from some strange harp
Strange symphony, and in their branching veins
The eloquent blood told an ineffable tale.
The beating of her heart was heard to fill
The pauses of her music, and her breath   170
Tumultuously accorded with those fits
Of intermitted song. Sudden she rose,
As if her heart impatiently endured
Its bursting burthen: at the sound he turned,
And saw by the warm light of their own life   175
Her glowing limbs beneath the sinuous veil
Of woven wind, her outspread arms now bare,

[13]The poet travels eastward, through Arabia and Persia, to the Indian Kashmir. As in *Prometheus Unbound* (1819), the external geography reflects a mental journey.

Her dark locks floating in the breath of night,
Her beamy bending eyes, her parted lips
Outstretched, and pale, and quivering eagerly.   180
His strong heart sunk and sickened with excess
Of love. He reared his shuddering limbs and quelled
His gasping breath, and spread his arms to meet
Her panting bosom: . . . she drew back a while,
Then, yielding to the irresistible joy,   185
With frantic gesture and short breathless cry
Folded his frame in her dissolving arms.
Now blackness veiled his dizzy eyes, and night
Involved and swallowed up the vision; sleep,
Like a dark flood suspended in its course,   190
Rolled back its impulse on his vacant brain.

  Roused by the shock he started from his trance—
The cold white light of morning, the blue moon
Low in the west, the clear and garish hills,
The distinct valley and the vacant woods,   195
Spread round him where he stood.[14] Whither have fled[15]
The hues of heaven that canopied his bower
Of yesternight? The sounds that soothed his sleep,
The mystery and the majesty of Earth,
The joy, the exultation? His wan eyes   200
Gaze on the empty scene as vacantly
As ocean's moon looks on the moon in heaven.
The spirit of sweet human love has sent
A vision to the sleep of him who spurned
Her choicest gifts. He eagerly pursues   205
Beyond the realms of dream that fleeting shade;
He overleaps the bounds. Alas! Alas!
Were limbs, and breath, and being intertwined
Thus treacherously? Lost, lost, for ever lost,
In the wide pathless desert of dim sleep,   210
That beautiful shape! Does the dark gate of death
Conduct to thy mysterious paradise,
O Sleep? Does the bright arch of rainbow clouds,

---

[14]Note the radical transition from the dream-lorn "vacant brain" (l. 191) to a now "vacant" waking world.

[15]Meaning "Where are . . .?" "Where have they gone?" *Ubi sunt* is a traditional elegiac formula, sounded by Wordsworth in his "Intimations" ode.

And pendent mountains seen in the calm lake,
Lead only to a black and watery depth, 215
While death's blue vault, with loathliest vapours hung,
Where every shade which the foul grave exhales
Hides its dead eye from the detested day,
Conducts, O Sleep, to thy delightful realms?
This doubt with sudden tide flowed on his heart, 220
The insatiate hope which it awakened, stung
His brain even like despair.

                    While daylight held
The sky, the Poet kept mute conference
With his still soul. At night the passion came,
Like the fierce fiend of a distempered dream, 225
And shook him from his rest, and led him forth
Into the darkness.—As an eagle grasped
In folds of the green serpent, feels her breast
Burn with the poison, and precipitates
Through night and day, tempest, and calm, and cloud, 230
Frantic with dizzying anguish, her blind flight
O'er the wide aëry wilderness: thus driven
By the bright shadow of that lovely dream,
Beneath the cold glare of the desolate night,
Through tangled swamps and deep precipitous dells, 235
Startling with careless step the moonlight snake,
He fled. Red morning dawned upon his flight,
Shedding the mockery of its vital hues
Upon his cheek of death. He wandered on
Till vast Aornos seen from Petra's steep 240
Hung o'er the low horizon like a cloud;
Through Balk, and where the desolated tombs
Of Parthian kings scatter to every wind
Their wasting dust, wildly he wandered on,
Day after day a weary waste of hours, 245
Bearing within his life the brooding care
That ever fed on its decaying flame.
And now his limbs were lean; his scattered hair
Sered by the autumn of strange suffering
Sung dirges in the wind; his listless hand 250
Hung like dead bone within its withered skin;
Life, and the lustre that consumed it, shone

As in a furnace burning secretly
From his dark eyes alone. The cottagers,
Who ministered with human charity   255
His human wants, beheld with wondering awe
Their fleeting visitant. The mountaineer,
Encountering on some dizzy precipice
That spectral form, deemed that the Spirit of wind
With lightning eyes, and eager breath, and feet   260
Disturbing not the drifted snow, had paused
In its career: the infant would conceal
His troubled visage in his mother's robe
In terror at the glare of those wild eyes,
To remember their strange light in many a dream   265
Of after-times; but youthful maidens, taught
By nature, would interpret half the woe
That wasted him, would call him with false names
Brother, and friend, would press his pallid hand
At parting, and watch, dim through tears, the path   270
Of his departure from their father's door.

    At length upon the lone Chorasmian shore[16]
He paused, a wide and melancholy waste
Of putrid marshes. A strong impulse urged
His steps to the sea-shore. A swan was there,   275
Beside a sluggish stream among the reeds.
It rose as he approached, and with strong wings
Scaling the upward sky, bent its bright course
High over the immeasurable main.
His eyes pursued its flight.—"Thou hast a home,   280
Beautiful bird; thou voyagest to thine home,
Where thy sweet mate will twine her downy neck
With thine, and welcome thy return with eyes
Bright in the lustre of their own fond joy.
And what am I that I should linger here,   285
With voice far sweeter than thy dying notes,
Spirit more vast than thine, frame more attuned
To beauty, wasting these surpassing powers
In the deaf air, to the blind earth, and heaven

[16]The region of the Caspian and Aral Sea, the Caucasus Mountains; in Shelley's time this area was believed to be the site of the Garden of Eden. It is also where Prometheus was said to have been tormented.

That echoes not my thoughts?" A gloomy smile   290
Of desperate hope wrinkled his quivering lips.[17]
For sleep, he knew, kept most relentlessly
Its precious charge, and silent death exposed,
Faithless perhaps as sleep, a shadowy lure,
With doubtful smile mocking its own strange charms.   295

    Startled by his own thoughts he looked around.
There was no fair fiend near him, not a sight
Or sound of awe but in his own deep mind.
A little shallop floating near the shore
Caught the impatient wandering of his gaze.   300
It had been long abandoned, for its sides
Gaped wide with many a rift, and its frail joints
Swayed with the undulations of the tide.
A restless impulse urged him to embark
And meet lone Death on the drear ocean's waste;   305
For well he knew that mighty Shadow loves
The slimy caverns of the populous deep.

    The day was fair and sunny, sea and sky
Drank its inspiring radiance, and the wind
Swept strongly from the shore, blackening the waves.   310
Following his eager soul, the wanderer
Leaped in the boat, he spread his cloak aloft
On the bare mast, and took his lonely seat,
And felt the boat speed o'er the tranquil sea
Like a torn cloud before the hurricane.   315

    As one that in a silver vision floats
Obedient to the sweep of odorous winds
Upon resplendent clouds, so rapidly
Along the dark and ruffled waters fled
The straining boat.—A whirlwind swept it on,   320
With fierce gusts and precipitating force,
Through the white ridges of the chafèd sea.
The waves arose. Higher and higher still
Their fierce necks writhed beneath the tempest's scourge
Like serpents struggling in a vulture's grasp.   325

---

[17]In the copy of this volume that he gave to Leigh Hunt, Shelley revised this line to read "Of desperate hope convulsed his curling lips."

Calm and rejoicing in the fearful war
Of wave ruining on wave, and blast on blast
Descending, and black flood on whirlpool driven
With dark obliterating course, he sate:
As if their genii were the ministers   330
Appointed to conduct him to the light
Of those belovèd eyes, the Poet sate
Holding the steady helm. Evening came on,
The beams of sunset hung their rainbow hues
High 'mid the shifting domes of sheeted spray   335
That canopied his path o'er the waste deep;
Twilight, ascending slowly from the east,
Entwined in duskier wreaths her braided locks
O'er the fair front and radiant eyes of day;
Night followed, clad with stars. On every side   340
More horribly the multitudinous streams
Of ocean's mountainous waste to mutual war
Rushed in dark tumult thundering, as to mock
The calm and spangled sky. The little boat
Still fled before the storm; still fled, like foam   345
Down the steep cataract of a wintry river;
Now pausing on the edge of the riven wave;
Now leaving far behind the bursting mass
That fell, convulsing ocean: safely fled—
As if that frail and wasted human form,   350
Had been an elemental god.

                    At midnight
The moon arose: and lo! the ethereal[18] cliffs
Of Caucasus, whose icy summits shone
Among the stars like sunlight, and around
Whose caverned base the whirlpools and the waves   355
Bursting and eddying irresistibly
Rage and resound for ever.—Who shall save?—
The boat fled on,—the boiling torrent drove,—
The crags closed round with black and jaggèd arms.
The shattered mountain overhung the sea,   360
And faster still, beyond all human speed,
Suspended on the sweep of the smooth wave,

---

[18]Ether is the highest region of the atmosphere.

The little boat was driven. A cavern there
Yawned, and amid its slant and winding depths
Ingulfed the rushing sea. The boat fled on   365
With unrelaxing speed.—"Vision and Love!"
The Poet cried aloud, "I have beheld
The path of thy departure. Sleep and death
Shall not divide us long!"

                      The boat pursued
The windings of the cavern. Daylight shone   370
At length upon that gloomy river's flow;
Now, where the fiercest war among the waves
Is calm, on the unfathomable stream
The boat moved slowly. Where the mountain, riven.
Exposed those black depths to the azure sky,   375
Ere yet the flood's enormous volume fell
Even to the base of Caucasus, with sound
That shook the everlasting rocks, the mass
Filled with one whirlpool all that ample chasm;
Stair above stair the eddying waters rose,   380
Circling immeasurably fast, and laved
With alternating dash the gnarlèd roots
Of mighty trees, that stretched their giant arms
In darkness over it. I' the midst was left,
Reflecting, yet distorting every cloud,   385
A pool of treacherous and tremendous calm.
Seized by the sway of the ascending stream,
With dizzy swiftness, round, and round, and round,
Ridge after ridge the straining boat arose,
Till on the verge of the extremest curve,   390
Where, through an opening of the rocky bank,
The waters overflow, and a smooth spot
Of glassy quiet mid those battling tides
Is left, the boat paused shuddering.—Shall it sink
Down the abyss? Shall the reverting stress   395
Of that resistless gulf embosom it?
Now shall it fall?—A wandering stream of wind,
Breathed from the west, has caught the expanded sail,
And, lo! with gentle motion, between banks
Of mossy slope, and on a placid stream,   400
Beneath a woven grove it sails, and, hark!

The ghastly torrent mingles its far roar,
With the breeze murmuring in the musical woods.
Where the embowering trees recede, and leave
A little space of green expanse, the cove   405
Is closed by meeting banks, whose yellow flowers[19]
For ever gaze on their own drooping eyes,
Reflected in the crystal calm. The wave
Of the boat's motion marred their pensive task,
Which nought but vagrant bird, or wanton wind,   410
Or falling spear-grass, or their own decay
Had e'er disturbed before. The Poet longed
To deck with their bright hues his withered hair,
But on his heart its solitude returned,
And he forbore. Not the strong impulse hid   415
In those flushed cheeks, bent eyes, and shadowy frame
Had yet performed its ministry: it hung
Upon his life, as lightning in a cloud
Gleams, hovering ere it vanish, ere the floods
Of night close over it.

                The noonday sun   420
Now shone upon the forest, one vast mass
Of mingling shade, whose brown magnificence
A narrow vale embosoms. There, huge caves,
Scooped in the dark base of their aëry rocks
Mocking[20] its moans, respond and roar for ever.   425
The meeting boughs and implicated[21] leaves
Wove twilight o'er the Poet's path, as led
By love, or dream, or god, or mightier Death,
He sought in Nature's dearest haunt, some bank,
Her cradle, and his sepulchre. More dark   430
And dark the shades accumulate. The oak,
Expanding its immense and knotty arms,
Embraces the light beech. The pyramids
Of the tall cedar overarching, frame
Most solemn domes within, and far below,   435

---

[19]River Narcissus, named for the legendary Greek youth who pined away while gazing, infatuated, at his own reflection in a stream.

[20]Echoing, perhaps with a sense of ridicule.

[21]Intertwined, literally "folded in."

Like clouds suspended in an emerald sky,
The ash and the acacia floating hang
Tremulous and pale. Like restless serpents, clothed
In rainbow and in fire, the parasites,
Starred with ten thousand blossoms, flow around   440
The grey trunks, and, as gamesome infants' eyes,
With gentle meanings, and most innocent wiles,
Fold their beams round the hearts of those that love.
These twine their tendrils with the wedded boughs
Uniting their close union; the woven leaves   445
Make net-work of the dark blue light of day,
And the night's noontide clearness, mutable
As shapes in the weird clouds. Soft mossy lawns
Beneath these canopies extend their swells,
Fragrant with perfumed herbs, and eyed with blooms   450
Minute yet beautiful. One darkest glen
Sends from its woods of musk-rose, twined with jasmine,
A soul-dissolving odour, to invite
To some more lovely mystery. Through the dell,
Silence and Twilight here, twin-sisters, keep   455
Their noonday watch, and sail among the shades,
Like vaporous shapes half seen; beyond, a well,
Dark, gleaming, and of most translucent wave,
Images all the woven boughs above,
And each depending leaf, and every speck   460
Of azure sky, darting between their chasms;
Nor aught else in the liquid mirror laves
Its portraiture, but some inconstant star
Between one foliaged lattice twinkling fair,
Or, painted bird, sleeping beneath the moon,   465
Or gorgeous insect floating motionless,
Unconscious of the day, ere yet his wings
Have spread their glories to the gaze of noon.

    Hither the Poet came. His eyes beheld
Their own wan light through the reflected lines   470
Of his thin hair, distinct in the dark depth
Of that still fountain; as the human heart,
Gazing in dreams over the gloomy grave,
Sees its own treacherous likeness there. He heard
The motion of the leaves, the grass that sprung   475

Startled and glanced and trembled even to feel
An unaccustomed presence, and the sound
Of the sweet brook that from the secret springs
Of that dark fountain rose. A Spirit seemed
To stand beside him—clothed in no bright robes 480
Of shadowy silver or enshrining light,
Borrowed from aught the visible world affords
Of grace, or majesty, or mystery;—
But, undulating woods, and silent well,
And leaping rivulet, and evening gloom 485
Now deepening the dark shades, for speech assuming,
Held commune with him,[22] as if he and it
Were all that was,—only . . . when his regard
Was raised by intense pensiveness, . . . two eyes,
Two starry eyes, hung in the gloom of thought, 490
And seemed with their serene and azure smiles
To beckon him.

                    Obedient to the light
That shone within his soul, he went, pursuing
The windings of the dell.—The rivulet
Wanton and wild, through many a green ravine 495
Beneath the forest flowed. Sometimes it fell
Among the moss with hollow harmony
Dark and profound. Now on the polished stones
It danced; like childhood laughing as it went:
Then, through the plain in tranquil wanderings crept, 500
Reflecting every herb and drooping bud
That overhung its quietness.—"O stream!
Whose source is inaccessibly profound,
Whither do thy mysterious waters tend?
Thou imagest my life. Thy darksome stillness, 505
Thy dazzling waves, thy loud and hollow gulfs,
Thy searchless fountain, and invisible course
Have each their type in me: and the wide sky,
And measureless ocean may declare as soon
What oozy cavern of what wandering cloud 510
Contains thy waters, as the universe
Tell where these living thoughts reside, when stretched

[22]Communicated through the holy access provided by natural piety.

Upon thy flowers my bloodless limbs shall waste
I' the passing wind!"

                      Beside the grassy shore
Of the small stream he went; he did impress   515
On the green moss his tremulous step, that caught
Strong shuddering from his burning limbs. As one
Roused by some joyous madness from the couch
Of fever, he did move; yet, not like him,
Forgetful of the grave, where, when the flame   520
Of his frail exultation shall be spent,
He must descend. With rapid steps he went
Beneath the shade of trees, beside the flow
Of the wild babbling rivulet; and now
The forest's solemn canopies were changed   525
For the uniform and lightsome[23] evening sky.
Grey rocks did peep from the spare moss, and stemmed
The struggling brook: tall spires of windlestrae[24]
Threw their thin shadows down the rugged slope,
And nought but gnarled roots[25] of ancient pines   530
Branchless and blasted, clenched with grasping roots
The unwilling soil. A gradual change was here,
Yet ghastly. For, as fast years flow away,
The smooth brow gathers, and the hair grows thin
And white, and where irradiate dewy eyes   535
Had shone, gleam stony orbs:—so from his steps
Bright flowers departed, and the beautiful shade
Of the green groves, with all their odorous winds
And musical motions. Calm, he still pursued
The stream, that with a larger volume now   540
Rolled through the labyrinthine dell; and there
Fretted a path through its descending curves
With its wintry speed. On every side now rose
Rocks, which, in unimaginable forms,
Lifted their black and barren pinnacles   545
In the light of evening, and, its precipice
Obscuring the ravine, disclosed above,

[23]Radiant.

[24]Withered grass.

[25]Although Shelley later changed this word to "stumps," I follow Mary Shelley's
texts of 1824 and 1839 in retaining "roots."

Mid toppling stones, black gulfs and yawning caves,
Whose windings gave ten thousand various tongues
To the loud stream. Lo! where the pass expands   550
Its stony jaws, the abrupt mountain breaks,
And seems, with its accumulated crags,
To overhang the world: for wide expand
Beneath the wan stars and descending moon
Islanded seas, blue mountains, mighty streams,   555
Dim tracts and vast, robed in the lustrous gloom
Of leaden-coloured even, and fiery hills
Mingling their flames with twilight, on the verge
Of the remote horizon. The near scene,
In naked and severe simplicity,   560
Made contrast with the universe. A pine,
Rock-rooted, stretched athwart the vacancy
Its swinging boughs, to each inconstant blast
Yielding one only response, at each pause
In most familiar cadence, with the howl   565
The thunder and the hiss of homeless streams
Mingling its solemn song, whilst the broad river,
Foaming and hurrying o'er its rugged path,
Fell into that immeasurable void
Scattering its waters to the passing winds.   570

Yet the grey precipice and solemn pine
And torrent, were not all;—one silent nook
Was there. Even on the edge of that vast mountain,
Upheld by knotty roots and fallen rocks,
It overlooked in its serenity   575
The dark earth, and the bending vault of stars.
It was a tranquil spot, that seemed to smile
Even in the lap of horror. Ivy clasped
The fissured stones with its entwining arms,
And did embower with leaves for ever green,   580
And berries dark, the smooth and even space
Of its inviolated floor, and here
The children of the autumnal whirlwind bore,
In wanton sport, those bright leaves, whose decay,
Red, yellow, or ethereally pale,   585
Rivals the pride of summer.[26] 'Tis the haunt

[26]Compare the opening stanzas of "Ode to the West Wind" (1819).

Of every gentle wind, whose breath can teach
The wilds to love tranquility. One step,
One human step alone, has ever broken
The stillness of its solitude:—one voice   590
Alone inspired its echoes;—even that voice
Which hither came, floating among the winds,
And led the loveliest among human forms
To make their wild haunts the depository
Of all the grace and beauty that endued   595
Its motions, render up its majesty,
Scatter its music on the unfeeling storm,
And to the damp leaves and blue cavern mould,
Nurses of rainbow flowers and branching moss,
Commit the colours of that varying cheek,   600
That snowy breast, those dark and drooping eyes.

　　The dim and hornèd[27] moon hung low, and poured
A sea of lustre on the horizon's verge
That overflowed its mountains. Yellow mist
Filled the unbounded atmosphere, and drank   605
Wan moonlight even to fulness: not a star
Shone, not a sound was heard; the very winds,
Danger's grim playmates, on that precipice
Slept, clasped in his embrace.—O, storm of death!
Whose sightless[28] speed divides this sullen night: 610
And thou, colossal Skeleton, that, still
Guiding its irresistible career
In thy devastating omnipotence,
Art king of this frail world, from the red field
Of slaughter, from the reeking hospital,   615
The patriot's sacred couch, the snowy bed
Of innocence, the scaffold and the throne,
A mighty voice invokes thee. Ruin calls
His brother Death. A rare and regal prey
He hath prepared, prowling around the world;   620
Glutted with which thou mayst repose, and men
Go to their graves like flowers or creeping worms,

[27]Crescent; by l. 654 the setting moon has drawn so close to the horizon that only
the two points remain visible.
[28]Blind, insensible.

Nor ever more offer at thy dark shrine
The unheeded tribute of a broken heart.

When on the threshold of the green recess   625
The wanderer's footsteps fell, he knew that death
Was on him. Yet a little, ere it fled,
Did he resign his high and holy soul
To images of the majestic past,
That paused within his passive being now,   630
Like winds that bear sweet music, when they breathe
Through some dim latticed chamber. He did place
His pale lean hand upon the rugged trunk
Of the old pine. Upon an ivied stone
Reclined his languid head, his limbs did rest,   635
Diffused and motionless, on the smooth brink
Of that obscurest chasm;—and thus he lay,
Surrendering[29] to their final impulses
The hovering powers of life. Hope and despair,
The torturers, slept; no mortal pain or fear   640
Marred his repose, the influxes of sense,
And his own being unalloyed by pain,
Yet feebler and more feeble, calmly fed
The stream of thought, till he lay breathing there
At peace, and faintly smiling:—his last sight   645
Was the great moon, which o'er the western line
Of the wide world her mighty horn suspended,
With whose dun beams inwoven darkness seemed
To mingle. Now upon the jaggèd hills
It rests, and still as the divided frame   650
Of the vast meteor sunk, the Poet's blood,
That ever beat in mystic sympathy
With nature's ebb and flow, grew feebler still:
And when two lessening points of light alone
Gleamed through the darkness, the alternate gasp   655
Of his faint respiration scarce did stir
The stagnate night:—till the minutest ray
Was quenched, the pulse yet lingered in his heart.
It paused—it fluttered. But when heaven remained
Utterly black, the murky shades involved   660

[29]In the final lines, "surrender" seems to modulate into a perhaps willed flight.

An image, silent, cold, and motionless,
As their own voiceless earth and vacant air.
Even as a vapour fed with golden beams
That ministered on sunlight, ere the west
Eclipses it, was now that wondrous frame—   665
No sense, no motion, no divinity—
A fragile lute, on whose harmonious strings
The breath of heaven did wander—a bright stream
Once fed with many-voicèd waves—a dream
Of youth, which night and time have quenched for ever,   670
Still, dark, and dry, and unremembered now.

O, for Medea's wondrous alchemy,
Which wheresoe'er it fell made the earth gleam
With bright flowers,[30] and the wintry boughs exhale
From vernal blooms fresh fragrance! O, that God,   675
Profuse of poisons, would concede the chalice
Which but one living man[31] has drained, who now,
Vessel of deathless wrath, a slave that feels
No proud exemption in the blighting curse
He bears, over the world wanders for ever,   680
Lone as incarnate death! O, that the dream
Of dark magician in his visioned[32] cave,
Raking the cinders of a crucible
For life and power, even when his feeble hand
Shakes in its last decay, were the true law   685
Of this so lovely world! But thou art fled
Like some frail exhalation; which the dawn
Robes in its golden beams,—ah! thou hast fled!
The brave, the gentle, and the beautiful,
The child of grace and genius. Heartless things   690
Are done and said i' the world, and many worms
And beasts and men live on, and mighty Earth
From sea and mountain, city and wilderness,
In vesper low or joyous orison,
Lifts still its solemn voice:—but thou art fled—   695

[30]In Greek mythology, Jason's wife, a sorceress, made a potion to restore Jason's father to youth; when some spilled on the ground, flowers sprang up.

[31]Ahasuerus, the Wandering Jew, a figure from Christian folklore. This shoemaker taunted Jesus on his way to Calvary and was condemned to eternal wandering until the second coming of Jesus. He is the subject of one of Shelley's earliest poems.

[32]Filled with visions or apparitions.

Thou canst no longer know or love the shapes
Of this phantasmal scene, who have to thee
Been purest ministers, who are, alas!
Now thou art not. Upon those pallid lips
So sweet even in their silence, on those eyes   700
That image sleep in death, upon that form
Yet safe from the worm's outrage, let no tear
Be shed—not even in thought. Nor, when those hues
Are gone, and those divinest lineaments,
Worn by the senseless wind, shall live alone   705
In the frail pauses of this simple strain,
Let not high verse, mourning the memory
Of that which is no more, or painting's woe
Or sculpture, speak in feeble imagery
Their own cold powers. Art and eloquence,   710
And all the shows o' the world are frail and vain
To weep a loss that turns their lights to shade.
It is a woe too "deep for tears,"[33] when all
Is reft at once, when some surpassing Spirit,
Whose light adorned the world around it, leaves   715
Those who remain behind, not sobs or groans,
The passionate tumult of a clinging hope;
But pale despair and cold tranquillity,
Nature's vast frame, the web of human things,
Birth and the grave, that are not as they were.   720

Mutability[1]

We are as clouds that veil the midnight moon;
     How restlessly they speed, and gleam, and quiver,
Streaking the darkness radiantly!—yet soon
     Night closes round, and they are lost for ever:

[33]In the concluding line of Wordsworth's "Ode: Intimations of Immortality," the poet, conscious of "man's mortality," turns his heart to the beauties of nature with "thoughts that do often lie too deep for tears."

[1]From the *Alastor* volume. The title-word means variableness, inconstancy, or fickleness. The poem recalls the *ubi sunt* tradition dating back to the Middle Ages and illustrated later in Edmund Spenser's posthumously published (1609) "mutability cantos," a projected seventh book of his *Faerie Queene* (1590, 1596).

Or like forgotten lyres,[2] whose dissonant strings   5
  Give various response to each varying blast,
To whose frail frame no second motion brings
  One mood or modulation like the last.

We rest.—A dream has power to poison sleep;
  We rise.—One wandering thought pollutes the day;   10
We feel, conceive or reason, laugh or weep;
  Embrace fond woe, or cast our cares away:

It is the same!—For, be it joy or sorrow,
  The path of its departure still is free:
Man's yesterday may ne'er be like his morrow;   15
  Nought may endure but Mutability.

from *On the Punishment of Death*

This work was probably written in 1814 or 1815.

A FRAGMENT

The first law which it becomes a Reformer to propose and support
at the approach of a period of great political change is the abolition
of the punishment of death.

It is sufficiently clear that revenge, retaliation, atonement, expi-
ation, are rules and motives so far from deserving a place in any enlightened system of political life that they are the chief sources of a
prodigious class of miseries in the domestic circles of society. It is
clear that however the spirit of legislation may appear to frame institutions upon more philosophical maxims, it has hitherto, in
those cases which are termed criminal, done little more than palli-
ate the spirit by gratifying a portion of it; and afforded a compromise between that which is best;—the inflicting of no evil upon a
sensitive being, without a decisively beneficial result in which he
should at least participate;—and that which is worst; that he
should be put to torture for the amusement of those whom he may
have injured, or may seem to have injured.

---

[2]Aeolian harps, or wind harps, whose tuned strings produce music when the wind
blows across them.

Omitting these remoter considerations, let us inquire what *Death* is; that punishment which is applied as a measure of transgressions of indefinite shades of distinction so soon as they shall have passed that degree and colour of enormity with which it is supposed no inferior infliction is commensurate.

And first, whether death is good or evil, a punishment or a reward, or whether it be wholly indifferent, no man can take upon himself to assert. [. . .]

The popular system of religion[1] suggests the idea that the mind after death will be painfully or pleasurably affected according to its determinations during life. However ridiculous and pernicious we must admit the vulgar accessories of this creed to be, there is a certain analogy, not wholly absurd, between the consequences resulting to an individual during life from the virtuous or vicious, prudent or imprudent, conduct of his external actions, to those consequences which are conjectured to ensue from the discipline and order of his internal thoughts as affecting his condition in a future state. [. . .] The philosopher is unable to determine whether our existence in a previous state has affected our present condition and abstains from deciding whether our present condition will affect us in that which may be future. That if we continue to exist the manner of our existence will be such as no inferences nor conjectures afforded by a consideration of our earthly experience can elucidate, is sufficiently obvious. The opinion that the vital principle within us, in whatever mode it may continue to exist, must lose that consciousness of definite and individual being which now characterizes it and become a unit in the vast sum of action and of thought which disposes and animates the universe and is called God, seems to belong to that class of opinion which has been designated as indifferent.

To compel a person to know all that can be known by the dead concerning that which the living fear, hope, or forget; to plunge him into the pleasure or pain which there awaits him; to punish or reward him in a manner and in a degree incalculable and incomprehensible by us; to disrobe him at once from all that intertexture of good and evil with which Nature seems to have clothed every form of individual existence, is to inflict on him the doom of death.

A certain degree of pain and terror usually accompany the infliction of death. This degree is infinitely varied by the infinite variety in the temperament and opinions of the sufferers. As a measure

---

[1]Christianity.

of punishment, strictly so considered, and as an exhibition which by its known effects on the sensibility of the sufferer is intended to intimidate the spectators from incurring a similar liability, it is singularly inadequate.

Firstly,—Persons of energetic character in whom, as in men who suffer for political crimes, there is a large mixture of enterprise and fortitude and disinterestedness and the elements, though misguided and disarranged, by which the strength and happiness of a nation might have been cemented, die in such a manner as to make death appear not evil but good. The death of what is called a traitor, that is, a person who from whatever motive would abolish the government of the day, is as often a triumphant exhibition of suffering virtue as the warning of a culprit. The multitude, instead of departing with a panic-stricken approbation of the laws which exhibited such a spectacle, are inspired with pity, admiration and sympathy; and the most generous among them feel an emulation to be the authors of such flattering emotions as they experience stirring in their bosoms. Impressed by what they see and feel, they make no distinctive between the motives which incited the criminals to the action for which they suffer or the heroic courage with which they turned into good that which their judges awarded to them as evil or the purpose itself of those actions, though that purpose may happen to be eminently pernicious. The laws in this case lose their sympathy, which it ought to be their chief object to secure, and in a participation of which consists their chief strength in maintaining those sanctions by which the parts of the social union are bound together so as to produce, as nearly as possible, the ends for which it is instituted.[2]

Secondly,—Persons of energetic character, in communities not modelled with philosophical skill to turn all the energies which they contain to the purposes of common good, are prone also to fall into the temptation of undertaking, and are peculiarly fitted for despising the perils attendant upon consummating, the most enormous crimes. Murder, rapes, extensive schemes of plunder are the actions of persons belonging to this class; and death is the penalty of conviction. But the coarseness of organization peculiar to men capable of committing acts wholly selfish is usually found to be associated with a proportionate insensibility to fear or pain. Their sufferings communicate to those of the spectators who may be liable to the com-

[2]Public executions diminished in England because criminals who died bravely or defiantly might seem heroic, and their deaths no more a deterrent. Angry crowds sometimes turned upon the executioners.

mission of similar crimes a sense of the lightness of that event, when closely examined, which at a distance, as uneducated persons are accustomed to do, probably they regarded with horror. But a great majority of the spectators are so bound up in the interests and the habits of social union that no temptation would be sufficiently strong to induce them to a commission of the enormities to which this penalty is assigned. The more powerful and the richer among them, [. . .] regard their own wrongs as in some degree avenged and their own rights secured by this punishment, inflicted as the penalty of whatever crime. [. . .] Men feel that their revenge is gratified and that their security is established by the extinction and the sufferings of beings in most respects resembling themselves; and their daily occupations constraining them to a precise form in all their thoughts, they come to connect inseparably the idea of their own advantage with that of the death and torture of others. It is manifest that the object of sane polity is directly the reverse;[3] and that laws founded upon reason should accustom the gross vulgar to associate their ideas of security and of interest with the reformation and the strict restraint, for that purpose alone, of those who might invade it.

The passion of revenge[4] is originally nothing more than an habitual perception of the ideas of the sufferings of the person who inflicts an injury as connected, as they are in a savage state or in such portions of society as are yet undisciplined to civilization, with security that that injury will not be repeated in future. This feeling, engrafted upon superstition and confirmed by habit, at last loses sight of the only object for which it may be supposed to have been implanted and becomes a passion and a duty to be pursued and fulfilled, even to the destruction of those ends to which it originally tended. The other passions, both good and evil, Avarice, Remorse, Love, Patriotism, present a similar appearance; and to this principle of the mind over-shooting the mark at which it aims we owe all that is eminently base or excellent in human nature. [. . .]

Nothing is more clear than that the infliction of punishment in general, in a degree which the reformation and the restraint of those who transgress the laws does not render indispensable, and none more than death, confirms all the inhuman and unsocial impulses of men. [. . .]

[3]While the powerful may enjoy executing their opponents, for Shelley, "sane" policy requires *reforming*, not executing, the criminal.

[4]Like Avarice, Remorse, Love, and Patriotism (mentioned later here), revenge becomes not the *means* to an end but that end.

The spectators who feel no abhorrence at a public execution but rather a self-applauding superiority and a sense of gratified indignation are surely excited to the most inauspicious emotions. The first reflection of such a one is the sense of his own internal and actual worth, as preferable to that of the victim, whom circumstances have led to destruction. The meanest wretch is impressed with a sense of his own comparative merit. He is one of those on whom the tower of Siloam fell not[5]—he is such a one as Jesus Christ found not in all Samaria, who, in his own soul, throws the first stone at the woman taken in adultery. The popular religion of the country takes its designation from that illustrious person whose beautiful sentiment I have quoted.[6] Any one who has stript from the doctrines of this person the veil of familiarity will perceive how adverse their spirit is to feelings of this nature.

To Wordsworth

This unconventional sonnet appeared in the Alastor *volume (1816). When in 1814 Wordsworth published his long narrative poem,* The Excursion, *he seemed to many younger poets to have abandoned the republican idealism of his youth. Shelley's sonnet-form acknowledged Wordsworth's own fondness for the form (he would write more than two hundred), but Shelley inverts the Petrarchan formula of octave-sestet (which Wordsworth liked), perhaps to signify Wordsworth's ideological inversion.*

Poet of Nature, thou hast wept to know
That things depart which never may return:
Childhood and youth, friendship and love's first glow,
Have fled like sweet dreams, leaving thee to mourn.
These common woes I feel. One loss is mine   5
Which thou too feel'st, yet I alone deplore.[1]

[5]In Luke 13.4, Jesus says that those people spared when the tower of Siloam (near Jerusalem) collapsed, killing 18, should not think themselves sinless just because they escaped death.

[6]Jesus, whose doctrines are perverted by institutional Christianity.

[1]Lament, but also disparage.

Thou wert as a lone star,[2] whose light did shine
On some frail bark in winter's midnight roar:
Thou hast like to a rock-built refuge stood
Above the blind and battling multitude: 10
In honoured poverty thy voice did weave
Songs consecrate to truth and liberty,[3]—
Deserting these, thou leavest me to grieve,
Thus having been, that thou shouldst cease to be.

Feelings of a Republican on the Fall of Bonaparte

*Composed in 1814 or 1815, after either Napoleon's abdication (1814)
or his defeat at Waterloo (1815). A "republican" advocates a participating government and opposes monarchy. Just as "To Wordsworth"
laments Wordsworth's departure from his youthful republican ideals,
this sonnet laments Napoleon's betrayal of the French Revolution's republican ideals. Napoleon's defeat produced the restoration of several
monarchies, in France and across Europe; such "customary" governments typically legalize tyranny, warfare, and the local oppressions au-
thorized by religious institutions.*

I hated thee, fallen tyrant! I did groan
To think that a most unambitious slave,
Like thou, shouldst dance and revel on the grave
Of Liberty. Thou mightst have built thy throne
Where it had stood even now: thou didst prefer   5
A frail and bloody pomp which Time has swept
In fragments towards Oblivion. Massacre,
For this I prayed, would on thy sleep have crept,
Treason and Slavery, Rapine, Fear, and Lust,
And stifled thee, their minister. I know   10
Too late, since thou and France are in the dust,
That Virtue owns a more eternal foe
Than Force or Fraud: old Custom, legal Crime,
And bloody Faith the foulest birth of Time.

[2]In his sonnet, "London, 1802," Wordsworth had written of Milton, "Thy soul was
like a Star and dwelt apart" (l. 9), and implies that he is Milton's heir as the moral,
spiritual, and political guide of his own time.

[3]Wordsworth's sonnet "London, 1802" and other political poems appeared in his *Poems, in Two Volumes* (1807), under the subheading, "Sonnets Dedicated to Liberty."

Hymn to Intellectual Beauty

Leigh Hunt published this poem in his liberal political weekly The Examiner *in January 1817. Audaciously giving his poem the genre of sacred poetry, Shelley proposes a spiritual alternative. The concept of intellectual beauty derives from Plato's distinction, in the* Symposium, *between the beauties registered on the senses and those apprehended by the mind, involving rational intellect and creative imagination. What is most ideal about the concept of intellectual beauty is also its greatest liability: it is a generative power, but it appears in the world of sense experience, and in poetry itself, only in elusive and transitory impressions.*

1.

The awful shadow of some unseen Power
    Floats though unseen among us,—visiting
    This various world with as inconstant[1] wing
As summer winds that creep from flower to flower,—
Like moonbeams that behind some piny mountain shower,   5
      It visits with inconstant glance
      Each human heart and countenance;
Like hues and harmonies of evening,—
      Like clouds in starlight widely spread,—
      Like memory of music fled,—   10
      Like aught that for its grace may be
Dear, and yet dearer for its mystery.

2.

Spirit of BEAUTY, that dost consecrate
    With thine own hues all thou dost shine upon
    Of human thought or form,—where art thou gone?   15
Why dost thou pass away and leave our state,
This dim vast vale of tears, vacant and desolate?
      Ask why the sunlight not for ever
      Weaves rainbows o'er yon mountain-river,
Why aught should fail and fade that once is shown,   20
      Why fear and dream and death and birth
      Cast on the daylight of this earth
      Such gloom,—why man has such a scope
For love and hate, despondency and hope?

---

[1]Variable, with a suggestion of unfaithful (see l. 62).

3.

No voice from some sublimer world hath ever   25
 To sage or poet these responses given—
 Therefore the names of Demon, Ghost,[2] and Heaven,
Remain the records of their vain endeavour,
Frail spells—whose uttered charm might not avail to sever,
  From all we hear and all we see,   30
  Doubt, chance, and mutability.
Thy light alone—like mist o'er mountains driven,
 Or music by the night-wind sent
 Through strings of some still instrument,[3]
  Or moonlight on a midnight stream, 35
Gives grace and truth to life's unquiet dream.

4.

Love, Hope, and Self-esteem, like clouds depart
 And come, for some uncertain moments lent.
 Man were immortal, and omnipotent,
Didst thou,[4] unknown and awful as thou art, 40
Keep with thy glorious train firm state within his heart.
  Thou messenger of sympathies,
  That wax and wane in lovers' eyes—
Thou—that to human thought art nourishment,
 Like darkness to a dying flame!   45
 Depart not as thy shadow came,
 Depart not—lest the grave should be,
Like life and fear, a dark reality.

5.

While yet a boy I sought for ghosts, and sped
 Through many a listening chamber, cave and ruin, 50
 And starlight wood, with fearful steps pursuing
Hopes of high talk with the departed dead.

[2]Shelley later changed the line to read ". . . God and ghosts. . . . " All these names, Shelley proposes, are "[f]rail spells" (l. 29) inadequate to answer "[d]oubt, chance, and mutability" (l. 31).

[3]Aeolean harp.

[4]If thou didst.

I called on poisonous names with which our youth is fed;[5]
    I was not heard—I saw them not—
    When musing deeply on the lot   55
Of life, at that sweet time when winds are wooing
      All vital things that wake to bring
      News of birds and blossoming,—
    Sudden, thy shadow fell on me;
I shrieked, and clasped my hands in ecstasy![6]   60

6.

I vowed that I would dedicate my powers
    To thee and thine—have I not kept the vow?
    With beating heart and streaming eyes, even now
I call the phantoms of a thousand hours
Each from his voiceless grave: they have in visioned bowers   65
      Of studious zeal or love's delight
      Outwatched with me the envious night—
They know that never joy illumed my brow
      Unlinked with hope that thou wouldst free
      This world from its dark slavery,   70
    That thou—O awful LOVELINESS,
Wouldst give whate'er these words cannot express.

7.

The day becomes more solemn and serene
    When noon is past—there is a harmony
    In autumn, and a lustre in its sky,   75
Which through the summer is not heard or seen,
As if it could not be, as if it had not been![7]
      Thus let thy power, which like the truth
      Of nature on my passive youth
Descended, to my onward life supply   80
    Its calm[8]—to one who worships thee,

[5]Referring to his youthful experiments in spiritual conjuration, Shelley equates these with the "names of God and ghosts and Heaven."

[6]Ecstasy means literally "standing outside," as if transported to a new reality.

[7]Wordsworth, "Ode: Intimations of Immortality": "The Clouds that gather round the setting sun / Do take a sober colouring from an eye / That hath kept watch over man's mortality; / Another race hath been, and other palms are won" (ll. 199–202).

[8]Recasting the last stanza of Wordsworth's ode, which anticipates immortality, Shelley hopes that the visionary visitations of his youth will sustain him throughout his life.

And every form containing thee,
Whom, SPIRIT fair, thy spells did bind
To fear himself,[9] and love all human kind.

Mont Blanc

Begun in July 1816 after traveling through the Chamounix Valley with Mary and Claire, this appeared in A History of a Six Weeks' Tour *(1817), a travel book coauthored with Mary. Shelley witnessed the scene from on a bridge over the Arve River. "Mont Blanc was before us, but it was covered with cloud," he wrote to his friend T. L. Peacock, 24 July 1816; the ravine was "so deep that the very roaring of the untameable Arve, which rolled through it, could not be heard above." As a result, "all was as much our own, as if we had been the creators of such impressions in the minds of others as now occupied our own."*

At nearly 16,000 feet, Mont Blanc is the highest peak in Europe; by 1816 few had reached its cloud-shrouded summit. In History, *Shelley described his poem as "an undisciplined overflowing of the soul" that attempts to "imitate" the wildness of the scenery and the feelings it generates. Shelley's language recalls Wordsworth's description of poetry as "the spontaneous overflow of powerful feeling" (Preface to* Lyrical Ballads, *1800). With image piled upon image, complex rhetorical constructions, anagrammatic transformations of words, blank verse and rhyme, and numerous philosophical inconsistencies, "Mont Blanc" reproduces for his reader the sensations he felt in viewing Mont Blanc.*

Lines Written in the Vale of Chamouni

I.

The everlasting universe of things[1]
Flows through the mind, and rolls its rapid waves,
Now dark—now glittering—now reflecting gloom—
Now lending splendour, where from secret springs
The source of human thought its tribute brings   5
Of waters,—with a sound but half its own,

---

[9]To fear overly self-involved behavior and neglect of social responsibilities, but also to be in awe of (as in "God-fearing").

---

[1]Traditional philosophy distinguishes between "things" (objects) and "ideas" (abstractions).

Such as a feeble brook will oft assume
In the wild woods, among the mountains lone,
Where waterfalls around it leap for ever,
Where woods and winds contend, and a vast river   10
Over its rocks ceaselessly bursts and raves.

II.

Thus thou, Ravine of Arve—dark, deep Ravine—
Thou many-coloured, many-voicèd vale,
Over whose pines, and crags, and caverns sail
Fast cloud-shadows and sunbeams: awful scene,   15
Where Power in likeness of the Arve comes down
From the ice-gulfs[2] that gird his secret throne,
Bursting through these dark mountains like the flame
Of lightning through the tempest;—thou dost lie,
Thy giant brood of pines around thee clinging,   20
Children of elder time, in whose devotion
The chainless winds still come and ever came
To drink their odours, and their mighty swinging
To hear—an old and solemn harmony;
Thine earthly rainbows stretched across the sweep   25
Of the aethereal waterfall, whose veil
Robes some unsculptured image;[3] the strange sleep
Which when the voices of the desert fail
Wraps all in its own deep eternity;—
Thy caverns echoing to the Arve's commotion,   30
A loud, lone sound no other sound can tame;
Thou art pervaded with that ceaseless motion,
Thou art the path of that unresting sound—
Dizzy Ravine! and when I gaze on thee
I seem as in a trance sublime and strange   35
To muse on my own separate fantasy,
My own, my human mind, which passively
Now renders and receives fast influencings,
Holding an unremitting interchange
With the clear universe of things around;   40
One legion of wild thoughts, whose wandering wings
Now float above thy darkness, and now rest

[2]The glaciers of the Mer de Glace (Sea of Ice).
[3]Rocks behind the waterfall.

Where that or thou art no unbidden guest,
In the still cave of the witch Poesy,
Seeking among the shadows that pass by   45
Ghosts of all things that are, some shade of thee,
Some phantom, some faint image;[4] till the breast
From which they fled recalls them, thou art there!

III.

Some say that gleams of a remoter world
Visit the soul in sleep,—that death is slumber,   50
And that its shapes the busy thoughts outnumber
Of those who wake and live.[5]—I look on high;
Has some unknown omnipotence unfurled
The veil of life and death? or do I lie
In dream, and does the mightier world of sleep   55
Spread far around and inaccessibly
Its circles? For the very spirit fails,
Driven like a homeless cloud from steep to steep
That vanishes among the viewless gales!
Far, far above, piercing the infinite sky,   60
Mont Blanc appears,[6]—still, snowy, and serene—
Its subject mountains their unearthly forms
Pile around it, ice and rock; broad vales between
Of frozen floods, unfathomable deeps,
Blue as the overhanging heaven, that spread   65
And wind among the accumulated steeps;
A desert peopled by the storms alone,
Save when the eagle brings some hunters bone,
And the wolf tracks her there—how hideously
Its shapes are heaped around! rude, bare, and high,   70
Ghastly, and scarred, and riven.—Is this the scene
Where the old Earthquake-dæmon[7] taught her young
Ruin? Were these their toys? or did a sea
Of fire envelop once this silent snow?

[4]In *The Republic*, Plato compares the mind to a cave, where what we "know" consists only of shadows cast upon the wall from a source of light outside.

[5]In the "Intimations" ode, Wordsworth writes, "Our birth is but a sleep and a forgetting" (l. 58) of a divine origin; Shelley proposes that dreams are a form of memory.

[6]Comes into view; impresses the mind.

[7]A spirit part human, part divine, often malicious (punning "demon").

None can reply—all seems eternal now. 75
The wilderness has a mysterious tongue
Which teaches awful[8] doubt, or faith so mild,
So solemn, so serene, that man may be,
But for[9] such faith, with nature reconciled;
Thou hast a voice, great Mountain, to repeal 80
Large codes of fraud and woe; not understood
By all, but which the wise, and great, and good
Interpret, or make felt, or deeply feel.

IV.

The fields, the lakes, the forests, and the streams,
Ocean, and all the living things that dwell 85
Within the daedal[10] earth; lightning, and rain,
Earthquake, and fiery flood, and hurricane,
The torpor of the year when feeble dreams
Visit the hidden buds, or dreamless sleep
Holds every future leaf and flower;—the bound 90
With which from that detested trance they leap;
The works and ways of man, their death and birth,
And that of him and all that his may be;
All things that move and breathe with toil and sound
Are born and die; revolve, subside, and swell. 95
Power dwells apart in its tranquillity,
Remote, serene, and inaccessible:
And *this*, the naked countenance of earth,
On which I gaze, even these primaeval mountains
Teach the adverting[11] mind. The glaciers creep 100
Like snakes that watch their prey, from their far fountains,
Slow rolling on; there, many a precipice,
Frost and the Sun in scorn of mortal power
Have piled: dome, pyramid, and pinnacle,
A city of death, distinct with many a tower 105
And wall impregnable of beaming ice.
Yet not a city, but a flood of ruin

[8]Awe-filled, awe-inspiring.
[9]Perhaps "only by means of," but perhaps nearly the opposite: "except for."
[10]Variously adorned (from the Greek for skillful and variegated).
[11]Attentive ("turning toward"). The scenery gives no direct evidence of God, just records the eternal, inexorable process of destruction and renewal.

Is there, that from the boundaries of the sky
Rolls its perpetual stream; vast pines are strewing
Its destined path, or in the mangled soil   110
Branchless and shattered stand; the rocks, drawn down
From yon remotest waste, have overthrown
The limits of the dead and living world,
Never to be reclaimed. The dwelling-place
Of insects, beasts, and birds, becomes its spoil;   115
Their food and their retreat for ever gone,
So much of life and joy is lost. The race
Of man flies far in dread; his work and dwelling
Vanish, like smoke before the tempests stream,
And their place is not known.[12] Below, vast caves   120
Shine in the rushing torrents restless gleam,
Which from those secret chasms in tumult welling
Meet in the vale, and one majestic River,
The breath and blood of distant lands, for ever
Rolls its loud waters to the ocean-waves,   125
Breathes its swift vapours to the circling air.

V.

Mont Blanc yet gleams on high:—the power is there,[13]
The still and solemn power of many sights,
And many sounds, and much of life and death.
In the calm darkness of the moonless nights,   130
In the lone glare of day, the snows descend
Upon that Mountain; none beholds them there,[14]
Nor when the flakes burn in the sinking sun,
Or the star-beams dart through them:—Winds contend
Silently there, and heap the snow with breath   135
Rapid and strong, but silently! Its home
The voiceless lightning in these solitudes

---

[12]See Psalms 103: "As for man, his days are as grass. . . . For the wind passeth over it, and it is gone; and the place thereof shall know it no more."

[13]Shelley daringly divides the couplet ("air / . . . there") across the stanza break.

[14]This scene of pure poetic imagination sets up the poem's concluding question, about the mind's agency in producing a sublimity that overpowers the mind. Shelley may be invoking the "immaterialist" notion advanced by Bishop George Berkeley (1685–1753) that the physical forms and phenomena of the natural world are always held in the mind of a creator God; or he may be implying that it takes a human mind, a poet's mind, to behold their reality.

Keeps innocently, and like vapour broods
Over the snow. The secret strength of things
Which governs thought, and to the infinite dome   140
Of Heaven is as a law, inhabits thee!
And what were thou, and earth, and stars, and sea,
If to the human mind's imaginings
Silence and solitude were vacancy?

July 23, 1816.

An Address to the People on the Death of the Princess Charlotte

Composed within a week of Princess Charlotte Augusta's childbed death (6 November 1817), sent to Shelley's publisher, Charles Ollier, but apparently not published. An unauthorized edition appeared in 1843.

Shelley juxtaposes the public mourning for the popular dead princess with the executions—on the day she died—of several Derbyshire rebels who led an unsuccessful uprising in June 1817. Betrayed by a government informer ("Oliver the Spy"), the leaders were hanged; their associates were transported to Australia. In his radical Black Dwarf, *Thomas Wooler wrote on 12 November:*

Those who do not permit an *alledged* state *necessity* to overpower the common principles of humanity, are astonished that the sentence of the wretched beings condemned at Derby should have been carried into effect, at a moment which the executioners of that sentence are eager to designate as one of the greatest national calamity. That the death of the Princess Charlotte should have been immediately followed by such a scene of blood as that exhibited upon the scaffold at Derby, is as shocking to the understanding, as it is abhorrent to the feelings. Was the vulture of law so eager for the banquet of mangled carcases, that it could not fast through the solemnity of those funeral preparations, which we are told will inhume *all the virtues* of humanity, and all the hopes of England? Was it decorous, at a moment, when ALL BUSINESS was desired to be suspended, that the EXECUTIONER ALONE should pursue his SANGUINARY AVOCATION; and that the AXE should be raised for human slaughter, while all the implements of peaceful industry were ordered to repose?

"WE PITY THE PLUMAGE, BUT FORGET THE DYING BIRD."[1]

I. The Princess Charlotte is dead. She no longer moves, nor thinks, nor feels.[2] She is as inanimate as the clay with which she is about to mingle. It is a dreadful thing to know that she is a putrid corpse, who but a few days since was full of life and hope; a woman young, innocent, and beautiful, snatched from the bosom of domestic peace, and leaving that single vacancy which none can die and leave not.

II. Thus much the death of the Princess Charlotte has in common with the death of thousands. How many women die in childbed and leave their families of motherless children and their husbands to live on, blighted by the remembrance of that heavy loss? How many women of active and energetic virtues; mild, affectionate, and wise, whose life is as a chain of happiness and union, which once being broken, leaves those whom it bound to perish, have died, and have been deplored with bitterness, which is too deep for words?[3] Some have perished in penury or shame, and their orphan baby has survived, a prey to the scorn and neglect of strangers. Men have watched by the bedside of their expiring wives, and have gone mad when the hideous death-rattle was heard within the throat, regardless of the rosy child sleeping in the lap of the unobservant nurse. The countenance of the physician had been read by the stare of this distracted husband, till the legible despair sunk into his heart. All this has been and is. You walk with a merry heart through the streets of this great city, and think not that such are the scenes acting all around you. You do not number in your thought the mothers who die in childbed. It is the most horrible of ruins:—In sickness, in old age, in battle, death comes as to his own home; but in the season of joy and hope, when life should succeed to life, and the assembled family expects one more, the youngest and the best beloved, that the wife, the mother—she for whom each member of the family was so dear to one another, should die!—Yet thousands

---

[1] "He pities the plumage, but forgets the dying bird," said Tom Paine, in *The Rights of Man* (1791), of Edmund Burke's lament for the fall of the French royal family in his *Reflections on the Revolution in France* (1790). The dying bird is the oppressed French people.

[2] Echoing Wordsworth's "A Slumber Did My Spirit Seal" (1800): "No motion has she now, no force, / She neither hears nor sees" (ll. 5–6).

[3] At the end of his "Intimations" ode, Wordsworth writes, "To me the meanest flower that blows can give / Thoughts that do often lie too deep for tears" (ll. 205–6; meanest: humblest; blows: blooms).

of the poorest poor, whose misery is aggravated by what cannot be spoken now, suffer this. And have they no affections? Do not their hearts beat in their bosoms, and the tears gush from their eyes? Are they not human flesh and blood?[4] Yet none weep for them—none mourn for them—none when their coffins are carried to the grave (if indeed the parish furnishes a coffin for all) turn aside and moralize upon the sadness they have left behind.

III. The Athenians did well to celebrate, with public mourning, the death of those who had guided the republic with their valour and their understanding, or illustrated[5] it with their genius. Men do well to mourn for the dead: it proves that we love something beside ourselves; and he must have a hard heart who can see his friend depart to rottenness and dust, and speed him without emotion on his voyage to "that bourne whence no traveller returns."[6] To lament for those who have benefited the State, is a habit of piety yet more favourable to the cultivation of our best affections. When Milton died it had been well that the universal English nation had been clothed in solemn black, and that the muffled bells had tolled from town to town. The French nation should have enjoined a public mourning at the deaths of Rousseau and Voltaire.[7] We cannot truly grieve for every one who dies beyond the circle of those especially dear to us; yet in the extinction of the objects of public love and admiration, and gratitude, there is something, if we enjoy a liberal mind, which has departed from within that circle. It were well done also, that men should mourn for any public calamity which has befallen their country or the world, though it be not death. This helps to maintain that connexion between one man and another, and all men considered as a whole, which is the bond of social life. There should be public mourning when those events take place which make all good men mourn in their hearts,—the rule of foreign or domestic tyrants, the abuse of public faith, the wresting of old and venerable laws[8] to the murder of the innocent, the established insecurity of all those, the flower of the nation, who cherish an unconquerable en-

[4]Echoing Shakespeare's Jew Shylock, proclaiming his humanity to a Christian court (*The Merchant of Venice*, 3.1).

[5]Dignified, made exemplary.

[6]Hamlet's description of the afterlife (*Hamlet*, 3.1.79–80); bourne: limit.

[7]Jean-Jacques Rousseau (1712–78), Voltaire (François-Marie Arouet, 1694–1778): celebrated French Enlightenment writers and philosophers, supporters of civil liberties and social reforms.

[8]The Magna Carta, the first British document against monarchal tyranny.

thusiasm for public good. Thus, if Horne Tooke and Hardy had been convicted of high treason,[9] it had been good that there had been not only the sorrow and the indignation which would have filled all hearts, but the external symbols of grief. When the French Republic was extinguished, the world ought to have mourned.

IV. But this appeal to the feelings of men should not be made lightly, or in any manner that tends to waste, on inadequate objects, those fertilising streams of sympathy, which a public mourning should be the occasion of pouring forth. This solemnity should be used only to express a wide and intelligible calamity, and one which is felt to be such by those who feel for their country and for mankind; its character ought to be universal, not particular.

V. The news of the death of the Princess Charlotte, and of the execution of Brandreth, Ludlam, and Turner,[10] arrived nearly at the same time. If beauty, youth, innocence, amiable manners, and the exercise of the domestic virtues could alone justify public sorrow when they are extinguished for ever, this interesting Lady would well deserve that exhibition. She was the last and the best of her race. But there were thousands of others equally distinguished as she, for private excellences, who have been cut off in youth and hope. The accident of her birth neither made her life more virtuous nor her death more worthy of grief. For the public she had done nothing, either good or evil; her education had rendered her incapable of either in a large and comprehensive sense. She was born a Princess; and those who are destined to rule mankind are dispensed with acquiring that wisdom and that experience which is necessary even to rule themselves. She was not like Lady Jane Grey,[11] or Queen Elizabeth, a woman of profound and various learning. She had accomplished nothing, and aspired to nothing, and could understand nothing respecting those great political questions which involve the happiness of those over whom she was destined to rule.[12] Yet this should not be

[9]Radicals John Horne Tooke (1736–1812) and Thomas Hardy (1752–1832) were prosecuted—and acquitted—for high treason in 1794 for publishing anti-government writings.

[10]Jeremiah Brandreth, Isaac Ludlam, and William Turner were the rebels executed for high treason on 6 Nov. 1817, the day Princess Charlotte died.

[11]Lady Jane Grey (1537–54), intellectual wife of Guildford Dudley and queen of England for nine days in 1553 following the death of Edward VI. Edward's Catholic sister Mary, his successor, had both arrested and executed.

[12]Though a friend to liberal reformers and an advocate of public benevolence, young Princess Charlotte was not politically active or effective.

said in blame, but in compassion: let us speak no evil of the dead. Such is the misery, such the impotence of royalty.—Princes are prevented from the cradle from becoming any thing which may deserve that greatest of all rewards next to a good conscience, public admiration and regret.

VI. The execution of Brandreth, Ludlam, and Turner, is an event of quite a different character from the death of the Princess Charlotte. These men were shut up in a horrible dungeon, for many months, with the fear of a hideous death and of everlasting hell thrust before their eyes; and at last were brought to the scaffold and hung. They too had domestic affections, and were remarkable for the exercise of private virtues. Perhaps their low station permitted the growth of those affections in a degree not consistent with a more exalted rank. They had sons, and brothers, and sisters, and fathers, who loved them, it should seem, more than the Princess Charlotte could be loved by those whom the regulations of her rank had held in perpetual estrangement from her. Her husband[13] was to her as father, mother, and brethren. Ludlam and Turner were men of mature years, and the affections were ripened and strengthened within them. What those sufferers felt shall not be said. But what must have been the long and various agony of their kindred may be inferred from Edward Turner, who, when he saw his brother dragged along upon the hurdle,[14] shrieked horribly and fell in a fit, and was carried away like a corpse by two men. How fearful must have been their agony, sitting in solitude on that day when the tempestuous voice of horror from the crowd, told them that the head so dear to them was severed from the body! Yes—they listened to the maddening shriek which burst from the multitude: they heard the rush of ten thousand terror-stricken feet, the groans and the hootings which told them that the mangled and distorted head was then lifted into the air. The sufferers were dead. What is death? Who dares to say that which will come after the grave?[15] Brandreth was calm, and evidently believed that the consequences of our errors were limited by that tremendous barrier. Ludlam and Turner were full of fears, lest God should plunge them in everlasting fire. Mr. Pickering, the clergyman, was evidently anx-

---

[13]Charlotte married Prince Leopold of Saxe-Cobourg in May 1816.

[14]Sled-like, laddered device for dragging the condemned to execution.

[15]"'Your death has eyes in his head—mine is not painted so.'—*Cymbeline*." [Shelley's note.] "Your death has eyes in his head then; I have not seen / Him so pictured," says a jailer to a condemned commoner (*Cymbeline* 5.5.268–69).

ious that Brandreth should not by a false confidence, lose the single opportunity of reconciling himself with the Ruler of the future world. None knew what death was, or could know. Yet these men were presumptuously thrust into that unfathomable gulf, by other men, who knew as little and who reckoned not the present or the future sufferings of their victims. Nothing is more horrible than that man should for any cause shed the life of man. For all other calamities[16] there is a remedy or a consolation. When that Power through which we live ceases to maintain the life which it has conferred, then is grief and agony, and the burthen which must be borne: such sorrow improves the heart. But when man sheds the blood of man, revenge, and hatred, and a long train of executions, and assassinations, and proscriptions, is perpetuated to remotest time.

VII. Such are the particular, and some of the general considerations depending on[17] the death of these men. But however deplorable, if it were a mere private or customary grief, the public, as the public, should not mourn. But it is more than this. The events which led to the death of those unfortunate men are a public calamity. I will not impute blame to the jury who pronounced them guilty of high treason, perhaps the law requires that such should be the denomination of their offence. Some restraint ought indeed to be imposed on those thoughtless men who imagine they can find in violence a remedy for violence, even if their oppressors had tempted them to this occasion of their ruin. They are instruments of evil, not so guilty as the hands that wielded them, but fit to inspire caution. But their death, by hanging and beheading, and the circumstances of which it is the characteristic and the consequence, constitute a calamity such as the English nation ought to mourn with an unassuageable grief.

VIII. Kings and their ministers have in every age been distinguished from other men by a thirst for expenditure and bloodshed. There existed in this country, until the American war, a check,[18] sufficiently feeble and pliant indeed, to this desolating propensity. Until America proclaimed itself a republic, England was perhaps the freest and most glorious nation subsisting on the surface of the earth. It was not what is to the full desirable that a nation should be, but all that it can be, when it does not govern itself. The consequences however of that fundamental defect soon became evident.

[16]Events of universal consequence.

[17]Relating to; associated with.

[18]The "Sinking Fund," an increasingly oppressive tax to reduce the national debt.

The government which the imperfect constitution of our representative assembly threw into the hands of a few aristocrats, improved the method of anticipating the taxes by loans, invented by the ministers of William III,[19] until an enormous debt had been created. In the war against the Republic of France, this policy was followed up, until now, the *mere interest* of the public debt amounts to more than twice as much as the lavish expenditure of the public treasure, for maintaining the standing army, and the royal family, and the pensioners, and the placemen.[20] The effect of this debt is to produce such an unequal distribution of the means of living, as saps the foundation of social union and civilized life. It creates a double aristocracy,[21] instead of one which was sufficiently burthensome before, and gives twice as many people the liberty of living in luxury and idleness, on the produce of the industrious and the poor. And it does not give them this because they are more wise and meritorious than the rest, or because their leisure is spent in schemes of public good, or in those exercises of the intellect and the imagination, whose creations ennoble or adorn a country. They are not like the old aristocracy men of pride and honour, *sans peur et sans tache*,[22] but petty piddling slaves who have gained a right to the title of public creditors, either by gambling in the funds,[23] or by subserviency to government, or some other villainous trade. They are not the "Corinthian capital of polished society,"[24] but the petty and creeping weeds which deface the rich tracery of its sculpture. The effect of this system is, that the day labourer gains no more now by working sixteen hours a day than he gained before by working eight. I put the thing in its simplest and most intelligible shape. The labourer, he that tills the ground and manufactures cloth, is the man who has to provide, out of what he would bring home to his wife and children, for the luxuries and comforts of those, whose claims are represented by an annuity of forty-four millions a year[25]

[19]The Bank of England, founded in 1694, subsidized wars with loans to be repaid through increasing taxes. William III and Queen Mary ruled 1689–1702.

[20]Government appointees.

[21]The hereditary aristocracy and the new *economic* one produced by industrialization.

[22]"Without fear and without stain."

[23]Borrowed funds incurred a national debt; gamblers are investors and speculators.

[24]"Nobility is a graceful ornament to the civil order. It is the Corinthian capital of polished society," (Burke, *Reflections*). In *Rights of Man*, Paine attacks this passage.

[25]*The Examiner* had recently estimated the debt at £40 million.

levied upon the English nation. Before, he supported the army and the pensioners, and the royal family, and the landholders; and this is a hard necessity to which it was well that he should submit. Many and various are the mischiefs flowing from oppression, but this is the representative of them all; namely, that one man is forced to labour for another in a degree not only not necessary to the support of the subsisting distinctions among mankind, but so as by the excess of the injustice to endanger the very foundations of all that is valuable in social order, and to provoke that anarchy which is at once the enemy of freedom, and the child and the chastiser of misrule. The nation, tottering on the brink of two chasms, began to be weary of a continuance of such dangers and degradations, and the miseries which are the consequence of them; the public voice loudly demanded a free representation of the people. It began to be felt that no other constituted body of men could meet the difficulties which impend. Nothing but the nation itself dares to touch the question as to whether there is any remedy or no to the annual payment of forty-four millions a year, beyond the necessary expenses of state, for ever and for ever. A nobler spirit also went abroad, and the love of liberty, and patriotism, and the self-respect attendant on those glorious emotions, revived in the bosoms of men. The government had a desperate game to play.[26]

IX. In the manufacturing districts of England discontent and disaffection had prevailed for many years; this was the consequence of that system of double aristocracy produced by the causes before mentioned. The manufacturers, the helots[27] of our luxury, are left by this system famished, without affections, without health, without leisure or opportunity for such instruction as might counteract those habits of turbulence and dissipation, produced by the precariousness and insecurity of poverty. Here was a ready field for any adventurer who should wish for whatever purpose to incite a few ignorant men to acts of illegal outrage. So soon as it was plainly seen that the demands of the people for a free representation must be conceded if some intimidation and prejudice were not conjured up, a conspiracy of the most horrible atrocity was laid in train. It is impossible to know how far the higher members of the government are involved in the guilt of their infernal agents. It is impossible to

---

[26]Radicals suspected that the government used spies and *agents provocateurs* (like Oliver) to undermine the reform movement by discrediting it among moderates.

[27]Manufacturers are factory workers; helots are serfs and bondsmen—virtual slaves.

know how numerous or how active they have been, or by what false hopes they are yet inflaming the untutored multitude to put their necks under the axe and into the halter. But thus much is known, that so soon as the whole nation lifted up its voice for parliamentary reform, spies were sent forth. These were selected from the most worthless and infamous of mankind, and dispersed among the multitude of famished and illiterate labourers. It was their business if they found no discontent to create it. It was their business to find victims, no matter whether right or wrong. It was their business to produce upon the public all impression, that if any attempt to attain national freedom, or to diminish the burthens of debt and taxation under which we groan, were successful, the starving multitude would rush in, and confound all orders and distinctions, and institutions and laws, in common ruin.[28] The inference with which they were required to arm the ministers was, that despotic power ought to be eternal. To produce this salutary impression, they betrayed some innocent and unsuspecting rustics into a crime whose penalty is a hideous death. A few hungry and ignorant manufacturers seduced by the splendid promises of these remorseless blood-conspirators, collected together in what is called rebellion against the state. All was prepared, and the eighteen dragoons[29] assembled in readiness, no doubt, conducted their astonished victims to that dungeon which they left only to be mangled by the executioner's hand. The cruel instigators of their ruin retired to enjoy the great revenues which they had earned by a life of villainy. The public voice was overpowered by the timid and the selfish, who threw the weight of fear into the scale of public opinion, and parliament confided anew to the executive government those extraordinary powers which may never be laid down, or which may be laid down in blood, or which the regularly constituted assembly of the nation must wrest out of their hands.[30] Our alternatives are a despotism, a revolution, or reform.

X. On the 7th of November, Brandreth, Turner, and Ludlam ascended the scaffold. We feel for Brandreth the less, because it seems he killed a man. But recollect who instigated him to the proceedings which led to murder. On the word of a dying man, Brandreth

---

[28]The government was happy to wield the specter of French Revolution and Terror.

[29]As reported in *The Examiner* on 9 November 1819.

[30]Probably the suspension of habeas corpus, which Parliament approved in March 1817 when it also passed the seditious Meetings Act to stifle dissent.

tells us, that "OLIVER *brought him to this*"—that, "*but for* OLIVER, *he would not have been there.*" See, too, Ludlam and Turner, with their sons and brothers, and sisters, how they kneel together in a dreadful agony of prayer. Hell is before their eyes, and they shudder and feel sick with fear, lest some unrepented or some wilful sin should seal their doom in everlasting fire. With that dreadful penalty before their eyes—with that tremendous sanction for the truth of all he spoke, Turner exclaimed loudly and distinctly, *while the executioner was putting the rope round his neck*, "THIS IS ALL OLIVER AND THE GOVERNMENT." What more he might have said we know not, because the chaplain prevented any further observations. Troops of horse, with keen and glittering swords, hemmed in the multitudes collected to witness this abominable exhibition. "When the stroke of the axe was heard, there was a burst of horror from the crowd.[31] The instant the head was exhibited, there was a tremendous shriek set up, and the multitude ran violently in all directions, as if under the impulse of sudden frenzy. Those who resumed their stations, groaned and hooted." It is a national calamity, that we endure men to rule over us, who sanction for whatever ends a conspiracy which is to arrive at its purpose through such a frightful pouring forth of human blood and agony. But when that purpose is to trample upon our rights and liberties for ever, to present to us the alternatives of anarchy and oppression, and triumph when the astonished nation accepts the latter at their hands, to maintain a vast standing army, and add, year by year, to a public debt, which, already, they know, cannot be discharged; and which, when the delusion that supports it fails,[32] will produce as much misery and confusion through all classes of society as it has continued to produce of famine and degradation to the undefended poor; to imprison and calumniate those who may offend them, at will; when this, if not the purpose, is the effect of that conspiracy, how ought we not to mourn?

XI. Mourn then People of England. Clothe yourselves in solemn black. Let the bells be tolled. Think of mortality and change. Shroud yourselves in solitude and the gloom of sacred sorrow. Spare no symbol of universal grief. Weep—mourn—lament. Fill the great City—fill the boundless fields, with lamentation and

[31] "These expressions are taken from *The Examiner*, Sunday, Nov. 9th." [Shelley's note.]
[32] The Sinking Fund and paper money create the illusion that the national debt can be retired.

the echo of groans. A beautiful Princess is dead:—she who should have been the Queen of her beloved nation, and whose posterity should have ruled it for ever. She loved the domestic affections, and cherished arts which adorn, and valour which defends. She was amiable and would have become wise, but she was young, and in the flower of youth the despoiler came. LIBERTY is dead. Slave! I charge thee disturb not the depth and solemnity of our grief by any meaner sorrow. If One has died who was like her that should have ruled over this land, like Liberty, young, innocent, and lovely, know that the power through which that one perished was God, and that it was a private grief. But *man* has murdered Liberty, and whilst the life was ebbing from its wound, there descended on the heads and on the hearts of every human thing, the sympathy of an universal blast and curse. Fetters heavier than iron weigh upon us, because they bind our souls. We move about in a dungeon more pestilential than damp and narrow walls, because the earth is its floor and the heavens are its roof. Let us follow the corpse of British Liberty slowly and reverentially to its tomb: and if some glorious Phantom should appear,[33] and make its throne of broken swords and sceptres and royal crowns trampled in the dust, let us say that the Spirit of Liberty has arisen from its grave and left all that was gross and mortal there, and kneel down and worship it as our Queen.

[33]Shelley reprises this image of attenuated hope at the end of his unpublishable sonnet "England in 1819" (see p. 80).

⌒ *Other Deaths in 1817*

Domestic crises and unrest pushed Britain to the brink of revolution. The economy, already slumping before Waterloo, was burdened by hundreds of thousands of returning veterans. Terrible weather in 1815 and 1816 led to crop failures, high prices, and widespread starvation. Rapid industrialization loaded the slums in manufacturing cities (Birmingham and Manchester). Mill workers dispossessed by new machinery turned on the machines, destroying them and burning factories. Many rioters were tried, convicted, executed, or sent to penal colonies. Even so, bands of pro-reform laborers and former soldiers continued to agitate, and the government responded not with remedies but with harsh laws against assembly and with treacherous *agents provocateurs*. At the village of Pentrich in 1817, one such agent provoked several Derbyshire workingmen to a protest. Dozens were arrested and imprisoned, and the three principal leaders were publicly executed.

Accouchement[1] and Decease of Her Royal Highness the Princess Charlotte

> *This monthly, founded by the Philosophical Society of London, published from 1782 to 1826. Its primary focus was literary, historical, and antiquarian, but it also offered national and international news. The princess and her new husband, Prince Leopold of Saxe-Cobourg, focused public hopes for a new, respectable monarchy—dashed by her childbed death and stillborn son.*

[1]Childbed.

The European Magazine, and London Review
(November 1817), pp. 383–85

> All Angel now!—Yet little less than all,
>   While yet a pilgrim in our world below!
> What 'vails it us that sweetness to recall,
>   Which hid its own to soothe all other woe;
> What 'vails it to tell, how Virtue's purest glow
>   Shone yet more lovely in a form so fair:
> And least of all,—What 'vails the world should know,
>   That this poor garland, 'twined to deck thy hair,
> Is hung upon thy hearse, to droop and wither there!
>   Walter Scott.[2]

The Princess Charlotte is no more!—"How many sorrows crowd into these few brief words!"[3]—How many dearly-cherished hopes and expectations do they annihilate for ever!—Torn from the world in the bloom of life, of enjoyment, and of prosperity, Her awful bereavement has affected us like the tremendous convulsion of an earthquake, or the sudden visitation of an overwhelming darkness.—It is with feelings of acute sorrow, to which our remembrance furnishes no parallel, that we enter upon the melancholy and unexpected duty of recording its particulars, and of announcing an event, which has absorbed every other solicitude, and rendered light every other grief.— An event which has removed from us a Princess who was truly the "expectancy and rose of our fair state,"[4]—but of whom, alas! nothing now remains but a sad remembrance, and a bitter regret.—It is our painful task to narrate an occurrence, as afflictive as is recorded in the annals of hereditary Monarchies,—the deaths of the only two presumptive heirs to the Crown in direct succession, the Mother and her child: The circumstances of whose dissolution are as affecting to private feelings, as the event itself may be esteemed publicly calamitous; for if there is an occasion on which the infliction of the universal doom excites peculiar sorrow, it is that wherein the more tender sex is alone exposed to pain and hazard; and if there is a station to which man might wish to be born, for the purpose of promoting the happiness of his fellow-creatures, it is that of the constitutional Sovereign of

---

[2]From *The Lord of the Isles* (1815), Canto Sixth, "Conclusion," stanza 2.1.

[3]*Ibid.*, stanza 1.6. "How many sorrows crowd / Into these two brief words."

[4]Ophelia on distracted Hamlet: "O, what a noble mind is here o'erthrown! . . . The expectancy and rose of the fair state" (3.1.150–52).

the British Empire. Under there circumstances we have lost a Prince, just before he saw the light, and a Princess in the prime of youth, and at the height of happiness.—A Princess, who was indeed beloved for every estimable virtue which could endear her to the British People, and who, now the grave has closed over her remains, is deplored with grief as unaffected as it is general. The blow has fallen too, at a moment when we were least prepared to meet its vengeance, and when she was about to add a new, and a more endearing claim to our attachment.—Her Royal Highness has been snatched from us, at an hour when the fond and eager anticipations of anxious loyalty were hailing her the Mother of "a line of Kings,"[5] were picturing her the future Sovereign of a people who loved, admired, and reverenced her. Those prospects, the inscrutable decrees of Heaven have rendered vain, and the ardency of disappointed hope serves now but to embitter present calamity. It has brought to us one other awful lesson of the insecurity of all human bliss, and the instability of all earthly greatness; it has proclaimed, that in the grave the Sovereign and the subject are alike undistinguished, and that rank, wealth, and happiness, are equally defenceless against the dire advances of Life's last foe. Like a blossom which expands but to give promise of its future loveliness, the lone bud has been severed from its native stem, and while the Parent root yet flourishes in strength and vigour, its opening leaves are withered by the passing blast, and every fond anticipation lies buried in the grave that hides its beauty. We have not only to mourn the loss of Her Royal Highness as our future Queen,—as the depositary of a Nation's hopes, and prayers, and affections,—as the presumptive heiress of a Realm in which she should sustain all the glory of her departed ancestors, but we have also to lament the wreck of all those fondly cherished expectations, with which we were prepared to congratulate her fulfilment of a Nation's dearest wishes, in becoming the living mother of a living child.—How dreadful now is the reverse!—

> "All things which we ordained festival,
> Turn from their office to black funeral;
> Our solemn hymns to sullen dirges change,
> Our bridal flowers serve for a buried corse,
> And all things change them to the contrary!"[6]

[5] *Macbeth* 3.1.59. Macbeth laments the witches' prophecy that Banquo would father a line of kings, leaving Macbeth excluded.

[6] Capulet comments on dead Juliet (see *Romeo and Juliet* 4.5.84–90).

On Her Royal Highness the hopes of the Nation had for many years fondly rested, and the shock has come upon us like one of those awful convulsions of Nature, where no warning voice is heard, until all around is ruin, and desolation, and death. Even yet, the flattering thought of its impossibility will sometimes start upon our listless moments, as if it were a dream too horrible for memory,—but again the sad reality returns, in all its distressing certainty of waking truth, and forces our conviction. The Princess was indeed an Englishwoman! and possessed a mind influenced by more than feminine firmness, and an heart which had abundantly profited by the instructions of her early youth. Had it pleased Providence she should ascend the British Throne, she would have brought to it the true spirit of an English Queen.— Proud of her country, she respected its manners,—she admired its Constitution,—and she venerated its Religion. Warmth and openness of heart marked her conduct through life; and when she found herself blessed with the husband of her choice,—when she found that choice justified by his virtues, she more than once declared herself the happiest woman in the kingdom!—That happiness is past; but we may confidently trust, that her mortal coronet, lined with thorns, dimmed by infirmity, and dislodged by death, is now exchanged for a diadem which shall know no change for ever and for ever!

Before entering upon the more interesting particulars of our painful task, it will be necessary to preface the melancholy detail by a concise account of the previous circumstances. Every thing indeed connected with the distressing subject, must excite a peculiar interest, and be read with peculiar feeling; for, all that remains of our once lovely Princess is now a breathless corpse. . . .

Derbyshire

> Founded in 1814, this influential Tory monthly applauded the most repressive government policies, though in the 1820s it softened sufficiently to attract liberal writers and readers.

from *New Monthly Magazine* 8.47 (December 1817), p. 458

Nov. 7th, the sentence of the law was carried into execution at Derby on Jeremiah Brandreth, William Turner and Isaac Ludlam, convicted of high treason. About noon the prisoners were brought to the front of the gaol; they appeared resigned to their fate, and after shaking each other by the hand, and taking leave of each other, the ropes were placed round their necks, and after a few awful minutes they were launched into eternity. The bodies hung about 40 minutes, when they were cut down, and the sentence of decapitation was carried into effect. As each head was severed from the body, the executioner held it up to the view of the spectators, and said—"Behold the head of a traitor!" The bodies were then put into the coffins prepared for them, and given to their friends.—As these men have been the first we have had to record as suffering for the high crime of treason, we most sincerely hope they will be the last; and that their fate will be sufficient to deter others from engaging in such unlawful combinations.

The Execution of Jeremiah Brandreth, 27, William Turner, 46, Isaac Ludlum, 52, for High Treason, at DERBY (1817)

Appearing just after the executions, this anonymous four-column broadside (a large sheet, c. 14 x 20 inches) was edged with the thick black band of mourning notices like those for Princess Charlotte. The printer's name was legally required to appear at the end of any document. The title spans the page, with a woodcut illustration atop the two middle columns.

THE STATE PRISONERS AT DERBY.

Derby, Nov. 6, 1817.

The criminals appeared in no respect materially different from what they had previously been. When the Chaplain visited Turner and Ludlam, he presented the latter with the book which had been already stated he wished to possess, in order to give it to his son— "Baxter's Call to the Unconverted." Ludlam received the little volume with expressions of thankfulness, and said it was a book from which he had derived much benefit himself, and he hoped the son for whom he intended it, and others of his family, would profit no less by it than he had done. . . . The manner of his death seemed frequently to fill him with unspeakable horror. He was sincerely penitent, but he appeared deficient in fortitude. By degrees, his mind became more tranquillised, and he took a just view of the crime for which he was about to suffer. Attempting to raise his thoughts to

Heaven in prayer that afternoon while supplicating his Maker to pardon his numerous sins, he extended his appeal to the Throne of Mercy, by imploring the Great Disposer of all Events, "to bless his native land . . . to incline the King to love his people . . . to make him beloved by them, and to save the nation from a recurrence of those commotions which had disturbed the public peace, and brought him to an untimely end."[. . .]

Turner in the course of this day was visited by several of his friends and relations. Like Ludlam, he was much wasted by imprisonment and sorrow. [. . .] He desired that an affectionate letter might be written, one that would be read with pleasure by those for whom he designed it when he should be no more; and to such letter he expressed a wish to affix his signature. [. . .] He did not explicitly confess his offence against his country as Ludlam had done, but he did not hesitate to admit that his conduct had been wrong.

Brandreth on this day exhibited a remarkable instance of fortitude. Few men in such circumstances have ever appeared so perfectly composed. There was nothing of levity, or of vivacity in his conduct, to call for reproof, but he was singularly tranquil, and he continued unshaken to the last. The Chaplain was astonished to find him thus serene. In his experience, he had never met with a man about to lay down his life for offences so aggravated, and under circumstances so peculiarly terrific, who could appear so little distressed, and whose mind was so completely made up to meet death without dismay. In conversing with the prisoner, he expressed surprise at finding him thus, . . . Brandreth replied, that he felt himself sustained beyond execution. He declared he had no fear, and did not at all shrink from the idea of mounting the scaffold. [. . .]

The Minister next endeavoured to impress him with a due sense of the guilt he had incurred in shedding the blood of a fellow creature. On this subject at least, he suggested, a full confession ought to be made. Brandreth was here as impenetrable as ever. He had endeavoured to make peace with GOD, and he did not see that it was necessary to make any statement for the satisfaction of man. To him it appeared that this was a question wholly between the ALMIGHTY and his own soul, and now that he was about to be snatched from earth, he cherished a confident hope that an arm of vengeance would not be interposed between him and Heaven. He repeated the declaration that he had no reluctance to mount the scaffold, and felt no dread of the morrow! In the evening, when he was again visited by the Chaplain, his manner and his language were the same, and no trace of emotion or fear could be discovered. During his confinement he once said, that but for Mr Oliver he never should have been there. He was pressed to explain these words, but refused to do so, and he never repeated the assertion, nor even mentioned the name of Mr. Oliver again.

THE EXECUTION

This morning Ludlam and Turner looked shocking wan and spiritless. They had watched the whole night in prayer and psalmsinging. At nine the Chaplain visited them, and assisted them in their devotions. [. . .] Their voices were dejected in the extreme.

Brandreth slept as usual, rose in good spirits, and shewed no sign of despondency or fear.

From an early hour in the morning the scaffolding and drop were erecting in front of the gaol, and a considerable number of persons were collected in the street quietly looking on, and listening with visible alarm to each sad note of preparation.

At half-past ten all the prisoners went to the Chapel. Ludlam and Turner looked like walking spectres. Brandreth stept forward firmly. All the other prisoners appeared to feel much sympathy. At the same moment the crowd without felt some trepidation on seeing the horse led into the gaol that was to draw the hurdle along the yard.

At half past eleven all the prisoners, excepting the three men to be executed, and George Weightman left in the Chapel. All held their handkerchiefs to their eyes, and sobbed deeply. Shortly after they had come into the yard, William Turner's brother, Edward, shrieked horribly, and was carried into a room by two men. The Chaplain then administered the sacrament to the four convicts.

At twelve precisely, Mr. Simpson, the Under Sheriff, appeared with a few javelin men, and a considerable number of special constables. The prisoners then descended from the Chapel to the room which Brandreth [. . .] had occupied. [. . .]

At a quarter past twelve the hurdle was drawn up at the door of this room, it was turned the flat side upwards, and the horse was now attached to it. Brandreth came into the yard [. . .] where, in a few minutes, he was joined by Turner . [. . .] Brandreth took Turner by the hand, and they kissed each other.

When they had thus embraced, Brandreth addressed his fellow-sufferer, [. . .] "Well," he said, "we shall now soon be above the sky, where there will be joy and glory for ever and ever in the presence of Jesus Christ." "Yes", Turner replied with enthusiasm, "there will be no sorrow there, all will be joy and felicity." The Chaplain encouraged these hopes, and assisted them with other consoling reflections till Ludlam was brought to the door of the passage. [. . .] Ludlam having passed them praying to himself, [. . .] they were summoned to the scaffold.

They passed along the passage leading towards that part of the prison in which Ludlam and Turner had been latterly confined, and were now placed in a row at the foot of a ladder, by which they were to be conducted to the platform. . . .

After a momentary pause, Mr. Pickering passed up the ladder with Brandreth, preceded by the executioner and his assistant.

On being brought to the scaffold, dispatch is mercy to the criminal. That the sufferers might yesterday be dismissed from life with the greatest possible expedition, after they were exposed to the gaze of the multitude, it was ordered that the three noozes [*sic*] should be formed, and the ends of the ropes tied to the suspending beam, so that when the sufferers were led forth nothing might remain to be done but pass each rope over the head of the man for whom it was destined, to pull down the caps, and let the drop fall.

On mounting the scaffold Brandreth exclaimed, "God be with you all and Lord Castlereagh." The cord by which he was to be suspended was tied too high, and on account of his shortness it became necessary to loosen it at the top to make it reach him. When his head was passed through it, and the knot placed behind the left ear, the rope being at the same time drawn moderately tight, the word was given for William Turner to be brought up; he ascended the ladder with a faultering step, and on reaching the platform, called out with an air of wildness, "This is all Oliver and the Government, the Lord have mercy on my soul." The halter was then placed about his neck, and he joined with the Minister in prayer. The third sufferer, Isaac Ludlam, was now brought up the ladder; he prayed, as he passed up, and while the rope was being placed about his neck he raised his voice in humble supplication to Heaven, in the following terms:— "O Lord, forgive my sins, and receive my soul, and grant that I may meet all this great concourse of people in Heaven. Bless the King of this nation, bless the people, bless all the people high and low, rich and poor, bound and free; yea, bless all, from the King upon his Throne down to the meanest subject in the realm; and may this awful dispensation be made a blessing to thousands and tens of thousands. O Lord, receive my spirit!" [. . .] The executioners put the caps on the heads of the unhappy men, and pulled them over their faces. Each of them exclaimed at this moment, "Into thy hands, O God! I commit my spirit." They continued to call on their Creator and Redeemer for mercy, and I. Ludlam was once more giving utterance to the last part of the prayer about inserted, when . . .

The drop fell a quarter before one, & at a quarter past one they were cut down. Brandreth's body was then laid upon the block, with the face downwards, and the head towards the street, in the full view of the people; the scaffold not being more than ten feet from the ground. The executioner raised the axe, and struck at the neck with all his force. At that instant there was a burst of horror from the crowd. The executioner then took up the head, and holding it by the hair, addressed the people, "Behold the head of Jeremiah Brandreth, the Traitor!"

The heads of Turner and Ludlam were exhibited in the same way. The heads and bodies were then thrown into the coffins, and interred at dusk in St. Werburgh's Church Yard, Derby.

[INNES, Printer, Manchester]

Ozymandias

The subject of Shelley's sonnet, Ozymandias (the Greek name for the pharaoh Ramses II), was Moses's opponent in Exodus. The British Museum had recently acquired a bust of Ramses II found near a ruined statue. Shelley and his friend Horace Smith staged a contest in the winter of 1817–18 to compose sonnets on this subject. Leigh Hunt published both poems in The Examiner *in the winter of 1818, signing Shelley's poem "Glirastes."*

I met a traveller from an antique land
Who said—"Two vast and trunkless legs of stone
Stand in the desart. . . . Near them on the sand,
Half sunk, a shatter'd visage lies, whose frown
And wrinkled lip and sneer of cold command   5
Tell that its sculptor well those passions read
Which yet survive, stamp'd on these lifeless things,[1]

[1]The sculptor understood well the passions that are preserved in the ruin; Shelley may also mean "yet survive" in the tyrants of modern Europe.

THE EXAMINER.

ORIGINAL POETRY.

OZYMANDIAS.

I met a Traveller from an antique land,
Who said, "Two vast and trunkless legs of stone
Stand in the desart. Near them, on the sand,
Half sunk, a shattered visage lies, whose frown,
And wrinkled lip, and sneer of cold command,
Tell that its sculptor well those passions read,
Which yet survive, stamped on these lifeless things,
The hand that mocked them, and the heart that fed:
And on the pedestal these words appear:
"My name is OZYMANDIAS, King of Kings."
Look on my works ye Mighty, and despair!
No thing beside remains. Round the decay
Of that Colossal Wreck, boundless and bare,
The lone and level sands stretch far away.

GLIRASTES.

THE POOR LAWS.

PLYMOUTH DOCK, OR PARISH OF STOKE DAMEREL.

From their peculiar situation, all sea-ports are more or less subject to the influx of strangers; but such places as Plymouth, Portsmouth, &c. feel the weight of the evil, as connected with the Poor Laws, in the extreme; as it is to those places the destitute make for, in the hope of finding employment, either on board the King's ships or merchant vessels; whilst many calculate to a certainty on being employed in his Majesty's arsenals; but after having travelled perhaps two or three hundred miles, and expended their last penny, their hopes are blasted, and their disappointment arrived to the highest pitch, they are compelled to apply to the parish.

Others again, arriving in the different vessels from abroad, disabled or enfeebled by age, are discharged to make room for more active and efficient men. These set themselves at the first place where they land; as also do women and children who have lost their husbands and fathers, and who have been sent home from the Continent or our Colonies.

To it is distressing list may be added, women with their families, who have followed their husbands to the place of embarkation, or who have come to visit them when there.

All these must be provided for by the parishes of such sea-ports, until their examinations are taken as to their different settlements.

This is the first and a very difficult step; for one half of the poor creatures who would wish to be removed, know no more about their husbands' or fathers' right of settlement, than the person who asks the question; whilst the other half, not wishing to be sent to their own parishes as paupers, contrive by every means to deceive.

After having made the necessary enquiries, by writing or otherwise, in this or that direction,—and in which it is as requisite to be as particular and cautious as if searching for the titles to an estate,—a clear settlement often appears to be made out, the paupers are forwarded to the place of destination, and the expence of conveyance and maintenance on the road is paid by the Overseers.

It is, however, two to one but a notice of appeal is given —something has occurred which was not known or could not be discovered, perhaps informality in the wording of the order, or what is worse than both, the paupers have been sent to the right parish; but a Township in that parish maintains its own poor, and the order should have been directed to the Overseers of such township.

This last calls loudly for some alteration, should nothing else be altered; the townships and parishes should be combined, or there should be *a book printed by authority*, stating the different hamlets, townships, or parishes who maintain their own poor.

No such book is extant; neither can Overseers by any means get at certain information on the subject; which is to be regretted more than any other defect in the Poor Laws: for in all cases parishes will and do take advantages of one another in this respect, urged on by their Solicitors, who are sure to gain by the contest.

It often happens, that rather than risk the enormous expenses of an appeal, distant as we are nearly fifty miles from the place where the Sessions for the County are held, this parish takes back paupers who do not belong to it; which circumstance is the more galling, inasmuch as the persons never resided in the parish, or ever did one act, by labour or otherwise, to benefit the town, but merely *slept a night or two, on their transfer from the ship to the shore.*

Two cases occurred lately, which will fully explain the above. William Johns, a seaman, was landed here ill; he was maintained a considerable time before his settlement could be found; when this was ascertained, a suspended order was made out, and he was kept in the Workhouse on a charge of four shillings per week, until fit to be removed to the parish of Madran. On his arrival at Penzance, which is in the parish of Madran, the Overseers gave notice of appeal, the grounds of which were, that his settlement was in the township of Penzance. This case was settled, by sending a person to the spot, who arranged it, with the loss of the suspension and expenses.

The other case was that of J. Dunn and family, born and settled in the parish of Falmouth. He was also ill, and remained in the Work-house under a suspended order, till being removed, notice of appeal was received, at the same time stating that Dunn was born in the town of Falmouth, but that the township maintained its own poor. Expenses of settling this were paid by this parish, who lost the suspension.

Enough then, one would suppose, has been said, to convince every mind, that sea-ports labour under disadvantages, as the Poor Laws now stand, and that something ought to be done to ameliorate their condition, and lessen, if possible, their burthen, by either *establishing County Workhouses*, and collecting an equitable Rate for their support; or by *Government taking the whole under their superintendance*, and collecting a Rate, in the manner the Assessed Taxes are now collected.

Lest that conviction should not be produced, the following case is added:—

A soldier, named Garland, returned from abroad a few months since, whose wife and child had been in the workhouse eighteen years. On taking his examination, it appeared that he had previously gained a settlement in Whitechapel, by renting 12l. per annum; and also a subsequent settlement in Gosport, of which circumstances his wife was not aware.

Thus have this Parish expended (calculated at only four shillings per week each) 374l. 8s.; which expence ought to have been borne by some other. To add to this regret felt on the occasion, the child, at the proper age, was bound an apprentice, and gained a settlement under that binding, when the indenture was cancelled by the Magistrates, on the ground of his being *non compos mentis*; and consequently this Parish has to maintain him as long as he lives.

So much for paupers who come to sea-ports, and perhaps only sleep a night or two in a town before they become chargeable.

Our strong argument might be used to influence the Government to take the Poor under their own superintendance and management; which is, that, during the

The Examiner, 11 January 1818, showing *Ozymandias*.

The hand that mock'd them and the heart that fed;
And on the pedestal these words appear:
'My name is Ozymandias, king of kings:[2]   10
Look on my works, ye Mighty, and despair!
Nothing beside remains. Round the decay
Of that colossal Wreck, boundless and bare,
The lone and level sands stretch far away."—

Lines Written among the Euganean Hills

Published in Rosalind and Helen, *1819. A prefatory "Advertisement"
reports that the poem was written near Padua, "after a day's excursion
among those lovely mountains which surround what was once the retreat, and where is now the sepulchre, of Petrarch" (Italian Renaissance
poet). These lines illustrate Shelley's "speed," a poetics of forward rush,
rapid accumulation, and enjambment. The long sentences (the first sentence extends 26 lines) across short lines, piling up modifying and qual-
ifying phrases, yield a remarkable sense of rapid forward motion.*

October, 1818.

Many a green isle needs must be
In the deep wide sea of Misery,
Or the mariner, worn and wan,
Never thus could voyage on—
Day and night, and night and day,   5
Drifting on his dreary way,
With the solid darkness black
Closing round his vessel's track;
Whilst above the sunless sky,
Big with clouds, hangs heavily,   10
And behind the tempest fleet
Hurries on with lightning feet,
Riving[1] sail, and cord, and plank,
Till the ship has almost drank
Death from the o'er-brimming deep;   15

[2]According to Diodorus, this was the actual boast; Shelley also mines the irony of
the modern Christian attribution to Jesus Christ of the term "king of kings."

---

[1]Tearing apart.

And sinks down, down, like that sleep
When the dreamer seems to be
Weltering[2] through eternity;
And the dim low line before
Of a dark and distant shore   20
Still recedes, as ever still
Longing with divided will,
But no power to seek or shun,
He is ever drifted on
O'er the unreposing wave   25
To the haven of the grave.
What, if there no friends will greet;
What, if there no heart will meet
His with love's impatient beat;
Wander wheresoe'er he may,   30
Can he dream before that day
To find refuge from distress
In friendship's smile, in love's caress?
Then 'twill wreak him little woe
Whether such there be or no: 35
Senseless[3] is the breast, and cold,
Which relenting love would fold;
Bloodless are the veins and chill
Which the pulse of pain did fill;
Every little living nerve   40
That from bitter words did swerve
Round the tortured lips and brow,
Are like sapless leaflets now
Frozen upon December's bough.

On the beach of a northern sea   45
Which tempests shake eternally,
As once the wretch there lay to sleep,
Lies a solitary heap,
One white skull and seven dry bones,
On the margin of the stones,   50
Where a few gray rushes stand,
Boundaries of the sea and land:
Nor is heard one voice of wail

[2]Tossed about.
[3]Unfeeling, irrational.

But the sea-mews,[4] as they sail
O'er the billows of the gale;   55
Or the whirlwind up and down
Howling, like a slaughtered town,
When a king in glory rides
Through the pomp of fratricides:
Those unburied bones around   60
There is many a mournful sound;
There is no lament for him,
Like a sunless vapour, dim,
Who once clothed with life and thought
What now moves nor murmurs not.   65

Aye, many flowering islands lie
In the waters of wide Agony:
To such a one this morn was led,
My bark by soft winds piloted:
'Mid the mountains Euganean   70
I stood listening to the paean[5]
With which the legioned rooks did hail
The sun's uprise majestical;
Gathering round with wings all hoar,
Through the dewy mist they soar   75
Like gray shades, till the eastern heaven
Bursts, and then, as clouds of even,
Flecked with fire and azure, lie
In the unfathomable sky,
So their plumes of purple grain,   80
Starred with drops of golden rain,
Gleam above the sunlight woods,
As in silent multitudes
On the morning's fitful gale
Through the broken mist they sail,   85
And the vapours cloven and gleaming
Follow, down the dark steep streaming,
Till all is bright, and clear, and still,
Round the solitary hill.

[4]See Archangel Michael's description of the Flood that will make Eden "an Island
salt and bare, / The haunt of Seals and Orcs, and Sea-mews' clang" (*PL* 11.834–35).
[5]Hymn.

Beneath is spread like a green sea   90
The waveless plain of Lombardy,
Bounded by the vaporous air,
Islanded by cities fair;
Underneath Day's azure eyes
Ocean's nursling, Venice lies,   95
A peopled labyrinth of walls,
Amphitrite's[6] destined halls,
Which her hoary sire now paves
With his blue and beaming waves.
Lo! the sun upsprings behind,   100
Broad, red, radiant, half-reclined
On the level quivering line
Of the waters crystalline;
And before that chasm of light,
As within a furnace bright,   105
Column, tower, and dome, and spire,
Shine like obelisks of fire,
Pointing with inconstant motion
From the altar of dark ocean
To the sapphire-tinted skies;   110
As the flames of sacrifice
From the marble shrines did rise,
As to pierce the dome of gold
Where Apollo spoke of old.[7]

Sun-girt City,[8] thou hast been   115
Ocean's child, and then his queen;
Now is come a darker day,
And thou soon must be his prey,
If the power that raised thee here
Hallow so thy watery bier.   120
A less drear ruin then than now,
With thy conquest-branded brow
Stooping to the slave of slaves
From thy throne, among the waves
Wilt thou be, when the sea-mew   125

[6]In Greek myth, the daughter of Oceanus and wife of Poseidon.
[7]The oracle of Apollo at Delphi.
[8]Venice.

Flies, as once before it flew,
O'er thine isles depopulate,
And all is in its ancient state,
Save where many a palace gate
With green sea-flowers overgrown   130
Like a rock of Ocean's own,
Topples o'er the abandoned sea
As the tides change sullenly.
The fisher on his watery way,
Wandering at the close of day,   135
Will spread his sail and seize his oar
Till he pass the gloomy shore,
Lest thy dead should, from their sleep
Bursting o'er the starlight deep,
Lead a rapid masque[9] of death   140
O'er the waters of his path.

Those who alone thy towers behold
Quivering through aërial gold,
As I now behold them here,
Would imagine not they were   145
Sepulchres, where human forms,
Like pollution-nourished worms,
To the corpse of greatness cling,
Murdered, and now mouldering:
But if Freedom should awake   150
In her omnipotence, and shake
From the Celtic Anarch's[10] hold
All the keys of dungeons cold,
Where a hundred cities lie
Chained like thee, ingloriously,   155
Thou and all thy sister band
Might adorn this sunny land,
Twining memories of old time
With new virtues more sublime;
If not, perish thou and they!—   160
Clouds which stain truth's rising day
By her sun consumed away—

[9]An elaborate court entertainment.
[10]Austrian tyranny; cf. l. 223. Italy was under Austrian domination.

Earth can spare ye: while like flowers,
In the waste of years and hours,
From your dust new nations spring   165
With more kindly blossoming.

Perish—let there only be
Floating o'er thy hearthless sea
As the garment of thy sky
Clothes the world immortally,   170
One remembrance, more sublime
Than the tattered pall of time,
Which scarce hides thy visage wan;—
That a tempest-cleaving Swan
Of the songs of Albion,   175
Driven from his ancestral streams
By the might of evil dreams,
Found a nest in thee;[11] and Ocean
Welcomed him with such emotion
That its joy grew his, and sprung   180
From his lips like music flung
O'er a mighty thunder-fit,
Chastening terror:—what though yet
Poesy's unfailing River,
Which through Albion winds forever   185
Lashing with melodious wave
Many a sacred Poet's grave,
Mourn its latest nursling fled?
What though thou with all thy dead
Scarce can for this fame repay   190
Aught thine own? oh, rather say
Though thy sins and slaveries foul
Overcloud a sunlike soul?
As the ghost of Homer clings
Round Scamander's[12] wasting springs;   195
As divinest Shakespeare's might
Fills Avon[13] and the world with light
Like omniscient power which he

---

[11]The residence of Byron (Albion's "tempest-cleaving Swan") in Venice.

[12]In the *Iliad*, a river near Troy.

[13]Stratford-on-Avon is Shakespeare's birthplace.

Imaged 'mid mortality;
As the love from Petrarch's urn,   200
Yet amid yon hills doth burn,
A quenchless lamp by which the heart
Sees things unearthly;—so thou art,
Mighty spirit—so shall be
The City that did refuge thee.   205

Lo, the sun floats up the sky
Like thought-wingèd Liberty,
Till the universal light
Seems to level plain and height;
From the sea a mist has spread,   210
And the beams of morn lie dead
On the towers of Venice now,
Like its glory long ago.
By the skirts of that gray cloud
Many-domèd Padua proud   215
Stands, a peopled solitude,
'Mid the harvest-shining plain,
Where the peasant heaps his grain
In the garner of his foe,
And the milk-white oxen slow   220
With the purple vintage strain,
Heaped upon the creaking wain,[14]
That the brutal Celt may swill
Drunken sleep with savage will;
And the sickle to the sword   225
Lies unchanged, though many a lord,
Like a weed whose shade is poison,
Overgrows this region's foison,[15]
Sheaves of whom are ripe to come
To destruction's harvest-home: 230
Men must reap the things they sow,
Force from force must ever flow,
Or worse; but 'tis a bitter woe
That love or reason cannot change
The despot's rage, the slave's revenge.   235

[14]Large, ox-drawn vehicle.
[15]Plentiful harvest.

Padua, thou within whose walls
Those mute guests at festivals,
Son and Mother, Death and Sin,
Played at dice for Ezzelin,[16]
Till Death cried, "I win, I win!"   240
And Sin cursed to lose the wager,
But Death promised, to assuage her,
That he would petition for
Her to be made Vice-Emperor,
When the destined years were o'er,   245
Over all between the Po
And the eastern Alpine snow,
Under the mighty Austrian.
Sin smiled so as Sin only can,
And since that time, ay, long before,   250
Both have ruled from shore to shore,—
That incestuous pair, who follow
Tyrants as the sun the swallow,
As Repentance follows Crime,
And as changes follow Time.   255
In thine halls the lamp of learning,
Padua, now no more is burning;
Like a meteor, whose wild way
Is lost over the grave of day,
It gleams betrayed and to betray: 260
Once remotest nations came
To adore that sacred flame,
When it lit not many a hearth
On this cold and gloomy earth:
Now new fires from antique light   265
Spring beneath the wide world's might;
But their spark lies dead in thee,
Trampled out by Tyranny.
As the Norway woodman quells,
In the depth of piny dells,   270
One light flame among the brakes,[17]

[16]Satan's daughter Sin, and his instantaneously begot son, Death, guard the gates of Hell (*PL* 2.684ff.). In Coleridge's *Rime of the Ancient Mariner* (1798–1817), Death and Death-in-Life determine the Mariner's fate with a cast of dice. Ezzelino da Romano (a 13th-c. tyrant), the oppressor of Venice and Padua.

[17]Woody brush.

While the boundless forest shakes,
And its mighty trunks are torn
By the fire thus lowly born:
The spark beneath his feet is dead,   275
He starts to see the flames it fed
Howling through the darkened sky
With a myriad tongues victoriously,
And sinks down in fear: so thou,
O Tyranny, beholdest now   280
Light around thee, and thou hearest
The loud flames ascend, and fearest:
Grovel on the earth; ay, hide
In the dust thy purple pride!

Noon descends around me now: 285
'Tis the noon of autumn's glow,
When a soft and purple mist
Like a vaporous amethyst,
Or an air-dissolvèd star
Mingling light and fragrance, far   290
From the curved horizon's bound
To the point of Heaven's profound,[18]
Fills the overflowing sky;
And the plains that silent lie
Underneath, the leaves unsodden   295
Where the infant Frost has trodden
With his morning-wingèd feet,
Whose bright print is gleaming yet;
And the red and golden vines,
Piercing with their trellised lines   300
The rough, dark-skirted wilderness;
The dun and bladed grass no less,
Pointing from this hoary tower
In the windless air; the flower
Glimmering at my feet; the line   305
Of the olive-sandalled Apennine
In the south dimly islanded;
And the Alps, whose snows are spread
High between the clouds and sun;

[18]Depth (a Miltonism).

And of living things each one;   310
And my spirit which so long
Darkened this swift stream of song,—
Interpenetrated lie
By the glory of the sky:
Be it love, light, harmony,   315
Odour, or the soul of all
Which from Heaven like dew doth fall,
Or the mind which feeds this verse
Peopling the lone universe.

Noon descends, and after noon   320
Autumn's evening meets me soon,
Leading the infantine moon,
And that one star,[19] which to her
Almost seems to minister
Half the crimson light she brings   325
From the sunset's radiant springs:
And the soft dreams of the morn
(Which like wingèd winds had borne
To that silent isle, which lies
Mid remembered agonies,   330
The frail bark[20] of this lone being)
Pass, to other sufferers fleeing,
And its ancient pilot, Pain,
Sits beside the helm again.

Other flowering isles must be   335
In the sea of Life and Agony:
Other spirits float and flee
O'er that gulf: even now, perhaps,
On some rock the wild wave wraps,
With folded wings they waiting sit   340
For my bark, to pilot it
To some calm and blooming cove,
Where for me, and those I love,
May a windless bower be built,
Far from passion, pain, and guilt,   345

[19]Venus, the evening star.

[20]Small boat.

In a dell mid lawny hills,
Which the wild sea-murmur fills,
And soft sunshine, and the sound
Of old forests echoing round,
And the light and smell divine   350
Of all flowers that breathe and shine:
We may live so happy there,
That the Spirits of the Air,
Envying us, may even entice
To our healing Paradise   355
The polluting multitude;
But their rage would be subdued
By that clime divine and calm,
And the winds whose wings rain balm
On the uplifted soul, and leaves   360
Under which the bright sea heaves;
While each breathless interval
In their whisperings musical
The inspired soul supplies
With its own deep melodies,   365
And the love which heals all strife
Circling, like the breath of life,
All things in that sweet abode
With its own mild brotherhood:
They, not it, would change; and soon   370
Every sprite beneath the moon
Would repent its envy vain,
And the earth grow young again.

Stanzas Written in Dejection—
December 1818, near Naples

The relationship between Percy and Mary, already stressed by the rigors of travel in Italy and by emotional estrangement, deteriorated further when their daughter Clara died (24 September 1818), for which Mary partially blamed Percy. In poor health at this time, he felt even more keenly his separation from friends like Leigh Hunt, Thomas Love Peacock, and others. The poem uses a modified Spenserian stanza (after Edmund Spenser's The Faerie Queene,*

1596, spectacularly refreshed by Byron in Childe Harold's Pilgrimage *[1812–18]). The title may allude to Coleridge's "Dejection: An
Ode" (1802).*

The sun is warm, the sky is clear,
The waves are dancing fast and bright,
Blue isles and snowy mountains wear
The purple noon's transparent might:
The breath of the moist earth is light   5
Around its unexpanded buds;
Like many a voice of one delight—
The winds, the birds, the ocean-floods—
The City's voice itself is soft, like Solitude's.

I see the deep's untrampled floor   10
With green and purple sea-weeds strown;
I see the waves upon the shore
Like light dissolved in star-showers thrown:
I sit upon the sands alone;
The lightning of the noon-tide ocean   15
Is flashing round me, and a tone
Arises from its measured motion—
How sweet! did any heart now share in my emotion.

Alas! I have nor hope nor health,
Nor peace within nor calm around,   20
Nor that content, surpassing wealth,
The sage in meditation found,
And walk'd with inward glory crown'd—
Nor fame, nor power, nor love, nor leisure;
Others I see whom these surround—   25
Smiling they live, and call life pleasure;
To me that cup has been dealt in another measure.[1]

[1] A rueful pun on "verse."

Yet now despair itself is mild
Even as the winds and waters are;
I could lie down like a tired child,   30
And weep away the life of care
Which I have borne, and yet must bear,—
Till death like sleep[2] might steal on me,
And I might feel in the warm air
My cheek grow cold, and hear the sea   35
Breathe o'er my dying brain its last monotony.

Some might lament that I were cold,
As I, when this sweet day is gone
Which my lost heart, too soon grown old,
Insults with this untimely moan—   40
They might lament—for I am one
Whom men love not, and yet regret:[3]
Unlike this day, which when the Sun
Shall on its cloudless glory set,
Will linger though enjoyed, like joy in Memory yet.   45

[2]"Death, like sleep" but also "death-like sleep."
[3]Have regret for; mourn.

Political Poems of 1819

Events in Britain were nearing a crisis by the summer of 1819. Growing resentment over the government's intransigence in the face of widespread calls for parliamentary reform to give greater representation to the working-class cities was fed by rising prices and increasing contempt for the Prince Regent, titular head of state (George III was deemed incompetent, by madness, in 1811). Bands of unemployed former soldiers were gathering throughout the country, and a demonstration by 50,000 citizens in Birmingham in July was followed by another peaceful gathering of 60,000–100,000 at St. Peter's Fields, near Manchester, on 16 August, featuring charismatic orator Henry Hunt. A local cavalry detachment of Army Hussars, along with the Manchester Yeomanry, many drunk, was sent to arrest Hunt and other speakers. The Hussars charged the crowd, wielding sabers and other weapons, killing at least six and wounding dozens, maybe hundreds, more, including women and children. The press and public reacted with shock and outrage at "Peterloo," a contemptuous parody of British triumphalism over Waterloo. Although the immediate effect was a suppression of the reform movement with new legislative strictures, Peterloo proved pivotal. Important leaders, such as Lord John Russell and Earl Grey, began to support reform and would help secure passage in 1832 of the First Reform Act. Shelley's "phantom" figures evoke this hope for the future.

Shelley learned about Peterloo from letters and newspaper reports he read in Italy. Thomas Love Peacock sent a letter, and Leigh Hunt sent press accounts, including the 22 and 29 August issues of *The Examiner*. Outraged, Shelley threw himself into a frenzy of writing "exoteric" poems—topical, explicitly political, and confrontational. He sent several to Hunt to put in *The Examiner*, but fearing a reprisal of the state persecution that had imprisoned him and others, Hunt demurred. Parliament's notorious Six Acts of 1819 stiffened penalties for "treasonous" or "seditious" words and licensed the seizure of private and public spaces. Such measures would spur a backlash and hasten progress toward the Reform Act of 1832, after whose passage Shelley's poems appeared posthumously. *The Mask of Anarchy* appeared in 1832 and the rest in Mary Shelley's 1839 edition, with headnotes. In her "Note on Poems of 1819," she wrote:

> Shelley loved the people, and respected them as often more virtuous, as always more suffering, and, therefore more deserving of sympathy, than the great. He believed that a clash between the two classes of society was inevitable, and he eagerly ranged himself on the people's side. He had an idea of publishing a series of poems adapted expressly to commemorate their circumstances and wrongs.—He wrote a few, but in those days of prosecution for libel, they could not be printed. They are not among the best of his productions, a writer being always shackled when he endeavours to write down to the comprehension of those who could not understand or feel a highly imaginative style; but they show his earnestness, and with what heartfelt compassion he went home to the direct point of wrong—that oppression is detestable, as being the parent of starvation, nakedness and ignorance. Besides these outpourings of compassion and indignation, he had meant to adorn the cause he loved with loftier poetry of glory and triumph—such is the scope of the Ode to the Assertors of Liberty. (3.206–7)

Lines Written During the Castlereagh Administration

This is the title that Shelley's cousin, Thomas Medwin, applied when he published the lines in The Athenaeum *in 1832. Viscount Castlereagh (Robert Stewart, 1739–1822) built his career as an opponent of Napoleonic France, serving as Secretary of War under Prime Ministers William Pitt (1805–6) and the Duke of Portland (1807–9), and then, from 1812, as Foreign Secretary in Lord Liverpool's unpopular ministry. One of the architects of the settlement that followed Waterloo (1815), he advocated a policy of nonintervention in other nations' affairs. The "Oppressor" (stanza 3) is not only Castlereagh's or Liverpool's administration but also the whole reactionary establishment. Castlereagh committed suicide the same year as Shelley drowned.*

The Massacre at Peterloo! or a Specimen of English Liberty.

Corpses are cold in the tomb;
Stones on the pavement are dumb;
Abortions are dead in the womb,
And their mothers look pale—like the death-white shore
    Of Albion,[1] free no more.   5

[1]Old mythic name for England; the white shore involves the chalk cliffs of Dover.

Her sons are as stones in the way—
They are masses of senseless clay[2]—
They are trodden, and move not away,—
The abortion with which she travaileth
    Is Liberty, smitten to death.   10

Then trample and dance, thou Oppressor!
For thy victim is no redresser;
Thou art sole lord and possessor
Of her corpses, and clods, and abortions—they pave
    Thy path to the grave.   15

Hearest thou the festival din
Of Death, and Destruction, and Sin,
And Wealth crying Havoc! within?
'Tis the bacchanal triumph that makes Truth dumb,
    Thine Epithalamium.[3]   20

Ay, marry thy ghastly wife!
Let Fear and Disquiet and Strife
Spread thy couch in the chamber of Life!
Marry Ruin, thou Tyrant! and Hell be thy guide
    To the bed of the bride!   25

Song: To the Men of England

Published in 1839, this song was a favorite in the working-class Chartist movement of the 1840s. Counseling passive civil disobedience, Shelley assumes that the oppressors will be shamed into reform. Even so, the insistent questions and declarations, a staple of radical rhetoric (cf. "An Ode, Written October 1819"), aim to excite workers to their righteous cause, and the form of the song seeks to give them a communal voice as well as ongoing inspiration.

Men of England, wherefore plough
For the lords who lay ye low?
Wherefore weave with toil and care
The rich robes your tyrants wear?

[2]Clay: poetic term for flesh, the physical body.
[3]A poem celebrating a wedding.

Wherefore feed, and clothe, and save, 5
From the cradle to the grave,
Those ungrateful drones who would
Drain your sweat—nay, drink your blood?

Wherefore, Bees of England,[1] forge
Many a weapon, chain, and scourge, 10
That these stingless drones[2] may spoil
The forced produce of your toil?

Have ye leisure, comfort, calm,
Shelter, food, love's gentle balm?
Or what is it ye buy so dear 15
With your pain and with your fear?

The seed ye sow, another reaps;
The wealth ye find, another keeps;
The robes ye weave, another wears;
The arms ye forge, another bears. 20

Sow seed,—but let no tyrant reap;
Find wealth,—let no impostor heap;
Weave robes,—let not the idle wear;
Forge arms,—in your defence to bear.

Shrink to your cellars, holes, and cells; 25
In halls ye deck another dwells.
Why shake the chains ye wrought? Ye see
The steel[3] ye tempered glance on ye.

---

[1] In his famous *Fable of the Bees* (1714), Bernard de Mandeville argues that society thrives not by benevolence, as Shelley (and Godwin) believed, but from personal acquisitiveness and the love of luxury.

[2] Nonworker, whose only role is to impregnate the queen. Shelley's term implies social and sexual impotence.

[3] Swords and sabers.

With plough and spade, and hoe and loom,
Trace your grave, and build your tomb,   30
And weave your winding-sheet, till fair
England be your sepulchre.[4]

England in 1819

*First published 1839, this sonnet (one long explosive sentence) is a
tacit homage to Sir Francis Burdett (1770–1844), aristocratic reformer
and member of Parliament. On his election in 1812, Burdett gave a
speech (published in* The Examiner*) referring to England's "Phantom
for a king," its "army of spies and informers," its "vague and sanguinary laws," and its "oppressed people." Shelley dedicated his early
unpublished poem,* The Wandering Jew *(1809–10), to Burdett, and in
early 1817 had his publisher send Burdett a copy of* A Proposal for
Putting Reform to the Vote Throughout the Kingdom.*

An old, mad, blind, despised, and dying king,[1]—
Princes,[2] the dregs of their dull race, who flow
Through public scorn,—mud from a muddy spring,—
Rulers who neither see, nor feel, nor know,
But leech-like[3] to their fainting country cling,   5
Till they drop, blind in blood, without a blow,—
A people starved and stabbed in the untilled field,[4]—
An army, which liberticide[5] and prey

---

[4]In Thomas Gray's *The Bard* (1757), in which a corpse is wrapped for burial, the
bard casts a spell, "the winding-sheet of Edward's race": the extinction of tyrants
and the survival of the champions of liberty, including the poets.

---

[1]George III ruled 1760–1811, when his madness required that the Prince of Wales
become Prince Regent. Shelley's language echoes King Lear's self-description on the
verge of madness: "a poor, infirm, weak, and despised old man" (*King Lear* 3.3.20).

[2]George III's sons were notoriously dissolute, promiscuous, and corrupt—an embar-
rassment to the King no less than to England itself.

[3]Leeches were common in medical practice to draw "bad blood": George III was
subjected to such treatment, but the body Shelley has in mind is England itself,
drained by leech-like political parasites.

[4]The Peterloo Massacre, 16 August 1819.

[5]The killing of liberty; this use to describe an action rather than a person is original
with Shelley (*OED*).

Makes as a two-edged sword to all who wield,—
Golden and sanguine laws[6] which tempt and slay;   10
Religion Christless, Godless—a book sealed;
A Senate,[7]—Time's worst statute unrepealed,—
Are graves, from which a glorious Phantom may
Burst, to illumine our tempestuous day.

Similes for Two Political Characters of 1819

> *First published in 1832 with this title. Shelley's title was "To S——th and C— —gh," for First Viscount Sidmouth (architect of the Peace of Amiens, 1802, and Home Secretary, 1812–22) and Viscount Castlereagh. Sidmouth was notoriously severe in dealing with civil disturbances; in 1817 he proposed suspending habeas corpus and restricting freedom of the press. After Peterloo he congratulated the troops that had attacked the crowd, and he introduced four of the Six Acts.*

As from an ancestral oak
   Two empty ravens sound their clarion,
Yell by yell, and croak by croak,
When they scent the noonday smoke
     Of fresh human carrion:—   5

As two gibbering night-birds flit
   From their bowers of deadly yew[1]
Through the night to frighten it,
When the moon is in a fit,
     And the stars are none, or few:—   10

As a shark and dog-fish[2] wait
   Under an Atlantic isle,

---

[6]Laws procured with money and enforced with bloodshed, or entrapment and death sentences.

[7]Parliament, still unreformed.

---

[1]Often planted in churchyards, the yew tree is an emblem of death and mourning.

[2]Small shark.

For the negro-ship,[3] whose freight
Is the theme of their debate,
      Wrinkling their red gills the while—   15

Are ye, two vultures sick for battle,
    Two scorpions under one wet stone,
Two bloodless wolves whose dry throats rattle,
Two crows perched on the murrained[4] cattle,
      Two vipers tangled into one.   20

National Anthem[1]

God prosper, speed, and save,
God raise from England's grave
      Her murdered Queen!
Pave with swift victory
The steps of Liberty,   5
Whom Britons own to be
      Immortal Queen.

See, she comes throned on high,
On swift Eternity!
      God save the Queen!   10
Millions on millions wait,
Firm, rapid, and elate,
On her majestic state!
      God save the Queen!

She is Thine[2] own pure soul   15
Moulding the mighty whole,—
      God save the Queen!
She is Thine own deep love

---

[3]Dead, dying, or diseased slaves were often cast overboard.
[4]Diseased carrion.

---

[1]A parody to the meter of *God Save the King* ("My Country, 'tis of thee" in the U.S.), in which the "murdered Queen" is Liberty.
[2]England's (and humanity's) "millions."

Rained[3] down from Heaven above,—
Wherever she rest or move,   20
    God save our Queen!

Wilder[4] her enemies
In their own dark disguise,—
    God save our Queen!
All earthly things that dare   25
Her sacred name to bear,
Strip them, as kings are, bare;
    God save the Queen!

Be her eternal throne
Built in our hearts alone—   30
    God save the Queen!
Let the oppressor hold
Canopied seats of gold;
She sits enthroned of old
    O'er our hearts Queen.   35

Lips touched by seraphim
Breathe out the choral hymn
    "God save the Queen!"
Sweet as if angels sang,
Loud as that trumpet's clang   40
Wakening the world's dead gang,[5]—
    God save the Queen!

An Ode, Written October 1819, Before the Spaniards Had Recovered Their Liberty

This is the title used in the PU *volume (1820); the original title was "Ode to the Assertors of Liberty." The seven-line* ababccc *stanza is unusual for an ode. Shelley links Peterloo to contemporary events in Spain, where King Ferdinand's reactionary measures alienated his supporters*

---

[3]Punning on "reigned."
[4]Bewilder, punning on "wilder," the comparative adjective (a joke on England's jingoism).
[5]The trumpet of the Last Judgment.

*and provoked an opposition that would erupt into a revolution in
1820, a short-lived "Liberty" extinguished in 1823.*

    Arise, arise, arise!
There is blood on the earth that denies ye bread;
    Be your wounds like eyes
To weep for the dead, the dead, the dead.
What other grief were it just to pay?   5
Your sons, your wives, your brethren, were they;
Who said they were slain on the battle day?

    Awaken, awaken, awaken!
The slave and the tyrant are twin-born foes;
    Be the cold chains shaken   10
To the dust where your kindred repose, repose:
Their bones in the grave will start and move,
When they hear the voices of those they love,
Most loud in the holy combat above.

    Wave, wave high the banner!   15
When Freedom is riding to conquest by:
    Though the slaves that fan her
Be Famine and Toil, giving sigh for sigh.
And ye who attend her imperial car,[1]
Lift not your hands in the banded[2] war,   20
But in her defence whose children ye are.

    Glory, glory, glory,
To those who have greatly suffered and done!
    Never name in story
Was greater than that which ye shall have won.   25
Conquerors have conquered their foes alone,
Whose revenge, pride, and power they have overthrown:
Ride ye, more victorious, over your own.[3]

---

[1]Chariot.

[2]Confederated, leagued.

[3]Note how the close rhymes in these four lines and the anagrams (won / own) enact
a drama of transformation even at the linguistic level.

Bind, bind every brow
With crownals of violet, ivy, and pine:[4]   30
    Hide the blood-stains now
With hues which sweet Nature has made divine:
Green strength, azure hope, and eternity:
But let not the pansy[5] among them be;
Ye were injured, and that means memory.   35

The Mask of Anarchy

Almost as soon as he learned of Peterloo, Shelley, in a self-described "torrent of indignation," wrote this poem and sent it to Leigh Hunt to put in The Examiner *on 23 September 1819. But in the atmosphere of persecution that gripped England, Hunt felt the risk was too great. It wasn't until 1832 that he published the poem, which he now retitled* The Masque of Anarchy *and ran without the subtitle. In his Introduction, Hunt stressed Shelley's inspired prophetic vision of nonviolence as the best means of achieving a transformative civic and constitutional reform. Shelley's title-word* Mask *satirizes the pernicious alliance of Church, King, and Government (Sidmouth and Castlereagh again) against the people. The female "Shape" that rises to speak the last half of the poem recalls the "Phantom of Liberty" at the end of* An Address to the People on the Death of the Princess Charlotte. *The poem's verse form of tetrameter couplets and triplets is based on the ballad, a popular form. The other literary form, reflected in the 1832 title, is the masque, a court performance of elaborate spectacle, usually to honor or flatter the reigning monarch, but turned by Shelley to mordant critique. Playing on "mask," Shelley suggests a facade, one that can be punctured, even unmasked.*

Written on the Occasion of the Massacre at Manchester

As I lay asleep in Italy
There came a voice from over the Sea,
And with great power it forth led me
To walk in the visions of Poesy.[1]

---

[4]Emblems, respectively, of modesty, athletic skill, and longevity or eternity.
[5]The pansy is named from the French *pensée*: thought.

---

[1]The dream-vision is a traditional form for allegorical prophecy, dating back to the Middle Ages; Shelley also used the genre for *Queen Mab*.

I met Murder on the way—   5
He had a mask like Castlereagh—
Very smooth he looked, yet grim;
Seven blood-hounds[2] followed him:

All were fat; and well they might
Be in admirable plight,   10
For one by one, and two by two,
He tossed them human hearts to chew
Which from his wide cloak he drew.

Next came Fraud, and he had on,
Like Eldon,[3] an ermined gown;   15
His big tears, for he wept well,
Turned to mill-stones as they fell.

And the little children, who
Round his feet played to and fro,
Thinking every tear a gem,   20
Had their brains knocked out by them.

Clothed with the Bible, as with light,
And the shadows of the night,
Like Sidmouth,[4] next, Hypocrisy
On a crocodile rode by.   25

And many more Destructions played
In this ghastly masquerade,
All disguised, even to the eyes,
Like Bishops, lawyers, peers, or spies.

---

[2]The European states that in 1815, as part of the resolution of the Napoleonic Wars, England agreed to allow to continue in the slave trade.

[3]The Lord Chancellor's garb of office was an ermine-trimmed robe. The post was held by the reactionary John Scott, Lord Eldon, famous for public weeping and for his notorious cruelty. It was he who in 1817 denied Shelley custody of Charles and Ianthe.

[4]As Home Secretary, Viscount Sidmouth raised large sums to build churches for the poor, whom he subjected to spies, informers, and brutal police actions.

Last came Anarchy: he rode   30
On a white horse, splashed with blood;
He was pale even to the lips,
Like Death in the Apocalypse.⁵

And he wore a kingly crown;
And in his grasp a sceptre shone;   35
On his brow this mark I saw—
"I am God, and King, and Law!"⁶

With a pace stately and fast,
Over English land he passed,
Trampling to a mire of blood   40
The adoring multitude.

And a mighty troop around,
With their trampling shook the ground,
Waving each a bloody sword,
For the service of their Lord.   45

And with glorious triumph, they
Rode through England proud and gay,
Drunk as with intoxication
Of the wine of desolation.

O'er fields and towns, from sea to sea,   50
Passed the Pageant swift and free,
Tearing up, and trampling down;
Till they came to London town.

And each dweller, panic-stricken,
Felt his heart with terror sicken   55
Hearing the tempestuous cry
Of the triumph of Anarchy.

---

⁵In St. John the Divine's vision of the apocalypse (Revelation 6.8), Death rides a pale horse as he vanquishes the earth with war and famine. The image was popular both in high art (Benjamin West's *Death on a Pale Horse*, 1783/1803) and in popular caricature (James Gillray's *Presages of the Millennium*, 1795). For Shelley, "Anarchy" is not the absence of government but its tyrannic abuse.

⁶The King is also the head of the Church of England.

For with pomp to meet him came,
Clothed in arms like blood and flame,
The hired murderers,[7] who did sing   60
"Thou art God, and Law, and King.

"We have waited, weak and lone
For thy coming, Mighty One!
Our purses are empty, our swords are cold,
Give us glory, and blood, and gold."   65

Lawyers and priests, a motley crowd,
To the earth their pale brows bowed;
Like a bad prayer not over loud,
Whispering—"Thou art Law and God."—

Then all cried with one accord,   70
"Thou art King, and God, and Lord;
Anarchy, to thee we bow,
Be thy name made holy now!"

And Anarchy, the Skeleton,
Bowed and grinned to every one,   75
As well as if his education
Had cost ten millions to the nation.[8]

For he knew the Palaces
Of our Kings were rightly his;
His the sceptre, crown, and globe,   80
And the gold-inwoven robe.

So he sent his slaves before
To seize upon the Bank and Tower,[9]
And was proceeding with intent
To meet his pensioned Parliament[10]   85

---

[7]The mercenaries wore the red-coat uniforms of the British army—a color chosen to camouflage blood.

[8]The Prince Regent's routine extravagant debts were consistently covered by Parliament.

[9]The Bank of England and the Tower of London, repository of the crown jewels.

[10]Parliament had been bribed with "pensions."

When one fled past, a maniac maid,
And her name was Hope, she said:
But she looked more like Despair,[11]
And she cried out in the air:

"My father Time is weak and gray   90
With waiting for a better day;
See how idiot-like he stands,
Fumbling with his palsied hands![12]

"He has had child after child,
And the dust of death is piled   95
Over every one but me—
Misery, oh, Misery!"

Then she lay down in the street,
Right before the horses' feet,
Expecting, with a patient eye,   100
Murder, Fraud, and Anarchy.

When between her and her foes
A mist, a light, an image rose,
Small at first, and weak, and frail
Like the vapour of a vale: 105

Till as clouds grow on the blast,
Like tower-crowned giants striding fast,
And glare with lightnings as they fly,
And speak in thunder to the sky,

It grew—a Shape arrayed in mail   110
Brighter than the Viper's scale,
And upborne on wings whose grain
Was as the light of sunny rain.[13]

[11]Literally, from the Latin, *de* + *sperare*, "loss of hope."

[12]This stanza is also a jibe at the still-living George III.

[13]The mail-armored viper evokes the revolutionary American colonial "Don't tread on me" banner. The morning star in the next stanza is not Venus, the manipulative goddess of sexual love, but the hope associated with a *morning* star.

On its helm, seen far away,
A planet, like the Morning's, lay;   115
And those plumes its light rained through
Like a shower of crimson dew.

With step as soft as wind it passed
O'er the heads of men—so fast
That they knew the presence there,   120
And looked,—but all was empty air.

As flowers beneath May's footstep waken,
As stars from Night's loose hair are shaken,
As waves arise when loud winds call,
Thoughts sprung where'er that step did fall.[14]   125

And the prostrate multitude
Looked—and ankle-deep in blood,
Hope, that maiden most serene,
Was walking with a quiet mien:

And Anarchy, the ghastly birth,   130
Lay dead earth upon the earth;
The Horse of Death tameless as wind
Fled, and with his hoofs did grind
To dust the murderers thronged behind.

A rushing light of clouds and splendour,   135
A sense awakening and yet tender
Was heard and felt—and at its close
These words of joy and fear arose

As if their own indignant Earth
Which gave the sons of England birth   140
Had felt their blood upon her brow,
And shuddering with a mother's throe

---

[14]Shelley implies that all change begins in awakened thought.

Had turnèd every drop of blood
By which her face had been bedewed
To an accent unwithstood,—   145
As if her heart had cried aloud:[15]

"Men of England, heirs of Glory,
Heroes of unwritten story,
Nurslings of one mighty Mother,
Hopes of her, and one another;   150

"Rise like Lions after slumber
In unvanquishable number,
Shake your chains to earth like dew
Which in sleep had fallen on you—
Ye are many—they are few.   155

"What is Freedom?—ye can tell
That which slavery is, too well—
For its very name has grown
To an echo of your own.

"'Tis to work and have such pay   160
As just keeps life from day to day
In your limbs, as in a cell
For the tyrants' use to dwell,

"So that ye for them are made
Loom, and plough, and sword, and spade,   165
With or without your own will bent
To their defence and nourishment.

"'Tis to see your children weak
With their mothers pine and peak,[16]
When the winter winds are bleak,—   170
They are dying whilst I speak.

---

[15]The exhortation that begins in l. 147 seems to come from the Earth (the natural world) as well as the people.

[16]Mourn and grow weaker.

"'Tis to hunger for such diet
As the rich man in his riot
Casts to the fat dogs that lie
Surfeiting[17] beneath his eye;   175

"'Tis to let the Ghost of Gold[18]
Take from Toil a thousandfold
More than e'er its substance could
In the tyrannies of old.

"Paper coin—that forgery   180
Of the title-deeds, which ye
Hold to something of the worth
Of the inheritance of Earth.

"'Tis to be a slave in soul
And to hold no strong control   185
Over your own wills, but be
All that others make of ye.[19]

"And at length when ye complain
With a murmur weak and vain
'Tis to see the Tyrant's crew   190
Ride over your wives and you—
Blood is on the grass like dew.

"Then it is to feel revenge
Fiercely thirsting to exchange
Blood for blood—and wrong for wrong—   195
Do not thus when ye are strong.[20]

---

[17]Bloated.

[18]Shelley advocated the gold standard, rather than the ghost of paper currency, often issued without adequate backing; the poor suffered from useless wages and rising costs for necessities.

[19]Shelley anticipates the Marxist view that workers are made into dehumanized instruments—passive, compliant subjects to King, Law, God.

[20]Progressive reformers such as Shelley, fearing a bloody French Revolution at home, counseled passive resistance and patience.

"Birds find rest, in narrow nest
When weary of their wingèd quest;
Beasts find fare, in woody lair
When storm and snow are in the air.[21]   200

"Asses, swine, have litter spread
And with fitting food are fed;
All things have a home but one—
Thou, Oh, Englishman, hast none![22]

"This is Slavery—savage men,   205
Or wild beasts within a den
Would endure not as ye do—
But such ills they never knew.

"What art thou Freedom? O! could slaves
Answer from their living graves   210
This demand—tyrants would flee
Like a dream's dim imagery:

"Thou art not, as impostors say,
A shadow soon to pass away,
A superstition, and a name   215
Echoing from the cave of Fame.[23]

"For the labourer thou art bread,
And a comely table spread
From his daily labour come
In a neat and happy home.   220

---

[21]Leigh Hunt's edition of *The Masque of Anarchy* includes this stanza, which Mary
Shelley did not include in *1839*:

Horses, oxen, have a home,
When from daily toil they come;
Household dogs, when the wind roars,
Find a home within warm doors.

[22]Jesus cryptically cautions a scribe who wants to join his ministry, "The foxes have
holes, and the birds of the air have nests; but the Son of Man hath not where to lay
his head" (Matthew 8.20).

[23]The goddess Fame (public reports) often deals in falsities; "superstition" is the
Protestant term for Roman Catholicism.

"Thou art clothes, and fire, and food
For the trampled multitude—
No—in countries that are free
Such starvation cannot be
As in England now we see.   225

"To the rich thou art a check,
When his foot is on the neck
Of his victim, thou dost make
That he treads upon a snake.[24]

"Thou art Justice—ne'er for gold   230
May thy righteous laws be sold
As laws are in England—thou
Shield'st alike the high and low.

"Thou art Wisdom—Freemen never
Dream that God will damn for ever   235
All who think those things untrue
Of which Priests make such ado.

"Thou art Peace—never by thee
Would blood and treasure wasted be
As tyrants wasted them, when all   240
Leagued to quench thy flame in Gaul.[25]

"What if English toil and blood
Was poured forth, even as a flood?
It availed, Oh, Liberty!
To dim, but not extinguish thee.   245

"Thou[26] art Love—the rich have kissed
Thy feet, and like him following Christ,
Give their substance to the free
And through the rough world follow thee,

[24]Another reference to the American revolutionary banner.

[25]The French Revolution.

[26]Not the wealthy but the *fortunate*—and perhaps both. Jesus unsuccessfully counsels a rich youth, "If thou wilt be perfect, go and sell that thou hast, and give to the poor, and thou shalt have treasure in heaven: and come and follow me" (Matthew 19.21).

"Or turn their wealth to arms, and make   250
War for thy belovèd sake
On wealth, and war, and fraud—whence they
Drew the power which is their prey.

"Science, Poetry, and Thought
Are thy lamps; they make the lot   255
Of the dwellers in a cot[27]
So serene, they curse it not.

"Spirit, Patience, Gentleness,
All that can adorn and bless
Art thou—let deeds, not words, express   260
Thine exceeding loveliness.

"Let a great Assembly be
Of the fearless and the free
On some spot of English ground
Where the plains stretch wide around.   265

"Let the blue sky overhead,
The green earth on which ye tread,
All that must eternal be
Witness the solemnity.

"From the corners uttermost   270
Of the bounds of English coast;
From every hut, village, and town
Where those who live and suffer moan
For others' misery or their own,

"From the workhouse[28] and the prison   275
Where pale as corpses newly risen,
Women, children, young and old
Groan for pain, and weep for cold—

[27]Cottage.

[28]Originally meant for vagrants and petty criminals, by 1819 they housed many poor and homeless, who were required to work, sometimes for subsidized poor wages. The horrific conditions were meant as a deterrent.

"From the haunts of daily life
Where is waged the daily strife   280
With common wants and common cares
Which sows the human heart with tares[29]—

"Lastly from the palaces
Where the murmur of distress
Echoes, like the distant sound   285
Of a wind alive around

"Those prison halls of wealth and fashion,
Where some few[30] feel such compassion
For those who groan, and toil, and wail
As must make their brethren pale—   290

"Ye who suffer woes untold,
Or to feel, or to behold
Your lost country bought and sold
With a price of blood and gold—

"Let a vast assembly be,   295
And with great solemnity
Declare with measured words that ye
Are, as God has made ye, free—

"Be your strong and simple words
Keen to wound as sharpened swords,   300
And wide as targes[31] let them be,
With their shade to cover ye.

"Let the tyrants pour around
With a quick and startling sound,
Like the loosening of a sea,   305
Troops of armed emblazonry.[32]

---

[29]Noxious weeds; for Jesus's parable of the tares in the wheatfield, see Matthew 13.24–30.

[30]Enlightened reformers.

[31]Lightweight shields or bucklers carried by medieval footsoldiers.

[32]Ornamented heraldry.

"Let the charged artillery drive
Till the dead air seems alive
With the clash of clanging wheels,
And the tramp of horses' heels.   310

"Let the fixèd bayonet
Gleam with sharp desire to wet
Its bright point in English blood
Looking keen as one for food.

"Let the horsemen's scimitars   315
Wheel and flash, like sphereless stars[33]
Thirsting to eclipse their burning
In a sea of death and mourning.

"Stand ye calm and resolute,
Like a forest close and mute,
With folded arms and looks which are   320
Weapons of unvanquished war,[34]

"And let Panic, who outspeeds
The career of armèd steeds
Pass, a disregarded shade   325
Through your phalanx undismayed.

"Let the laws of your own land,
Good or ill, between ye stand
Hand to hand, and foot to foot,
Arbiters of the dispute,   330

---

[33]Meteors. Scimitars are curved Turkish swords.

[34]"[F]olded arms" means both retracted weapons and a stance of passive resistance.
As Satan is fomenting rebellion in Heaven, it is Archangel Abdiel who stands thus,
at the end of Book 5 of *PL*.

"The old laws of England[35]—they
Whose reverend heads with age are gray,
Children of a wiser day;
And whose solemn voice must be
Thine own echo—Liberty!   335

"On those who first should violate
Such sacred heralds in their state
Rest the blood that must ensue,
And it will not rest on you.

"And if then the tyrants dare   340
Let them ride among you there,
Slash, and stab, and maim, and hew,—
What they like, that let them do.

"With folded arms and steady eyes,
And little fear, and less surprise,   345
Look upon them as they slay
Till their rage has died away.

"Then they will return with shame
To the place from which they came,
And the blood thus shed will speak   350
In hot blushes on their cheek.

"Every woman in the land
Will point at them as they stand—
They will hardly dare to greet
Their acquaintance in the street.   355

"And the bold, true warriors
Who have hugged Danger in wars
Will turn to those who would be free,
Ashamed of such base company.

---

[35]Radical writers and orators frequently appealed to the "old laws of England," by which they generally meant the Magna Carta and the compact between the nobles and the monarch by which King John was enabled to rule. The radicals believed that recent governments had abrogated these traditional rights.

"And that slaughter to the Nation   360
Shall steam up like inspiration,
Eloquent, oracular;
A volcano heard afar.

"And these words shall then become
Like Oppression's thundered doom   365
Ringing through each heart and brain,
Heard again—again—again—

"Rise like Lions after slumber
In unvanquishable number—
Shake your chains to earth like dew   370
Which in sleep had fallen on you—
Ye are many—they are few."

⁓ *Politics and Violence in the Regency*

The Regency, named for Prince Regent George, later George IV (1821), was a politically volatile decade. The costly Napoleonic Wars concluded with Napoleon's defeat at Waterloo, June 1815. When the leaders of the victorious nations assembled in London to carve up Europe, all were cheered by great crowds—except the Prince Regent. Scorned and hissed, despised as an immoral spendthrift, he had to resort to disguise and circuitous routes. Demand for parliamentary reform led to widespread demonstrations, which the government suppressed, often violently: at Pentrich in 1817, the leaders of a popular uprising were executed (see p. 54). Reform agitation boiled over in Manchester in 1819, resulting in the Peterloo Massacre. By then, Shelley was a prominent expatriate in Italy. He kept abreast of English news and kept sending poems back to Leigh Hunt; however, despite Shelley's urging, Hunt could not risk publishing the poems. Selections from the press presented here, including political poetry, reflect varying shades of political opinion, from conservative to radical. The poetry appeals to a popular readership, with an uncomplicated vocabulary and forms taken from songs, hymns, and playful rhymes.

The Constitution

Radical journalist Thomas Wooler's weekly Black Dwarf *(1817–24) published brilliant satires and parodies. By 1819, upwards of 10,000 copies reached a largely working-class readership. Fearing such influence, the government arrested Wooler in 1817; he was acquitted on one charge and partially exonerated on another. The title involves multiple puns: Britain's pride in its strength, its constitutive elements, its guaranteed liberties. Britain has no paper constitution—just a set of laws.*

from *Black Dwarf* 1.1 (29 January 1817)

In ancient times, when Britain stood,
Surrounded by her shield, the flood,[1]
And every champion of her right,
Stood forth in naked, native might,
                    To guard her constitution.   5

The Roman eagle, half disarm'd,
And Caesar's self, shrunk back alarm'd,
Beneath the force of freedom's hand,
And baffl'd fled the British strand,[2]
                    Foil'd by her constitution.   10

But fell dissention[3] spread around,
And tainted Freedom's hallow'd ground;
And foes, whom force had not avail'd,
O'er Freedom's erring sons prevail'd,
                    And quench'd her constitution.   15

Long time the sport of every wave,
Of every hostile hand the slave,
Imperial Britain prostrate lay,
And felt no power, and held no sway,
                    Subdued her constitution.   20

Till Alfred[4] rose, the wise, the great,
And wak'd to life a morbid state:
Rais'd honor from the blood-stain'd earth,
And gave the British Navy birth,
                    To guard her constitution.   25

---

[1]Protected as an island.

[2]Shore. In the 5th c., the Romans left Britain; it has not been conquered since.

[3]Civil wars and dynastic conflicts, 5th–8th c.

[4]Pious and progressive 9th-c. King Alfred the Great defended England from the Vikings, formulated a code of laws, and fostered learning.

Yet Britain's hapless, thoughtless sons,
The dupes of many a royal dunce,
Abandon'd Freedom's rays divine,
And bent before an idol's shrine,
          Instead of constitution.   30

But oft a beam of sacred light
Broke thro' the darkness of her night,
And oft it spread with rapid flame,
And struck through every languid frame
          A spark of constitution.   35

And oft a stronger, brighter blaze,
O'ercame a monarch's weaker rays,
And taught the minions of a crown,
That England's fairest, best renown,
          Was in her constitution.   40

But modern wiles, and impious men,
Have veil'd the awful shrine again,
And Britain with indignant eye,
Sees rapine flourish, freedom die,
          Beneath her constitution.   45

Rise, from the trance of death arise,
Ye patriots, erst[5] the sacrifice
To Britain's rights, on land or wave,
And teach your anxious sons to save
          The wreck of constitution.   50

One hour, by every patriot blest,
Gave us a sacred pledge of rest;
And still the scaffold, and the tomb,
Should be the impious wretch's doom,
          Who strikes at constitution.   55

[5]Earliest.

from *The Annual Register* (1819)

A little before noon on the 16th August, the first body of reformers began to arrive on the scene of action, which was a piece of ground called St. Peters Field, adjoining a church of that name in the town of Manchester. These persons bore two banners, surmounted with caps of liberty, and bearing the inscriptions, 'no corn laws', 'annual parliaments', 'universal suffrage', 'vote by ballot'. Some of these flags, after being paraded round the field, were planted in the cart on which the speakers stood; but others remained in different parts of the crowd. Numerous large bodies of reformers continued to arrive from the towns in the neighbourhood of Manchester till about one o clock, all preceded by flags and many of them in regular marching order, five deep. Two clubs of female reformers advanced, one of them numbering more than 150 members and bearing a white silk banner. One body of reformers timed their steps to the sound of a bugle with much of a disciplined air; another had assumed to itself the motto of the illustrious Wallace; 'God armeth the patriot'. A band of special constables assumed a position on the field without resistance. The congregated multitude now amounted to a number roundly computed at 80,000, and the arrival of the hero of the day was impatiently expected. At length, Mr. Hunt made his appearance, and after a rapturous greeting, was incited to preside; he signified his assent, and mounting a scaffolding, began to harangue his admirers. He had not proceeded far, when the appearance of the yeomanry cavalry advancing towards the area in a brisk trot, excited a panic in the outskirts of the meeting. They entered the enclosure, and after pausing a moment to recover their disordered ranks, and breathe their horses, they drew their swords, and brandished them fiercely in the air. The multitude, by the direction of their leaders, gave three cheers to show that they were undaunted by this intrusion, and the orator had just resumed his speech to assure the people that this was only a trick to disturb the meeting, and to exhort them to stand firm, when the cavalry dashed into the crowd, making for the cart on which the speakers were placed. The multitude offered no resistance, they fell back on all sides. The commanding officer then approaching Mr. Hunt, and brandishing his sword, told him that he was his prisoner. Mr. Hunt, after enjoining the people to tranquillity, said he would readily surrender to any civil officer on showing his warrant, and Mr. Nadin, the principal police officer, received him in charge. Another person named Johnson, was likewise apprehended, and a few of the mob, some others against whom there were warrants, escaped in the crowd. A cry now arose among the military of, 'have at their flags' and they dashed down not only those in the cart, but the other dispersed in the field; cutting to right and left to get at them. The people began running in all directions; and from this moment the yeomanry lost all command of temper; numbers were trampled under the feet of men and horses; many, both men and women were cut down by sabres; several, and a peace officer and a female in the number, slain on the spot. The whole number of persons injured amounted to between three and four hundred. The populace threw a few stones and brick bats in their retreat, but in less than ten minutes, the ground was entirely cleared of its former occupants, and filled by various bodies of military, both horse and foot.

Disturbances at Manchester [Peterloo]

Leigh Hunt published this essay in The Examiner *within days of the vicious attack upon the participants in a pro-reform demonstration at Manchester on 16 August 1819. Hunt's account in particular seems to have prompted Shelley to work in earnest on a collection of purely political poems in a "common" style (he called them "exoteric" poems), which he intended for Hunt to publish in England. He eventually published* The Masque of Anarchy *in 1832, and Mary Shelley included other of the poems in her editions of Shelley's poetry. Hunt's essay employs the rhetoric of righteous indignation in its attack on the government and its agents, arguing that the government's resistance to reform reflects its indebtedness to the interests of the aristocracy and its hostility to the poor and the working classes. Hunt reads the attack on the demonstrators as an attack upon the constitution by a government bent on usurping the legitimate rights and powers of the citizens, an argument that appears in radical rhetoric throughout the period. Hunt introduces many images and phrases upon which Shelley visibly drew in his poems, most notably* The Mask of Anarchy, *the title of which may be indebted to Hunt's reference to the "seat-selling violators of the British Constitution" as "Men in the brazen Masks of power."*

from *The Examiner* (22 August 1819)

The long irritated sufferings of the Reformers, and the eagerness of power to avail itself of the first opportunity to attack them, have at length given rise to a disturbance at Manchester. The reader will see the particulars in our paper of today. Before we say a word further, we remind our readers of the taunts and provocations thrown out by the Government papers, in consequence of the peaceableness of the Smithfield meeting.[1] That peaceableness was called cowardice. The grossest political ill-treatment, joined with starvation, was not enough for the poorer part of the Reformers. They were to be insulted with charges of *cowardice*, in proportion to their very *patience*. Never let this be forgotten, when tumult is talked of.

Now the multitude which assembled at Manchester could not forget these reproaches when coming to the place of meeting. It was impossible. Every hostile look,—every face of sneering or threatening assumption, every spot in which they had slaved to little purpose, till they were not even allowed to slave any longer,—must have reminded them of all they had borne and suffered, this last provocation included. If they made some counter-signs, who is to wonder? But they did nothing. They assembled peaceably; and the speakers were proceeding as quietly as at the ridiculed Meeting in Smithfield, when according to all accounts but *one* (which every succeeding account has contradicted), a body of military dashed through them sword in hand, trampled down opposition, bruised and wounded many, and bore off the flags and the speakers to the county jail. Some lives have certainly been lost. The sensation in the Metropolis is great and bitter. Not only the papers in opposition to Government, but every one, we believe, not actually committed with the seat-sellers in power, gave way to a burst of astonishment and indignation. Can any thing, in fact, on the face of the transaction, afford a more revolting specimen of impatient, violent, arbitrary feeling on the part of the retainers of Government? Or one more foolish as well as violent? For they talk of the revolutionary tendencies of the conduct of the Reformers; but how can revolutionary tendencies be more excited than by government's lawlessly drawing the sword, and being the first to shed blood systematically? We say lawlessly, and first; for every account we have seen subsequent to that of the *Courier*[2] affirms that an hour had certainly not elapsed (one says not more than twenty minutes) between the

---

[1] A reform meeting conducted by Henry Hunt at Smithfield, London, 21 July 1819.

[2] This liberal London daily newspaper condemned the Peterloo violence. The London *Times* account was widely corroborated by witnesses.

reading of the Riot Act[3] and the charge of the soldiery. And where after all, was the Riot Act read? Who heard it? The account sent up to the *Times* newspaper by a gentleman who obtained a place for convenience sake on the hustings, and who in the infinite hurry of the government-officers was arrested with the leaders of the meeting, says that nobody knew any thing about the Riot Act; and concludes it must have been read by the Magistrates to one another in-doors. Granting even for the sake of argument that the Riot Act was known to have been read, we have other questions to ask. Why was it not acted upon before? If the meeting was illegal, why not have prevented it? If the inflammatory inscriptions on the flags are the plea for interference, why not have seized them on the road? By all accounts but the one before mentioned (which appeared in a paper notoriously violent in favour of the seat-sellers, and in the habit of publishing the most exaggerated statements about the Reformers), there does not seem to have been the least reason for the interference of the military; and if so, we leave our readers to judge of the dilemma with which the Government have hampered themselves, and of the dangerous provocation which such an *example* is likely to give to the Reformers. . . .

It is even affirmed in the *Courier*'s account, that had it not been for the deputy-constable, "it is certain Mr. HUNT would not now have been alive, *for the military were determined to cut him to pieces*!" These are the literal words. The military determined to cut a man to pieces for saying what they do not like! . . . Suppose Mr. HUNT *had* been cut to pieces:—do we think that thousands and thousands of Englishmen would any longer have contented themselves with tamely looking on; or with execrations, or with brickbats and staves? No, most assuredly. They would have risen in the irresistible might of their numbers; and every soldier would have been dragged off his horse, and massacred on the spot. "People cannot bear every thing;" as a soldier himself was heard to say the other day in the streets. . . .

We lament as much as any human being possibly can the effusion of human blood, and all those first causes of wilfulness and injustice which give rise to it; but the seat-selling violators of the British Constitution can see, with philosophy enough, whole oceans of blood shed for the security of their own guilty power, or the restoration of a tyrannical dynasty; and the interested hypocritical howl raised by

---

[3]The Riot Act (1714) permitted local authorities to demand that any group of 12 or more either disperse or face police action.

their hirelings at the fatal consequences of a disturbance to a few individuals, excites in us nothing but anger and disgust.

We write this article to tell them that their eternal beggings of the question, always *against* the poor and the Reformers, in *favour* of the rich and the corrupt, form nothing but a provoking and disgusting contrast with the warrantable demands and most unwarrantable sufferings of those calumniated poor. We will just give a few specimens of the matter, to shew how their flimsy pretences are seen through; and how much additional bitterness and fever they must throw into the cup of their country's sorrow.

To repeat what we have just alluded to. With what feelings can these Men in the Brazen Masks of power dare to speak lamentingly of the wounds or even the death received by a constable or a soldier or any other person concerned against an assemblage of Englishmen irritated by every species of wrong and insult, public and private? With what feelings can they dare to speak of such things in such a tone, after they have so long been inciting the whole world under false pretences to shed their blood in the impudent cause of Divine Right? After they have been hallooing, and shouting, and clapping their "deluded countrymen" on the back, and *paying* them to make charge after charge upon their fellow-creatures with bloody swords and bayonets, not for poverty's sake and right, but that hereditary masters and their hirelings might wallow to all eternity at their pleasure in superfluities and wrong? Those masters *knew* their pretences to be false;—they knew them to be so, and tacitly avowed it, for when they had succeeded in their object, they came forward with an avowal of their real object. Yet though the pretexts of the war were false, the wants of it superfluous, the means of sustaining it exhausting, the modes most bloody and full of carnage, and the real object of it too infamous to be avowed, what despot, aristocratical or oligarchical, what slave, grinning or serious, prosing, poetical, or pathetical, ever scrupled to

Cry Havoc! and let slip the dogs of war![4]

Who said that human beings were not to be cut down, shot, and trampled upon?—that towns and districts were not to be thrown into the most horrible consternation?—that mothers were not to be

---

[4]After the assassination of Julius Caesar, Antony predicts civil war (*Julius Caesar* 3.1.268). Havoc is license to all-out violence.

deprived of their children, and children of their fathers and each other?—that mothers were not to be seduced away from their work, men pressed whether they wished it or not into the sea-conscriptions, and hearts broken at home as well as torn asunder abroad? Who ever said that cities were not to be fired?—that thousands of living human bodies were not to be blown up in the air?—that arms and legs were not to be split off, bones shattered, bodies cut in two, faces carried away, bowels torn out, and dying men left to rave, and shriek out "water!" and beg for GOD's sake to be put out of their misery? What canting hireling, even while pretending to shake something in his head at the "lamentable necessity" of war, ever thought of actually doing any thing but inflaming and carrying it on? Nay, who ever thought of not doing his best to recommend the grace and glory of dying in war, of meeting one's fate upon "the field of honour," and of helping as many as possible of his fellow-creatures and even countrymen to meet them? So that it is an innocent, admirable, and desirable thing for thousands of human beings to slaughter and be slaughtered for the greater security of a corrupt Government but if the corruptions of that Government provoke a half-starved populace to the destruction of a single constable or a soldier, we are allowed to return to our abstract lamentations on the shedding of blood! In the former case, "Carnage is GOD's daughter;"—so says a pathetic court poet.[5] In the latter, a single fatal blow is all that is diabolical:—so says a grinning court buffoon.

O ye recommenders, in times like these, of the reconciling influence of the reading of Scriptures,—Scripture which tells us that "it is easier for a camel to go through the eye of a needle than for a rich man to enter the kingdom of GOD,"—is there not another text about a camel, that would be still less seasonable than this,— a text where it says, "Ye hypocrites! who strain at a gnat, and swallow a camel!"[6]

The Corruptionists assume at every step that they are in the right, and at every step they stumble upon a betrayal to the contrary. In the ministerial paper which contains accounts of the proceedings at Manchester, there is an advertisement from a "loyal" meeting at Middlewich.[7] The persons present at it, with a happy ne-

---

[5]Wordsworth's phrase in his triumphal *Ode, 1815*, celebrating the British victory at Waterloo, the battle sardonically parodied in "Peterloo."

[6]So Jesus lectures (Matthew 19.24 and 23.24).

[7]Cheshire village.

glect of those aristocratical assumptions of good grammar which "the loyal" are so apt to contradict, talk of being "*convinced of,* and happy in, our happy and glorious Constitution in Church and State." What they mean by being convinced of a glorious Constitution, we leave them to explain. By the glorious Constitution in Church and State they of course mean Non-residence, Pluralities, and seat-selling. But observe these loyal beggars of the question. They say that being "convinced of, and happy in, our excellent and glorious Constitution," they "hereby declare their willingness to come forward to the utmost of their power in support of his Majesty's Government." Suppose then that they were *not* "convinced of, and" *not* "happy in our excellent and glorious Constitution," we are to conclude they would *not* willingly come forward. Now we do not know how many solid reasons these gentlemen may have for the blissfulness of their bad grammar, but the meeters at Manchester are certainly not convinced of, and happy in, said misnomer called the Constitution, and therefore according to these very loyalists, they are justified in not agreeing with them.

At the same meeting it was said to be "the bounded duty of every loyal subject to stand forth in defence of our *happy* and glorious Constitution" (they would call it a pea-green constitution, if the epithet would make a shew) "against *seditionists*, traitors, and conspirators, who under THE SPECIOUS PRETEXT of Parliamentary Reform, are endeavouring to subvert all that is dear and valuable to us as Englishmen, and to bring about a national Revolution." This is the vague style in which any courtiers can write on any occasion. They wrote so in the time of James II,[8] previously to the Revolution now affectedly called glorious by men of this very stamp. By "all that is dear and valuable," they meant "popery and servility." It now means *master*-conspiracies, places under government, and security from every species of responsibility. But there is something else "dear and valuable," which has nothing to do with such superabundance; and that is, "meat, clothes, and fire." These are dear and valuable to the poor; and Reform is dear and valuable to them, in proportion as they think it will help to restore them. What is meant by the words "specious *pretext*"? Observe the unconscious self-betrayal skulking under this phrase. Why is Reform such a *specious* pretext, but because its claims are founded in justice? and

---

[8]Britain's last Roman Catholic monarch was deposed in the so-called Glorious Revolution of 1688, a nonviolent regime change.

why, when Reform is so specious, do these men always hasten to confound it with Revolution? Would Reform be so specious, if there were no such monstrous and anti-constitutional inequalities as at present exist,—no taxation without representation, no responsibility of ministers, no seat-selling, no privileged *master*-conspiracies, while those of the workmen are so heavily visited? No; and they know it instinctively, though intellectually they say nothing.

Stanzas Occasioned by the Manchester Massacre!
from *Black Dwarf* (25 August 1819)

Oh, weep not for those who are freed
From bondage[1] so frightful as ours!
Let *tyranny* mourn for the deed,
And howl o'er the prey she devours!

The mask[2] for a century worn,   5
Has fallen from her visage at last;
Of all its sham attributes shorn,
Her reign of delusion is past.

In native deformity now
Behold her, how shatter'd and weak!   10
With *murder* impress'd on her brow,
And *cowardice* blanching her cheek.

With guilt's gloomy terrors bow'd down,
She scowls on the smile of the slave!
She shrinks at the patriot's frown;   15
She *dies* in the grasp of the brave.

Then brief be our wail for the dead,
Whose blood has seal'd tyranny's doom;
And the tears that affliction will shed,
Let vengeance, bright flashes illume.   20

---

[1]Suggests both the Egyptian bondage of the Jews and contemporary slaves.
[2]Shelley used the same image in *The Mask of Anarchy* (p. 84).

And shame on the passionless thing
Whose soul can *now* slumber within him!
To slavery still let him cling,
For liberty scorns to win him.

Her manlier spirits arouse   25
At the summons so frightfully given!
And glory exults in their vows,
While virtue records them in Heaven.

August 21.   HIBERNICUS.[3]

---

[3]The pseudonym recalls Exul Hibernicus, Latin name of an Irish stranger in Charlemagne's Europe who wrote didactic poems in plain language, and also hibernation, a sleep before (perhaps political) awakening.

Shelley and
Political Caricature

The Six Acts of late 1819 had a chilling effect on the radical and reformist press. For his brilliant anti-government satires, Thomas Wooler, publisher of the *Black Dwarf* (1817–24), had been tried in 1817 for seditious libel; his acquittal was widely cheered. William Hone, also tried and acquitted in 1817 on the same charge, wrote and published *The Political House That Jack Built* (1819), a pamphlet illustrated with engravings by George Cruikshank—part of Hone's ongoing assault on the Prince Regent and the Liverpool ministry's oppressive measures. It was a spectacular success, selling about 100,000 copies by 1821. Cruikshank's vicious cartoon of the Regent adapts, or alludes to, James Gillray's famous caricature print, *A Voluptuary Under the Horrors of Digestion* (1792), to convey popular contempt; it appeared in Hone's and Cruikshank's widely read pamphlet, *The Queen's Matrimonial Ladder* (1820). These fearless pamphlets influenced the political poetry of Shelley and his contemporaries, which put into play many of the same images and rhetoric.

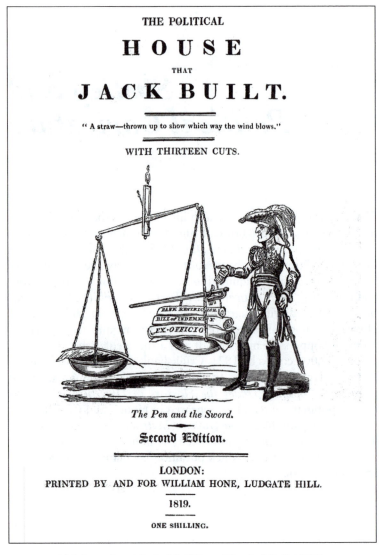

Title Page, from *The Political House That Jack Built* (1819).

" Portentous, unexampled, unexplain'd !
——————— —— What man seeing this,
And having human feelings, does not blush,
And hang his head, to think himself a man ?
——————— I cannot rest
A silent witness of the headlong rage,
Or heedless folly, by which thousands die——
Bleed gold for Ministers to sport away."

THESE ARE

THE PEOPLE

all tatter'd and torn,

Who curse the day

wherein they were born,

On account of Taxation

too great to be borne,

And pray for relief,

from night to morn ;

Who, in vain, Petition

in every form,

These Are the People, from *The Political House That Jack Built* (1819).

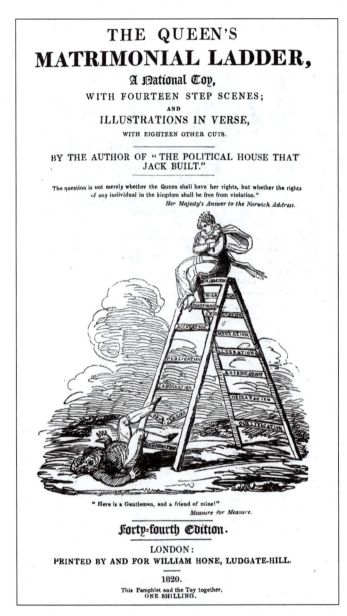

THE QUEEN'S
MATRIMONIAL LADDER,
𝔄 𝔑ational 𝔗oy,
WITH FOURTEEN STEP SCENES;
AND
ILLUSTRATIONS IN VERSE,
WITH EIGHTEEN OTHER CUTS.

BY THE AUTHOR OF "THE POLITICAL HOUSE THAT
JACK BUILT."

"The question is not merely whether the Queen shall have her rights, but whether the rights
of any individual in the kingdom shall be free from violation."
Her Majesty's Answer to the Norwich Address.

" Here is a Gentleman, and a friend of mine!"
Measure for Measure.

𝔉orty=fourth 𝔈dition.

LONDON:
PRINTED BY AND FOR WILLIAM HONE, LUDGATE-HILL.
1820.
This Pamphlet and the Toy together,
ONE SHILLING.

Title Page, from *The Queen's Matrimonial Ladder* (1820).

Qualification, from *The Queen's Matrimonial Ladder* (1820).

Prometheus Unbound

Dating from 1818–19, Prometheus Unbound *poses many challenges, from its length and form to the text's many variants. But Shelley's great lyrical drama advances a remarkably straightforward thesis: to renovate the world, each individual must embrace love and reject whatever harms others. Its story concerns a bloodless revolution against tyranny by an exemplary and self-sacrificing hero, Prometheus. In Act I, he revokes his curse on his tormentor Jupiter, who had had him pinioned atop the Caucasus mountains for refusing to divulge the secret that he alone knew: that Jupiter would be superseded by his more powerful son. Tormented physically (a bird of prey gnaws at his liver, which regenerates overnight) and mentally (by a thirst for vengeance), Prometheus refuses revenge, because it levels the victim with his opponent, and images Jesus, whose forgiveness of injury represents a liberating moral fortitude.*

Shelley called PU a "lyrical drama" for several reasons. He linked his drama to a lost play by Aeschylus (c. 525–456 BCE) in which Prometheus is liberated and vindicated. The "lyric" element follows the emphasis on feeling over action in Wordsworth's and Coleridge's Lyrical Ballads *(1798–1805), and it also reflects the combination of drama, music, and poetry in this extraordinary work. The Shelleys regularly attended operas while in Italy, but PU is not written for staging. Its closest analogues might be the oratorio, or the celebratory movements, odes, and choruses of Beethoven's symphonies.*

Shelley had been thinking about Prometheus long before beginning PU in 1818. He read Aeschylus at Oxford (1810–11), and he and Byron discussed Aeschylus and the Prometheus myth in Switzerland in 1816, as Mary Shelley began Frankenstein, *which she subtitled "The Modern Prometheus." Once he began, Shelley worked for eighteen months, completing the first three acts in the spring of 1819. He then turned to other projects,* The Cenci, *and the political poetry prompted by events back in England. Later in 1819 he composed Act 4. The first three acts are a dramatically coherent unit in themselves, with an arc of passion—Prometheus's forgiveness—that concludes with the Spirit of the Earth and the Spirit of the Hour announcing a new millennium. The fourth act, a grand hymn of celebration, drives toward another apocalyptic announcement, proclaimed by Demogorgon: destiny or historical necessity.*

As in Greek drama, much of the "action" is not staged, only reported. The key event is the moral revolution in Prometheus, as he turns from a desire for vengeance against Jupiter. Shelley opens the drama just before, with Prometheus repenting his curse. Although his supporters misinterpret this as surrender, Prometheus knows better and resists even the temptation to despair represented in the Furies' description of suffering, crucified Jesus.

The central figure in Act 2 is Asia, the embodiment of unconditional love. Also on hand is Panthea, whose dream of Prometheus's transfiguration is patterned on Jesus's (recounted in Matthew 17.1–19, Mark 9.2–8, and Luke 9.28–36). Her dreams prepare for the shadowy and enigmatic Demogorgon, who recounts to Asia the history of Jupiter's tyranny. Asia in turn recounts Prometheus's gifts to humanity and predicts an ideal state governed by her and Prometheus. Act 3 treats the overthrow of Jupiter, and Hercules's liberation of Prometheus, who retires with Asia to the oracular cave, seat of their eternal bliss, while the universe undergoes a spectacular transformation. Finally, the Spirit of the Hour announces humanity's transformation, a perfection that radiates throughout the universe. This is where Shelley paused in the spring of 1819. In the fall he decided to write a final act (4), a single scene of polyphonic apostrophe to Love and its effects. It concludes with Demogorgon's description of the moral and intellectual revolution that will ensure mankind against any future tyranny.

PU was imperfectly printed when first published and subsequently edited and revised by Mary Shelley and others from often conflicting manuscripts. There is no definitive text. For details of the manuscripts and printed editions, see The Poems of Shelley (2000), *edited by Kelvin Everest, vol. 2.*

A Lyrical Drama in Four Acts

AUDISNE HÆC AMPHIARAE, SUB TERRAM ABDITE?[1]

Preface

The Greek tragic writers, in selecting as their subject any portion of their national history or mythology, employed in their treatment of it a certain arbitrary discretion. They by no means conceived themselves bound to adhere to the common interpretation or to imitate in story as in title their rivals and predecessors. Such a system would have amounted to a resignation of those claims to preference over their competitors which incited the composition. The Agamemnonian story was exhibited on the Athenian theatre with as many variations as dramas.

I have presumed to employ a similar license. The Prometheus Unbound of Æschylus supposed the reconciliation of Jupiter with his victim as the price of the disclosure of the danger threatened to

---

[1] "Do you hear all of this, Amphiarus, hidden away under the earth?" Aeschylus's lost play, *Epigoni*; quoted in Cicero's *Tusclulan Disputations*. The epigraph appears on the *PU* volume's title page. Shelley rejects Aeschylus's claim that pain must be accepted.

his empire by the consummation of his marriage with Thetis. Thetis, according to this view of the subject, was given in marriage to Peleus, and Prometheus, by the permission of Jupiter, delivered from his captivity by Hercules. Had I framed my story on this model, I should have done no more than have attempted to restore the lost drama of Æschylus; an ambition which, if my preference to this mode of treating the subject had incited me to cherish, the recollection of the high comparison such an attempt would challenge might well abate. But, in truth, I was averse from a catastrophe so feeble as that of reconciling the Champion with the Oppressor of mankind. The moral interest of the fable, which is so powerfully sustained by the sufferings and endurance of Prometheus, would be annihilated if we could conceive of him as unsaying his high language and quailing before his successful and perfidious adversary. The only imaginary being, resembling in any degree Prometheus, is Satan; and Prometheus is, in my judgment, a more poetical character than Satan, because, in addition to courage, and majesty, and firm and patient opposition to omnipotent force, he is susceptible of being described as exempt from the taints of ambition, envy, revenge, and a desire for personal aggrandizement, which, in the hero of Paradise Lost, interfere with the interest. The character of Satan engenders in the mind a pernicious casuistry[2] which leads us to weigh his faults with his wrongs, and to excuse the former because the latter exceed all measure. In the minds of those who consider that magnificent fiction with a religious feeling it engenders something worse. But Prometheus is, as it were, the type of the highest perfection of moral and intellectual nature impelled by the purest and the truest motives to the best and noblest ends.

This Poem was chiefly written upon the mountainous ruins of the Baths of Caracalla, among the flowery glades and thickets of odoriferous blossoming trees, which are extended in ever winding labyrinths upon its immense platforms and dizzy arches suspended in the air. The bright blue sky of Rome, and the effect of the vigorous awakening spring in that divinest climate, and the new life with which it drenches the spirits even to intoxication, were the inspiration of this drama.

The imagery which I have employed will be found, in many instances, to have been drawn from the operations of the human mind, or from those external actions by which they are expressed.

---

[2]Belief that circumstances alter judgments about right and wrong. Shelley is thinking of Milton's Satan (*PL*).

This is unusual in modern poetry, although Dante and Shakespeare are full of instances of the same kind; Dante indeed more than any other poet, and with greater success. But the Greek poets, as writers to whom no resource of awakening the sympathy of their contemporaries was unknown, were in the habitual use of this power; and it is the study of their works (since a higher merit would probably be denied me) to which I am willing that my readers should impute this singularity.

One word is due in candor to the degree in which the study of contemporary writings may have tinged my composition, for such has been a topic of censure with regard to poems far more popular, and indeed more deservedly popular, than mine.[3] It is impossible that any one, who inhabits the same age with such writers as those who stand in the foremost ranks of our own, can conscientiously assure himself that his language and tone of thought may not have been modified by the study of the productions of those extraordinary intellects. It is true that, not the spirit of their genius, but the forms in which it has manifested itself, are due less to the peculiarities of their own minds than to the peculiarity of the moral and intellectual condition of the minds among which they have been produced. Thus a number of writers possess the form, whilst they want the spirit of those whom, it is alleged, they imitate; because the former is the endowment of the age in which they live, and the latter must be the uncommunicated lightning of their own mind.

The peculiar style of intense and comprehensive imagery which distinguishes the modern literature of England has not been, as a general power, the product of the imitation of any particular writer. The mass of capabilities remains at every period materially the same; the circumstances which awaken it to action perpetually change. If England were divided into forty republics, each equal in population and extent to Athens, there is no reason to suppose but that, under institutions not more perfect than those of Athens, each would produce philosophers and poets equal to those who (if we except Shakespeare) have never been surpassed. We owe the great writers of the golden age of our literature to that fervid awakening of the public mind which shook to dust the oldest and most oppressive form of the Christian religion. We owe Milton to the progress and development of the same spirit: the sacred Milton was, let it

[3]Shelley wrote the rest of the Preface after reading a savage review of *The Revolt of Islam* (1818) accusing him of plagiarism and immorality.

ever be remembered, a republican and a bold inquirer into morals and religion. The great writers of our own age are, we have reason to suppose, the companions and forerunners of some unimagined change in our social condition or the opinions which cement it. The cloud of mind is discharging its collected lightning, and the equilibrium between institutions and opinions is now restoring or is about to be restored.

As to imitation, poetry is a mimetic art. It creates, but it creates by combination and representation. Poetical abstractions are beautiful and new, not because the portions of which they are composed had no previous existence in the mind of man or in Nature, but because the whole produced by their combination has some intelligible and beautiful analogy with those sources of emotion and thought and with the contemporary condition of them. One great poet is a masterpiece of Nature which another not only ought to study but must study. He might as wisely and as easily determine that his mind should no longer be the mirror of all that is lovely in the visible universe as exclude from his contemplation the beautiful which exists in the writings of a great contemporary. The pretence of doing it would be a presumption in any but the greatest; the effect, even in him, would be strained, unnatural and ineffectual. A poet is the combined product of such internal powers as modify the nature of others, and of such external influences as excite and sustain these powers; he is not one, but both. Every man's mind is, in this respect, modified by all the objects of Nature and art; by every word and every suggestion which he ever admitted to act upon his consciousness; it is the mirror upon which all forms are reflected and in which they compose one form. Poets, not otherwise than philosophers, painters, sculptors and musicians, are, in one sense, the creators, and, in another, the creations, of their age. From this subjection the loftiest do not escape. There is a similarity between Homer and Hesiod, between Æschylus and Euripides, between Virgil and Horace, between Dante and Petrarch, between Shakespeare and Fletcher, between Dryden and Pope; each has a generic resemblance under which their specific distinctions are arranged. If this similarity be the result of imitation, I am willing to confess that I have imitated.

Let this opportunity be conceded to me of acknowledging that I have what a Scotch philosopher[4] characteristically terms a 'passion for reforming the world:' what passion incited him to write and pub-

---

[4]Robert Forsyth, *Principles of Moral Science* (1805).

lish his book he omits to explain. For my part I had rather be damned with Plato and Lord Bacon than go to Heaven with Paley and Malthus.[5] But it is a mistake to suppose that I dedicate my poetical compositions solely to the direct enforcement of reform, or that I consider them in any degree as containing a reasoned system on the theory of human life. Didactic poetry is my abhorrence; nothing can be equally well expressed in prose that is not tedious and supererogatory in verse. My purpose has hitherto been simply to familiarize the highly refined imagination of the more select classes of poetical readers with beautiful idealisms of moral excellence; aware that, until the mind can love, and admire, and trust, and hope, and endure, reasoned principles of moral conduct are seeds cast upon the highway of life which the unconscious passenger tramples into dust, although they would bear the harvest of his happiness.[6] Should I live to accomplish what I purpose, that is, produce a systematical history of what appear to me to be the genuine elements of human society, let not the advocates of injustice and superstition flatter themselves that I should take Æschylus rather than Plato as my model.

The having spoken of myself with unaffected freedom will need little apology with the candid; and let the uncandid consider that they injure me less than their own hearts and minds by misrepresentation. Whatever talents a person may possess to amuse and instruct others, be they ever so inconsiderable, he is yet bound to exert them: if his attempt be ineffectual, let the punishment of an unaccomplished purpose have been sufficient; let none trouble themselves to heap the dust of oblivion upon his efforts; the pile they raise will betray his grave which might otherwise have been unknown.

DRAMATIS PERSONÆ

Prometheus.	Demogorgon.
Jupiter.	Asia, Panthea, Ione: Oceanides
The Earth.	Hercules.
Ocean.	The Phantasm of Jupiter.
Apollo.	The Spirit of the Earth.
Mercury.	The Spirit of the Moon.
	Spirits of the Hours.
	Spirits. Echoes. Fauns. Furies.

[5]Shelley disliked William Paley (1743–1805) and Robert Malthus (1766–1834) for using religion and economics to justify social injustice.

[6]See the Parable of the Sower, Matthew 13.3–9.

ACT I

Scene.—A Ravine of Icy Rocks in the Indian Caucasus. Prometheus is discovered bound to the Precipice. Panthea and Ione are seated at his feet. Time, night. During the Scene, morning slowly breaks.

PROMETHEUS.

Monarch of Gods and Dæmons,[1] and all Spirits
But One, who throng those bright and rolling Worlds
Which Thou and I alone of living things
Behold with sleepless eyes! regard this Earth
Made multitudinous with thy slaves, whom thou   5
Requitest for knee-worship, prayer, and praise,
And toil, and hecatombs[2] of broken hearts,
With fear and self-contempt and barren hope.
Whilst me, who am thy foe, eyeless in hate,
Hast thou made reign and triumph, to thy scorn,   10
O'er mine own misery and thy vain revenge.
Three thousand years of sleep-unsheltered hours,
And moments aye divided by keen pangs
Till they seemed years, torture and solitude,
Scorn and despair,—these are mine empire:[3]—   15
More glorious far than that which thou surveyest
From thine unenvied throne, O Mighty God!
Almighty, had I deigned to share the shame
Of thine ill tyranny, and hung not here
Nailed to this wall of eagle-baffling mountain,   20
Black, wintry, dead, unmeasured; without herb,
Insect, or beast, or shape or sound of life.
Ah me! alas, pain, pain ever, for ever!

No change, no pause, no hope! Yet I endure.
I ask the Earth, have not the mountains felt?   25
I ask yon Heaven, the all-beholding Sun,
Has it not seen? The Sea, in storm or calm,
Heaven's ever-changing Shadow, spread below,

---

[1]Spirits between humans and gods; Shelley links Jupiter with Old Testament Jehovah.

[2]Massive public sacrifices.

[3]Some antiquarian scientists theorized the rise and fall of civilizations in 3,000-year cycles, which would make the play's action contemporary.

Have its deaf waves not heard my agony?
Ah me! alas, pain, pain ever, for ever! 30

The crawling glaciers pierce me with the spears
Of their moon-freezing crystals, the bright chains
Eat with their burning cold into my bones.
Heaven's wingèd hound, polluting from thy lips
His beak in poison not his own, tears up 35
My heart; and shapeless sights come wandering by,
The ghastly people of the realm of dream,
Mocking me: and the Earthquake-fiends are charged
To wrench the rivets from my quivering wounds
When the rocks split and close again behind: 40
While from their loud abysses howling throng
The genii of the storm, urging the rage
Of whirlwind, and afflict me with keen hail.
And yet to me welcome is day and night,
Whether one breaks the hoar frost of the morn, 45
Or starry, dim, and slow, the other climbs
The leaden-coloured east; for then they lead
The wingless, crawling hours,[4] one among whom
—As some dark Priest hales[5] the reluctant victim—
Shall drag thee, cruel King, to kiss the blood 50
From these pale feet, which then might trample thee
If they disdained not such a prostrate slave.
Disdain! Ah no! I pity thee. What ruin
Will hunt thee undefended through wide Heaven!
How will thy soul, cloven to its depth with terror, 55
Gape like a hell within! I speak in grief,
Not exultation, for I hate no more,
As then ere misery made me wise. The curse
Once breathed on thee I would recall.[6] Ye Mountains,
Whose many-voicèd Echoes, through the mist 60
Of cataracts, flung the thunder of that spell!
Ye icy Springs, stagnant with wrinkling frost,
Which vibrated to hear me, and then crept
Shuddering through India! Thou serenest Air,
Through which the Sun walks burning without beams! 65

[4]Hours (embodied time) are usually portrayed winged.
[5]Drags forcibly.
[6]Remember and take back (recant).

And ye swift Whirlwinds, who on poisèd wings
Hung mute and moveless o'er yon hushed abyss,
As thunder, louder than your own, made rock
The orbèd world! If then my words had power,
Though I am changed so that aught evil wish   70
Is dead within; although no memory be
Of what is hate, let them not lose it now!
What was that curse? for ye all heard me speak.

FIRST VOICE: *from the Mountains*
Thrice three hundred thousand years
    O'er the Earthquake's couch we stood: 75
Oft, as men convulsed with fears,
    We trembled in our multitude.

SECOND VOICE: *from the Springs*
Thunderbolts had parched our water,
    We had been stained with bitter blood,
And had run mute, 'mid shrieks of slaughter,   80
    Thro' a city and a solitude.

THIRD VOICE: *from the Air*
I had clothed, since Earth uprose,
    Its wastes in colours not their own,
And oft had my serene repose
    Been cloven by many a rending groan.   85

FOURTH VOICE: *from the Whirlwinds*
We had soared beneath these mountains
    Unresting ages; nor had thunder,
Nor yon volcano's flaming fountains,
    Nor any power above or under
    Ever made us mute with wonder.   90

FIRST VOICE
    But never bowed our snowy crest
    As at the voice of thine unrest.

SECOND VOICE
Never such a sound before
To the Indian waves we bore.

A pilot asleep on the howling sea   95
Leaped up from the deck in agony,
And heard, and cried, "Ah, woe is me!"
And died as mad as the wild waves be.

                    THIRD VOICE
By such dread words from Earth to Heaven
My still realm was never riven: 100
When its wound was closed, there stood
Darkness o'er the day like blood.

                    FOURTH VOICE
       And we shrank back: for dreams of ruin
       To frozen caves our flight pursuing
       Made us keep silence—thus—and thus—   105
       Though silence is as hell to us.

                    THE EARTH
The tongueless Caverns of the craggy hills
Cried, "Misery!" then; the hollow Heaven replied,
"Misery!" And the Ocean's purple waves,
Climbing the land, howled to the lashing winds,   110
And the pale nations heard it, "Misery!"

                    PROMETHEUS
I heard a sound of voices: not the voice
Which I gave forth.—Mother,[7] thy sons and thou
Scorn him, without whose all-enduring will
Beneath the fierce omnipotence of Jove,   115
Both they and thou had vanished, like thin mist
Unrolled on the morning wind. Know ye not me,
The Titan? He who made his agony
The barrier to your else all-conquering foe?
O rock-embosomed lawns, and snow-fed streams,   120
Now seen athwart frore[8] vapours, deep below,
Through whose o'ershadowing woods I wandered once
With Asia, drinking life from her loved eyes;

[7]Associating motherhood with Earth (and fatherhood with sky) originates with Hesiod's *Theogony*.

[8]Frozen.

Why scorns the spirit which informs[9] ye, now
To commune with me? me alone, who checked,   125
As one who checks a fiend-drawn charioteer,
The falsehood and the force of him who reigns
Supreme, and with the groans of pining slaves
Fills your dim glens and liquid wildernesses:
Why answer ye not, still? Brethren!

           THE EARTH

                        They dare not.   130

           PROMETHEUS
Who dares? for I would hear that curse again.
Ha, what an awful whisper rises up!
'Tis scarce like sound: it tingles through the frame
As lightning tingles, hovering ere it strike.
Speak, Spirit! from thine inorganic voice   135
I only know that thou art moving near
And love.[10] How cursed I him?

           THE EARTH
                        How canst thou hear
Who knowest not the language of the dead?

           PROMETHEUS
Thou art a living spirit; speak as they.

           THE EARTH
I dare not speak like life, lest Heaven's fell King   140
Should hear, and link me to some wheel of pain
More torturing than the one whereon I roll.[11]
Subtle thou art and good, and though the Gods
Hear not this voice, yet thou art more than God,
Being wise and kind: earnestly hearken now.   145

---

[9]Indwells and shapes.

[10]Love me.

[11]Ixion was tortured by being bound to a wheel in Hades.

PROMETHEUS
Obscurely through my brain, like shadows dim,
Sweep awful[12] thoughts, rapid and thick. I feel
Faint, like one mingled in entwining love;
Yet 'tis not pleasure.

THE EARTH
              No, thou canst not hear:
Thou art immortal, and this tongue is known   150
Only to those who die.

PROMETHEUS
              And what art thou,
O, melancholy Voice?

THE EARTH
              I am the Earth,
Thy mother; she within whose stony veins,
To the last fibre of the loftiest tree
Whose thin leaves trembled in the frozen air,   155
Joy ran, as blood within a living frame,
When thou didst from her bosom, like a cloud
Of glory, arise, a spirit of keen joy!
And at thy voice her pining sons uplifted
Their prostrate brows from the polluting dust,   160
And our almighty Tyrant with fierce dread
Grew pale, until his thunder chained thee here.
Then, see those million worlds which burn and roll
Around us: their inhabitants beheld
My spherèd light wane in wide Heaven; the sea   165
Was lifted by strange tempest, and new fire
From earthquake-rifted mountains of bright snow
Shook its portentous hair beneath Heaven's frown;
Lightning and Inundation vexed the plains;
Blue thistles bloomed in cities; foodless toads   170
Within voluptuous chambers panting crawled:
When Plague had fallen on man, and beast, and worm,
And Famine; and black blight on herb and tree;
And in the corn, and vines, and meadow-grass,
Teemed ineradicable poisonous weeds   175

[12]Awe-inspiring, with a sense of terror.

Draining their growth, for my wan breast was dry
With grief; and the thin air, my breath, was stained
With the contagion of a mother's hate
      Breathed on her child's destroyer; ay, I heard
Thy curse, the which, if thou rememberest not,   180
Yet my innumerable seas and streams,
Mountains, and caves, and winds, and yon wide air,
And the inarticulate people of the dead,
Preserve, a treasured spell. We meditate
In secret joy and hope those dreadful words,   185
But dare not speak them.

      PROMETHEUS
          Venerable Mother!
All else who live and suffer take from thee
Some comfort; flowers, and fruits, and happy sounds,
And love, though fleeting; these may not be mine.
But mine own words, I pray, deny me not.   190

      THE EARTH
They shall be told. Ere Babylon was dust,
The Magus Zoroaster,[13] my dead child,
Met his own image walking in the garden.
That apparition, sole of men, he saw.
For know there are two worlds of life and death: 195
One that which thou beholdest; but the other
Is underneath the grave, where do inhabit
The shadows of all forms that think and live
Till death unite them and they part no more;
Dreams and the light imaginings of men,   200
And all that faith creates or love desires,
Terrible, strange, sublime and beauteous shapes.
There thou art, and dost hang, a writhing shade,
'Mid whirlwind-peopled mountains; all the gods
Are there, and all the powers of nameless worlds,   205
Vast, sceptred phantoms; heroes, men, and beasts;
And Demogorgon,[14] a tremendous gloom;

---

[13]Persian prophet Zoroaster (c. 600 BCE) opposed light and fire to darkness and evil.
Meeting one's likeness was an omen of death.
[14]In *PL* (2.965) Demogorgon is inexorable determinism.

And he, the supreme Tyrant, on his throne
Of burning gold. Son, one of these shall utter
The curse which all remember. Call at will   210
Thine own ghost, or the ghost of Jupiter,
Hades or Typhon,[15] or what mightier Gods
From all-prolific Evil, since thy ruin
Have sprung, and trampled on my prostrate sons.
Ask, and they must reply: so the revenge   215
Of the Supreme may sweep through vacant shades,[16]
As rainy wind through the abandoned gate
Of a fallen palace.

PROMETHEUS
   Mother, let not aught
Of that which may be evil, pass again
My lips, or those of aught resembling me.—   220
Phantasm of Jupiter, arise, appear!

IONE
My wings are folded o'er mine ears:
My wings are crossèd o'er mine eyes:
Yet through their silver shade appears,
And through their lulling plumes arise,   225
  A Shape, a throng of sounds;
   May it be no ill to thee
  O thou of many wounds!
Near whom, for our sweet sister's[17] sake,
Ever thus we watch and wake.   230

PANTHEA[18]
The sound is of whirlwind underground,
Earthquake, and fire, and mountains cloven;
The shape is awful like the sound,
Clothed in dark purple, star-inwoven.
  A sceptre of pale gold   235

[15]Hades: Jupiter's brother, ruler of the underworld. Typhon: hundred-headed monster whom Jupiter confined beneath Mt. Etna.

[16]Ghosts.

[17]Asia.

[18]"All goddesses," suggesting pantheism.

To stay steps proud, o'er the slow cloud
His veinèd hand doth hold.
Cruel he looks, but calm and strong,
Like one who does, not suffers wrong.

PHANTASM OF JUPITER
Why have the secret powers of this strange world 240
Driven me, a frail and empty phantom, hither
On direst storms? What unaccustomed sounds
Are hovering on my lips, unlike the voice
With which our pallid race hold ghastly talk
In darkness? And, proud sufferer, who art thou? 245

PROMETHEUS
Tremendous Image, as thou art must be
He whom thou shadowest forth. I am his foe,
The Titan. Speak the words which I would hear,
Although no thought inform thine empty voice.

THE EARTH
Listen! And though your echoes must be mute, 250
Gray mountains, and old woods, and haunted springs,
Prophetic caves, and isle-surrounding streams,
Rejoice to hear what yet ye cannot speak.

PHANTASM
A spirit seizes me and speaks within:
It tears me as fire tears a thunder-cloud. 255

PANTHEA
See, how he lifts his mighty looks, the Heaven
Darkens above.

IONE
He speaks! O shelter me!

PROMETHEUS
I see the curse on gestures proud and cold,
And looks of firm defiance, and calm hate,
And such despair as mocks itself with smiles, 260
Written as on a scroll: yet speak: Oh, speak!

PHANTASM

Fiend, I defy thee! with a calm, fixed mind,
　All that thou canst inflict I bid thee do;
Foul Tyrant both of Gods and Human-kind,
　　One only being shalt thou not subdue.　　　　265
　　　Rain then thy plagues upon me here,
　　　Ghastly disease, and frenzying fear;
　　　And let alternate frost and fire
　　　Eat into me, and be thine ire
Lightning, and cutting hail, and legioned forms　　270
Of furies, driving by upon the wounding storms.

Aye, do thy worst. Thou art Omnipotent.
　O'er all things but thyself I gave thee power,
And my own will.[19] Be thy swift mischiefs sent
　　To blast mankind, from yon ethereal tower.　　275
　　　Let thy malignant spirit move
　　　In darkness over those I love:
　　　On me and mine I imprecate[20]
　　　The utmost torture of thy hate;
And thus devote to sleepless agony,　　　　280
This undeclining head while thou must reign on high.

But thou, who art the God and Lord: O, thou,
　Who fillest with thy soul this world of woe,
To whom all things of Earth and Heaven do bow
　　In fear and worship: all-prevailing foe!　　285
　　　I curse thee! let a sufferer's curse
　　　Clasp thee, his torturer, like remorse;
　　　Till thine Infinity shall be
　　　A robe of envenomed agony;
And thine Omnipotence a crown of pain,[21]　　290
To cling like burning gold round thy dissolving brain.

---

[19]Latinate syntax: I gave you power over all things but yourself and my will.

[20]Invoke, pray for, call down (as a curse).

[21]In Greek myth, Hercules is killed by a poisoned tunic from the centaur Nessus;
Medea kills Jason's wife Creusa with a cursed dress. The passage also alludes to the
robe and crown of thorns used to mock Jesus and suggests the general curse of
monarchy.

Heap on thy soul, by virtue of this Curse,
    Ill deeds, then be thou damned, beholding good;
Both infinite as is the universe,
    And thou, and thy self-torturing solitude.   295
        An awful image of calm power
        Though now thou sittest, let the hour
        Come, when thou must appear to be
        That which thou art internally;
And after many a false and fruitless crime   300
Scorn track thy lagging fall through boundless space and time.
                        [*The Phantasm vanishes*]

PROMETHEUS
Were these my words, O Parent?

THE EARTH
                They were thine.

PROMETHEUS
    It doth repent me: words are quick and vain;
Grief for awhile is blind, and so was mine.
    I wish no living thing to suffer pain.   305

THE EARTH
    Misery, Oh misery to me,
    That Jove at length should vanquish thee.[22]
    Wail, howl aloud, Land and Sea,
    The Earth's rent heart shall answer ye.
Howl, Spirits of the living and the dead,   310
Your refuge, your defence lies fallen and vanquishèd.

FIRST ECHO
Lies fallen and vanquishèd?

SECOND ECHO
              Fallen and vanquishèd!

---

[22]Earth and her echoes assume repentance means capitulation.

IONE

Fear not—'tis but some passing spasm,
    The Titan is unvanquished still.   315
But see, where through the azure chasm
    Of yon forked and snowy hill
Trampling the slant winds on high
    With golden-sandalled feet, that glow
Under plumes of purple dye,   320
Like rose-ensanguined[23] ivory,
    A Shape comes now,
Stretching on high from his right hand
    A serpent-cinctured wand.[24]

PANTHEA

'Tis Jove's world-wandering herald, Mercury.   325

IONE

And who are those with hydra tresses[25]
    And iron wings that climb the wind,
Whom the frowning God represses
    Like vapours steaming up behind,
Clanging loud, an endless crowd—   330

PANTHEA

These are Jove's tempest-walking hounds,[26]
Whom he gluts with groans and blood,
When charioted on sulphurous cloud
He bursts Heaven's bounds.

IONE

Are they now led, from the thin dead   335
On new pangs to be fed?

---

[23]Blood-colored, blood-stained.

[24]The serpent-wrapped staff is the traditional emblem of Mercury, messenger of the gods, and later became the physician's emblem.

[25]The hydra has many heads; the image evokes Medusa's snakehead.

[26]The Furies.

PANTHEA
The Titan looks as ever, firm, not proud.

FIRST FURY
Ha! I scent life!

SECOND FURY
Let me but look into his eyes!

THIRD FURY
The hope of torturing him smells like a heap
Of corpses, to a death-bird after battle.   340

FIRST FURY
Darest thou delay, O Herald! take cheer, Hounds
Of Hell—what if the Son of Maia[27] soon
Should make us food and sport—who can please long
The Omnipotent?

MERCURY
                    Back to your towers of iron,
And gnash, beside the streams of fire and wail,[28]   345
Your foodless teeth! Geryon,[29] arise! and Gorgon,
Chimæra, and thou Sphinx, subtlest of fiends
Who ministered to Thebes Heaven's poisoned wine,
Unnatural love, and more unnatural hate:
These shall perform your task.

FIRST FURY
                          Oh, mercy! mercy!   350
We die with our desire—drive us not back!

MERCURY
Crouch then in silence.—
                    Awful Sufferer!

[27]Jupiter; Maia is the brightest star in the constellation Pleiades.

[28]Wailing; the Furies expected to feed on Prometheus.

[29]Three-headed man-eating monster killed by Hercules. Mercury summons the Gorgon Medusa, whose gaze turned men to stone; the dragon-like monster Chimera; and the Sphinx, who cursed Oedipus with "unnatural love," an unintended marriage to his own mother.

To thee unwilling, most unwillingly
I come, by the great Father's will driven down,
To execute a doom of new revenge. 355
Alas! I pity thee, and hate myself
That I can do no more.—Aye from thy sight
Returning, for a season, Heaven seems Hell,
So thy worn form pursues me night and day,
Smiling reproach. Wise art thou, firm and good, 360
But vainly wouldst stand forth alone in strife
Against the Omnipotent; as yon clear lamps
That measure and divide the weary years
From which there is no refuge, long have taught
And long must teach. Even now thy Torturer arms 365
With the strange might of unimagined pains
The powers who scheme slow agonies in Hell,
And my commission is to lead them here,
Or what more subtle, foul, or savage fiends
People the abyss, and leave them to their task. 370
Be it not so! There is a secret known
To thee, and to none else of living things,
Which may transfer the sceptre of wide Heaven,
The fear of which perplexes the Supreme:
Clothe it in words, and bid it clasp his throne 375
In intercession; bend thy soul in prayer,
And like a suppliant in some gorgeous fane,[30]
Let the will kneel within thy haughty heart:
For benefits and meek submission tame
The fiercest and the mightiest. 380

PROMETHEUS
                          Evil minds
Change good to their own nature. I gave all
He has; and in return he chains me here
Years, ages, night and day: whether the Sun
Split my parched skin, or in the moony night
The crystal-wingèd snow cling round my hair— 385
Whilst my belovèd race is trampled down
By his thought-executing[31] ministers.

---

[30]Temple.
[31]Acting out; destroying (a dark pun).

Such is the tyrant's recompense: 'tis just:
He who is evil can receive no good;
And for a world bestowed, or a friend lost,   390
He can feel hate, fear, shame—not gratitude:
He but requites me for his own misdeed.
Kindness to such is keen reproach, which breaks
With bitter stings the light sleep of Revenge.
Submission, thou dost know I cannot try: 395
For what submission but that fatal word,
The death-seal of mankind's captivity—
Like the Sicilian's hair-suspended sword,[32]
Which trembles o'er his crown—would he accept,
Or could I yield?—which yet I will not yield.   400
Let others flatter Crime, where it sits throned
In brief Omnipotence: secure are they:
For Justice, when triumphant, will weep down
Pity, not punishment, on her own wrongs,
Too much avenged by those who err. I wait,   405
Enduring thus, the retributive hour
Which since we spake is even nearer now.—
But hark, the hell-hounds clamour. Fear delay:
Behold! Heaven lowers[33] under thy Father's frown.

MERCURY
Oh, that we might be spared—I to inflict   410
And thou to suffer! Once more answer me:
Thou knowest not the period[34] of Jove's power?

PROMETHEUS
I know but this, that it must come.

MERCURY
        Alas!
Thou canst not count thy years to come of pain?

---

[32]When Damocles called Dionysius the Elder, ruler of ancient Syracuse, the world's happiest man, Dionysius challenged him to trade places. Mounting the throne, Damocles saw a sword suspended over his head by a single horsehair.

[33]Crouches, skulks.

[34]The timespan; the termination.

PROMETHEUS
They last while Jove must reign: nor more, nor less   415
Do I desire or fear.

MERCURY
                    Yet pause, and plunge
Into Eternity, where recorded time,
Even all that we imagine, age on age,
Seems but a point, and the reluctant mind
Flags wearily in its unending flight,   420
Till it sink, dizzy, blind, lost, shelterless;
Perchance it has not numbered the slow years
Which thou must spend in torture, unreprieved?

PROMETHEUS
Perchance no thought can count them—yet they pass.

MERCURY
If thou might'st dwell among the Gods the while   425
Lapped in voluptuous joy?—

PROMETHEUS
                            I would not quit
This bleak ravine, these unrepentant pains.

MERCURY
Alas! I wonder at, yet pity thee.

PROMETHEUS
Pity the self-despising slaves of Heaven,
Not me, within whose mind sits peace serene,   430
As light in the sun, throned. How vain is talk!
Call up the fiends.

IONE
                    O, sister, look! White fire
Has cloven to the roots yon huge snow-loaded cedar;
How fearfully God's thunder howls behind!

MERCURY
I must obey his words and thine—alas!   435
Most heavily remorse hangs at my heart!

PANTHEA

See where the child of Heaven, with wingèd feet,
Runs down the slanted sunlight of the dawn.

IONE

Dear sister, close thy plumes over thine eyes
Lest thou behold and die—they come: they come   440
Blackening the birth of day with countless wings,
And hollow underneath, like death.

FIRST FURY

                Prometheus!

SECOND FURY

Immortal Titan!

THIRD FURY

       Champion of Heaven's slaves!

PROMETHEUS

He whom some dreadful voice invokes is here,
Prometheus, the chained Titan.—Horrible forms,   445
What and who are ye? Never yet there came
Phantasms so foul through monster-teeming Hell
From the all-miscreative brain of Jove;
Whilst I behold such execrable shapes,
Methinks I grow like what I contemplate,   450
And laugh and stare in loathsome sympathy.

FIRST FURY

We are the ministers of pain, and fear,
And disappointment, and mistrust, and hate,
And clinging crime; and as lean dogs pursue
Through wood and lake some struck and sobbing fawn,   455
We track all things that weep, and bleed, and live,
When the great King betrays them to our will.

PROMETHEUS

Oh! many fearful natures in one name,
I know ye; and these lakes and echoes know
The darkness and the clangour of your wings.   460

But why more hideous than your loathèd selves
Gather ye up in legions from the deep?

SECOND FURY

We knew not that—Sisters, rejoice, rejoice!

PROMETHEUS

Can aught exult in its deformity?

SECOND FURY

The beauty of delight makes lovers glad,   465
Gazing on one another—so are we.
As from the rose which the pale priestess kneels
To gather for her festal crown of flowers
The aëreal crimson falls, flushing her cheek—
So from our victim's destined agony   470
The shade which is our form invests us round,
Else we are shapeless as our Mother Night.

PROMETHEUS

I laugh your power, and his who sent you here,
To lowest scorn.—Pour forth the cup of pain.

FIRST FURY

Thou thinkest we will rend thee bone from bone?   475
And nerve from nerve, working like fire within?

PROMETHEUS

Pain is my element, as hate is thine;
Ye rend me now: I care not.

SECOND FURY

                  Dost imagine
We will but laugh into thy lidless[35] eyes?

PROMETHEUS

I weigh not what ye do, but what ye suffer,   480
Being evil. Cruel was the Power which called
You, or aught else so wretched, into light.

[35]Unable to close; sleepless.

THIRD FURY

Thou think'st we will live through thee, one by one,
Like animal life, and though we can obscure not
The soul which burns within, that we will dwell   485
Beside it, like a vain loud multitude
Vexing the self-content of wisest men—
That we will be dread thought beneath thy brain,
And foul desire round thine astonished heart,
And blood within thy labyrinthine veins   490
Crawling like agony?

PROMETHEUS
           Why, ye are thus now;
Yet am I king over myself, and rule
The torturing and conflicting throngs within,
As Jove rules you when Hell grows mutinous.

CHORUS OF FURIES

From the ends of the Earth, from the ends of the earth,   495
Where the night has its grave and the morning its birth,
        Come, Come, Come!
O ye who shake hills with the scream of your mirth,
When cities sink howling in ruin, and ye
Who with wingless footsteps trample the Sea,   500
And close upon Shipwreck and Famine's track,
Sit chattering with joy on the foodless wreck;
        Come, Come, Come!
    Leave the bed, low, cold, and red,
    Strewed beneath a nation dead;   505
    Leave the hatred—as in ashes
      Fire is left for future burning,—
    It will burst in bloodier flashes
      When ye stir it, soon returning:
    Leave the self-contempt implanted   510
    In young spirits, sense-enchanted,
      Misery's yet unkindled fuel;
    Leave Hell's secrets half unchanted
      To the maniac dreamer; cruel
    More than ye can be with hate   515
      Is he with fear.
        Come, Come, Come!

We are steaming up from Hell's wide gate
And we burthen the blast of the atmosphere,
But vainly we toil till ye come here.   520

> IONE
Sister, I hear the thunder of new wings.

> PANTHEA
These solid mountains quiver with the sound
Even as the tremulous air: their shadows make
The space within my plumes more black than night.

> FIRST FURY
> Your call was as a wingèd car   525
> Driven on whirlwinds fast and far;
> It rapt[36] us from red gulfs of war—

> SECOND FURY
> From wide cities, famine-wasted—

> THIRD FURY
> Groans half heard, and blood untasted—

> FOURTH FURY
> Kingly conclaves stern and cold,   530
> Where blood with gold is bought and sold—

> FIFTH FURY
> From the furnace, white and hot,
> In which—

> A FURY
>   Speak not: whisper not:
> I know all that ye would tell,
> But to speak might break the spell   535
> Which must bend the Invincible,
>   The stern of thought;
> He yet defies the deepest power of Hell.

> A FURY
Tear the veil!—

[36]Carried forcibly.

ANOTHER FURY
   It is torn.

CHORUS
           The pale stars of the morn
Shine on a misery, dire to be borne.   540
Dost thou faint, mighty Titan? We laugh thee to scorn.
Dost thou boast the clear knowledge thou waken'dst for man?
Then was kindled within him a thirst which outran
Those perishing waters; a thirst of fierce fever,
Hope, love, doubt, desire—which consume him for ever.   545
       One[37] came forth of gentle worth
       Smiling on the sanguine earth;
       His words outlived him, like swift poison
           Withering up truth, peace, and pity.
       Look! where round the wide horizon   550
           Many a million-peopled city
       Vomits smoke in the bright air.
       Hark that outcry of despair!
       'Tis his mild and gentle ghost
           Wailing for the faith he kindled: 555
       Look again, the flames almost
           To a glow-worm's lamp have dwindled:
       The survivors round the embers
           Gather in dread.
              Joy, Joy, Joy!   560
Past ages crowd on thee, but each one remembers,
And the future is dark, and the present is spread
Like a pillow of thorns for thy slumberless head.

      SEMICHORUS I
      Drops of bloody agony flow
      From his white and quivering brow.   565
      Grant a little respite now—
      See a disenchanted Nation[38]
      Springs like day from desolation;
      To Truth its state is dedicate,
      And Freedom leads it forth, her mate;   570

[37]Jesus, whose "words" are perverted by institutional Christianity.
[38]Post-Revolutionary France, or any idealized political state fallen to ruin.

A legionèd band of linkèd brothers
Whom Love calls children—

SEMICHORUS II
                                        'Tis another's—
See how kindred murder kin!
'Tis the vintage-time for Death and Sin:
Blood, like new wine, bubbles within   575
            Till Despair smothers
The struggling World—which slaves and tyrants win.
                    [*All the Furies vanish, except one.*]

IONE
Hark, sister! what a low yet dreadful groan
Quite unsuppressed is tearing up the heart
Of the good Titan—as storms tear the deep,   580
And beasts hear the Sea moan in inland caves.
Darest thou observe how the fiends torture him?

PANTHEA
Alas! I looked forth twice, but will no more.

IONE
What didst thou see?

PANTHEA
                    A woful sight—a youth
With patient looks nailed to a crucifix.   585

IONE
What next?

PANTHEA
                    The Heaven around, the Earth below
Was peopled with thick shapes of human death,
All horrible, and wrought by human hands,
And some appeared the work of human hearts,
For men were slowly killed by frowns and smiles: 590
And other sights too foul to speak and live
Were wandering by. Let us not tempt worse fear
By looking forth—those groans are grief enough.

FURY

Behold an emblem—those who do endure
Deep wrongs for man, and scorn, and chains, but heap   595
Thousand-fold torment on themselves and him.

PROMETHEUS

Remit the anguish of that lighted stare—
Close those wan lips—let that thorn-wounded brow
Stream not with blood—it mingles with thy tears!
Fix, fix those tortured orbs in peace and death,   600
So thy sick throes shake not that crucifix,
So those pale fingers play not with thy gore.—
O, horrible! Thy name[39] I will not speak,
It hath become a curse. I see, I see,
The wise, the mild, the lofty, and the just,   605
Whom thy slaves hate for being like to thee,
Some hunted by foul lies from their heart's home,
An early-chosen, late-lamented home;
As hooded ounces cling to the driven hind;[40]
Some linked to corpses in unwholesome cells: 610
Some—Hear I not the multitude laugh loud?—
Impaled in lingering fire: and mighty realms
Float by my feet, like sea-uprooted isles,
Whose sons are kneaded down in common blood
By the red light of their own burning homes.   615

FURY

Blood thou canst see, and fire; and canst hear groans;
Worse things, unheard, unseen, remain behind.

PROMETHEUS

Worse?

FURY

        In each human heart terror survives
The ravin it has gorged: the loftiest fear
All that they would disdain to think were true: 620
Hypocrisy and custom make their minds
The fanes of many a worship, now outworn.

[39]Christ, as in "Christianity."

[40]Ounces: leopards, hooded until released to hunt; hind: female deer.

They dare not devise good for man's estate,
And yet they know not that they do not dare.
The good want power, but to weep barren tears.   625
The powerful goodness want: worse need for them.
The wise want love; and those who love want wisdom;
And all best things are thus confused to ill.
Many are strong and rich—and would be just,—
But live among their suffering fellow-men   630
As if none felt—they know not what they do.[41]

PROMETHEUS
Thy words are like a cloud of wingèd snakes;
And yet I pity those they torture not.

FURY
Thou pitiest them? I speak no more!

[*Vanishes.*]

PROMETHEUS
                  Ah woe!
Ah woe! Alas! pain, pain ever, for ever!   635
I close my tearless eyes, but see more clear
Thy works within my woe-illumèd mind,
Thou subtle tyrant! Peace is in the grave—
The grave hides all things beautiful and good—
I am a God and cannot find it there—   640
Nor would I seek it: for, though dread revenge,
This is defeat, fierce king, not victory.
The sights with which thou torturest gird my soul
With new endurance, till the hour arrives
When they shall be no types of things which are.   645

PANTHEA
Alas! what sawest thou more?

PROMETHEUS
               There are two woes:
To speak, and to behold; thou spare me one.
Names are there, Nature's sacred watchwords—they

[41]Ironic echo of Jesus on the cross: "Father, forgive them; for they know not what they do" (Luke 23.34).

Were borne aloft in bright emblazonry;
The nations thronged around, and cried aloud,   650
As with one voice, "Truth, liberty, and love!"
Suddenly fierce confusion fell from heaven
Among them—there was strife, deceit, and fear:
Tyrants rushed in, and did divide the spoil.
This was the shadow of the truth I saw.   655

THE EARTH
I felt thy torture, son; with such mixed joy
As pain and virtue give.—To cheer thy state
I bid ascend those subtle and fair spirits,
Whose homes are the dim caves of human thought,
And who inhabit, as birds wing the wind,   660
Its world-surrounding æther:[42] they behold
Beyond that twilight realm, as in a glass,
The future—may they speak comfort to thee!

PANTHEA
Look, Sister, where a troop of spirits gather,
Like flocks of clouds in spring's delightful weather,   665
Thronging in the blue air!

IONE
                    And see! more come,
Like fountain-vapours when the winds are dumb,
That climb up the ravine in scattered lines.
And hark! is it the music of the pines?
Is it the lake? is it the waterfall?   670

PANTHEA
'Tis something sadder, sweeter far than all.

CHORUS OF SPIRITS
From unremembered ages we
Gentle guides and guardians be
Of heaven-oppressed mortality—
And we breathe, and sicken not,   675
The atmosphere of human thought:
Be it dim, and dank, and gray

[42]Highest atmosphere.

Like a storm-extinguished day
Travelled o'er by dying gleams;
    Be it bright as all between   680
Cloudless skies and windless streams,
    Silent, liquid, and serene—
As the birds within the wind,
    As the fish within the wave,
As the thoughts of man's own mind   685
    Float through all above the grave,
We make there our liquid lair,
Voyaging cloudlike and unpent[43]
Through the boundless element—
Thence we bear the prophecy   690
Which begins and ends in thee!

IONE

More yet come, one by one: the air around them
Looks radiant as the air around a star.

FIRST SPIRIT

On a battle-trumpet's blast
I fled hither, fast, fast, fast,   695
'Mid the darkness upward cast—
From the dust of creeds outworn,
From the tyrant's banner torn,
Gathering 'round me, onward borne,
There was mingled many a cry—   700
Freedom! Hope! Death! Victory!
Till they faded through the sky
And one sound—above, around,
One sound beneath, around, above,
Was moving; 'twas the soul of Love;   705
'Twas the hope, the prophecy,
Which begins and ends in thee.

SECOND SPIRIT

A rainbow's arch[44] stood on the sea,
Which rocked beneath, immovably;

[43]Released, unpenned.

[44]An inversion of the symbol of God's covenant with Man after the Flood.

And the triumphant Storm did flee,   710
Like a conqueror, swift and proud,
Between, with many a captive cloud,
A shapeless, dark and rapid crowd,
Each by lightning riven in half.—
I heard the thunder hoarsely laugh.—   715
Mighty fleets were strewn like chaff
And spread beneath a hell of death
O'er the white waters. I alit
On a great ship lightning-split,
And speeded hither on the sigh   720
Of one who gave an enemy
His plank—then plunged aside to die.[45]

   THIRD SPIRIT
I sate beside a sage's bed,
And the lamp was burning red
Near the book where he had fed,   725
When a Dream with plumes of flame,
To his pillow hovering came,
And I knew it was the same
Which had kindled long ago
Pity, eloquence, and woe;   730
And the world awhile below
Wore the shade, its lustre made.
It has borne me here as fleet
As Desire's lightning feet:
I must ride it back ere morrow,   735
Or the sage will wake in sorrow.

   FOURTH SPIRIT
On a Poet's lips I slept
Dreaming like a love-adept
In the sound his breathing kept;
Nor seeks nor finds he mortal blisses   740
But feeds on the aëreal kisses
Of shapes that haunt thought's wildernesses.
He will watch from dawn to gloom
The lake-reflected sun illume

[45]A shipwrecked mariner selflessly gives his buoyant plank to an enemy and drowns.

The yellow bees in the ivy-bloom,   745
Nor heed nor see, what things they be;
But from these create he can
Forms more real than living man,
Nurslings of immortality!—
One of these awakened me,   750
And I sped to succour[46] thee.

IONE

Behold'st thou not two shapes from the East and West
Come, as two doves to one belovèd nest,
Twin nurslings of the all-sustaining air
On swift still wings glide down the atmosphere?   755
And, hark! their sweet, sad voices! 'tis despair
Mingled with love, and then dissolved in sound.—

PANTHEA

Canst thou speak, sister? all my words are drowned.

IONE

Their beauty gives me voice. See how they float
On their sustaining wings of skiey grain,   760
Orange and azure deepening into gold:
Their soft smiles light the air like a star's fire.

CHORUS OF SPIRITS

Hast thou beheld the form of Love?

FIFTH SPIRIT

                          As over wide dominions
I sped, like some swift cloud that wings the wide air's wildernesses,
That planet-crested shape swept by on lightning-braided pinions,[47]   765
Scattering the liquid joy of life from his ambrosial[48] tresses:
His footsteps paved the world with light—but as I passed 'twas fading,
And hollow Ruin yawned behind: great sages bound in madness,
And headless patriots, and pale youths who perished, unupbraiding,
Gleamed in the night. I wandered o'er, till thou, O King of sadness,
Turned by thy smile the worst I saw to recollected gladness.

[46]Succor: give solace and encouragement to.
[47]Feathers, wings.
[48]Heavenly.

SIXTH SPIRIT

Ah, sister! Desolation is a delicate thing:
It walks not on the earth, it floats not on the air,
But treads with lulling footstep, and fans with silent wing
The tender hopes which in their hearts the best and gentlest bear;[49] 775
Who, soothed to false repose by the fanning plumes above
And the music-stirring motion of its soft and busy feet,
Dream visions of aëreal joy, and call the monster, Love,
And wake, and find the shadow Pain—as he whom now we greet.

CHORUS

Though Ruin now Love's shadow be, 780
Following him, destroyingly,
On Death's white and wingèd steed,[50]
Which the fleetest cannot flee—
Trampling down both flower and weed,
Man and beast, and foul and fair, 785
Like a tempest through the air;
Thou shalt quell this horseman grim,
Woundless though in heart or limb.—

PROMETHEUS

Spirits! how know ye this shall be?

CHORUS

In the atmosphere we breathe— 790
As buds grow red when the snow-storms flee,
From Spring gathering up beneath,
Whose mild winds shake the elder brake,
And the wandering herdsmen know
That the white-thorn soon will blow— 795
Wisdom, Justice, Love, and Peace,
When they struggle to increase,
Are to us as soft winds be
To shepherd boys—the prophecy
Which begins and ends in thee. 800

[49]In Plato's *Symposium*, which Shelley had translated, Love (not Desolation) dwells within and treads upon the softest of things.

[50]An image from the Apocalypse, the subject of a painting by Benjamin West exhibited in London in 1817.

IONE
Where are the Spirits fled?

PANTHEA
           Only a sense
Remains of them, like the Omnipotence
Of music, when the inspired voice and lute
Languish, ere yet the responses are mute,
Which through the deep and labyrinthine soul,   805
Like echoes through long caverns, wind and roll.

PROMETHEUS
How fair these air-born shapes! and yet I feel
Most vain all hope but love; and thou art far,
Asia! who, when my being overflowed,
Wert like a golden chalice to bright wine   810
Which else had sunk into the thirsty dust.
All things are still—alas! how heavily
This quiet morning weighs upon my heart;
Though I should dream I could even sleep with grief
If slumber were denied not. I would fain   815
Be what it is my destiny to be,
The saviour and the strength of suffering man,
Or sink into the original gulf of things:
There is no agony, and no solace left;
Earth can console, Heaven can torment no more.   820

PANTHEA
Hast thou forgotten one who watches thee
The cold dark night, and never sleeps but when
The shadow of thy spirit falls on her?

PROMETHEUS
I said all hope was vain but love—thou lovest.

PANTHEA
Deeply in truth—but the Eastern star looks white,   825
And Asia waits in that far Indian vale,
The scene of her sad exile—rugged once
And desolate and frozen, like this ravine;
But now invested with fair flowers and herbs,

And haunted by sweet airs and sounds, which flow   830
Among the woods and waters, from the æther[51]
Of her transforming presence—which would fade
If it were mingled not with thine.—Farewell!

ACT II
SCENE I

Morning. A lovely Vale in the Indian Caucasus. Asia alone.

ASIA

From all the blasts of heaven thou hast descended—
Yes, like a spirit, like a thought, which makes
Unwonted[1] tears throng to the horny[2] eyes,
And beatings haunt the desolated heart,
Which should have learnt repose,—thou hast descended   5
Cradled in tempests; thou dost wake, O Spring!
O child of many winds! As suddenly
Thou comest as the memory of a dream,
Which now is sad because it hath been sweet;
Like genius, or like joy which riseth up   10
As from the earth, clothing with golden clouds
The desert of our life. . . .
This is the season, this the day, the hour;
At sunrise thou shouldst come, sweet sister mine,
Too long desired, too long delaying, come!   15
How like death-worms the wingless moments crawl!
The point of one white star[3] is quivering still
Deep in the orange light of widening morn
Beyond the purple mountains. through a chasm
Of wind-divided mist the darker lake   20
Reflects it—now it wanes—it gleams again
As the waves fade, and as the burning threads
Of woven cloud unravel in pale air.
'Tis lost! and through yon peaks of cloud-like snow

---

[51]The element breathed by the gods; a "diviner air."

---

[1]Rare.

[2]Tough, shell-like, perhaps from being always open.

[3]The morning star, Venus, dimmed by the dawning sun.

The roseate sunlight quivers—hear I not   25
The Æolian music of her sea-green plumes
Winnowing⁴ the crimson dawn?

                                  [Panthea enters.]
                    I feel, I see
Those eyes which burn through smiles that fade in tears,
Like stars half quenched in mists of silver dew.—
Belovèd and most beautiful, who wearest   30
The shadow of that soul by which I live,
How late thou art! the spherèd sun had climbed
The sea; my heart was sick with hope, before
The printless air felt thy belated plumes.

      PANTHEA
Pardon, great Sister! but my wings were faint   35
With the delight of a remembered dream,
As are the noontide plumes of summer winds
Satiate with sweet flowers. I was wont to sleep
Peacefully, and awake refreshed and calm
Before the sacred Titan's fall, and thy   40
Unhappy love, had made through use and pity
Both love and woe familiar to my heart
As they had grown to thine: erewhile⁵ I slept
Under the glaucous⁶ caverns of old Ocean
Within dim bowers of green and purple moss,   45
Our young Ione's soft and milky arms
Locked then, as now, behind my dark, moist hair,
While my shut eyes and cheek were pressed within
The folded depth of her life-breathing bosom:
But not as now, since I am made the wind   50
Which fails beneath the music that I bear
Of thy most wordless converse; since dissolved
Into the sense with which love talks, my rest
Was troubled and yet sweet—my waking hours
Too full of care and pain.

---

⁴Sifting to separate grain from chaff.
⁵Formerly.
⁶Pale gray-greenish.

ASIA
                        Lift up thine eyes,   55
And let me read[7] thy dream.—

PANTHEA
                                As I have said
With our sea-sister at his feet I slept.
The mountain mists, condensing at our voice
Under the moon, had spread their snowy flakes,
From the keen ice shielding our linkèd sleep.   60
Then two dreams came. One, I remember not.
But in the other his pale wound-worn limbs
Fell from Prometheus, and the azure night
Grew radiant with the glory of that form
Which lives unchanged within, and his voice fell   65
Like music which makes giddy the dim brain,
Faint with intoxication of keen joy:
"Sister of her whose footsteps pave the world
With loveliness—more fair than aught but her,
Whose shadow thou art—lift thine eyes on me."   70
I lifted them—the overpowering light
Of that immortal shape was shadowed o'er
By love; which, from his soft and flowing limbs,
And passion-parted lips, and keen faint eyes,
Steamed forth like vaporous fire; an atmosphere   75
Which wrapped me in its all-dissolving power,
As the warm æther of the morning sun
Wraps ere it drinks some cloud of wandering dew.
I saw not—heard not—moved not—only felt
His presence flow and mingle through my blood   80
Till it became his life, and his grew mine,
And I was thus absorbed—until it past,
And like the vapours when the sun sinks down,
Gathering again in drops upon the pines
And tremulous as they, in the deep night   85
My being was condensed; and as the rays
Of thought were slowly gathered, I could hear
His voice, whose accents lingered ere they died
Like footsteps of weak melody: thy name
Among the many sounds alone I heard   90

[7]Discern; interpret.

Of what might be articulate; though still
I listened through the night when sound was none.
Ione wakened then, and said to me:
"Canst thou divine what troubles me to-night?
I always knew what I desired before,   95
Nor ever found delight to wish in vain.
But now I cannot tell thee what I seek;
I know not—something sweet, since it is sweet
Even to desire—it is thy sport, false sister;
Thou hast discovered some enchantment old   100
Whose spells have stolen my spirit as I slept
And mingled it with thine;—for when just now
We kissed, I felt within thy parted lips
The sweet air that sustained me, and the warmth
Of the life-blood, for loss of which I faint,   105
Quivered between our intertwining arms."
I answered not, for the Eastern star grew pale,
But fled to thee.

            ASIA
            Thou speakest, but thy words
Are as the air: I feel them not: oh, lift
Thine eyes, that I may read his written soul!   110

            PANTHEA
I lift them though they droop beneath the load
Of that they would express—what canst thou see
But thine own fairest shadow imaged there?

            ASIA
Thine eyes are like the deep, blue, boundless Heaven
Contracted to two circles underneath   115
Their long, fine lashes—dark, far, measureless,—
Orb within orb, and line through line inwoven.—

            PANTHEA
Why lookest thou as if a spirit past?

            ASIA
There is a change: beyond their inmost depth
I see a shade—a shape—'tis He,[8] arrayed   120

[8]Prometheus (with a suggestion of Jesus).

In the soft light of his own smiles, which spread
Like radiance from the cloud-surrounded moon.
Prometheus, it is thou—depart not yet!
Say not those smiles that we shall meet again
Within that bright pavilion which their beams   125
Shall build o'er the waste world? The dream is told.
What shape is that between us? Its rude⁹ hair
Roughens the wind that lifts it, its regard
Is wild and quick, yet 'tis a thing of air,
For through its gray robe gleams the golden dew   130
Whose stars the noon has quenched not.

DREAM

Follow! Follow!

PANTHEA

It is mine other dream.—

ASIA

It disappears.

PANTHEA

It passes now into my mind. Methought
As we sate here, the flower-infolding buds
Burst on yon lightning-blasted almond-tree,¹⁰   135
When swift from the white Scythian wilderness¹¹
A wind swept forth wrinkling the Earth with frost:
I looked, and all the blossoms were blown down;
But on each leaf was stamped—as the blue bells
Of Hyacinth tell Apollo's written grief¹²—   140
O, *follow, follow!*

Asia

As you speak, your words
Fill, pause by pause, my own forgotten sleep
With shapes. Methought among these lawns together

⁹Wild, unbound.

¹⁰The healthy almond tree is a biblical symbol of hope; see Jeremiah 1.11–12: ". . . I
see the rod of an almond tree"; Panthea sees the hope Prometheus embodies.

¹¹In Aeschylus's play, Prometheus is fettered in the Scythian wilderness.

¹²The wind-god Zephyrus killed Hyacinth, whom Apollo loved; Apollo turned his
blood into the hyacinth, whose petals are marked with the Greek letters for "woe."

We wandered, underneath the young gray dawn,
And multitudes of dense white fleecy clouds   145
Were wandering in thick flocks along the mountains
Shepherded by the slow, unwilling wind;
And the white dew on the new-bladed grass,
Just piercing the dark earth, hung silently—
And there was more which I remember not: 150
But on the shadows of the morning clouds,
Athwart the purple mountain slope, was written
Follow, O, follow! as they vanished by;
And on each herb from which Heaven's dew had fallen,
The like was stamped as with a withering fire;   155
A wind arose among the pines—it shook
The clinging music from their boughs, and then
Low, sweet, faint sounds, like the farewell of ghosts,
Were heard—O, *follow, follow, follow me!*
And then I said: "Panthea, look on me."   160
But in the depth of those belovèd eyes
Still I saw, *follow, follow!*

        Echo
              Follow, follow!

        Panthea
The crags, this clear spring morning, mock our voices
As they were spirit-tongued.

        Asia
              It is some being
Around the crags.—What fine clear sounds! O, list!   165

        Echoes *unseen*
        Echoes we—listen!
          We cannot stay:
        As dew-stars glisten
          Then fade away—
            Child of Ocean![13]   170

---

[13]Panthea, Ione, and Asia are daughters of Oceanus.

ASIA

Hark! Spirits speak. The liquid responses
Of their aëreal[14] tongues yet sound.—

PANTHEA

I hear.

ECHOES

O, follow, follow,
    As our voice recedeth
Through the caverns hollow,   175
    Where the forest spreadeth;
        [*More distant.*]
O, follow, follow!
Through the caverns hollow,
As the song floats thou pursue,
Where the wild bee never flew,   180
Through the noontide darkness deep,
By the odour-breathing sleep
Of faint night flowers, and the waves
At the fountain-lighted caves,
While our music, wild and sweet,   185
Mocks thy gently falling feet,
    Child of Ocean!

ASIA

Shall we pursue the sound?—It grows more faint
And distant.

PANTHEA

List!—the strain floats nearer now.

ECHOES

In the world unknown   190
    Sleeps a voice unspoken;
By thy step alone
    Can its rest be broken;
        Child of Ocean!

[14]Light as air. Notice how Shelley's rhymes (ll. 166–69) sound the fading echoes.

ASIA

How the notes sink upon the ebbing wind!   195

ECHOES
    O, follow, follow!
    Through the caverns hollow,
As the song floats thou pursue,
By the woodland noontide dew;
By the forest, lakes, and fountains,   200
Through the many-folded mountains;
To the rents, and gulfs, and chasms,
Where the Earth reposed from spasms,
On the day when He and thou
Parted—to commingle now   205
Child of Ocean!

        ASIA

Come, sweet Panthea—link thy hand in mine,
And follow, ere the voices fade away.

SCENE II

A Forest, intermingled with Rocks and Caverns.
Asia and Panthea pass into it. Two young Fauns[15]
are sitting on a Rock listening.

SEMICHORUS I OF SPIRITS
The path through which that lovely twain
    Have past, by cedar, pine, and yew,
    And each dark tree that ever grew,
    Is curtained out from Heaven's wide blue;
Nor sun, nor moon, nor wind, nor rain,   5
        Can pierce its interwoven bowers,
    Nor aught, save where some cloud of dew,
Drifted along the earth-creeping breeze,
Between the trunks of the hoar[16] trees,
        Hangs each a pearl in the pale flowers   10

---

[15]Mythical woodland creatures with men's bodies and goat-like ears, tail, horns, and hooves.

[16]Ancient.

Of the green laurel, blown anew;[17]
And bends, and then fades silently,
One frail and fair anemone:[18]
Or when some star of many a one
That climbs and wanders through steep night,   15
Has found the cleft through which alone
Beams fall from high those depths upon
Ere it is borne away, away,
By the swift Heavens that cannot stay—
It scatters drops of golden light,   20
Like lines of rain that ne'er unite:
And the gloom divine is all around,
And underneath is the mossy ground.

SEMICHORUS II
There the voluptuous nightingales,
   Are awake through all the broad noonday.   25
When one with bliss or sadness fails—
     And through the windless ivy-boughs,
   Sick with sweet love, droops dying away
On its mate's music-panting bosom—
Another from the swinging blossom,   30
     Watching to catch the languid close
   Of the last strain, then lifts on high
   The wings of the weak melody,
Till some new strain of feeling bear
   The song, and all the woods are mute;   35
When there is heard through the dim air
The rush of wings, and rising there
   Like many a lake-surrounded flute,
Sounds overflow the listener's brain
So sweet, that joy is almost pain.   40

SEMICHORUS I
There those enchanted eddies play
   Of echoes, music-tongued, which draw,

---

[17]The laurel (bay), sacred to Apollo, provided leaves for garlands awarded to the greatest poets; blown anew: recently bloomed.

[18]In Greek mythology, Adonis, beloved of Aphrodite, was killed by jealous Ares disguised as a boar. As Aphrodite carried his body away, crimson anemones sprang up from his blood. The wind that opens the blossoms also blows the petals away.

By Demogorgon's mighty law,[19]
With melting rapture, or sweet awe,
All spirits on that secret way;   45
    As inland boats are driven to Ocean
Down streams made strong with mountain-thaw:
    And first there comes a gentle sound
    To those in talk or slumber bound,
And wakes the destined—soft emotion   50
Attracts, impels them: those who saw
    Say from the breathing Earth behind
    There steams a plume-uplifting wind
Which drives them on their path, while they
    Believe their own swift wings and feet   55
The sweet desires within obey:
And so they float upon their way
Until, still sweet but loud and strong,
The storm of sound is driven along,
    Sucked up and hurrying—as they fleet   60
    Behind, its gathering billows meet
And to the fatal mountain bear
Like clouds amid the yielding air.

        FIRST FAUN
Canst thou imagine where those spirits live
Which make such delicate music in the woods?   65
We haunt within the least frequented caves
And closest coverts, and we know these wilds,
Yet never meet them, though we hear them oft:
Where may they hide themselves?

        SECOND FAUN
                            'Tis hard to tell:
I have heard those more skilled in spirits say,   70
The bubbles,[20] which the enchantment of the sun
Sucks from the pale faint water-flowers that pave
The oozy bottom of clear lakes and pools,
Are the pavilions where such dwell and float

[19]Historical inevitability; destiny.

[20]Contemporary science believed that hydrogen released by underwater vegetation during hot weather bubbled to the surface and burst into the air.

Under the green and golden atmosphere   75
Which noontide kindles through the woven leaves;
And when these burst, and the thin fiery air,
The which they breathed within those lucent domes,
Ascends to flow like meteors through the night,
They ride on them, and rein their headlong speed,   80
And bow their burning crests, and glide in fire
Under the waters of the Earth again.

      First Faun
If such live thus, have others other lives,
Under pink blossoms or within the bells
Of meadow flowers, or folded violets deep,   85
Or on their dying odours, when they die,
Or in the sunlight of the spherèd dew?

      Second Faun
Aye, many more which we may well divine.
But, should we stay to speak, noontide would come,
And thwart Silenus[21] find his goats undrawn,   90
And grudge to sing those wise and lovely songs
Of Fate, and Chance, and God, and Chaos old,
And Love, and the chained Titan's woful doom,
And how he shall be loosed, and make the earth
One brotherhood—delightful strains which cheer   95
Our solitary twilights, and which charm
To silence the unenvying nightingales.

SCENE III

A Pinnacle of Rock among Mountains. Asia and Panthea.

      Panthea
Hither the sound has borne us—to the realm
Of Demogorgon, and the mighty portal,
Like a volcano's meteor-breathing chasm,
Whence the oracular vapour is hurled up
Which lonely men drink wandering in their youth,   5

---

[21]Companion and tutor of pleasure-loving Dionysus, a cheerful old drunkard. Undrawn: not yet milked.

And call truth, virtue, love, genius, or joy—
That maddening wine of life, whose dregs they drain
To deep intoxication, and uplift
Like Mænads[22] who cry loud, Evoe! Evoe!
The voice which is contagion to the world.   10

      ASIA
Fit throne for such a Power! Magnificent!
How glorious art thou, Earth! And if thou be
The shadow of some Spirit lovelier still,
Though evil stain its work, and it should be
Like its creation, weak yet beautiful,   15
I could fall down and worship that and thee.—
Even now my heart adoreth.—Wonderful!
Look, Sister, ere the vapour dim thy brain:
Beneath is a wide plain of billowy mist,
As a lake, paving in the morning sky,   20
With azure waves which burst in silver light,
Some Indian vale. Behold it, rolling on
Under the curdling[23] winds, and islanding
The peak whereon we stand, midway, around,
Encinctured[24] by the dark and blooming forests,   25
Dim twilight-lawns, and stream-illumèd caves,
And wind-enchanted shapes of wandering mist;
And far on high the keen sky-cleaving mountains
From icy spires of sun-like radiance fling
The dawn, as lifted Ocean's dazzling spray,   30
From some Atlantic islet scattered up,
Spangles the wind with lamp-like water-drops.
The vale is girdled with their walls—a howl
Of cataracts from their thaw-cloven ravines,
Satiates the listening wind, continuous, vast,   35
Awful as silence.—Hark! the rushing snow!
The sun-awakened avalanche! whose mass,
Thrice sifted by the storm, had gathered there

---

[22]Dionysus's female worshipers, often intoxicated to fatal destructiveness. *Evoe* is their rallying cry.

[23]Curd-like in appearance.

[24]Belted, girdled.

Flake after flake, in Heaven-defying minds
As thought by thought is piled, till some great truth   40
Is loosened, and the nations echo round,
Shaken to their roots, as do the mountains now.

PANTHEA

Look, how the gusty sea of mist is breaking
In crimson foam, even at our feet!—it rises
As Ocean at the enchantment of the moon   45
Round foodless men wrecked on some oozy isle.

ASIA

The fragments of the cloud are scattered up—
The wind that lifts them disentwines my hair—
Its billows now sweep o'er mine eyes—my brain
Grows dizzy—I see thin shapes within the mist.   50

PANTHEA

A countenance with beckoning smiles—there burns
An azure fire within its golden locks—
Another and another—hark! they speak!²⁵

SONG OF SPIRITS

To the Deep, to the Deep,
        Down, Down!   55
    Through the shade of Sleep,
    Through the cloudy strife
    Of Death and of Life;
    Through the veil and the bar
    Of things which seem and are   60
Even to the steps of the remotest Throne,
        Down, Down!

²⁵Shelley first ended the scene here, then added the Song of Spirits, with its sonic and
verbal repetitions, anaphora (repeated first words), rhyme, and accumulating similes.

While the sound whirls around,
    Down, Down!
As the fawn draws the hound,   65
As the lightning the vapour,
As a weak moth the taper;
Death, Despair; Love, Sorrow;
Time both; to-day, to-morrow;
As steel obeys the Spirit of the stone,   70
    Down, Down!

Through the gray, void Abysm,
    Down, Down!
Where the air is no prism
And the moon and stars are not   75
And the cavern-crags wear not
The radiance of Heaven,
Nor the gloom to Earth given,
Where there is One pervading, One alone,
    Down, Down!   80

In the depth of the deep,
    Down, Down!
Like veiled Lightning asleep,
Like the spark nursed in embers,
The last look Love remembers,   85
Like a diamond, which shines
On the dark wealth of mines,
A spell is treasured but for thee alone —
    Down, Down!

We have bound thee, we guide thee   90
    Down, Down!
With the bright form beside thee—
Resist not the weakness—
Such strength is in meekness—
That the Eternal, the Immortal,   95
Must unloose through life's portal
The snake-like Doom coiled underneath his throne
    By that alone.

SCENE IV[26]

The Cave of Demogorgon. Asia and Panthea.

PANTHEA
What vèiled form sits on that ebon throne?

ASIA
The veil has fallen.

PANTHEA
         I see a mighty Darkness
Filling the seat of power, and rays of gloom
Dart round, as light from the meridian Sun.
Ungazed upon and shapeless:—neither limb,   5
Nor form, nor outline, yet we feel it is
A living Spirit.[27]

DEMOGORGON
        Ask what thou wouldst know.

ASIA
What canst thou tell?

DEMOGORGON
          All things thou dar'st demand.

ASIA
Who made the living world?

DEMOGORGON
        God.

---

[26]Asia's visit to Demogorgon's cave is patterned on the hero's journey to the underworld in traditional epics. It was believed that when seawater (Asia is Oceanus's daughter) came into contact with volcanic magma, an eruption would result. Volcanic eruptions are frequent images in the political writing of Shelley's era, for intellectual and political revolution.

[27]Shelley evokes Milton's Death: "The other shape, / If shape it might be call'd that shape had none / Distinguishable in member, joynt, or limb, / Or substance might be call'd that shadow seem'd, / For each seem'd either; black it stood as Night . . ." (*PL* 2.666–70).

ASIA

                              Who made all
That it contains—thought, passion, reason, will,   10
Imagination?

DEMOGORGON
God: Almighty God.

ASIA
Who made that sense which, when the winds of Spring
In rarest visitation, or the voice
Of one belovèd heard in youth alone,
Fills the faint eyes with falling tears which dim   15
The radiant looks of unbewailing flowers,
And leaves this peopled earth a solitude
When it returns no more?

DEMOGORGON
                    Merciful God.

ASIA
And who made terror, madness, crime, remorse,
Which from the links of the great chain of things,   20
To every thought within the mind of man
Sway and drag heavily—and each one reels
Under the load towards the pit of death;
Abandoned hope, and love that turns to hate;
And self-contempt, bitterer to drink than blood;   25
Pain, whose unheeded and familiar speech
Is howling, and keen shrieks, day after day;
And Hell, or the sharp fear of Hell?

DEMOGORGON
                    He reigns.[28]

ASIA
Utter his name—a world pining in pain
Asks but his name: curses shall drag him down.   30

---

[28]Like a traditional oracle, Demogorgon responds with cryptic answers.

DEMOGORGON

He reigns.

ASIA

I feel, I know it—who?

DEMOGORGON

He reigns.

ASIA

Who reigns? There was the Heaven and Earth at first,
And Light and Love;—then Saturn, from whose throne
Time[29] fell, an envious shadow: such the state
Of the earth's primal spirits beneath his sway,   35
As the calm joy of flowers and living leaves
Before the wind or sun has withered them
And semivital worms; but he refused
The birthright of their being, knowledge, power,
The skill which wields the elements, the thought   40
Which pierces this dim universe like light,
Self-empire, and the majesty of love;
For thirst of which they fainted. Then Prometheus
Gave wisdom, which is strength, to Jupiter,
And with this law alone, "Let man be free,"   45
Clothed him with the dominion of wide Heaven.
To know nor faith, nor love, nor law; to be
Omnipotent but friendless is to reign;
And Jove now reigned; for on the race of man
First famine, and then toil, and then disease,   50
Strife, wounds, and ghastly death unseen before,
Fell; and the unseasonable seasons drove
With alternating shafts of frost and fire,
Their shelterless, pale tribes to mountain caves:
And in their desert hearts fierce wants he sent,   55
And mad disquietudes, and shadows idle
Of unreal good, which levied mutual war,
So ruining the lair wherein they raged.
Prometheus saw, and waked the legioned hopes

[29] A pun on Saturn's Greek name, Kronos, and Time (Chronos).

Which sleep within folded Elysian flowers,[30]   60
Nepenthe, Moly, Amaranth,[31] fadeless blooms,
That they might hide with thin and rainbow wings
The shape of Death; and Love he sent to bind
The disunited tendrils of that vine
Which bears the wine of life, the human heart;   65
And he tamed fire, which like some beast of prey
Most terrible, but lovely, played beneath
The frown of man, and tortured to his will
Iron and gold, the slaves and signs of power,
And gems and poisons, and all subtlest forms   70
Hidden beneath the mountains and the waves.
He gave man speech,[32] and speech created thought,
Which is the measure of the Universe;
And Science struck the thrones of Earth and Heaven,
Which shook but fell not; and the harmonious mind   75
Poured itself forth in all-prophetic song;
And music lifted up the listening spirit
Until it walked, exempt from mortal care,
Godlike, o'er the clear billows of sweet sound;
And human hands first mimicked and then mocked,   80
With moulded limbs more lovely than its own,
The human form, till marble grew divine;
And mothers, gazing, drank the love men see
Reflected in their race—behold, and perish.—
He told the hidden power of herbs and springs,   85
And Disease drank and slept.—Death grew like sleep.—
He taught the implicated[33] orbits woven
Of the wide-wandering stars; and how the Sun
Changes his lair, and by what secret spell
The pale moon is transformed, when her broad eye   90
Gazes not on the interlunar[34] sea:
He taught to rule, as life directs the limbs,
The tempest-wingèd chariots of the Ocean,

[30]Heroes enjoyed an afterlife in the Elysian Fields.

[31]Nepenthe ("no pain") yields a drug of forgetfulness; Moly, an herb that Homer said protected Odysseus from Circe's magical spells; Amaranth, a heavenly flower.

[32]Among the gifts Prometheus gave to humanity, thus incurring Jupiter's wrath.

[33]Interfolded.

[34]Dark period between the old and new moon.

And the Celt knew the Indian. Cities then
Were built, and through their snow-like columns flowed   95
The warm winds, and the azure æther shone,
And the blue sea and shadowy hills were seen.
Such the alleviations of his state
Prometheus gave to man—for which he hangs
Withering in destined pain—but who rains[35] down   100
Evil, the immedicable plague, which, while
Man looks on his creation like a God
And sees that it is glorious, drives him on,
The wreck of his own will, the scorn of Earth,
The outcast, the abandoned, the alone?—   105
Not Jove: while yet his frown shook Heaven, aye when
His adversary from adamantine chains
Cursed him, he trembled like a slave. Declare
Who is his master? Is he too a slave?

DEMOGORGON
All spirits are enslaved which serve things evil.   110
Thou knowest if Jupiter be such or no.

ASIA
Whom calledst thou God?

DEMOGORGON
                I spoke but as ye speak—
For Jove is the supreme of living things.

ASIA
Who is the master of the slave?

DEMOGORGON
                —If the Abysm
Could vomit forth its secrets:—But a voice   115
Is wanting, the deep truth is imageless;[36]
For what would it avail to bid thee gaze

---

[35]The pun (rain / reign) calls attention to how Shelley also uses rhyme to link
Prometheus (pain) with Jupiter (rain).

[36]Shelley's metaphysical point: Truth transcends even this image-rich work.

On the revolving world? What to bid speak
Fate, Time, Occasion, Chance, and Change?—To these
All things are subject but eternal Love.   120

      ASIA

So much I asked before, and my heart gave
The response thou hast given; and of such truths
Each to itself must be the oracle.—
One more demand; and do thou answer me
As mine own soul would answer, did it know   125
That which I ask.—Prometheus shall arise
Henceforth the Sun of this rejoicing world:
When shall the destined hour arrive?

      DEMOGORGON

               Behold!

      ASIA

The rocks are cloven, and through the purple night
I see Cars drawn by rainbow-wingèd steeds   130
Which trample the dim winds—in each there stands
A wild-eyed charioteer urging their flight.
Some look behind, as fiends pursued them there,
And yet I see no shapes but the keen stars:
Others, with burning eyes, lean forth, and drink   135
With eager lips the wind of their own speed,
As if the thing they loved fled on before,
And now—even now they clasped it. Their bright locks
Stream like a comet's flashing hair: they all
Sweep onward.—

      DEMOGORGON

         These are the immortal Hours,   140
Of whom thou didst demand.—One waits for thee.

      ASIA

A Spirit with a dreadful countenance
Checks its dark chariot by the craggy gulf.
Unlike thy brethren—ghastly charioteer,
Who art thou? Whither wouldst thou bear me? Speak!   145

SPIRIT

I am the shadow of a destiny
More dread than is my aspect—ere yon planet
Has set, the Darkness which ascends with me
Shall wrap in lasting night Heaven's kingless throne.

ASIA

What meanest thou?

PANTHEA

          That terrible shadow floats   150
Up from its throne, as may the lurid smoke
Of earthquake-ruined cities o'er the sea.—
Lo! it ascends the Car; the coursers fly
Terrified: watch its path among the stars
Blackening the night!

ASIA

         Thus I am answered—strange!   155

PANTHEA

See, near the verge, another chariot stays:[37]
An ivory shell inlaid with crimson fire
Which comes and goes within its sculptured rim
Of delicate strange tracery—the young spirit
That guides it has the dove-like eyes of hope;   160
How its soft smiles attract the soul!—as light
Lures wingèd insects through the lampless air.

SPIRIT[38]

    My coursers are fed with the lightning,
        They drink of the whirlwind's stream,
    And when the red morning is bright'ning   165
        They bathe in the fresh sunbeam;
        They have strength for their swiftness I deem,
            Then ascend with me, Daughter of Ocean.
    I desire—and their speed makes night kindle;
        I fear—they outstrip the Typhoon;   170

[37]Verge: horizon; stays: awaits.

[38]The spirit of the hour whom Demogorgon has told Asia "waits for thee" (l. 141).

Ere the cloud piled on Atlas[39] can dwindle
    We encircle the earth and the moon:
    We shall rest from long labours at noon:
        Then ascend with me, Daughter of Ocean.

SCENE V

The Car pauses within a Cloud on the top of a snowy Mountain.
Asia, Panthea, and the Spirit of the Hour.

SPIRIT

On the brink of the night and the morning
    My coursers are wont to respire;[40]
But the Earth has just whispered a warning
    That their flight must be swifter than fire:
    They shall drink the hot speed of desire!   5

ASIA

Thou breathest on their nostrils—but my breath
Would give them swifter speed.

SPIRIT

                Alas! it could not.

PANTHEA

Oh Spirit! pause, and tell whence is the light
Which fills this cloud? the sun is yet unrisen.

SPIRIT

The sun will rise not until noon.[41]—Apollo   10
Is held in heaven by wonder—and the light
Which fills this vapour, as the aëreal hue
Of fountain-gazing roses fills the water,
Flows from thy mighty sister.

PANTHEA

            Yes, I feel—

[39]When Titan Atlas refused to allow Perseus to rest in his orchard, Perseus turned him into a mountain, leaving him to bear the universe's weight on his shoulders.

[40]Accustomed to rest; literally, "breathe again." (Latin)

[41]The volcanic eruption has obscured the sun (Apollo).

ASIA

What is it with thee, sister? Thou art pale.   15

PANTHEA

How thou art changed! I dare not look on thee;
I feel but see thee not. I scarce endure
The radiance of thy beauty. Some good change
Is working in the elements, which suffer
Thy presence thus unveiled.—The Nereids[42] tell   20
That on the day when the clear hyaline[43]
Was cloven at thine uprise, and thou didst stand
Within a veinèd shell, which floated on
Over the calm floor of the crystal sea,
Among the Ægean isles, and by the shores   25
Which bear thy name; love, like the atmosphere
Of the sun's fire filling the living world,
Burst from thee, and illumined Earth and Heaven
And the deep ocean and the sunless caves
And all that dwells within them; till grief cast   30
Eclipse upon the soul[44] from which it came:
Such art thou now; nor is it I alone,
Thy sister, thy companion, thine own chosen one,
But the whole world which seeks thy sympathy.
Hearest thou not sounds i' the air which speak the love   35
Of all articulate beings? Feelest thou not
The inanimate winds enamoured of thee?—List!

[*Music.*]

ASIA

Thy words are sweeter than aught else but his[45]
Whose echoes they are—yet all love is sweet,
Given or returned. Common as light is love,   40
And its familiar voice wearies not ever.
Like the wide Heaven, the all-sustaining air,
It makes the reptile equal to the God:
They who inspire it most are fortunate,

[42]Water nymphs.
[43]Smooth sea, clear sky.
[44]Perhaps punning on soul / *sol* (sun).
[45]Prometheus's.

As I am now; but those who feel it most   45
Are happier still, after long sufferings,
As I shall soon become.

      PANTHEA
           List! Spirits speak.

      VOICE (*in the air, singing*)
Life of Life![46] thy lips enkindle
    With their love the breath between them;
And thy smiles before they dwindle   50
    Make the cold air fire; then screen them
In those looks, where whoso gazes
Faints, entangled in their mazes.

Child of Light! thy limbs are burning
    Through the vest which seems to hide them;   55
As the radiant lines of morning
    Through the clouds ere they divide them;
And this atmosphere divinest
Shrouds thee wheresoe'er thou shinest.

Fair are others;—none beholds thee,   60
    But thy voice sounds low and tender
Like the fairest—for it folds thee
    From the sight, that liquid splendour,
And all feel, yet see thee never,
As I feel now, lost for ever!   65

Lamp of Earth! where'er thou movest
    Its dim shapes are clad with brightness,
And the souls of whom thou lovest
    Walk upon the winds with lightness,
Till they fail, as I am failing,   70
Dizzy, lost, yet unbewailing!

      ASIA
      My soul is an enchanted Boat,
      Which, like a sleeping swan, doth float

---

[46]After this initial abstraction, the images immediately become sensual.

Upon the silver waves of thy sweet singing;
    And thine doth like an Angel sit   75
    Beside a helm conducting it,
Whilst all the winds with melody are ringing.
    It seems to float ever —for ever—
    Upon that many-winding River,
    Between mountains, woods, abysses,   80
    A Paradise of wildernesses!
Till like one in slumber bound,
Borne to the Ocean, I float down, around,
Into a Sea profound, of ever-spreading sound:

    Meanwhile thy Spirit lifts its pinions   85
    In Music's most serene dominions;
Catching the winds that fan that happy heaven.
    And we sail on, away, afar,
    Without a course—without a star—
But, by the instinct of sweet Music driven   90
    Till through Elysian garden islets
    By thee, most beautiful of pilots,
    Where never mortal pinnace[47] glided,
    The boat of my desire is guided—
Realms where the air we breathe is Love,   95
Which in the winds and on the waves doth move,
Harmonizing this Earth with what we feel above.

    We have passed Age's icy caves,
    And Manhood's dark and tossing waves,
And Youth's smooth ocean, smiling to betray;   100
    Beyond the glassy gulfs we flee
    Of shadow-peopled Infancy,
Through Death and Birth, to a diviner day,
    A Paradise of vaulted bowers,
    Lit by downward-gazing flowers,   105
    And watery paths that wind between
    Wildernesses calm and green,
Peopled by shapes too bright to see,
And rest, having beheld—somewhat like thee;
Which walk upon the sea, and chant melodiously!   110

[47]Small, light boat.

ACT III
SCENE I

*Heaven. Jupiter on his Throne;[1]
Thetis and the other Deities assembled.*

JUPITER
Ye congregated powers of heaven, who share
The glory and the strength of him ye serve,
Rejoice! henceforth I am omnipotent.
All else had been subdued to me—alone
The soul of man, like unextinguished fire,   5
Yet burns towards Heaven with fierce reproach and doubt
And lamentation, and reluctant prayer,
Hurling up insurrection, which might make
Our antique empire insecure, though built
On eldest faith, and Hell's coeval,[2] fear;   10
And though my curses through the pendulous[3] air,
Like snow on herbless peaks, fall flake by flake[4]
And cling to it—though under my wrath's night
It climbs the crags of life, step after step,
Which wound it, as ice wounds unsandalled feet,   15
It yet remains supreme o'er misery,
Aspiring, unrepressed, yet soon to fall:
Even now have I begotten a strange wonder,
That fatal child,[5] the terror of the Earth,
Who waits but till the destined Hour arrive,   20
Bearing from Demogorgon's vacant throne
The dreadful might of ever-living limbs
Which clothed that awful spirit unbeheld—
To redescend, and trample out the spark.

---

[1]Book 2 of *PL* opens with Satan enthroned in Hell, boasting to his confederates—
the pattern for Jupiter, unaware that his reign is already over and full of pride, Satan's sin as well as a common character flaw of the protagonist of Greek tragedy.
The entire scene is packed with ironies against Jupiter's pride, since the revolution
has already begun.

[2]Born at the same time.

[3]Overhanging, drooping.

[4]Compare Asia's image of the avalanche that already occurred among the rebellious
spirits (2.3.37, p. 163).

[5]The child that results from Jupiter's rape of Thetis proves "fatal" to him by displacing
him. Shelley deliberately aligns Jupiter with Herod, who fears news of Christ's birth.

Pour forth heaven's wine, Idæan Ganymede,[6]   25
And let it fill the Dædal[7] cups like fire,
And from the flower-inwoven soil divine
Ye all-triumphant harmonies arise,
As dew from Earth under the twilight stars:
Drink! be the nectar circling through your veins   30
The soul of joy, ye ever-living Gods,
Till exultation burst in one wide voice
Like music from Elysian winds.—
                         And thou
Ascend beside me, veilèd in the light
Of the desire which makes thee one with me,   35
Thetis, bright image of eternity!—
When thou didst cry, "Insufferable might!
God! Spare me! I sustain not the quick flames,
The penetrating presence; all my being,
Like him whom the Numidian seps did thaw   40
Into a dew with poison,[8] is dissolved,
Sinking through its foundations"—even then
Two mighty spirits, mingling, made a third
Mightier than either—which unbodied now
Between us floats, felt although unbeheld,   45
Waiting the incarnation, which ascends—
Hear ye the thunder of the fiery wheels
Griding[9] the winds?—from Demogorgon's throne.—
Victory! Victory! Feel'st thou not, O World,
The Earthquake of his chariot thundering up   50
Olympus?[10]

        [The Car of the Hour arrives. Demogorgon
     descends, and moves towards the Throne of Jupiter.]

     Awful shape, what art thou? Speak!

[6]The gods' eternally young cupbearer; envious of his beauty, Zeus kidnapped him from Mount Ida (hence "Idæan").

[7]Intricately wrought, as if by Daedalus, creator of the Labyrinth.

[8]In *Pharsalia*, 1st-c. Roman poet Lucan tells a story about Sabellus, who dissolves into a pool of venom after he is bitten by a seps, a poisonous desert snake. Recall Hamlet's wish, after his father's death and mother's remarriage, that his "too too solid flesh would melt, / Thaw and resolve itself into a dew" (1.2.132–33).

[9]Grating noisily.

[10]Though missing its import, Jupiter feels the volcanic eruption that has occurred simultaneously in Act 2.

DEMOGORGON
Eternity—Demand no direr name.
Descend, and follow me down the abyss.
I am thy child, as thou wert Saturn's child;
Mightier than thee: and we must dwell together   55
Henceforth in darkness.—Lift thy lightnings not.
The tyranny of Heaven none may retain,
Or reassume, or hold, succeeding thee:
Yet if thou wilt, as 'tis the destiny
Of trodden worms to writhe till they are dead—   60
Put forth thy might.

JUPITER
                    Detested prodigy!
Even thus beneath the deep Titanian prisons
I trample thee! Thou lingerest?[11]
                              Mercy! mercy!
No pity—no release, no respite! Oh,
That thou wouldst make mine enemy my judge,   65
Even where he hangs, seared by my long revenge,
On Caucasus—he would not doom me thus.—
Gentle and just and dreadless, is he not
The monarch of the world?—What then art thou?
No refuge! no appeal!
                      Sink with me then—   70
We two will sink on the wide waves of ruin,
Even as a vulture and a snake outspent[12]
Drop, twisted in inextricable fight,
Into a shoreless sea.—Let Hell unlock
Its mounded Oceans of tempestuous fire,   75
And whelm on them into the bottomless void
This desolated world and thee and me,
The conqueror and the conquered, and the wreck
Of that for which they combated.
                              Ai![13] Ai!

[11]In the *Theogony*, Hesiod (c. 700 BCE) forecasts Jupiter's overthrow. Following their defeat by Jupiter and his generation, the Titans (including Demogorgon) were imprisoned underground in Tartarus, which legend associated with Sicily and the region around Mount Etna. Jupiter does not realize that further resistance is futile.

[12]A well-known image, frequent in Shelley, of mutual assured destruction.

[13]Greek lamentation.

The elements obey me not. I sink   80
Dizzily down—ever, for ever, down—
And, like a cloud, mine enemy above
Darkens my fall with victory!—Ai, Ai!

SCENE II[14]

The Mouth of a great River in the Island Atlantis. Ocean is
discovered reclining near the Shore; Apollo stands beside him.

OCEAN
He fell, thou sayest, beneath his conqueror's frown?

APOLLO
Ay, when the strife was ended which made dim
The orb I rule, and shook the solid stars,[15]
The terrors of his eye illumined Heaven
With sanguine light, through the thick ragged skirts   5
Of the victorious Darkness, as he fell:
Like the last glare of day's red agony,
Which, from a rent among the fiery clouds,
Burns far along the tempest-wrinkled Deep.

OCEAN
He sunk to the abyss? To the dark void?   10

APOLLO
An[16] eagle so caught in some bursting cloud
On Caucasus, his thunder-baffled wings
Entangled in the whirlwind, and his eyes
Which gazed on the undazzling sun, now blinded
By the white lightning, while the ponderous hail   15
Beats on his struggling form, which sinks at length
Prone, and the aëreal ice clings over it.

OCEAN
Henceforth the fields of Heaven-reflecting sea
Which are my realm, will heave, unstained with blood,

[14]As in Greek drama, this scene reports off-stage action.
[15]Apollo rules the sun; stars were thought to be in fixed (solid) positions.
[16](Like) an.

Beneath the uplifting winds—like plains of corn 20
Swayed by the summer air; my streams will flow
Round many-peopled continents, and round
Fortunate isles; and from their glassy thrones
Blue Proteus[17] and his humid nymphs shall mark
The shadow of fair ships, as mortals see 25
The floating bark of the light-laden moon
With that white star,[18] its sightless pilot's crest,
Borne down the rapid sunset's ebbing sea;
Tracking their path no more by blood and groans,
And desolation, and the mingled voice 30
Of slavery and command[19]—but by the light
Of wave-reflected flowers, and floating odours,
And music soft, and mild, free, gentle voices,
And sweetest music—such as spirits love.

APOLLO

And I shall gaze not on the deeds which make 35
My mind obscure with sorrow, as Eclipse
Darkens the sphere I guide—but list, I hear
The small, clear, silver lute of the young Spirit
That sits i' the Morning star.

OCEAN
      Thou must away?
Thy steeds will pause at even—till when farewell: 40
The loud Deep calls me home even now to feed it
With azure calm out of the emerald urns
Which stand for ever full beside my throne.
Behold the Nereids under the green sea,
Their wavering limbs borne on the wind-like stream, 45
Their white arms lifted o'er their streaming hair
With garlands pied[20] and starry sea-flower crowns,
Hastening to grace their mighty Sister's joy.
       [A sound of waves is heard.]

[17]Ancient sea god who alters his form to avoid capture; humid nymphs: Naiads.

[18]Venus, the morning star.

[19]Shelley's condemnation of British naval imperialism and the commercial slave trade (outlawed in Britain in 1807, but still legal in other countries, including the U.S.).

[20]Many-colored.

It is the unpastured Sea hungering for Calm.
Peace, Monster—I come now. Farewell.

APOLLO

Farewell!   50

SCENE III

*Caucasus. Prometheus, Hercules, Ione, the Earth, Spirits,
Asia, and Panthea, borne in the Car with the Spirit of the Hour.
Hercules unbinds Prometheus, who descends.*

HERCULES[21]

Most glorious among Spirits, thus doth strength
To wisdom, courage, and long-suffering love,
And thee, who art the form they animate,
Minister like a slave.

PROMETHEUS

Thy gentle words

Are sweeter even than freedom long desired   5
And long delayed.

Asia, thou light of life,
Shadow of beauty unbeheld: and ye,
Fair sister nymphs, who made long years of pain
Sweet to remember, through your love and care:
Henceforth we will not part. There is a Cave,[22]   10
All overgrown with trailing odorous plants,
Which curtain out the day with leaves and flowers,
And paved with veinèd emerald, and a fountain
Leaps in the midst with an awakening sound.
From its curved roof the mountain's frozen tears   15
Like snow or silver or long diamond spires
Hang downward, raining forth a doubtful light:
And there is heard the ever-moving air,
Whispering without from tree to tree, and birds,
And bees; and all around are mossy seats,   20
And the rough walls are clothed with long soft grass;

[21]In Aeschylus, Hercules (Herakles) kills the tormenting eagle and frees Prometheus;
Shelley skips the bird-murder.

[22]Prometheus's vision of a world beyond time and history—his paradise.

A simple dwelling, which shall be our own;
Where we will sit and talk of time and change,
As the world ebbs and flows, ourselves unchanged—
What can hide man from Mutability?[23]—   25
And if ye sigh, then I will smile; and thou,
Ione, shalt chant fragments of sea-music,
Until I weep, when ye shall smile away
The tears she brought, which yet were sweet to shed.
We will entangle buds and flowers and beams   30
Which twinkle on the fountain's brim, and make
Strange combinations out of common things,
Like human babes in their brief innocence;
And we will search, with looks and words of love,
For hidden thoughts, each lovelier than the last,   35
Our unexhausted spirits, and like lutes
Touched by the skill of the enamoured wind,
Weave harmonies divine, yet ever new,
From difference sweet where discord cannot be;
And hither come, sped on the charmèd winds,   40
Which meet from all the points of Heaven, as bees
From every flower aëreal Enna feeds,
At their known island-homes in Himera,[24]
The echoes of the human world, which tell
Of the low voice of love, almost unheard,   45
And dove-eyed pity's murmured pain, and music,
Itself the echo of the heart, and all
That tempers or improves man's life, now free;
And lovely apparitions,—dim at first,
Then radiant—as the mind, arising bright   50
From the embrace of beauty (whence the forms
Of which these are the phantoms) casts on them
The gathered rays which are reality—
Shall visit us, the progeny immortal
Of Painting, Sculpture, and rapt Poesy,   55
And arts, though unimagined, yet to be.[25]
The wandering voices and the shadows these

---

[23]Shelley's "Mutability" (pp. 25–26) treats this painful human dilemma.
[24]Enna: the Sicilian meadow from which Hades abducted Persephone to the underworld; Himera: a nearby village.
[25]Shelley's belief that art, love, and beauty attune the mind to the ideal.

Of all that man becomes, the mediators
Of that best worship, love, by him and us
Given and returned, swift shapes and sounds, which grow   60
More fair and soft as man grows wise and kind,
And, veil by veil, evil and error fall:
Such virtue has the cave and place around.

                                      [Turning to the Spirit of the Hour.]
For thee, fair Spirit, one toil remains. Ione,
Give her that curvèd shell,[26] which Proteus old   65
Made Asia's nuptial boon, breathing within it
A voice to be accomplished, and which thou
Didst hide in grass under the hollow rock.

            IONE
Thou most desired Hour, more loved and lovely
Than all thy sisters, this is the mystic shell;   70
See the pale azure fading into silver
Lining it with a soft yet glowing light:
Looks it not like lulled music sleeping there?

            SPIRIT
It seems in truth the fairest shell of Ocean:
Its sound must be at once both sweet and strange.   75

            PROMETHEUS
Go, borne over the cities of mankind
On whirlwind-footed coursers: once again
Outspeed the sun around the orbèd world;
And as thy chariot cleaves the kindling air,
Thou breathe into the many-folded Shell,   80
Loosening its mighty music;—it shall be
As thunder mingled with clear echoes.—Then
Return and thou shalt dwell beside our cave.

                                            [Kissing the ground]
And thou, O, Mother Earth!—

            THE EARTH
                    I hear—I feel—
Thy lips are on me, and their touch runs down   85

---

[26]Shelley interpolates a pun on "Shelley" and his family coat-of-arms, involving three conch shells. To "breathe into" the shell, like Proteus (who could foresee the future), is to "inspire," announcing Jupiter's fall and the new millennium.

Even to the adamantine[27] central gloom
Along these marble nerves—'tis life, 'tis joy,
And through my withered, old, and icy frame
The warmth of an immortal youth shoots down
Circling.—Henceforth the many children fair   90
Folded in my sustaining arms—all plants,
And creeping forms, and insects rainbow-winged,
And birds and beasts and fish and human shapes
Which drew disease and pain from my wan bosom,
Draining the poison of despair—shall take   95
And interchange sweet nutriment; to me
Shall they become like sister-antelopes
By one fair dam, snow-white and swift as wind,
Nursed among lilies near a brimming stream.
The dew-mists of my sunless sleep shall float   100
Under the stars like balm: night-folded flowers
Shall suck unwithering hues in their repose:
And men and beasts in happy dreams shall gather
Strength for the coming day, and all its joy:
And death shall be the last embrace of her   105
Who takes the life she gave, even as a mother
Folding her child, says, "Leave me not again."

                ASIA
Oh, mother! wherefore speak the name of death?
Cease they to love, and move, and breathe, and speak,
Who die?[28]

            THE EARTH
            It would avail not to reply:
Thou art immortal, and this tongue is known
But to the uncommunicating dead.—
Death is the veil which those who live call life:
They sleep—and it is lifted:[29] and meanwhile
In mild variety the seasons mild   115
With rainbow-skirted showers, and odorous winds,
And long blue meteors cleansing the dull night,

---

[27]Indestructible.

[28]A question considered in *On Life* (see pp. 219).

[29]This imagery is also in Shelley's sonnet "Lift not the painted veil" (p. 232).

And the life-kindling shafts of the keen Sun's
All-piercing bow, and the dew-mingled rain
Of the calm moonbeams, a soft influence mild,   120
Shall clothe the forests and the fields—aye, even
The crag-built deserts of the barren deep—
With ever-living leaves, and fruits, and flowers.
And thou! There is a Cavern[30] where my spirit
Was panted forth in anguish whilst thy pain   125
Made my heart mad, and those who did inhale it
Became mad too, and built a Temple there,
And spoke and were oracular, and lured
The erring nations round to mutual war,
And faithless faith, such as Jove kept with thee;   130
Which breath now rises, as amongst tall weeds
A violet's exhalation, and it fills
With a serener light and crimson air
Intense yet soft the rocks and woods around;
It feeds the quick growth of the serpent vine   135
And the dark linkèd ivy tangling wild
And budding, blown, or odour-faded blooms
Which star the winds with points of coloured light,
As they rain through them, and bright golden globes
Of fruit, suspended in their own green heaven,   140
And through their veinèd leaves and amber stems
The flowers whose purple and translucid bowls
Stand ever mantling[31] with aëreal dew,
The drink of spirits; and it circles round,
Like the soft waving wings of noonday dreams,   145
Inspiring calm and happy thoughts, like mine,
Now thou art thus restored. This Cave is thine.
Arise! Appear!
            [*A Spirit rises in the likeness of a winged child.*]
            This is my torch-bearer;
Who let his lamp out in old time with gazing
On eyes from which he kindled it anew   150
With love, which is as fire, sweet Daughter mine,
For such is that within thine own.—Run, Wayward,

---

[30]The "mighty portal" Panthea described in 2.3.2–10, now transformed and associated with the oracle's cave at Delphi.

[31]Frothing.

And guide this company beyond the peak
Of Bacchic Nysa,[32] Mænad-haunted mountain,
And beyond Indus[33] and its tribute rivers,   155
Trampling the torrent streams and glassy lakes
With feet unwet, unwearied, undelaying,
And up the green ravine, across the vale,
Beside the windless and crystalline pool,
Where ever lies, on unerasing waves,   160
The image of a temple built above,
Distinct with column, arch, and architrave[34]
And palm-like capital, and over-wrought,
And populous with most living imagery—
Praxitelean shapes,[35] whose marble smiles   165
Fill the hushed air with everlasting love.
It is deserted now, but once it bore
Thy name, Prometheus; there the emulous youths
Bore to thy honour through the divine gloom
The lamp which was thine emblem; even as those   170
Who bear the untransmitted torch of hope
Into the grave, across the night of life,
As thou hast borne it most triumphantly
To this far goal of Time. Depart, farewell.
Beside that temple is the destined cave.   175

SCENE IV

A Forest. In the Background a Cave. Prometheus, Asia,
Panthea, Ione, and the Spirit of the Earth.[36]

IONE

Sister, it[37] is not earthly: how it glides
Under the leaves! how on its head there burns
A light, like a green star, whose emerald beams

[32]Region of Bacchus and his attendants.

[33]River in India flowing into the Arabian Sea.

[34]Horizontal beam atop pillars and posts.

[35]As if by Greek sculptor Praxiteles (c. 400–330 BCE), famous for the Athenian Parthenon.

[36]This scene was the original conclusion; hence the long closing speech by the Spirit of the Hour, who may be the Spirit of the Earth transformed and so not recognized.

[37]The Spirit of the Earth, an electric force.

Are twined with its fair hair! how, as it moves,
The splendour drops in flakes upon the grass!   5
Knowest thou it?

PANTHEA
          It is the delicate spirit
That guides the earth through Heaven. From afar
The populous constellations call that light
The loveliest of the planets; and sometimes
It floats along the spray of the salt sea,   10
Or makes its chariot of a foggy cloud,
Or walks through fields or cities while men sleep,
Or o'er the mountain tops, or down the rivers,
Or through the green waste wilderness, as now,
Wondering at all it sees. Before Jove reigned   15
It loved our sister Asia, and it came
Each leisure hour to drink the liquid light
Out of her eyes, for which it said it thirsted
As one bit by a dipsas,[38] and with her
It made its childish confidence, and told her   20
All it had known or seen, for it saw much,
Yet idly reasoned what it saw; and called her—
For whence it sprung it knew not, nor do I—
"Mother, dear Mother."

THE SPIRIT OF THE EARTH (*running to Asia*)
          Mother, dearest Mother!
May I then talk with thee as I was wont?[39]   25
May I then hide my eyes in thy soft arms,
After thy looks have made them tired of joy?
May I then play beside thee the long noons,
When work is none in the bright silent air?

ASIA
I love thee, gentlest being, and henceforth   30
Can cherish thee unenvied.—Speak, I pray:
Thy simple talk once solaced, now delights.

---

[38]Tropical serpent whose bite caused terrible thirst.
[39]Used to.

SPIRIT OF THE EARTH
Mother, I am grown wiser, though a child
Cannot be wise like thee, within this day;
And happier too; happier and wiser both.   35
Thou knowest that toads and snakes and loathly worms
And venomous and malicious beasts, and boughs
That bore ill berries in the woods, were ever
An hindrance to my walks o'er the green world,
And that, among the haunts of humankind   40
Hard-featured men, or with proud, angry looks
Or cold, staid gait, or false and hollow smiles
Or the dull sneer of self-loved ignorance
Or other such foul masks,[40] with which ill thoughts
Hide that fair being whom we spirits call man;   45
And women too, ugliest of all things evil,—
Though fair, even in a world where thou art fair
When good and kind, free and sincere like thee,—
When false or frowning made me sick at heart
To pass them, though they slept, and I unseen.   50
Well—my path lately lay through a great City
Into the woody hills surrounding it.
A sentinel was sleeping at the gate:
When there was heard a sound, so loud, it shook
The towers amid the moonlight, yet more sweet   55
Than any voice but thine, sweetest of all;
A long long sound, as it would never end:
And all the inhabitants leaped suddenly
Out of their rest, and gathered in the streets,
Looking in wonder up to Heaven, while yet   60
The music pealed along. I hid myself
Within a fountain in the public square,
Where I lay like the reflex of the moon
Seen in a wave under green leaves—and soon
Those ugly human shapes and visages   65
Of which I spoke as having wrought me pain,
Passed floating through the air, and fading still
Into the winds that scattered them; and those
From whom they passed seemed mild and lovely forms

[40]As in *The Mask of Anarchy* (pp. 84–99).

After some foul disguise had fallen—and all   70
Were somewhat changed—and after brief surprise
And greetings of delighted wonder, all
Went to their sleep again: and when the dawn
Came—wouldst thou think that toads and snakes and efts,[41]
Could e'er be beautiful?—yet so they were,   75
And that with little change of shape or hue:
All things had put their evil nature off:
I cannot tell my joy, when o'er a lake
Upon a drooping bough with nightshade twined,
I saw two azure halcyons[42] clinging downward   80
And thinning one bright bunch of amber berries,
With quick long beaks, and in the deep there lay
Those lovely forms imaged as in a sky;
So, with my thoughts full of these happy changes
We meet again, the happiest change of all.   85

> ASIA

And never will we part, till thy chaste Sister
Who guides the frozen and inconstant moon
Will look on thy more warm and equal light
Till her heart thaw like flakes of April snow
And love thee.

> SPIRIT OF THE EARTH
>   What; as Asia loves Prometheus?   90

> ASIA

Peace, Wanton—thou art yet not old enough.
Think ye by gazing on each other's eyes
To multiply your lovely selves, and fill
With spherèd fires the interlunar air?

[41]Small lizards or newts.

[42]No longer poisonous, nightshade's berries feed the halcyons (a normally fish-eating kingfisher). The millennial Promethean universe is vegetarian. A "halcyon" calm was considered only temporary.

SPIRIT OF THE EARTH
Nay, Mother, while my sister trims[43] her lamp   95
'Tis hard I should go darkling.[44]

ASIA
                    —Listen; look!
                    [*The Spirit of the Hour enters.*]

PROMETHEUS
We feel what thou hast heard and seen—yet speak.

SPIRIT OF THE HOUR
Soon as the sound had ceased whose thunder filled
The abysses of the sky and the wide earth,
There was a change: the impalpable thin air   100
And the all-circling sunlight were transformed,
As if the sense of love dissolved in them
Had folded itself round the spherèd world.
My vision then grew clear, and I could see
Into the mysteries of the Universe.   105
Dizzy as with delight I floated down,
Winnowing[45] the lightsome air with languid plumes,
My coursers sought their birthplace in the sun,
Where they henceforth will live exempt from toil,
Pasturing flowers of vegetable fire—   110
And where my moonlike car will stand within
A temple, gazed upon by Phidian[46] forms
Of thee, and Asia and the Earth, and me,
And you fair nymphs looking the love we feel,—
In memory of the tidings it has borne,—   115
Beneath a dome fretted with graven flowers,
Poised on twelve columns of resplendent stone,
And open to the bright and liquid sky.
Yoked to it by an amphisbaenic[47] snake

[43]Prepares for lighting.

[44]In the dark.

[45]Blowing the chaff from the usable grain.

[46]Phidias (5th c. BCE), the greatest Greek sculptor. Shelley studied architectural artifacts in the Vatican Museum and the Roman Pantheon.

[47]With a head at each end, capable of moving in either direction.

The likeness of those wingèd steeds will mock   120
The flight from which they find repose.—Alas,
Whither has wandered now my partial[48] tongue
When all remains untold which ye would hear!—
As I have said, I floated to the Earth:
It was, as it is still, the pain of bliss   125
To move, to breathe, to be; I wandering went
Among the haunts and dwellings of mankind,
And first was disappointed not to see
Such mighty change as I had felt within
Expressed in outward things; but soon I looked,   130
And behold! thrones were kingless, and men walked
One with the other even as spirits do,
None fawned, none trampled; hate, disdain, or fear,
Self-love or self-contempt on human brows
No more inscribed, as o'er the gate of hell,   135
"All hope abandon ye who enter here";[49]
None frowned, none trembled, none with eager fear
Gazed on another's eye of cold command
Until the subject of a tyrant's will
Became, worse fate, the abject[50] of his own,   140
Which spurred him, like an outspent horse, to death.
None wrought his lips in truth-entangling lines
Which smiled the lie his tongue disdained to speak;
None, with firm sneer, trod out in his own heart
The sparks of love and hope till there remained   145
Those bitter ashes, a soul self-consumed,
And the wretch crept a vampire among men,
Infecting all with his own hideous ill.
None talked that common, false, cold, hollow talk
Which makes the heart deny the *yes* it breathes,   150
Yet question that unmeant hypocrisy
With such a self-mistrust as has no name.
And women, too, frank, beautiful, and kind
As the free Heaven which rains fresh light and dew
On the wide earth, past: gentle radiant forms,   155
From custom's evil taint exempt and pure;

[48]Favorably biased, partisan.
[49]In Dante's *Inferno* (3.9), these words appear over Hell's gate.
[50]Outcast.

Speaking the wisdom once they could not think,
Looking emotions once they feared to feel
And changed to all which once they dared not be,
Yet being now, made Earth like Heaven—nor pride,   160
Nor jealousy nor envy nor ill shame,
The bitterest of those drops of treasured gall,
Spoilt the sweet taste of the nepenthe,[51] love.

Thrones, altars, judgement-seats, and prisons; wherein
And beside which, by wretched men were borne   165
Sceptres, tiaras, swords, and chains, and tomes
Of reasoned wrong glozed on[52] by ignorance,
Were like those monstrous and barbaric shapes,
The ghosts of a no more remembered fame,
Which from their unworn obelisks[53] look forth   170
In triumph o'er the palaces and tombs
Of those who were their conquerors, mouldering round,
These imaged to the pride of Kings and Priests
A dark yet mighty faith, a power as wide
As is the world it wasted, and are now   175
But an astonishment;[54] even so the tools
And emblems of its last captivity,
Amid the dwellings of the peopled Earth,
Stand, not o'erthrown, but unregarded now.
And those foul shapes,[55] abhorred by God and man,—   180
Which under many a name and many a form
Strange, savage, ghastly, dark and execrable
Were Jupiter, the tyrant of the world;
And which the nations panic-stricken served
With blood, and hearts broken by long hope, and love   185
Dragged to his altars soiled and garlandless,
And slain amid men's unreclaiming tears,
Flattering the thing they feared, which fear was hate,—
Frown, mouldering fast, o'er their abandoned shrines.

[51]Pain-abolishing drug.

[52]Glossed, interpreted.

[53]Inscribed columns, ten of which had been brought to Rome from Egypt; in 1819 the hieroglyphs were still undecipherable.

[54]A wonder (with a pun on the literal meaning, "stone").

[55]Tyrannical religious authority, including contemporary. "Foul shape" is Milton's description of Sin (PL).

The painted veil, by those who were, called life,   190
Which mimicked,[56] as with colours idly spread,
All men believed or hoped, is torn aside—
The loathsome mask has fallen, the man remains
Sceptreless, free, uncircumscribed, but man
Equal, unclassed, tribeless, and nationless,   195
Exempt from awe, worship, degree,—the King
Over himself; just, gentle, wise—but man
Passionless? no—yet free from guilt or pain
Which were, for his will made or suffered them,
Nor yet exempt, though ruling them like slaves,   200
From chance, and death, and mutability,
The clogs[57] of that which else might oversoar
The loftiest star of unascended Heaven,
Pinnacled dim in the intense inane.[58]

ACT IV[1]

*Scene.—A Part of the Forest near the Cave
of Prometheus. Panthea and Ione are sleeping:
they awaken gradually during the first Song.*

VOICE OF UNSEEN SPIRITS
The pale Stars are gone,—
For the Sun, their swift Shepherd,
To their folds them compelling,
In the depths of the Dawn,
Hastes, in meteor-eclipsing array, and they flee   5
Beyond his blue dwelling,
As fawns flee the leopard.
But where are ye?

[*A Train of dark Forms and Shadows passes by confusedly, singing.*]

Here, oh, here!
We bear the bier   10

[56]See "Lift not the painted veil" (p. 232).

[57]Weights (to prevent rapid motion).

[58]Vacancy. Shelley makes a sublime term from a usually derogatory adjective.

---

[1]Added in fall 1819. Especially after the Peterloo Massacre (August), Shelley felt the
need for another statement of visionary hope and regeneration.

Of the Father of many a cancelled year![2]
      Spectres we
      Of the dead Hours be,
We bear Time[3] to his tomb in eternity.

      Strew, oh, strew   15
      Hair, not yew!
Wet the dusty pall with tears, not dew!
      Be the faded flowers
      Of Death's bare bowers
Spread on the corpse of the King of Hours!   20

      Haste, oh, haste!
      As shades are chased,
Trembling, by Day, from Heaven's blue waste.
      We melt away,
      Like dissolving spray,   25
From the children of a diviner day,
      With the lullaby
      Of winds that die
On the bosom of their own harmony!

      IONE
      What dark forms were they?   30

      PANTHEA
      The past Hours weak and grey
      With the spoil which their toil
         Raked together
From the conquest but One could foil.

      IONE
      Have they past?

      PANTHEA
              They have past;   35
      They outspeeded the blast;
      While 'tis said, they are fled—

---

[2]Jupiter. Shelley plays a rhetorical pun on "Hear / Here" (cf. "Ode to the West Wind," pp. 224–27).

[3]Jupiter's term.

IONE
Whither, oh, whither?

PANTHEA
To the dark, to the past, to the dead.

VOICE OF UNSEEN SPIRITS
Bright clouds float in Heaven,   40
Dew-stars gleam on Earth,
Waves assemble on Ocean,
They are gathered and driven
By the Storm of delight, by the panic of glee!
They shake with emotion—   45
They dance in their mirth—
But where are ye?

The pine boughs are singing
Old songs with new gladness,
The billows and fountains   50
Fresh music are flinging
Like the notes of a spirit from land and from sea;
The storms mock the mountains
With the thunder of gladness.
But where are ye?   55

IONE
What charioteers are these?

PANTHEA
Where are their chariots?

SEMICHORUS OF HOURS[4]
The voice of the Spirits of Air and of Earth
Has drawn back the figured curtain of sleep
Which covered our being and darkened our birth
In the deep—

A VOICE
In the deep?

SEMICHORUS II
Oh, below the deep.   60

[4]Free humanity's future.

SEMICHORUS I

An hundred ages we had been kept
Cradled in visions of hate and care,
And each one who waked as his brother slept,
Found the truth—

SEMICHORUS II

    Worse than his visions were!

SEMICHORUS I

We have heard the lute of Hope in sleep,   65
We have known the voice of Love in dreams,
We have felt the wand of Power, and leap—

SEMICHORUS II

As the billows leap in the morning beams!

CHORUS

Weave the dance on the floor of the breeze,
    Pierce with song Heaven's silent light,   70
Enchant the Day that too swiftly flees,
    To check its flight ere the cave of Night.

Once the hungry Hours were hounds
    Which chased the day like a bleeding deer,
And it limped and stumbled with many wounds   75
    Through the nightly dells of the desart year.

But now—oh weave the mystic measure
    Of music, and dance, and shapes of light,
Let the Hours, and the Spirits of might and pleasure,
    Like the clouds and sunbeams, unite.   80

A VOICE

                Unite!

PANTHEA

See, where the Spirits of the human mind
Wrapped in sweet sounds, as in bright veils, approach.

CHORUS OF SPIRITS

We join the throng
Of the dance and the song,

By the whirlwind of gladness borne along;   85
  As the flying-fish leap
  From the Indian deep,[5]
And mix with the sea-birds, half asleep.

   CHORUS OF HOURS
Whence come ye, so wild and so fleet,
For sandals of lightning are on your feet,   90
And your wings are soft and swift as thought,
And your eyes are as love which is veilèd not?

   CHORUS OF SPIRITS
  We come from the mind
  Of human kind
Which was late so dusk, and obscene,[6] and blind,   95
  Now 'tis an Ocean
  Of clear emotion,
A Heaven of serene and mighty motion.

  From that deep Abyss
  Of wonder and bliss,   100
Whose caverns are chrystal palaces;
  From those skiey towers
  Where Thought's crowned powers
Sit watching your dance, ye happy Hours!

  From the dim recesses   105
  Of woven caresses,
Where lovers catch ye by your loose tresses,—
  From the azure isles,
  Where sweet Wisdom smiles,
Delaying your ships with her syren wiles.   110

  From the temples high
  Of Man's ear and eye,
Roofed over Sculpture and Poesy;
  From the murmurings

---

[5]Indian Ocean.
[6]Repulsive (Latin, *obscenus*).

Of the unsealed springs   115
Where Science bedews her Dædal[7] wings.

Years after years,
Through blood, and tears,
And a thick hell of hatreds and hopes and fears,
We waded and flew,   120
And the islets were few
Where the bud-blighted flowers of happiness grew.

Our feet now, every palm,[8]
Are sandalled with calm,
And the dew of our wings is a rain of balm;   125
And beyond our eyes
The human love lies
Which makes all it gazes on Paradise.

CHORUS OF SPIRITS AND HOURS
Then weave the web of the mystic measure;
From the depths of the sky and the ends of the Earth,   130
Come, swift Spirits of might and of pleasure,
Fill the dance and the music of mirth,
As the waves of a thousand streams rush by
To an Ocean of splendour and harmony!

CHORUS OF SPIRITS
Our spoil is won,   135
Our task is done,
We are free to dive, or soar, or run;
Beyond and around
Or within the bound
Which clips the world with darkness round.   140

We'll pass the Eyes
Of the starry skies
Into the hoar[9] Deep to colonize;
Death, Chaos and Night,

[7]Intricately wrought.
[8]Sole.
[9]Ancient.

From the sound of our flight,   145
Shall flee, like mist from a Tempest's might.

And Earth, Air and Light,
And the Spirit of Might,
Which drives round the Stars in their fiery flight;
And Love, Thought, and Breath,   150
The powers that quell Death,
Wherever we soar shall assemble beneath.

And our singing shall build
In the Void's loose field
A world for the Spirit of Wisdom to wield;   155
We will take our plan
From the new world of man
And our work shall be called the Promethean.

CHORUS OF HOURS
Break the dance, and scatter the song;
Let some depart, and some remain.   160

SEMICHORUS I
We, beyond Heaven, are driven along—

SEMICHORUS II
Us, the inchantments of Earth retain—

SEMICHORUS I
Ceaseless and rapid and fierce and free
With the Spirits which build a new earth and sea,
And a Heaven where yet Heaven could never be—   165

SEMICHORUS II
Solemn and slow and serene and bright
Leading the Day and outspeeding the Night
With the powers of a world of perfect light—

SEMICHORUS I
We whirl, singing loud, round the gathering sphere,
Till the trees and the beasts and the clouds appear   170
From its chaos made calm by love, not fear—

SEMICHORUS II
We encircle the Oceans and Mountains of Earth,
And the happy forms of its death and birth
Change to the music of our sweet mirth.

CHORUS OF HOURS AND SPIRITS
Break the dance, and scatter the song—   175
    Let some depart, and some remain;
Wherever we fly we lead along
In leashes, like starbeams, soft yet strong,
    The clouds that are heavy with Love's sweet rain.

PANTHEA
Ha! they are gone!

IONE
              Yet feel you no delight   180
From the past sweetness?

PANTHEA
                 As the bare green hill
When some soft cloud vanishes into rain,
Laughs with a thousand drops of sunny water
To the unpavilioned[10] sky!

IONE
                Even whilst we speak
New notes arise. What is that awful sound?   185

PANTHEA
'Tis the deep music of the rolling world
Kindling within the strings of the waved air
Æolian modulations.[11]

IONE
            Listen too,
How every pause is filled with under-notes,
Clear, silver, icy, keen, awakening tones   190

[10]Cloudless.
[11]Aeolus is god of the winds.

Which pierce the sense and live within the soul
As the sharp stars pierce winter's crystal air
And gaze upon themselves within the sea.

PANTHEA
But see where through two openings in the forest
Which hanging branches overcanopy,   195
And where two runnels[12] of a rivulet,
Between the close moss violet-inwoven,
Have made their path of melody, like sisters
Who part with sighs that they may meet in smiles,
Turning their dear disunion to an isle   200
Of lovely grief, a wood of sweet sad thoughts;
Two visions of strange radiance float upon
The Ocean-like enchantment of strong sound,
Which flows intenser, keener, deeper yet
Under the ground and through the windless air.   205

IONE
I see a chariot like that thinnest boat,
In which the Mother of the Months is borne
By ebbing light into her western cave,
When she upsprings from interlunar dreams;[13]
O'er which is curved an orblike canopy   210
Of gentle darkness, and the hills and woods,
Distinctly seen through that dusk aery veil
Regard[14] like shapes in an enchanter's glass;
Its wheels are solid clouds, azure and gold,
Such as the genii of the thunderstorm   215
Pile on the floor of the illumined sea
When the Sun rushes under it; they roll
And move and grow as with an inward wind.
Within it sits a wingèd Infant, white
Its countenance, like the whiteness of bright snow,   220
Its plumes are as feathers of sunny frost,
Its limbs gleam white, through the wind-flowing folds
Of its white robe, woof[15] of ethereal pearl.

[12]Channels, branches.
[13]The old moon is dimly visible in the new moon's crescent.
[14]Appear.
[15]Weaving.

Its hair is white,—the brightness of white light
Scattered in strings, yet its two eyes are Heavens   225
Of liquid darkness, which the Deity
Within seems pouring, as a storm is poured
From jaggèd clouds, out of their arrowy lashes,
Tempering the cold and radiant air around,
With fire that is not brightness;[16] in its hand   230
It sways a quivering moonbeam, from whose point
A guiding power directs the chariot's prow
Over its wheelèd clouds, which as they roll
Over the grass and flowers and waves, wake sounds,
Sweet as a singing rain of silver dew.   235

PANTHEA
And from the other opening in the wood
Rushes with loud and whirlwind harmony
A sphere, which is as many thousand spheres,
Solid as chrystal, yet through all its mass
Flow, as through empty space, music and light: 240
Ten thousand orbs involving and involved,
Purple and azure, white and green and golden,
Sphere within sphere, and every space between
Peopled with unimaginable shapes,
Such as ghosts dream dwell in the lampless deep,   245
Yet each inter-transpicuous,[17] and they whirl
Over each other with a thousand motions
Upon a thousand sightless[18] axles spinning
And with the force of self-destroying swiftness,
Intensely, slowly, solemnly roll on—   250
Kindling with mingled sounds, and many tones,
Intelligible words and music wild.—
With mighty whirl the multitudinous Orb
Grinds the bright brook into an azure mist
Of elemental subtlety, like light,   255
And the wild odour of the forest flowers,
The music of the living grass and air,

---

[16]Sir Humphrey Davy (1778–1829) speculated that the moon produced infrared rays, heat without light.

[17]Transparent.

[18]Invisible.

The emerald light of leaf-entangled beams
Round its intense yet self-conflicting speed,[19]
Seem kneaded into one aëreal mass   260
Which drowns the sense. Within the Orb itself,
Pillowed upon its alabaster arms,
Like to a child o'erwearied with sweet toil,
On its own folded wings, and wavy hair,
The Spirit of the Earth is laid asleep,   265
And you can see its little lips are moving,
Amid the changing light of their own smiles,
Like one who talks of what he loves in dream.—

IONE
'Tis only mocking the orb's harmony.

PANTHEA
And from a star upon its forehead, shoot,   270
Like swords of azure fire, or golden spears
With tyrant-quelling myrtle[20] overtwined,
Embleming Heaven and Earth united now,
Vast beams like spokes of some invisible wheel
Which whirl as the Orb whirls, swifter than thought,   275
Filling the abyss with sun-like lightenings,
And perpendicular now, and now transverse,
Pierce the dark soil, and as they pierce and pass,
Make bare the secrets of the earth's deep heart—
Infinite mines of adamant and gold,   280
Valueless[21] stones, and unimagined gems,
And caverns on crystalline columns poised
With vegetable silver[22] overspread,
Wells of unfathomed fire, and water springs
Whence the great Sea, even as a child is fed,   285
Whose vapours clothe Earth's monarch mountain-tops
With kingly, ermine snow. The beams flash on
And make appear the melancholy ruins

[19]In different directions, at different speeds.
[20]Sacred to Venus, symbolizing love.
[21]Invaluable, beyond measure.
[22]Both Milton (*PL* 4.218–20) and Southey (in *Thalaba the Destroyer*, 1812) term perfect gold "vegetable gold."

Of cancelled cycles; anchors, beaks of ships;
Planks turned to marble; quivers, helms and spears,   290
And gorgon-headed targes,[23] and the wheels
Of scythèd[24] chariots, and the emblazonry
Of trophies, standards and armorial beasts,
Round which Death laughed, sepulchred emblems
Of dead Destruction, ruin within ruin!   295
The wrecks beside of many a city vast,
Whose population which the Earth grew over
Was mortal but not human; see, they lie,
Their monstrous works and uncouth skeletons,
Their statues, homes and fanes; prodigious shapes   300
Huddled in gray annihilation, split,
Jammed in the hard black deep; and over these,
The anatomies[25] of unknown wingèd things,
And fishes which were isles of living scale,
And serpents, bony chains, twisted around   305
The iron crags, or within heaps of dust
To which the tortuous strength of their last pangs
Had crushed the iron crags;—and over these
The jaggèd alligator and the might
Of earth-convulsing behemoth,[26] which once   310
Were monarch beasts, and on the slimy shores,
And weed-overgrown continents of earth,
Increased and multiplied like summer worms
On an abandoned corpse, till the blue globe
Wrapped deluge round it like a cloak, and they   315
Yelled, gaspt and were abolished; or some God
Whose throne was in a Comet, past, and cried—
"Be not!"[27]—and like my words they were no more.

THE EARTH
The joy, the triumph, the delight, the madness,
The boundless, overflowing, bursting gladness,   320

[23]Shields with images of the female Gorgons, to terrify and even petrify opponents.
[24]Bladed wheeled, to destroy the spokes of an opponent's wheels.
[25]Skeletons.
[26]See Job 40.15–24.
[27]Shelley eerily anticipates the modern theory that attributes dinosaurs' extinction to a catastrophic meteor impact.

The vaporous exultation not to be confined!
    Ha! Ha! the animation of delight
    Which wraps me, like an atmosphere of light,
And bears me as a cloud is borne by its own wind.

           THE MOON
        Brother mine, calm wanderer,   325
        Happy globe of land and air,
Some Spirit is darted like a beam from thee
        Which penetrates my frozen frame
        And passes with the warmth of flame—
With love, and odour, and deep melody   330
        Through me, through me!—

           THE EARTH
Ha! ha! the caverns of my hollow mountains,
My cloven fire-crags, sound-exulting fountains
Laugh with a vast and inextinguishable laughter.
    The Oceans and the Desarts and the Abysses   335
    Of the deep air's unmeasured wildernesses,
Answer from all their clouds and billows, echoing after.

    They cry aloud as I do.—"Sceptred Curse,[28]
    Who all our green and azure Universe
Threatenedst to muffle round with black destruction, sending 340
    A solid cloud to rain hot thunderstones,
    And splinter and knead down my children's bones,
All I bring forth, to one void mass battering and blending,

    "Until each crag-like tower and storied column,
    Palace and Obelisk and Temple solemn,   345
My imperial mountains crowned with cloud and snow and fire,
    My sea-like forests, every blade and blossom
    Which finds a grave or cradle in my bosom,
Were stamped by thy strong hate into a lifeless mire,

    "How art thou sunk, withdrawn, covered—drunk up 350
    By thirsty nothing, as the brackish[29] cup
Drained by a Desart-troop—a little drop for all!

[28]Jupiter, or any tyrant.
[29]Salty, life-killing.

And from beneath, around, within, above,
Filling thy void annihilation, Love
Bursts in like light on caves cloven by the thunder-ball."   355

    THE MOON
The Snow upon my lifeless mountains
Is loosened into living fountains,
My solid Oceans flow and sing and shine:
    A spirit from my heart bursts forth,
    It clothes with unexpected birth   360
My cold bare bosom—oh! it must be thine
      On mine, on mine!

    Gazing on thee I feel, I know
    Green stalks burst forth, and bright flowers grow
And living shapes upon my bosom move: 365
    Music is in the sea and air,
    Wingèd clouds soar here and there,
Dark with the rain new buds are dreaming of:
      'Tis love, all love!

    THE EARTH
    It interpenetrates my granite mass,   370
    Through tangled roots and trodden clay doth pass
Into the utmost leaves and delicatest flowers;
    Upon the winds, among the clouds 'tis spread,
    It wakes a life in the forgotten dead,
They breathe a spirit up from their obscurest bowers   375

    And like a storm bursting its cloudy prison
    With thunder and with whirlwind, has arisen
Out of the lampless caves of unimagined being,
    With earthquake shock and swiftness making shiver
    Thought's stagnant chaos, unremoved for ever,   380
Till Hate and Fear and Pain, light-vanquished shadows, fleeing,

    Leave Man, who was a many-sided mirror,
    Which could distort to many a shape of error,
This true fair world of things—a Sea reflecting Love;
    Which over all his kind, as the Sun's Heaven   385
    Gliding o'er Ocean, smooth, serene and even,
Darting from starry depths radiance and life, doth move,

Leave Man, even as a leprous child is left
Who follows a sick beast to some warm cleft
Of rocks, through which the might of healing springs is poured;[30] 390
  Then when it wanders home with rosy smile
  Unconscious, and its mother fears awhile
It is a Spirit—then weeps on her child restored.

  Man, oh, not men! a chain of linkèd thought,
  Of love and might to be divided not,   395
Compelling the elements with adamantine stress—
  As the Sun rules, even with a tyrant's gaze,
  The unquiet Republic of the maze
Of Planets, struggling fierce towards Heaven's free wilderness.

  Man, one harmonious Soul of many a soul,   400
  Whose nature is its own divine control,
Where all things flow to all, as rivers to the sea;
  Familiar acts are beautiful through love;
  Labour and Pain and Grief in life's green grove
Sport like tame beasts—none knew how gentle they could be! 405

  His Will, with all mean passions, bad delights,
  And selfish cares, its trembling satellites,
A spirit ill to guide, but mighty to obey,
  Is as a tempest-wingèd ship, whose helm
  Love rules, through waves which dare not overwhelm,   410
Forcing life's wildest shores to own its sovereign sway.

  All things confess his strength.—Through the cold mass
  Of marble and of colour his dreams pass;
Bright threads whence mothers weave the robes their children wear;
  Language is a perpetual Orphic song,   415
  Which rules with Dædal harmony a throng
Of thoughts and forms, which else senseless and shapeless were.[31]

[30]In English legend, leprous King Bladud is banished and becomes a swine-herder. When he bathes with them in warm springs, he finds his leprosy cured and then founds the city of Bath on the site.

[31]Orpheus could charm inanimate nature with his song. Daedal: intricate.

    The Lightning is his slave; Heaven's utmost deep
    Gives up her stars, and like a flock of sheep
They pass before his eye, are numbered and roll on!   420
    The Tempest is his steed,—he strides the air;
    And the abyss shouts from her depth laid bare,
"Heaven, hast thou secrets? Man unveils me; I have none."

      THE MOON
    The shadow of white Death has past
    From my path in Heaven at last,   425
A clinging shroud of solid frost and sleep—
    And through my newly-woven bowers
    Wander happy paramours
Less mighty, but as mild as those who keep
      Thy vales more deep.   430

      THE EARTH
    As the dissolving warmth of Dawn may fold
    A half unfrozen dew-globe, green, and gold
And chrystalline, till it becomes a wingèd mist
    And wanders up the vault of the blue Day,
    Outlives the moon, and on the Sun's last ray   435
Hangs o'er the Sea—a fleece of fire and amethyst—

      THE MOON
    Thou art folded, thou art lying
    In the light which is undying
Of thine own joy and Heaven's smile divine;
    All suns and constellations shower   440
    On thee a light, a life, a power
Which doth array thy sphere—thou pourest thine
      On mine, on mine!

      THE EARTH
    I spin beneath my pyramid of night[32]
    Which points into the heavens dreaming delight,   445
Murmuring victorious joy in my enchanted sleep;
    As a youth lulled in love-dreams, faintly sighing,
    Under the shadow of his beauty lying
Which round his rest a watch of light and warmth doth keep.

---

[32]Conical shadow cast into space by the sun's rays on a planet.

THE MOON

As in the soft and sweet eclipse,   450
  When soul meets soul on lovers' lips,
High hearts are calm, and brightest eyes are dull;
  So when thy shadow falls on me
  Then am I mute and still,—by thee
Covered; of thy love, Orb most beautiful,   455
  Full, oh, too full!—

  Thou art speeding round the Sun,
  Brightest World of many a one,
  Green and azure sphere which shinest
  With a light which is divinest   460
  Among all the lamps of Heaven
  To whom life and light is given;
  I, thy chrystal paramour
  Borne beside thee by a power
  Like the polar Paradise,   465
  Magnet-like of lovers' eyes;
  I, a most enamoured maiden
  Whose weak brain is overladen
  With the pleasure of her love—
  Maniac-like around thee move   470
  Gazing, an insatiate bride,
  On thy form from every side
  Like a Mænad round the cup
  Which Agave[33] lifted up
  In the weird Cadmæan forest.—   475
  Brother, wheresoe'er thou soarest
  I must hurry, whirl and follow
  Through the Heavens wide and hollow,
  Sheltered by the warm embrace
  Of thy soul from hungry space,   480
  Drinking from thy sense and sight
  Beauty, majesty, and might,
  As a lover or a chameleon
  Grows like what it looks upon,
  As a violet's gentle eye   485

---

[33]Cadmus's daughter, Agave, killed her son Pentheus in a frenzy with the Bacchic Maenads.

Gazes on the azure sky
Until its hue grows like what it beholds,
As a gray and watery mist
Glows like solid amethyst
Athwart the western mountain it enfolds,   490
When the sunset sleeps
Upon its snow—

THE EARTH
And the weak day weeps
That it should be so.
O gentle Moon, the voice of thy delight   495
Falls on me like thy clear and tender light
Soothing the seaman, borne the summer night
Through isles for ever calm;
O gentle Moon, thy chrystal accents pierce
The caverns of my Pride's deep Universe,   500
Charming the tiger Joy, whose tramplings fierce
Made wounds which need thy balm.

PANTHEA
I rise as from a bath of sparkling water,
A bath of azure light, among dark rocks,
Out of the stream of sound—   505

IONE
                              Ah me! sweet sister,
The stream of sound has ebbed away from us
And you pretend to rise out of its wave
Because your words fall like the clear soft dew
Shaken from a bathing wood-nymph's limbs and hair.

PANTHEA
Peace! peace!—a mighty Power, which is as Darkness,   510
Is rising out of Earth, and from the sky
Is showered like Night, and from within the air
Bursts, like eclipse which had been gathered up
Into the pores of sunlight—the bright Visions
Wherein the singing spirits rode and shone   515
Gleam like pale meteors through a watery night.

IONE
There is a sense of words upon mine ear—

PANTHEA
An universal sound like words. Oh, list!

DEMOGORGON
Thou, Earth, calm Empire of a happy Soul,
    Sphere of divinest shapes and harmonies,   520
Beautiful orb! gathering as thou dost roll
    The Love which paves thy path along the skies:

THE EARTH
I hear,—I am as a drop of dew that dies!

DEMOGORGON
Thou Moon, which gazest on the nightly Earth
    With wonder, as it gazes upon thee,   525
Whilst each to men and beasts and the swift birth
    Of birds, is beauty, love, calm, harmony:

THE MOON
I hear—I am a leaf shaken by thee!

DEMOGORGON
Ye Kings of suns and stars, Dæmons and Gods,
    Ætherial Dominations, who possess   530
Elysian, windless, fortunate abodes
    Beyond Heaven's constellated wilderness:

A VOICE: *from above*
Our great Republic hears; we are blest, and bless.

DEMOGORGON
Ye happy Dead, whom beams of brightest verse
    Are clouds to hide, not colours to portray,   535
Whether your nature is that Universe
    Which once Ye saw and suffered—

A VOICE: *from beneath*
                        Or as they
Whom we have left, we change and pass away.—

DEMOGORGON

Ye elemental Genii, who have homes
    From man's high mind even to the central stone   540
Of sullen lead; from Heaven's star-fretted domes
    To the dull weed some sea-worm battens[34] on—

A CONFUSED VOICE

We hear—thy words waken Oblivion.

DEMOGORGON

Spirits, whose homes are flesh—ye beasts and birds—
    Ye worms and fish—ye living leaves and buds—   545
Lightning and Wind—and ye untameable herds,
    Meteors and mists, which throng Air's solitudes:

A VOICE

Thy voice to us is wind among still woods.

DEMOGORGON

Man, who wert once a despot and a slave,—
    A dupe and a deceiver,—a Decay,   550
A Traveller from the cradle to the grave
    Through the dim night of this immortal Day:

ALL

Speak—thy strong words may never pass away.

DEMOGORGON

This is the Day which down the void Abysm
At the Earth-born's spell yawns for Heaven's Despotism,   555
    And Conquest is dragged captive through the Deep;
Love from its awful throne of patient power
In the wise heart, from the last giddy hour
    Of dread endurance, from the slippery, steep,
And narrow verge of crag-like Agony, springs   560
And folds over the world its healing wings.

[34]Feeds.

Gentleness, Virtue, Wisdom, and Endurance,—
These are the seals[35] of that most firm assurance
Which bars the pit over Destruction's strength;
And if,[36] with infirm hand, Eternity,   565
Mother of many acts and hours, should free
    The serpent that would clasp her with his length,—
These are the spells by which to reassume
An empire o'er the disentangled Doom.

To suffer woes which Hope thinks infinite;   570
To forgive wrongs darker than Death or Night;
    To defy Power, which seems Omnipotent;
To love, and bear; to hope till Hope creates
From its own wreck the thing it contemplates;
    Neither to change nor falter nor repent: 575
This, like thy glory, Titan! is to be
Good, great and joyous, beautiful and free;
This is alone Life, Joy, Empire, and Victory.

---

[35]Seals: signs, protective coverings. In Revelations, an angel binds the dragon, casts him into an abyss, and sets a seal upon him to confine him there (20.1–3).

[36]Shelley's sense of history keeps him from any confidence, even in this visionary mode, that tyranny will never recur.

~Prometheus and Romanticism

Perhaps the most important myth for the British Romantics was that of Prometheus, who is a prototype not only of Jesus, a martyr and benefactor of humanity, but also of Satanic defiance of a tyrannical god. He combines both, though Shelley emphasizes the former. Prometheus was the focus of much Romantic-era imaginative writing, from J. W. von Goethe in the 1770s to Byron and Mary Shelley in 1816–18. The full title of Mary's famous novel is *Frankenstein; or, The Modern Prometheus*.

In the earliest treatment, in Aeschylus's lost play (c. fifth century BCE), Prometheus is the Titan who steals fire from heaven and gives it to man, elevating humanity above the beasts and, by metaphysical implication, giving man the light of civilization. Yet fire may rage with destructive energy too. Ben Franklin was dubbed "the modern Prometheus" for capturing lightning and inaugurating the science of electricity. Napoleon was deemed a Prometheus in both liberating European peoples from monarchal oppression and in bringing twenty years of destructive war to Europe. For Byron, Prometheus joins the gallery of Byronic heroes (along with Satan and Napoleon)—a defiant, existential sufferer. In 1801 Beethoven composed the score for the ballet *The Creatures of Prometheus* (Op. 43). Rubens's famous early painting of *Prometheus and the Eagle* (1611–12) was widely reproduced throughout the eighteenth century. British artists John Flaxman and George Romney and their transplanted Swiss colleague Henry Fuseli sketched versions of Prometheus in the 1770s, as did Richard Cosway in the 1780s. In 1786 the British sculptor Thomas Banks produced his remarkable *The Fallen Titan*. Flaxman returned to the theme in the 1790s, along with poet William Blake. Prometheus also figured into political cartoons by James Gillray and others well into the 1820s.

Prometheus—Johann Wolfgang von Goethe, 1773
(Translated by Stephen C. Behrendt)

Cover thy wide heavens, Zeus,
With misty clouds,
And, like the boy who lops off
The heads of the thistles,
Play among oaks and mountain-peaks;   5
Yet thou must leave
My earth still intact;
My little cottage, too, not built by thee;
This hearth belongs to me.
Its warm glow   10
Envied by thee.

I know nothing more worthless
Under the sun, than ye gods!
Ye nourish with pain,
With strict sacrifices   15
And devoted prayers,
Your own majesty:
Ye would all starve,
If children and beggars
Were not such gullible fools.   20

Once, when a child
And ignorant about almost everything,
I raised my bewildered gaze
Toward the sun, as if somewhere up there
An ear waited to hear my woe,   25
A heart, like mine,
To pity the oppressed.

Who helped me
Against the Titans' insolence?
Who saved me from death,   30
From slavery?
Didst thou not do all of this on thy own,
My sacred, glowing heart?
And didst thou not glow, too, young and good,
With misplaced gratitude   35
To him who sleeps above?

I honor thee? Why?
Hast thou ever lightened
Man's heavy burden?
Hast thou comforted terrified man,   40
Wiped his tears?
Was it not all-powerful Time
That framed me to be a man,
And eternal Fate
That masters me and thee alike?   45

Didst thou ever imagine
I should learn to hate life itself,
Fly to deserts,
Because not all the blossoms
Of my dreams grew ripe?   50

Here I sit, now, forming mortals
In my own image—
A race that resembles me,
To suffer, to weep,
To enjoy, to be glad,   55
And to scorn thee,
As I do!

Prometheus—George Gordon, Lord Byron, 1816

I.

Titan! to whose immortal eyes
    The sufferings of mortality
    Seen in their sad reality,
Were not as things that gods despise;
What was thy pity's recompense?
A silent suffering, and intense;
The rock, the vulture, and the chain,
All that the proud can feel of pain,
The agony they do not show,
The suffocating sense of woe,   10
    Which speaks but in its loneliness,
And then is jealous lest the sky

Should have a listener, nor will sigh
    Until its voice is echoless.[1]

II.

Titan! to thee the strife was given
    Between the suffering and the will,
    Which torture where they cannot kill;
And the inexorable Heaven,
And the deaf tyranny of Fate,
The ruling principle of Hate.   20
Which for its pleasure doth create
The things it may annihilate,
Refused thee even the boon to die:
The wretched gift eternity
Was thine—and thou hast borne it well.
All that the Thunderer[2] wrung from thee
Was but the menace which flung back
On him the torments of thy rack;
The fate thou didst so well foresee,
But would not to appease him tell;   30
And in thy Silence was his Sentence,
And in his Soul a vain repentance,
And evil dread so ill dissembled
That in his hand the lightnings trembled.

III.

Thy Godlike crime was to be kind,
    To render with thy precepts less
    The sum of human wretchedness,
And strengthen Man with his own mind;
But baffled as thou wert from high,
Still in thy patient energy,   40
In the endurance, and repulse
    Of thine impenetrable Spirit,
Which Earth and Heaven could not convulse,
    A mighty lesson we inherit:

---

[1]Tantalizing syntactic anticipation of Demogorgon's observation that "the deep truth is imageless" (*PU* 2.4.116).

[2]Jupiter's weapon is thunder; this is also Satan's name for God (*PL* 2.28).

Thou art a symbol and a sign
    To Mortals of their fate and force;
Like thee, Man is in part divine,
    A troubled stream from a pure source;
And Man in portions can foresee[3]
His own funereal destiny;   50
His wretchedness, and his resistance,
And his sad unallied existence:
To which his Spirit may oppose
Itself—and equal to all woes,
    And a firm will, and a deep sense,
Which even in torture can descry
    Its own concenter'd recompense,
Triumphant where it dares defy,
And making Death a Victory.

                                        Diodati,[4] July, 1816

On Life

Written in 1819; related to Shelley's unfinished Philosophical View of Reform. *Published in 1840, with Mary Shelley's note:*

> How powerful—how almost appalling, in its vivid reality of representation, is the essay on "Life." Shelley was a disciple of the Immaterial Philosophy of Berkeley. This theory gave unity and grandeur to his ideas, while it opened a wide field for his imagination. The creation, such as it was perceived by his mind—a unit in immensity, was slight and narrow compared with the interminable forms of thought that might exist beyond, to be perceived perhaps hereafter by his own mind; or which are perceptible to other minds that fill the universe, not of space in the material sense, but of infinity in the immaterial one. Such ideas are, in some degree, developed in his poem entitled "Heaven" and when he makes one of the interlocutors exclaim,
>
> > "Peace! the abyss is wreathed in scorn
> > Of thy presumption, atom-born," ["Ode to Heaven," ll. 37–39]

[3]Pun on Prometheus's name (which means "fore-knowledge").
[4]Byron's villa on Lake Geneva, where Mary Shelley conceived *Frankenstein*.

> he expresses his despair of being able to conceive, far less express, all of variety, majesty, and beauty which is veiled from our imperfect senses in the unknown realm, the mystery of which his poetic vision sought in vain to penetrate.

Life and the world, or whatever we call that which we are and feel, is an astonishing thing. The mist of familiarity obscures from us the wonder of our being. We are struck with admiration at some of its transient modifications; but it is itself the great miracle. What are changes of empires, the wreck of dynasties with the opinions which supported them; what is the birth and the extinction of religions and of political systems to life? What are the revolutions of the globe which we inhabit, and the operations of the elements of which it is composed, compared with life? What is the universe of stars, and suns, of which this inhabited earth is one and their motions and their destiny compared with life? Life, the great miracle, we admire not,[1] because it is so miraculous. It is well that we are thus shielded by the familiarity of what is at once so certain and so unfathomable, from an astonishment which would otherwise absorb and overawe the functions of that which is its object.

If any artist I do not say had executed but had merely conceived in his mind the system of the sun and the stars and planets, they not existing, and had painted to us in words or upon canvas the spectacle now afforded by the nightly cope[2] of Heaven and illustrated it by the wisdom of astronomy, great would be our admiration. Or had he imagined the scenery of this earth, the mountains, the seas and the rivers, and the grass and the flowers and the variety of the forms and masses of the leaves of the woods and the colours which attend the setting and the rising sun, and the hues of the atmosphere, turbid or serene, these things not before existing, truly we should have been astonished, and it would not have been a vain boast to have said of such a man, "Non merita nome di creatore, sennon Iddio ed il Poeta."[3] But now these things are looked on with little wonder and to be conscious of them with intense delight is esteemed to be the distinguishing mark of a refined and extraordinary person. The multitude of men care not for them. It is thus with Life—that which includes all.

What is life? Thoughts and feelings arise, with or without our will, and we employ words to express them. We are born, and our

[1]Wonder at.

[2]Cloak.

[3]"No one deserves the name of Creator but God and the Poet" (attributed to Tasso). See also *A Defence of Poetry* (p. 317).

birth is unremembered and our infancy remembered but in fragments. We live on and in living we lose the apprehension of life.
How vain is it to think that words can penetrate the mystery of our
being. Rightly used they may make evident our ignorance to ourselves, and this is much. For what are we? Whence do we come,
and whither do we go? Is birth the commencement, is death the
conclusion of our being? What is birth and death?

The most refined abstractions of logic conduct to a view of life
which, though startling to the apprehension, is in fact that which
the habitual sense of its repeated combinations has extinguished in
us. It strips, as it were, the painted curtain from this scene of things.
I confess that I am one of those who am unable to refuse my assent
to the conclusions of those philosophers who assert that nothing
exists but as it is perceived.[4]

It is a decision against which all our persuasions struggle, and we
must be long convicted[5] before we can be convinced that the solid
universe of external things is "such stuff as dreams are made of."[6]
The shocking absurdities of the popular philosophy of mind and matter, its fatal consequences in morals, their violent dogmatism concerning the source of all things, had early conducted me to materialism.[7]
This materialism is a seducing system to young and superficial minds.
It allows its disciples to talk and dispenses them from thinking. But I
was discontented with such a view of things as it afforded; man is a
being of high aspirations "looking both before and after," whose
"thoughts wander through eternity,"[8] disclaiming alliance with tran-
sience and decay, incapable of imagining to himself annihilation, existing but in the future and the past, being, not what he is, but what he
has been and shall be. Whatever may be his true and final destination,
there is a spirit within him at enmity with nothingness and dissolution. This is the character of all life and being.—Each is at once the
centre and the circumference; the point to which all things are referred,
and the line in which all things are contained.—Such contemplations
as these materialism and the popular philosophy of mind and matter
alike forbid; they are only consistent with the intellectual system.

[4]The famous maxim of empiricist philosopher George Berkeley (1685–1753).
[5]Given proof.
[6]Prospero on the illusion of life; *The Tempest* 4.1.156–57.
[7]The scientifically verifiable.
[8]Hamlet's phrase about the mental capacity that distinguishes humanity and compels him to action (*Hamlet* 4.4.37), linked to fallen angel Belial's sense of consciousness (*PL* 2.148).

It is absurd to enter into a long recapitulation of arguments sufficiently familiar to those inquiring minds whom alone a writer on ab-
struse subjects can be conceived to address. Perhaps the most clear
and vigorous statement of the intellectual system is to be found in Sir
W. Drummond's Academical Questions.[9] After such an exposition it
would be idle to translate into other words what could only lose its
energy and fitness by the change. Examined point by point and word
by word, the most discriminating intellects have been able to discern
no train of thoughts in the process of reasoning, which does not conduct inevitably to the conclusion which has been stated.

What follows from the admission? It establishes no new truth, it
gives us no additional insight into our hidden nature, neither its action nor itself. Philosophy, impatient as it may be to build, has much
work yet remaining as pioneer[10] for the overgrowth of ages. It makes
one step towards this object; it destroys error, and the roots of error.
It leaves, what it is too often the duty of the reformer in political and
ethical questions to leave, a vacancy. It reduces the mind to that freedom in which it would have acted, but for the misuse of words and
signs, the instruments of its own creation.—By signs, I would be understood in a wide sense, including what is properly meant by that
term, and what I peculiarly mean. In this latter sense, almost all familiar objects are signs, standing not for themselves but for others, in
their capacity of suggesting one thought which shall lead to a train of
thoughts.—Our whole life is thus an education of error.

Let us recollect our sensations as children.[11] What a distinct and
intense apprehension had we of the world and of ourselves. Many of
the circumstances of social life were then important to us which are
now no longer so. But that is not the point of comparison on which
I mean to insist. We less habitually distinguished all that we saw and
felt from ourselves. They seemed as it were to constitute one mass.
There are some persons who in this respect are always children.
Those who are subject to the state called reverie feel as if their nature
were dissolved into the surrounding universe, or as if the surrounding universe were absorbed into their being. They are conscious of
no distinction. And these are states which precede or accompany or
follow an unusually intense and vivid apprehension of life. As men

[9]This 1805 treatise contested Berkeley's empiricist philosophy.

[10]Forerunner; Shelley implies underminer (digger-up).

[11]Shelley is aware of Wordsworth's "Ode: Intimations of Immortality from Recollections of Early Childhood."

grow up this power commonly decays, and they become mechanical and habitual agents.[12] Thus feelings and then reasonings are the combined result of a multitude of entangled thoughts, and of a series of what are called impressions, blunted by reiteration.

The view of life presented by the most refined deductions of the intellectual philosophy, is that of unity. Nothing exists but as it is perceived. The difference is merely nominal between those two classes of thought which are vulgarly distinguished by the names of ideas and of external objects. Pursuing the same thread of reasoning, the existence of distinct individual minds similar to that which is employed in now questioning its own nature, is likewise found to be a delusion. The words *I*, *you*, *they* are not signs of any actual difference subsisting between the assemblage of thoughts thus indicated, but are merely marks employed to denote the different modifications of the one mind. Let it not be supposed that this doctrine conducts to the monstrous presumption that I, the person who now write and think, am that one mind. I am but a portion of it. The words *I*, and *you*, and *they* are grammatical devices invented simply for arrangement and totally devoid of the intense and exclusive sense usually attached to them. It is difficult to find terms adequate to express so subtle a conception as that to which the intellectual philosophy has conducted us. We are on that verge where words abandon us, and what wonder if we grow dizzy to look down the dark abyss of—how little we know.

The relations of *things* remain unchanged, by whatever system. By the word *things* is to be understood any object of thought, that is, any thought upon which any other thought is employed, with an apprehension of distinction. The relations of these remain unchanged; and such is the material of our knowledge.

What is the cause of life?—that is, how was it preceded, or what agencies distinct from life have acted or act upon life? All recorded generations of mankind have wearily busied themselves in inventing answers to this question; and the result has been—Religion. Yet, that the basis of all things cannot be, as the popular philosophy alleges, mind, is sufficiently evident. Mind, as far as we have any experience of its properties—and beyond that experience how vain is argument—cannot create, it can only perceive. It is said also to be the Cause. But cause is only a word expressing a certain state of the human mind with regard to the manner in which two thoughts are apprehended to be related to each other.—If any one desires to know

---

[12]Actors and doers.

how unsatisfactorily the popular philosophy employs itself upon this great question, they need only impartially reflect upon the manner in which thoughts develope themselves in their minds.—It is infinitely improbable that the cause of mind, that is, of existence, is similar to mind. It is said that mind produces motion and it might as well have been said that motion produces mind.

Ode to the West Wind

Begun in October 1819 and published with PU *(1820) with this note:*

> *This poem was conceived and chiefly written in a wood that skirts the Arno, near Florence, and on a day when that tempestuous wind, whose temperature is at once mild and animating, was collecting the vapours which pour down the autumnal rains. They began, as I foresaw, at sunset with a violent tempest of hail and rain, attended by that magnificent thunder and lightning peculiar to the Cisalpine regions.*

> *Shelley's ode is composed of sonnet-stanzas, using for the first twelve lines the complicated interlocking* terza rima *stanza form of Dante's* Divine Comedy *(1308–21):* aba / bcb / cdc / ded / ee. *Because weather (and seasonal transformation) arrives on the west wind, it is a harbinger of change. The ode is all the more powerful for its honest questioning about whether the metaphor of nature's eternal cycle of seasons can be mapped onto human history, or whether the real transformation is from the winter of mortal life to the rebirth of eternal spring. Either way, Shelley hopes and prays for a poet's voice of inspired breath to sound the fiery trumpet and awaken the symbolically dead world.*

I

O wild West Wind, thou breath of Autumn's being,
Thou, from whose unseen presence the leaves dead
Are driven, like ghosts from an enchanter fleeing,

Yellow, and black, and pale, and hectic[1] red,
Pestilence-stricken multitudes![2] O thou   5
Who chariotest to their dark wintry bed

---

[1]Diseased.
[2]The four colors evoke human races.

The wingéd seeds, where they lie cold and low,
Each like a corpse within its grave, until
Thine azure sister of the Spring[3] shall blow

Her clarion[4] o'er the dreaming earth, and fill   10
(Driving sweet buds like flocks to feed in air)
With living hues and odours plain and hill:

Wild Spirit, which art moving everywhere;
Destroyer and Preserver;[5] Hear, oh hear![6]

II

Thou on whose stream, 'mid the steep sky's commotion,   15
Loose clouds like earth's decaying leaves are shed,
Shook from the tangled boughs of heaven and ocean,

Angels[7] of rain and lightning! there are spread
On the blue surface of thine airy surge,
Like the bright hair uplifted from the head   20

Of some fierce Mænad,[8] ev'n from the dim verge
Of the horizon to the zenith's height—
The locks of the approaching storm.[9] Thou dirge[10]

Of the dying year, to which this closing night
Will be the dome of a vast sepulchre,   25
Vaulted with all thy congregated might

Of vapours, from whose solid atmosphere
Black rain, and fire, and hail, will burst: Oh hear!

[3]Spring's gentle west wind. Traditionally, both the autumnal and the spring winds were personified as masculine. Shelley makes the spring wind female, like "Liberty."

[4]Small war trumpet (and its sound); the image evokes the trumpet of the Last Judgment in stanza 5.

[5]The names of two Hindu gods known from recent translations by Sir William Jones (1746–94).

[6]This slight off-rhyme strengthens the pun on *hear* as *here.*

[7]Literally, messengers.

[8]Female follower of Bacchus, god of wine.

[9]The wild hair of the frenzied Maenad seems imaged in the thundercloud.

[10]Song of mourning, often at a burial.

III

Thou who didst waken from his summer-dreams
The blue Mediterranean, where he lay,   30
Lull'd by the coil of his crystalline streams,

Beside a pumice isle in Baiæ's bay,[11]
And saw in sleep old palaces and towers
Quivering within the wave's intenser day,

All overgrown with azure moss, and flowers   35
So sweet, the sense faints picturing them! Thou
For whose path the Atlantic's level powers[12]

Cleave themselves into chasms, while far below
The sea-blooms and the oozy woods which wear
The sapless foliage of the ocean, know   40

Thy voice, and suddenly grow gray with fear
And tremble and despoil[13] themselves: Oh hear!

IV

If I were a dead leaf thou mightest bear;
If I were a swift cloud to fly with thee;
A wave to pant beneath thy power, and share   45

The impulse of thy strength, only less free
Than Thou, O uncontrollable! If even
I were as in my boyhood, and could be

The comrade of thy wanderings over heaven,
As then, when to outstrip thy skiey speed   50
Scarce seem'd a vision,—I would ne'er have striven[14]

---

[11]Site of ancient Roman ruins.

[12]"The phenomenon alluded to at the conclusion of the third stanza is well known to naturalists. The vegetation at the bottom of the sea, of rivers, and of lakes, sympathizes with that of the land in the change of seasons, and is consequently influenced by the winds which announce it." [Shelley's note.]

[13]Disrobe.

[14]Strive: "to contend in rivalry; to seek to surpass another or each other; to compete in a trial of strength or skill" (*OED*).

As thus with thee in prayer in my sore need.
Oh! lift me as a wave, a leaf, a cloud!
I fall upon the thorns of life![15] I bleed!

A heavy weight of hours has chain'd and bow'd   55
One too like thee—tameless, and swift, and proud.

V

Make me thy lyre, ev'n as the forest is:
What if my leaves are falling like its own![16]
The tumult of thy mighty harmonies

Will take from both a deep autumnal tone,   60
Sweet though in sadness. Be thou, Spirit fierce,
My spirit! be thou me,[17] impetuous one!

Drive my dead thoughts over the universe,
Like wither'd leaves, to quicken[18] a new birth;
And, by the incantation of this verse,   65

Scatter, as from an unextinguish'd hearth
Ashes and sparks, my words among mankind!
Be through my lips to unawaken'd earth

The trumpet of a prophecy! O Wind,
If Winter comes, can Spring be far behind?[19]   70

---

[15]Evoking both Jesus' tormenting crown of thorns and the classical gesture of falling upon one's sword in a suicide of honor in the face of defeat. Shelley knew Byron's lines, "The thorns which I have reap'd are of the tree / I planted: they have torn me, and I bleed" (Byron, *Childe Harold's Pilgrimage*, Canto IV [1818], ll. 88–89).

[16]The use of "leaves" is a pun: the forest's storm-driven falling leaves are a metaphor for tree leaves, but also metaphorically for the "leaves" of Shelley's books of poetry.

[17]Shelley's *me* (objective case) gains a stressed rhyme with *be* and also reflects a willingness to be made an object.

[18]Make happen more quickly, but also give (or restore) life, to animate (as the soul or the body).

[19]Although the question is often regarded as merely rhetorical (a question that assumes assent), it may voice real uncertainty. Spring always follows winter, guaranteeing nature's rebirth; guarantees of human spiritual and moral regeneration are less certain. And the apocalyptic trumpet, like the capitalized nouns, suggest a rebirth in eternity, out of human time and history.

To a Sky-Lark

Shelley composed this work in late June 1820, near Leghorn (Livorno). The European skylark was famed for singing only while in flight, and so high that it was invisible. It provided Shelley with an ideal symbol for the divinely inspired poet, with deliberate reference to Plato's Phaedrus *(which Shelley had read and may have translated), which images a winged soul. Shelley's unusual stanza form attempts to suggest the skylark's whirling flight and its distinctive trilling song, even as the poetry itself—in questions, serial similes, and surreal imagery—suggests the inadequacy of language to such inspiration.*

Hail to thee, blithe Spirit!
    Bird thou never wert—
That from heaven, or near it
    Pourest thy full heart
In profuse strains of unpremeditated art.[1]   5

Higher still and higher
    From the earth thou springest,
Like a cloud of fire,[2]
    The blue deep thou wingest,
And singing still dost soar, and soaring ever singest.   10

In the golden lightning
    Of the sunken Sun—
O'er which clouds are brightening,
    Thou dost float and run;
Like an unbodied joy whose race is just begun.   15

The pale purple even[3]
    Melts around thy flight,
Like a star of Heaven
    In the broad day-light
Thou art unseen,—but yet I hear thy shrill delight: 20

[1]Milton calls *PL* "unpremeditated verse" (9.24).
[2]Lit (colored) from beneath by the setting sun; in the Old Testament, God appears as a column of fire.
[3]Evening.

Keen as are the arrows
    Of that silver sphere,
Whose intense lamp narrows
    In the white dawn clear[4]
Until we hardly see—we feel that it is there.   25

All the earth and air
    With thy voice is loud,
As, when night is bare,
    From one lonely cloud
The moon rains out her beams—and heaven is overflow'd.   30

What thou art we know not;
    What is most like thee?
From rainbow clouds there flow not
    Drops so bright to see
As from thy presence showers a rain of melody;—   35

Like a Poet hidden
    In the light of thought,
Singing hymns unbidden,
    Till the world is wrought
To sympathy[5] with hopes and fears it heeded not: 40

Like a high-born maiden
    In a palace-tower,
Soothing her love-laden
    Soul in secret hour
With music sweet as love—which overflows her bower: 45

Like a glow-worm golden
    In a dell of dew,
Scattering unbeholden
    Its aerial[6] hue
Among the flowers and grass, which screen it from the view: 50

---

[4]Venus, the morning star, whose light disappears as the sun rises.
[5]Fellow-feeling.
[6]Airy; light, ethereal.

Like a rose embower'd
   In its own green leaves—
By warm winds deflower'd[7]—
   Till the scent it gives
Makes faint with too much sweet these heavy-wingéd thieves: 55

Sound of vernal[8] showers
   On the twinkling grass,
Rain-awaken'd flowers,
   All that ever was
Joyous, and clear, and fresh, thy music doth surpass.   60

Teach us, Sprite or Bird,
   What sweet thoughts are thine:
I have never heard
   Praise of love or wine
That panted forth a flood of rapture so divine: 65

Chorus Hymeneal[9]
   Or triumphal chaunt
Match'd with thine would be all
   But an empty vaunt,
A thing wherein we feel there is some hidden want.   70

What objects are the fountains
   Of thy happy strain?
What fields or waves or mountains?
   What shapes of sky or plain?
What love of thine own kind? what ignorance of pain?[10]   75

With thy clear keen joyance
   Languor cannot be—
Shadow of annoyance
   Never came near thee:
Thou lovest—but ne'er knew love's sad satiety.   80

[7]Unpetaled, made sexually generative in spreading pollen.

[8]Springtime.

[9]Wedding hymn.

[10]The ode begins to pivot away from the equating human poetry and skylark song.

Waking or asleep
    Thou of death must deem
Things more true and deep
    Than we mortals dream,
Or how could thy notes flow in such a chrystal stream?   85

We look before and after,[11]
    And pine for what is not—
Our sincerest laughter
    With some pain is fraught—
Our sweetest songs are those that tell of saddest thought.   90

Yet if we could scorn
    Hate and pride and fear;
If we were things born
    Not to shed a tear,
I know not how thy joy we ever should come near.[12]   95

Better than all measures[13]
    Of delightful sound—
Better than all treasures
    That in books are found—
Thy skill to poet were,[14] thou Scorner of the ground!   100

Teach me half the gladness
    That thy brain must know,
Such harmonious madness[15]
    From my lips would flow,
The world should listen then—as I am listening now.   105

---

[11]Hamlet identified this as human consciousness (*Hamlet* 4.4.37).

[12]Joy emerges in tandem with the inevitability of pain and sadness.

[13]Considerations, meters.

[14]Would be in comparison.

[15]In his *Ion* and *Phaedrus*, Plato suggests that poetic inspiration is a form of madness in which the poet loses conscious control and is directed by the inspiring spirit or vision. At the same time, there is a suggestion of an inverse ratio of inspiration and communicability—that the most intense inspirations will sound like madness and be unintelligible to "the world."

Sonnet ["Lift not the painted veil"]

Probably written in 1819 or early 1820, this sonnet revisits, much less idealistically, the skepticism about human existence Shelley articulated in "Hymn to Intellectual Beauty" (1816). In PU the Earth says, "Death is the veil which those who live call life: / They sleep—and it is lifted" (3.3.113–14). Shelley inverts the form of the Petrarchan sonnet, putting the sestet before the octave—an inversion that corresponds to others: life on earth is not "Life" in the ideal; those living in this world are spiritually dead, awaiting an awakening. Plato described life in this world as mere illusions, false art, memory of a transcendental ideal.

Lift not the painted veil which those who live
Call Life: though unreal shapes be pictured there,
And it but mimic all we would believe
With colours idly spread,—behind, lurk Fear
And Hope, twin Destinies; who ever weave   5
Their shadows, o'er the chasm, sightless[1] and drear.
I knew one who had lifted it—he sought,
For his lost heart was tender, things to love,
But found them not, alas! nor was there aught
The world contains, the which he could approve.   10
Through the unheeding many he did move,
A splendour among shadows, a bright blot
Upon this gloomy scene—a Spirit that strove
For truth, and like the Preacher[2] found it not.

Sonnet: Political Greatness

First published in 1824 as "Political Greatness," but Shelley titled it "Sonnet: To the Republic of Benevento" when he wrote it (probably) late in 1820, after the Carbonari revolt against the Bourbon King Ferdinand of Naples in July 1820. Benevento, northeast of Naples, was one of two Italian principalities that drove out the Roman garrisons and disavowed the pope, establishing itself as an independent republic. In the spring of 1821 the Austrian army crushed the revolution, making the 1824 publication distinctively elegiac.

[1]Invisible.
[2]The gloomy "Preacher" in Ecclesiastes 1.2 says, "Vanity of vanities, all is vanity."

Nor happiness, nor majesty, nor fame,
Nor peace, nor strength, nor skill in arms or arts,
Shepherd those herds whom tyranny makes tame;
Verse echoes not one beating of their hearts,
History is but the shadow of their shame,   5
Art veils her glass, or from the pageant starts[1]
As to oblivion their blind millions fleet,[2]
Staining that Heaven with obscene imagery
Of their own likeness. What are numbers knit
By force or custom? Man who man would be,   10
Must rule the empire of himself; in it
Must be supreme, establishing his throne
On vanquished will, quelling the anarchy
Of hopes and fears, being himself alone.

Ode to Liberty

> *This is the closing poem in* PU, *probably composed in spring 1820, in response to the popular uprising in Spain that began on 1 January, abolishing the reactionary post-Napoleonic monarchy and establishing a democratic monarchy. Shelley anticipated this bloodless revolution in "An Ode, Written October 1819, Before the Spaniards Had Recovered Their Liberty." "Ode to Liberty" portrays the revolution as the latest event in the history of Liberty, from its rise in Athens and Rome, through the Middle Ages and the English Revolution (including both Cromwell and Milton), to the American and French Revolutions, with hope for the future. Composed as an address to the spirit of Liberty, the "Ode" invokes its models in Pindaric odes to athletic victory (fifth century BCE), William Collins's "Ode to Liberty" (1747), and Thomas Gray's "The Progress of Poesy" (1757). Its concluding position in the volume gives Shelley's "Ode" the force of a summary prophecy.*

> Yet, Freedom, yet, thy banner, torn but flying,
> Streams like a thunder-storm against the wind.
> — BYRON.[1]

[1] Art either veils (obscures) the glass (mirror) in which she reveals this shameful history (the pageant), or she recoils from the image altogether.
[2] Rush blindly.

---

[1] *Childe Harold's Pilgrimage*, Canto IV (1818), stanza 98, an homage to Byron's championship of political liberty.

I.

A glorious people vibrated again
   The lightning of the nations: Liberty
From heart to heart, from tower to tower, o'er Spain,
   Scattering contagious fire into the sky,
Gleamed. My soul spurned the chains of its dismay,   5
      And in the rapid plumes of song
      Clothed itself, sublime and strong,
(As a young eagle soars the morning clouds among.)
   Hovering in verse o'er its accustomed prey;[2]
      Till from its station in the Heaven of fame   10
   The Spirit's whirlwind rapped[3] it, and the ray
Of the remotest sphere of living flame
Which paves the void was from behind it flung,
   As foam from a ship's swiftness, when there came
   A voice out of the deep: I will record the same.[4]   15

II.

The Sun and the serenest Moon sprang forth:
   The burning stars of the abyss were hurled
Into the depths of Heaven. The dædal[5] earth,
   That island in the ocean of the world,
Hung in its cloud of all-sustaining air: 20
      But this divinest universe
      Was yet a chaos and a curse,
For thou wert not: but, power from worst producing worse,
   The spirit of the beasts was kindled there,
      And of the birds, and of the watery forms,   25
   And there was war among them, and despair
      Within them, raging without truce or terms:
The bosom of their violated nurse[6]
   Groaned, for beasts warred on beasts, and worms on worms,
   And men on men; each heart was as a hell of storms.   30

---

[2]Shelley uses a conventional image of inspired prophecy.

[3]Carried forcibly; enraptured.

[4]Shelley's poet represents himself as transcribing an inspired dream-vision.

[5]Intricately created. In contrast to Genesis, Shelley imagines creation in a fallen state before the birth of Liberty ("thou," l. 23).

[6]Earth; Nature.

III.

Man, the imperial shape, then multiplied
    His generations under the pavilion
Of the Sun's throne: palace and pyramid,
    Temple and prison, to many a swarming million
Were, as to mountain-wolves their raggèd caves.   35
        This human living multitude
          Was savage, cunning, blind, and rude,
For thou wert not; but o'er the populous solitude,
    Like one fierce cloud over a waste of waves,
        Hung Tyranny; beneath, sate deified   40
    The sister-pest,[7] congregator of slaves;
        Into the shadow of her pinions wide
Anarchs[8] and priests, who feed on gold and blood
    Till with the stain their inmost souls are dyed,
    Drove the astonished herds of men from every side.   45

IV.

The nodding promontories, and blue isles,
    And cloud-like mountains, and dividuous waves
Of Greece, basked glorious in the open smiles
    Of favouring Heaven: from their enchanted caves
Prophetic echoes flung dim melody.   50
        On the unapprehensive[9] wild
          The vine, the corn, the olive mild,
Grew savage yet, to human use unreconciled;
    And, like unfolded flowers beneath the sea,
        Like the man's thought dark in the infant's brain,   55
    Like aught that is which wraps what is to be,
        Art's deathless dreams lay veiled by many a vein
Of Parian stone;[10] and, yet a speechless child,
    Verse murmured, and Philosophy did strain
    Her lidless eyes for thee; when o'er the Ægean main   60

[7]Organized institutional religion.
[8]False rulers.
[9]Uncomprehending, unbothered.
[10]Greek sculptors' favorite marble.

V.

Athens arose: a city such as vision
    Builds from the purple crags and silver towers
Of battlemented cloud, as in derision
    Of kingliest masonry: the ocean-floors
Pave it; the evening sky pavilions[11] it;   65
        Its portals are inhabited
        By thunder-zonèd winds, each head
Within its cloudy wings with sun-fire garlanded,—
    A divine work! Athens, diviner yet,
        Gleamed with its crest of columns, on the will   70
    Of man, as on a mount of diamond, set;
        For thou wert,[12] and thine all-creative skill
Peopled, with forms[13] that mock the eternal dead
    In marble immortality, that hill[14]
    Which was thine earliest throne and latest oracle.   75

VI.

Within the surface of Time's fleeting river
    Its wrinkled image lies, as then it lay
Immovably unquiet, and for ever
    It trembles, but it cannot pass away!
The voices of thy bards and sages thunder   80
        With an earth-awakening blast
        Through the caverns of the past:
Religion veils her eyes; Oppression shrinks aghast:
    A wingèd sound of joy, and love, and wonder,
        Which soars where Expectation never flew,   85
    Rending the veil of space and time asunder!
        One ocean feeds the clouds, and streams, and dew;
One Sun illumines Heaven; one Spirit vast
    With life and love makes chaos ever new,
    As Athens doth the world with thy delight renew.[15]   90

[11]Canopies.

[12]Existed.

[13]Sculptural likenesses.

[14]The Acropolis.

[15]Athens's poetry and philosophy survives its demise as a civilization.

VII.

Then Rome was, and from thy deep bosom fairest,
    Like a wolf-cub from a Cadmæan Mænad,[16]
She drew the milk of greatness, though thy dearest
    From that Elysian food was yet unweanèd;
And many a deed of terrible uprightness   95
        By thy sweet love was sanctified;
            And in thy smile, and by thy side,
Saintly Camillus lived, and firm Atilius[17] died.
        But when tears stained thy robe of vestal whiteness,
            And gold prophaned thy Capitolian throne,[18]   100
        Thou didst desert, with spirit-wingèd lightness,
            The senate of the tyrants: they sunk prone
Slaves of one tyrant: Palatinus sighed
    Faint echoes of Ionian song;[19] that tone
    Thou didst delay to hear, lamenting to disown.   105

VIII.

From what Hyrcanian[20] glen or frozen hill,
    Or piny promontory of the Arctic main,
Or utmost islet inaccessible,
    Didst thou lament the ruin of thy reign,
Teaching the woods and waves, and desert rocks,   110
        And every Naiad's[21] ice-cold urn,
            To talk in echoes sad and stern
Of that sublimest lore which man had dared unlearn?[22]
    For neither didst thou watch the wizard flocks

---

[16]"See the Bacchæ of Euripides." [Shelley's note.] In *The Bacchæ*, Bacchus's followers, the Maenads, led by Cadmus's daughter, suckle wolf-cubs. Athens remains Liberty's favorite despite the rise of other cultures like Rome.

[17]Though publicly disgraced, Camillus defended Rome against the Gauls in 387 BCE; Attilus, whom Horace praised, led the Roman legions against the Carthaginians, who tortured him to death.

[18]Rome's decline from republic (with its seat of power on the Capitoline hill) to empire (the Palatine hill).

[19]Roman poets, especially Horace and Virgil, whose works Shelley believed followed Athenian models.

[20]Wilderness region in present-day Iran.

[21]Water nymphs.

[22]"Unlearned" after the Roman empire.

Of the Scald's dreams, nor haunt the Druid's sleep.[23]   115
What if the tears rained through thy shattered locks
    Were quickly dried? for thou didst groan, not weep,[24]
When from its sea of death, to kill and burn,
    The Galilean serpent forth did creep,
    And made thy world an undistinguishable heap.[25]   120

IX.

A thousand years the Earth cried, "Where art thou?"
    And then the shadow of thy coming fell
On Saxon Alfred's olive-cinctured brow:[26]
    And many a warrior-peopled citadel,
Like rocks which fire lifts out of the flat deep,   125
        Arose in sacred Italy,
        Frowning o'er the tempestuous sea
Of kings, and priests, and slaves, in tower-crowned majesty;[27]
    That multitudinous anarchy did sweep
        And burst around their walls, like idle foam,   130
    Whilst from the human spirit's deepest deep
        Strange melody with love and awe struck dumb
Dissonant arms; and Art, which cannot die,
    With divine wand traced on our earthly home
    Fit imagery to pave Heaven's everlasting dome.   135

X.

Thou huntress swifter than the Moon![28] thou terror
    Of the world's wolves! thou bearer of the quiver,
Whose sunlike shafts pierce tempest-wingèd Error,
    As light may pierce the clouds when they dissever[29]
In the calm regions of the orient day!   140

---

[23]Scalds: medieval Scandinavian poets; Druids: medieval Celtic priests.

[24]Felt but did not surrender to sorrow.

[25]Institutional Christianity, which reduces Liberty to dogma.

[26]Alfred the Great (870–901) united Britain, made peace with the Danes, and fostered learning.

[27]Shelley attributes the rise of medieval city-states to their resistance to the domination by emperors and popes, an assertion of liberty that encouraged the arts.

[28]Liberty, tyranny's antagonist, is superior to Diana, goddess of the moon.

[29]Part; separate.

Luther[30] caught thy wakening glance;
  Like lightning, from his leaden lance
Reflected, it dissolved the visions of the trance
  In which, as in a tomb, the nations lay;
    And England's prophets hailed thee as their queen,   145
  In songs whose music cannot pass away,
    Though it must flow forever: not unseen
Before the spirit-sighted countenance
  Of Milton didst thou pass, from the sad scene
Beyond whose night he saw, with a dejected mien.[31]   150

XI.

The eager hours and unreluctant years
  As on a dawn-illumined mountain stood,
Trampling to silence their loud hopes and fears,
  Darkening each other with their multitude,
And cried aloud, "Liberty!" Indignation   155
    Answered Pity from her cave;
    Death grew pale within the grave,
And Desolation howled to the destroyer, Save!
  When like Heaven's Sun girt by the exhalation
    Of its own glorious light, thou didst arise,   160
  Chasing thy foes from nation unto nation
    Like shadows: as if day had cloven the skies
At dreaming midnight o'er the western wave,
  Men started, staggering with a glad surprise,
  Under the lightnings of thine unfamiliar[32] eyes.   165

XII.

Thou Heaven of earth! what spells could pall thee then
  In ominous eclipse? a thousand years
Bred from the slime of deep Oppression's den,
  Dyed all thy liquid light with blood and tears,
Till thy sweet stars could weep the stain away;   170
    How like Bacchanals of blood

---

[30]The Reformation, personified in Martin Luther, who broke the Roman Catholic Church's grip on Europe.

[31]Blind Milton felt he spent his eyesight in the service of Liberty. He was part of the government that executed Charles I. His enemies said that his blindness was God's punishment; Shelley credits him for the spiritual insight for which he prayed in *PL*.

[32]Unfamiliar, because to oppressed humanity tyranny seems natural.

Round France, the ghastly vintage, stood
Destruction's sceptred slaves, and Folly's mitred brood![33]
  When one, like them, but mightier far than they,
   The Anarch of thine own bewildered powers,[34]   175
  Rose: armies mingled in obscure array,
   Like clouds with clouds, darkening the sacred bowers
Of serene Heaven. He, by the past pursued,
  Rests with those dead, but unforgotten hours,
  Whose ghosts scare victor kings in their ancestral towers. 180

XIII.

England yet sleeps: was she not called of old?
  Spain calls her now, as with its thrilling thunder
Vesuvius wakens Ætna, and the cold
  Snow-crags by its reply are cloven in sunder:[35]
O'er the lit waves every Æolian isle   185
    From Pithecusa to Pelorus[36]
    Howls, and leaps, and glares in chorus:
They cry, "Be dim; ye lamps of Heaven suspended o'er us!"
  Her chains[37] are threads of gold, she need but smile
    And they dissolve; but Spain's were links of steel, 190
  Till bit to dust by virtue's keenest file.
    Twins of a single destiny! appeal
To the eternal years enthroned before us
  In the dim West; impress us from a seal,
  All ye have thought and done! Time cannot dare conceal. 195

XIV.

Tomb of Arminius![38] render up thy dead
  Till, like a standard from a watch-tower's staff,
His soul may stream over the tyrant's head;

---

[33]European monarchs, aristocrats, and clergy who opposed the French Revolution.

[34]Napoleon, an Anarch (tyrant) who emerged from revolutionary Liberty's descent into the Reign of Terror. After championing Liberty in opposition to various monarchies, he turned emperor and tyrant.

[35]Split, divided.

[36]Italian islands.

[37]England's oppressions.

[38]Arminius, founder of Germanic independence, led the annihilation of a Roman legion in 9 CE.

Thy victory shall be his epitaph,
Wild Bacchanal of truth's mysterious wine,   200
      King-deluded Germany,
        His dead spirit lives in thee.
Why do we fear or hope? thou art already free!
   And thou,[39] lost Paradise of this divine
      And glorious world! thou flowery wilderness!   205
   Thou island of eternity! thou shrine
      Where Desolation, clothed with loveliness,
Worships the thing thou wert! O Italy,
   Gather thy blood into thy heart; repress
   The beasts who make their dens thy sacred palaces.   210

XV.

Oh, that the free would stamp the impious name
   Of KING into the dust! or write it there,
So that this blot upon the page of fame
   Were as a serpent's path, which the light air
Erases, and the flat sands close behind!   215
      Ye[40] the oracle have heard:
      Lift the victory-flashing sword,
And cut the snaky knots of this foul gordian[41] word,
   Which, weak itself as stubble, yet can bind
      Into a mass, irrefragably[42] firm,   220
   The axes and the rods[43] which awe mankind;
      The sound has poison in it, 'tis the sperm
Of what makes life foul, cankerous,[44] and abhorred;
   Disdain not thou,[45] at thine appointed term,
   To set thine armèd heel on this reluctant[46] worm.   225

[39]Italy.

[40]You who are free.

[41]"KING" (l. 212); when it was foretold that anyone who could untie the knot tied by the Phrygian King Gordias would conquer Asia, Alexander the Great severed it with his sword.

[42]Indisputably.

[43]*Fasces*, rods bound around an axe, Roman symbols of authority; hence "fascist," a brutal authoritarian.

[44]Cancerous.

[45]Hesitate not (addressed to Liberty).

[46]Unwilling.

XVI.

Oh, that the wise from their bright minds would kindle
    Such lamps within the dome of this dim world,
That the pale name of PRIEST might shrink and dwindle
    Into the hell from which it first was hurled,
A scoff of impious pride from fiends impure;   230
        Till human thoughts might kneel alone,
        Each before the judgement-throne
Of its own aweless soul, or of the Power unknown![47]
    O, that the words which make the thoughts obscure
        From which they spring, as clouds of glimmering dew   235
From a white lake blot Heaven's blue portraiture,
        Were stripped of their thin masks and various hue
And frowns and smiles and splendours not their own,
    Till in the nakedness of false and true
    They stand before their Lord,[48] each to receive its due!   240

XVII.

He[49] who taught man to vanquish whatsoever
    Can be between the cradle and the grave
Crowned him the King of Life. Oh, vain endeavour!
    If on his own high will, a willing slave,
He has enthroned the oppression and the oppressor.   245
        What if earth can clothe and feed
        Amplest millions at their need,
And power in thought be as the tree within the seed?
    Or what if Art, an ardent intercessor,
        Driving on fiery wings to Nature's throne,   250
    Checks the great mother stooping to caress her,
        And cries: "Give me, thy child, dominion
Over all height and depth"? if Life can breed
    New wants, and wealth from those who toil and groan,
    Rend of thy gifts and hers a thousandfold for one!   255

[47]Cf. the unseen "power" ("Hymn to Intellectual Beauty"). Power is in the soul of each, and connected to some invisible animating force.

[48]The thoughts behind the inadequate words.

[49]Prometheus; perhaps also Christ.

XVIII.

Come, Thou, but lead out of the inmost cave
    Of man's deep spirit, as the morning-star
Beckons the Sun from the Eoan[50] wave,
    Wisdom. I hear the pennons of her car[51]
Self-moving, like cloud charioted by flame;   260
        Comes she[52] not, and come ye not,
        Rulers of eternal thought,
To judge, with solemn truth, life's ill-apportioned lot?
    Blind Love, and equal Justice, and the Fame
        Of what has been, the Hope of what will be?   265
    O Liberty! if such could be thy name
        Wert thou disjoined from these, or they from thee:
If thine or theirs were treasures to be bought
    By blood or tears, have not the wise and free
    Wept tears, and blood like tears?—The solemn harmony   270

XIX.

Paused, and the Spirit of that mighty singing
    To its abyss was suddenly withdrawn;[53]
Then, as a wild swan, when sublimely winging
    Its path athwart the thunder-smoke of dawn,
Sinks headlong through the aëreal golden light   275
        On the heavy-sounding plain,
        When the bolt has pierced its brain;
As summer clouds dissolve, unburthened of their rain;
    As a far taper fades with fading night,
        As a brief insect dies with dying day,—   280
    My song, its pinions disarrayed of might,
        Drooped; o'er it closed the echoes far away
Of the great voice which did its flight sustain,
    As waves which lately paved his watery way
    Hiss round a drowner's head in their tempestuous play.   285

---

[50]Eastern; Eos is goddess of the dawn.

[51]Pennons: banners; car: chariot bearing the sun.

[52]Wisdom.

[53]The inspiring vision ends, the poet's inspiration fails, but his fading song reverberates in the powerful enjambments.

Peter Bell the Third

*This political satire on William Wordsworth, written in summer and
fall 1819, is contemporary with* The Cenci, PU, *and the explicit political poems of that period.* Wordsworth's Peter Bell, *mostly written in
1798, was published in April 1819, dedicated to the Poet Laureate,
Robert Southey, who (like Coleridge, also satirized by Shelley) had also
turned conservative. It describes the redemption of an immoral potter
by the example of an ass's faithfulness to its dead master, and was
bruited by its poet as a permanent contribution to "the Literature of
my Country" and widely ridiculed by liberals and radicals.*

*Before Wordsworth's poem actually appeared, word had gotten
out. Keats's and Shelley's friend John Hamilton Reynolds published a
parody,* Peter Bell: A Lyrical Ballad, *which Keats reviewed for Hunt's*
Examiner. *The parody whetted public appetite for Wordsworth's poem,
which appeared shortly afterward and sold well—to the chagrin of liberals. Hunt called it "a didactic little horror." Although Shelley read the
reviews of Wordsworth's poem in Italy, it is not clear that he read the
poem itself before composing his own, sending it to Hunt in November
1819 with instructions for his usual publisher, Charles Ollier, to publish
it immediately, but without Shelley's name. Shelley was planning the
English publication of* The Cenci, *the* PU *volume, and other projects,
and he did not wish to compromise himself as the author of* Peter Bell
the Third. *Ollier did not publish the poem; it first appeared in 1839.*

Shelley's Peter Bell *attacks not only Wordsworth's pompous sermo-
nizing and poets fallen away from the radical principles of their youth
but also a plethora of contemporary political and social perversions:
royal despotism, corrupt ministries, a discredited Parliament, regressive
taxation policies, and prostitution, lawyers, judges, bailiffs, chancel-
lors, and bishops. For all this, however, Shelley's counter-attack worries
about the fate of poets in increasingly conservative England. Shelley is
also uneasy with the genre of venomous satire as perhaps too injurious.
Although Shelley told Hunt that his poem was a mere partisan "squib"
upon which he had "only expended a few days," it bristles with artistic
brilliance in its allusive texture, its sharp satire, and dazzling wordplay.*

By Miching Mallecho, Esq.

Is it a party in a parlour,
Crammed just as they on earth were crammed,
  Some sipping punch—some sipping tea;
  But, as you by their faces see,
All silent, and all—damned!
                    Peter Bell, by W. Wordsworth.[1]

[1]This stanza, originally at the end of Part 1 of Wordsworth's poem, widely criticized, and deleted from later editions.

Ophelia: What means this, my lord?
Hamlet: Marry, this is miching mallecho; it means mischief.[2]

Dedication
To Thomas Brown, Esq., the Younger, H. F.[3]

Dear Tom—Allow me to request you to introduce Mr. Peter Bell to the respectable family of the Fudges. Although he may fall short of those very considerable personages in the more active properties which characterize the Rat and the Apostate,[4] I suspect that even you, their historian, will confess that he surpasses them in the more peculiarly legitimate qualification of intolerable dulness.

[*You know Mr. Examiner Hunt. That murderous and smiling villain at the mere sound of whose voice our susceptible friend the Quarterly fell into a paroxysm of eleutherophobia and foamed so much acrid gall that it burned the carpet in Mr. Murray's upper room, and eating a hole in the floor fell like rain upon our poor friend's head, who was scampering from room to room like a bear with a swarm of bees on his nose:—it caused an incurable ulcer and our poor friend has worn a wig ever since. Well, this monkey suckled with tyger's milk, this odious thief, liar, scoundrel, coxcomb and monster presented me to two of the Mr. Bells. Seeing me in his presence they of course uttered very few words and those with much caution. I scarcely need observe that they only kept company with him—at least I can certainly answer for one of them—in order to observe whether they could not borrow colours from any particulars of his private life for the denunciation they mean to make of him, ans the member of an "infamous and black conspiracy for diminishing the authority of that venerable canon, which forbids any man to mar his grandmother"; the effect of which in this our moral and religious nation is likely to answer the purpose of the controversy.*][5] My intimacy with the

---

[2]*Hamlet* 3.2.148–49 Hamlet refers to his mousetrap play to catch the conscience of murderous King Claudius. *Mallecho* is based on a Spanish word for "evil deed."

[3]Thomas Moore published his popular satire, *The Fudge Family in Paris* (1818), under the pseudonym "Thomas Brown, the Younger." "H. F." ("Historian of the Fudges") mocks Wordsworth's dedication to "Robert Southey, Esq. P. L.," (Poet Laureate).

[4]Reynolds's parody and Wordsworth's *Peter Bell*. Apostate: one fallen away from faith.

[5]In *1839* Mary Shelley suppressed this passage not only for its attack on the conservative establishment publisher John Murray (Byron's publisher) but also for the gleeful satire of Leigh Hunt ("Mr. Examiner Hunt") from the Tory point of view, which by *1839* she feared might mistakenly have been taken seriously. Shelley's coinage *eleutherophobia* denotes "fear of freedom's defenders."

younger Mr. Bell naturally sprung from this introduction to his brothers. And in presenting him to you, I have the satisfaction of being able to assure you that he is considerably the dullest of the three.

There is this particular advantage in an acquaintance with any one of the Peter Bells, that if you know one Peter Bell, you know three Peter Bells; they are not one, but three; not three, but one. An awful mystery, which, after having caused torrents of blood, and having been hymned by groans enough to deafen the music of the spheres, is at length illustrated to the satisfaction of all parties in the theological world, by the nature of Mr. Peter Bell.

Peter is a polyhedric Peter, or a Peter with many sides. He changes colours like a chameleon, and his coat like a snake. He is a Proteus[6] of a Peter. He was at first sublime, pathetic, impressive, profound; then dull; then prosy and dull; and now dull—o so dull! it is an ultra-legitimate dulness.

You will perceive that it is not necessary to consider Hell and the Devil as supernatural machinery. The whole scene of my epic is in "this world which is"—so Peter informed us before his conversion to *White Obi*[7]—

> the world of all of us, *and where*
> *We find our happiness, or not at all.*

Let me observe that I have spent six or seven days in composing this sublime piece;—the orb of my moonlike genius has made the fourth part of its revolution round the dull earth which you inhabit, driving you mad, while it has retained its calmness and its splendour, and I have been fitting this its last phase "to occupy a permanent station in the literature of my country."

Your works, indeed, dear Tom, sell better; but mine are far superior. The public is no judge; posterity sets all to rights.

Allow me to observe that so much has been written of Peter Bell, that the present history can be considered only, like the *Iliad*, as a continuation of that series of cyclic poems, which have already been candidates for bestowing immortality upon, at the same time that they receive it from, his character and adventures. In this point of view I have violated no rule of syntax in beginning my composition with a conjunction; the full stop which closes the

---

[6]Prophetic sea god who changes shape to elude enemies.
[7]"White magic," Christianity.

poem continued by me being, like the full stops at the end of the *Iliad* and *Odyssey*, a full stop of a very qualified import.

Hoping that the immortality which you have given to the Fudges, you will receive from them; and in the firm expectation, that when London shall be an habitation of bitterns;[8] when St. Paul's and Westminster Abbey shall stand, shapeless and nameless ruins, in the midst of an unpeopled marsh; when the piers of Waterloo Bridge shall become the nuclei of islets of reeds and osiers,[9] and cast the jagged shadows of their broken arches on the solitary stream,—some transatlantic commentator will be weighing in the scales of some new and now unimagined system of criticism, the respective merits of the Bells and the Fudges, and their historians. I remain, dear Tom, Yours sincerely,

Miching Mallecho.

December 1, 1819.

P.S.—Pray excuse the date of place; so soon as the profits of the publication come in, I mean to hire lodgings in a more respectable street.[10]

Prologue

Peter Bells, one, two and three,
O'er the wide world wandering be.—
First, the antenatal Peter,[11]
Wrapped in weeds of the same metre,
The so-long-predestined raiment   5
Clothed in which to walk his way meant
The second Peter; whose ambition
Is to link the proposition,
As the mean of two extremes—
(This was learned from Aldric's[12] themes)   10
Shielding from the guilt of schism
The orthodoxal syllogism;
The First Peter—he who was
Like the shadow in the glass

[8]Marsh birds.
[9]Willows.
[10]Prefaces are customarily signed by name, date, and place of residence.
[11]Reynolds's poem, born first.
[12]Henry Aldrich's textbook, *Artis Logicae Compendium* (1691).

Of the second, yet unripe, 15
His substantial antitype.—
Then came Peter Bell the Second,
Who henceforward must be reckoned
The body of a double soul,
And that portion of the whole 20
Without which the rest would seem
Ends of a disjointed dream.—
And the Third is he who has
O'er the grave been forced to pass
To the other side, which is,— 25
Go and try else,—just like this.
Peter Bell the First was Peter
Smugger, milder, softer, neater,
Like the soul before it is
Born from that world into this. 30
The next Peter Bell was he,
Predevote,[13] like you and me,
To good or evil as may come;
His was the severer doom,—
For he was an evil Cotter,[14] 35
And a polygamic Potter.[15]
And the last is Peter Bell,
Damned since our first parents fell,
Damned eternally to Hell—
Surely he deserves it well! 40

PART FIRST

Death

And Peter Bell, when he had been
    With fresh-imported Hell-fire warmed,
Grew serious—from his dress and mien

---

[13]Foredoomed.

[14]Cottage-dweller (Scots dialect).

[15]"The oldest scholiasts read—

        A *dodecagamic* Potter.

This is at once descriptive and more megalophonous—but the alliteration of the texts had captivated the vulgar ears of the heard [*sic*] of later commentators." [Shelley's note.] Polygamic: multiple-wived; dodecagamic: with 12 wives; megalophonous: of imposing sound.

'Twas very plainly to be seen
    Peter was quite reformed.   5

His eyes turned up, his mouth turned down;
    His accent caught a nasal twang;
He oiled his hair;[16] there might be heard
The grace of God in every word
    Which Peter said or sang.   10

But Peter now grew old, and had
    An ill no doctor could unravel;
His torments almost drove him mad;—
Some said it was a fever bad—
    Some swore it was the gravel.[17]   15

His holy friends then came about,
    And with long preaching and persuasion
Convinced the patient that, without
The smallest shadow of a doubt,
    He was predestined to damnation.   20

They said—"Thy name is Peter Bell;
    Thy skin is of a brimstone hue;
Alive or dead—ay, sick or well—
The one God made to rhyme with hell;
    The other, I think, rhymes with you."   25

Then Peter set up such a yell!—
    The nurse, who with some water gruel
Was climbing up the stairs, as well
As her old legs could climb them—fell,
    And broke them both—the fall was cruel.   30

The Parson from the casement lept
    Into the lake of Windermere[18]—
And many an eel—though no adept

[16]"To those who have not duly appreciated the distinction between *whale* and *Russia* oil this attribute might rather seem to belong to the Dandy than the Evangelic. The effect, when to the windward, is indeed so similar, that it requires a subtle Naturalist to discriminate the animals. They belong, however, to distinct genera." [Shelley's note.] Russia oil is expensive; both were strong smelling.

[17]Kidney stones (Shelley suffered from them).

[18]In Wordsworth's Lake District. Casement: a large framed window.

In God's right reason for it—kept
    Gnawing his kidneys half a year.   35

And all the rest rushed through the door,
    And tumbled over one another,
And broke their skulls.—Upon the floor
Meanwhile sat Peter Bell, and swore,
    And cursed his father and his mother;   40

And raved of God, and sin, and death,
    Blaspheming like an infidel;
And said, that with his clenchèd teeth
He'd seize the earth from underneath,
    And drag it with him down to hell.   45

As he was speaking came a spasm,
    And wrenched his gnashing teeth asunder;
Like one who sees a strange phantasm
He lay,—there was a silent chasm
    Between his upper jaw and under.   50

And yellow death lay on his face;
    And a fixed smile that was not human
Told, as I understand the case,
That he was gone to the wrong place:—
    I heard all this from the old woman.   55

Then there came down from Langdale Pike[19]
    A cloud, with lightning, wind and hail;
It swept over the mountains like
An ocean,—and I heard it strike
    The woods and crags of Grasmere vale.   60

And I saw the black storm come
    Nearer, minute after minute;
Its thunder made the cataracts[20] dumb;
With hiss, and clash, and hollow hum,
    It neared as if the Devil was in it.   65

[19]Mountain range near Wordsworth's home in Grasmere.
[20]Waterfalls.

The Devil was in it:—he had bought
    Peter for half-a-crown;[21] and when
The storm which bore him vanished, nought
That in the house that storm had caught
    Was ever seen again.   70

The gaping neighbours came next day—
    They found all vanished from the shore:
The Bible, whence he used to pray,
Half scorched under a hen-coop lay;
    Smashed glass—and nothing more!   75

PART SECOND

The Devil

The Devil, I safely can aver,
    Has neither hoof, nor tail, nor sting;
Nor is he, as some sages swear,
A spirit, neither here nor there,
    In nothing—yet in everything.   80

He is—what we are; for sometimes
    The Devil is a gentleman;
At others a bard bartering rhymes
For sack;[22] a statesman spinning crimes;
    A swindler, living as he can;   85

A thief, who cometh in the night,
    With whole boots and net pantaloons,
Like some one whom it were not right
To mention;—or the luckless wight
    From whom he steals nine silver spoons.[23]   90

But in this case he did appear
    Like a slop-merchant from Wapping,[24]

[21]Coin worth 2 shillings (20 shillings = £1).

[22]Sherry. The Poet Laureate was paid with a butt of sack, about 125 gallons.

[23]In 1735 Edward Cullen was executed for stealing nine silver spoons and some stockings from Margaret Yates's home in Covent Garden. Shelley may be alluding to this story, but ll. 88–89 suggest a contemporary reference.

[24]Slop-merchant: a seller of cheap, ready-made clothes; Wapping: a poor area of East London where many seamen lived.

And with smug face, and eye severe,
On every side did perk[25] and peer
    Till he saw Peter dead or napping.   95

He had on an upper Benjamin[26]
    (For he was of the driving schism)
In the which he wrapped his skin
From the storm he travelled in,
    For fear of rheumatism.   100

He called the ghost out of the corse;[27]—
    It was exceedingly like Peter,—
Only its voice was hollow and hoarse—
It had a queerish look of course—
    Its dress too was a little neater.   105

The Devil knew not his name and lot;
    Peter knew not that he was Bell:
Each had an upper stream of thought,
Which made all seem as it was not;
    Fitting itself to all things well.   110

Peter thought he had parents dear,
    Brothers, sisters, cousins, cronies,
In the fens of Lincolnshire;
He perhaps had found them there
    Had he gone and boldly shown his   115

Solemn phiz[28] in his own village;
    Where he thought oft when a boy
He'd clomb the orchard walls to pillage
The produce of his neighbour's tillage,
    With marvellous pride and joy.   120

And the Devil thought he had,
    'Mid the misery and confusion

[25]Preen.
[26]Carriage-driver's short overcoat.
[27]Corpse.
[28]Slang: physiognomy (face).

Of an unjust war, just made
A fortune by the gainful trade
Of giving soldiers rations bad—   125
    The world is full of strange delusion—

That he had a mansion planned
    In a square like Grosvenor Square,[29]
That he was aping fashion, and
That he now came to Westmoreland   130
    To see what was romantic[30] there.

And all this, though quite ideal,—
    Ready at a breath to vanish,—
Was a state not more unreal
Than the peace he could not feel,   135
    Or the care he could not banish.

After a little conversation,
    The Devil told Peter, if he chose,
He'd bring him to the world of fashion
By giving him a situation   140
    In his own service—and new clothes.

And Peter bowed, quite pleased and proud,
    And after waiting some few days
For a new livery—dirty yellow
Turned up with black—the wretched fellow   145
    Was bowled[31] to Hell in the Devil's chaise.

PART THIRD
Hell

Hell is a city much like London—
    A populous and a smoky city;
There are all sorts of people undone,
And there is little or no fun done;   150
    Small justice shown, and still less pity.

[29]Stylish new section of West London, named for wealthy Lord Grosvenor.

[30]Westmoreland is Wordsworth country—picturesque and exotic (romantic) from an urban perspective.

[31]Wheeled. Livery: uniform of one's employer.

There is a Castles, and a Canning,
    A Cobbett, and a Castlereagh;[32]
All sorts of caitiff corpses planning
All sorts of cozening for trepanning[33]   155
    Corpses less corrupt than they.

There is a [Southey],[34] who has lost
    His wits, or sold them, none knows which;
He walks about a double ghost,
And though as thin as Fraud almost—   160
    Ever grows more grim and rich.

There is a Chancery Court;[35] a King;
    A manufacturing mob; a set
Of thieves who by themselves are sent
Similar thieves to represent;[36]   165
    An army; and a public debt.

Which last is a scheme of paper money,[37]
    And means—being interpreted—
"Bees, keep your wax—give us the honey,
And we will plant, while skies are sunny,   170
    Flowers, which in winter serve instead."

There is a great talk of revolution—
    And a great chance of despotism—
German soldiers—camps—confusion—
Tumults—lotteries—rage—delusion—   175
    Gin—suicide—and methodism;[38]

---

[32]John Castle, government spy and *agent provocateur*; George Canning, witty writer for the conservative *Anti-Jacobin Review* and later prime minister; William Cobbett, radical journalist and pamphleteer; Viscount Castlereagh (John Stewart), powerful and unpopular Foreign Secretary (see *The Mask of Anarchy*, p. 85).

[33]Caitiff: vile; cozening; cheating; trepanning: swindling.

[34]The name was later crossed out in the printer's copy.

[35]Presided over by the Lord Chancellor, this court handled disputes between individuals. In 1817 Lord Chancellor Eldon denied Shelley custody of his first two children.

[36]Parliament, controlled by wealthy landowners.

[37]See Shelley's *A Philosophical View of Reform* (1819–20) for his critique of the monetary system. Bees (l. 169) are Britain's workers.

[38]New popular religion, famous for evangelical conversions.

Taxes too, on wine and bread,
    And meat, and beer, and tea, and cheese,
From which those patriots pure[39] are fed,
Who gorge before they reel to bed   180
    The tenfold essence of all these.

There are mincing women, mewing,
    (Like cats, who amant miserè,[40])
Of their own virtue, and pursuing
Their gentler sisters to that ruin,   185
    Without which—what were chastity?[41]

Lawyers—judges—old hobnobbers
    Are there—bailiffs—chancellors—
Bishops—great and little robbers—
Rhymesters—pamphleteers—stock-jobbers[42]—   190
    Men of glory in the wars,—

Things whose trade is, over ladies
    To lean, and flirt, and stare, and simper,
Till all that is divine in woman
Grows cruel, courteous, smooth, inhuman,   195
    Crucified 'twixt a smile and whimper.

Thrusting, toiling, wailing, moiling,[43]
    Frowning, preaching—such a riot!
Each with never-ceasing labour,
Whilst he thinks he cheats his neighbour,   200
    Cheating his own heart of quiet.

[39]A dig at the selfish elite.

[40]Misery of love (because in heat). "One of the attributes in Linnaeus's description of the Cat. To a similar cause the caterwauling of more than one species of this genus is to be referred;—except indeed that the poor quadruped is compelled to quarrel with its own pleasures, whilst the biped is supposed only to quarrel with those of others." [Shelley's note.]

[41]"What would this husk and excuse for a Virtue be without its kernal prostitution, or the kernal prostitution without this husk of a Virtue? I wonder the Women of the Town do not form an association, like the Society for the Suppression of Vice, for the support of what may be considered the 'King, church, and Constitution' of their order. But this subject is almost too horrible for a joke.—" [Shelley's note.] The Society for the Suppression of Vice, founded in 1804 with support from the Evangelical Christian Member of Parliament William Wilberforce, to counteract vice and immorality and to save young minds from impure and licentious publications.

[42]Stockbrokers.

[43]Labor in mud and mire; "toil and moil" was a common working-class expression.

And all these meet at levees;[44]—
    Dinners convivial and political;—
Suppers of epic poets;—teas,
Where small talk dies in agonies;—   205
    Breakfasts professional and critical;

Lunches and snacks so aldermanic
    That one would furnish forth ten dinners,
Where reigns a Cretan-tonguèd panic,[45]
Lest news Russ, Dutch, or Alemannic[46]   210
    Should make some losers, and some winners;—

At conversazioni[47]—balls—
    Conventicles[48]—and drawing-rooms—
Courts of law—committees—calls
Of a morning—clubs—book-stalls—   215
    Churches—masquerades—and tombs.

And this is Hell—and in this smother
    All are damnable and damned;
Each one damning, damns the other
They are damned by one another,   220
    By none other are they damned.

'Tis a lie to say, "God damns!"[49]
    Where was Heaven's Attorney General
When they first gave out such flams?[50]
Let there be an end of shams,   225
    They are mines of poisonous mineral.

Statesmen damn themselves to be
    Cursed; and lawyers damn their souls

[44]Formal morning receptions by members of the royal family—usually just for men; dinner: a midday meal.

[45]Cretan is a term for a liar.

[46]German.

[47]High-toned gathering for conversations.

[48]Nonconformist or dissenting religious meetings, sometimes illegal.

[49]It is not God who does so. "This libel on our national oath, and this accusation of all our countrymen of being in the daily practice of solemnly asseverating the most enormous falsehood I fear deserves the notice of a more active Attorney General than that here alluded to." [Shelley's note.]

[50]Fanciful notions.

To the auction of a fee;
Churchmen damn themselves to see   230
    God's sweet love in burning coals.

The rich are damned, beyond all cure,
    To taunt, and starve, and trample on
The weak and wretched; and the poor
Damn their broken hearts to endure   235
    Stripe[51] on stripe, with groan on groan.

Sometimes the poor are damned indeed
    To take,—not means for being blessed,—
But Cobbett's snuff, revenge;[52] that weed
From which the worms that it doth feed   240
    Squeeze less than they before possessed.

And some few,[53] like we know who,
    Damned—but God alone knows why—
To believe their minds are given
To make this ugly Hell a Heaven;   245
    In which faith they live and die.

Thus, as in a town, plague-stricken,
    Each man be he sound or no
Must indifferently sicken;
As when day begins to thicken,   250
    None knows a pigeon from a crow,—

So good and bad, sane and mad,
    The oppressor and the oppressed;
Those who weep to see what others
Smile to inflict upon their brothers;   255
    Lovers, haters, worst and best;

All are damned—they breathe an air,
    Thick, infected, joy-dispelling:
Each pursues what seems most fair,
Mining like moles, through mind, and there   260

[51]Lashings.

[52]Journalist William Cobbett (1763–1835) called for the poor to avenge their oppression—a policy Shelley opposed.

[53]Visionary reformers; Satan would make a Heaven of Hell (*PL* 1.254).

Scoop palace-caverns vast, where Care
    In thronèd state is ever dwelling.

PART FOURTH

Sin

Lo, Peter in Hell's Grosvenor Square,
    A footman in the Devil's service![54]
And the misjudging world would swear   265
That every man in service there
    To virtue would prefer vice.

But Peter, though now damned, was not
    What Peter was before damnation.
Men oftentimes prepare a lot   270
Which ere it finds them, is not what
    Suits with their genuine station.

All things that Peter saw and felt
    Had a peculiar aspect to him;
And when they came within the belt   275
Of his own nature, seemed to melt,
    Like cloud to cloud, into him.

And so the outward world uniting
    To that within him, he became
Considerably uninviting   280
To those who, meditation slighting,
    Were moulded in a different frame.

And he scorned them, and they scorned him;
    And he scorned all they did; and they
Did all that men of their own trim[55]   285
Are wont to do to please their whim,
    Drinking, lying, swearing, play.

Such were his fellow-servants; thus
    His virtue, like our own, was built

[54]Wordsworth, having entered "polite society" and conservative politics, and having accepted a government patronage position, is in such service. The ensuing descriptions of Peter apply also to Wordsworth, Shelley implies.

[55]Manner.

Too much on that indignant fuss   290
Hypocrite Pride stirs up in us
    To bully one another's guilt.

He had a mind which was somehow
    At once circumference and centre
Of all he might or feel or know;   295
Nothing went ever out, although
    Something did ever enter.

He had as much imagination
    As a pint-pot;—he never could
Fancy another situation,   300
From which to dart his contemplation,
    Than that wherein he stood.

Yet his was individual mind,
    And new created all he saw
In a new manner, and refined   305
Those new creations, and combined
    Them, by a master-spirit's law.

Thus—though unimaginative—
    An apprehension clear, intense,
Of his mind's work, had made alive   310
The things it wrought on; I believe
    Wakening a sort of thought in sense.

But from the first 'twas Peter's drift
    To be a kind of moral eunuch,[56]
He touched the hem of Nature's shift,   315
Felt faint—and never dared uplift
    The closest, all-concealing tunic.

She laughed the while, with an arch smile,
    And kissed him with a sister's kiss,
And said—"My best Diogenes,[57]   320
I love you well—but, if you please,
    Tempt not again my deepest bliss.

[56]A eunuch is a castrated man, with no sexual appetite. Byron used the term derisively for Southey and Castlereagh.

[57]Philosopher Diogenes (c. 412–323 BCE) famously renounced physical pleasure; some contemporaries attributed his boast to vanity, not philosophy.

'Tis you are cold—for I, not coy,
    Yield love for love, frank, warm, and true;
And Burns, a Scottish peasant boy—   325
His errors prove it—knew my joy
    More, learnèd friend, than you.[58]

'*Bocca bacciata non perde ventura,*
    Anzi rinnuova come fa la luna:[59]—
So thought Boccaccio, whose sweet words might cure a   330
Male prude, like you, from what you now endure, a
    Low-tide in soul, like a stagnant laguna."

Then Peter rubbed his eyes severe,
    And smoothed his spacious forehead down
With his broad palm;—'twixt love and fear,   335
He looked, as he no doubt felt, queer,
    And in his dream sate down.

The Devil was no uncommon creature;
    A leaden-witted thief—just huddled
Out of the dross and scum of nature;   340
A toad-like lump of limb and feature,
    With mind, and heart, and fancy muddled.

He was that heavy, dull, cold thing,
    The spirit of evil well may be:
A drone[60] too base to have a sting;   345
Who gluts, and grimes his lazy wing,
    And calls lust, luxury.

Now he was quite the kind of wight[61]
    Round whom collect, at a fixed æra,[62]
Venison, turtle, hock,[63] and claret,—   350
Good cheer—and those who come to share it—
    And best East Indian madeira!

[58]Robert Burns, a sexually frank Scots poet.

[59]"A mouth was never the worse for having been kissed; / Instead, it renews itself as the moon does." Boccaccio, *Decameron* 2.7.

[60]Nonworking male bee whose only function is to impregnate the queen.

[61]Derogatory term for a man.

[62]Era.

[63]A white German wine.

It was his fancy to invite
   Men of science, wit, and learning,
Who came to lend each other light;   355
He proudly thought that his gold's might
   Had set those spirits burning.

And men of learning, science, wit,
   Considered him as you and I
Think of some rotten tree, and sit   360
Lounging and dining under it,
   Exposed to the wide sky.

And all the while, with loose fat smile,
   The willing wretch sat winking there,
Believing 'twas his power that made   365
That jovial scene—and that all paid
   Homage to his unnoticed chair.

Though to be sure this place was Hell;
   He was the Devil—and all they—
What though the claret circled well,   370
And wit, like ocean, rose and fell?—
   Were damned eternally.

PART FIFTH

Grace

Among the guests who often stayed
   Till the Devil's petits-soupers,[64]
A man[65] there came, fair as a maid,   375
And Peter noted what he said,
   Standing behind his master's chair.

He was a mighty poet—and
   A subtle-souled psychologist;
All things he seemed to understand,   380
Of old or new—of sea or land—
   But his own mind—which was a mist.

[64]Little intimate meals.

[65]Shelley's portrait of Coleridge (whom he never met) as poet, thinker, and meta-physician reflects the contemporary view of him both as genius and as fuzzy thinker.

This was a man who might have turned
    Hell into Heaven[66]—and so in gladness
A Heaven unto himself have earned;   385
But he in shadows undiscerned
    Trusted,—and damned himself to madness.

He spoke of poetry, and how
    "Divine it was—a light—a love—
A spirit which like wind doth blow   390
As it listeth, to and fro;
    A dew rained down from God above;

A power which comes and goes like dream,
    And which none can ever trace—
Heaven's light on earth—Truth's brightest beam."[67]   395
And when he ceased there lay the gleam
    Of those words upon his face.

Now Peter, when he heard such talk,
    Would, heedless of a broken pate,
Stand like a man asleep, or balk[68]   400
Some wishing guest of knife or fork,
    Or drop and break his master's plate.

At night he oft would start and wake[69]
    Like a lover, and began
In a wild measure songs to make   405
On moor, and glen, and rocky lake,
    And on the heart of man—

And on the universal sky—
    And the wide earth's bosom green,—
And the sweet, strange mystery   410
Of what beyond these things may lie,
    And yet remain unseen.

[66]Like Milton's Satan; Coleridge's opium addiction created hell instead.

[67]Cf. John 3.8: "The wind bloweth where it listeth, and thou hearest the sound thereof, but canst not tell whence it cometh, and whither it goeth: so is every one that is born of the Spirit." Coleridge was famed for his enrapturing conversation.

[68]Deprive.

[69]This and the following passages are woven with phrases and allusions of Wordsworth that Shelley most admired and often echoes, especially *Tintern Abbey* and the "Intimations" ode.

For in his thought he visited
    The spots in which, ere dead and damned,
He his wayward life had led; 415
Yet knew not whence the thoughts were fed
    Which thus his fancy crammed.

And these obscure remembrances
    Stirred such harmony in Peter,
That, whensoever he should please, 420
He could speak of rocks and trees
    In poetic metre.

For though it was without a sense
    Of memory, yet he remembered well
Many a ditch and quick-set fence; 425
Of lakes he had intelligence,
    He knew something of heath and fell.[70]

He had also dim recollections
    Of pedlars tramping on their rounds;
Milk-pans and pails; and odd collections 430
Of saws,[71] and proverbs; and reflections
    Old parsons make in burying-grounds.

But Peter's verse was clear, and came
    Announcing from the frozen hearth
Of a cold age, that none might tame 435
The soul of that diviner flame
    It augured to the Earth:

Like gentle rains, on the dry plains,
    Making that green which late was gray,
Or like the sudden moon, that stains 440
Some gloomy chamber's window-panes
    With a broad light like day.

For language was in Peter's hand
    Like clay while he was yet a potter;
And he made songs for all the land, 445

[70]Heath: uncultivated flatlands; fell: uplands.
[71]Sayings.

Sweet both to feel and understand,
  As pipkins[72] late to mountain Cotter.

And Mr. —,[73] the bookseller,
  Gave twenty pounds for some;—then scorning
A footman's yellow coat to wear,[74]   450
Peter, too proud of heart, I fear,
  Instantly gave the Devil warning.

Whereat the Devil took offence,
  And swore in his soul a great oath then,
That for his damned impertinence   455
He'd bring him to a proper sense
  Of what was due to gentlemen!

PART SIXTH

Damnation

"O that mine enemy had written
  A book!"—cried Job:[75]—a fearful curse,
If to the Arab, as the Briton,   460
'Twas galling to be critic-bitten:—
  The Devil to Peter wished no worse.

When Peter's next new book found vent,
  The Devil to all the first Reviews
A copy of it slyly sent,   465
With five-pound note as compliment,
  And this short notice—"Pray abuse."[76]

Then *seriatim*,[77] month and quarter,
  Appeared such mad tirades.—One said—
"Peter seduced Mrs. Foy's daughter,   470

---

[72]Small pots.

[73]Probably the publisher of *Lyrical Ballads*, Joseph Cottle (playing on "Cotter," l. 447).

[74]Wordsworth was in no one's service in 1798–1805.

[75]Job's adversary is God; God's book is the Bible, which contains the Book of Job.

[76]Romantic-era literary periodicals, often allied with political and religious parties; publishing firms were frequently bribed to publish prejudicial, often abusive reviews.

[77]One after another (Latin).

Then drowned the mother in Ullswater,[78]
    The last thing as he went to bed."

Another—"Let him shave his head!
    Where's Dr. Willis?[79]—Or is he joking?
What does the rascal mean or hope,   475
No longer imitating Pope,
    In that barbarian Shakespeare poking?"[80]

One more, "Is incest not enough?
    And must there be adultery too?
Grace after meat? Miscreant[81] and Liar!   480
Thief! Blackguard! Scoundrel! Fool! Hell-fire
    Is twenty times too good for you.

"By that last book of yours we think
    You've double damned yourself to scorn;
We warned you whilst yet on the brink   485
You stood. From your black name will shrink
    The babe that is unborn."

All these Reviews the Devil made
    Up in a parcel, which he had
Safely to Peter's house conveyed.   490
For carriage, tenpence Peter paid—
    Untied them—read them—went half mad.

"What!" cried he, "this is my reward
    For nights of thought, and days of toil?
Do poets, but to be abhorred   495
By men of whom they never heard,
    Consume their spirits' oil?

What have I done to them?—and who
    Is Mrs. Foy? 'Tis very cruel
To speak of me and Betty so!   500

[78]Betty Foy: mother in Wordsworth's "The Idiot Boy"; Ullswater: in the Lake District.

[79]The physician who treated George III's madness; shaving the head was one of many futile treatments.

[80]Pope was Byron's favorite. Many 18th-c. critics considered Shakespeare "barbaric" (for vulgar diction, profanity, and violations of decorum).

[81]Depraved villain.

Adultery! God defend me! Oh!
    I've half a mind to fight a duel."

"Or," cried he, a grave look collecting,
    "Is it my genius, like the moon,
Sets those who stand her face inspecting,   505
That face within their brain reflecting,
    Like a crazed bell-chime, out of tune?"[82]

For Peter did not know the town,
    But thought, as country readers do,
For half a guinea or a crown,   510
He bought oblivion or renown
    From God's own voice[83] in a review.

All Peter did on this occasion
    Was, writing some sad stuff in prose.
It is a dangerous invasion   515
When poets criticize; their station
    Is to delight, not pose.[84]

The Devil then sent to Leipsic fair
    For Born's translation of Kant's book;[85]
A world of words, tail foremost, where   520
Right—wrong—false—true—and foul—and fair
    As in a lottery-wheel are shook.

Five thousand crammed octavo pages
    Of German psychologics,—he
Who his *furor verborum*[86] assuages   525
Thereon, deserves just seven months' wages
    More than will e'er be due to me.

---

[82]Ophelia's claim at Hamlet's strange behavior, his "sovereign reason, / Like sweet bells jangled, out of tune . . ." (3.1.165–66).

[83]"*Vox populi, vox dei.* As Mr. Godwin truly observes of a more famous saying, of *some merit as a popular maxim, but totally destitute of philosophical accuracy.*" [Shelley's note.] The phrase means "the voice of the people is the voice of God." A guinea is worth a pound and a shilling. A crown is worth five shillings (¼£).

[84]Roman poet Horace said poets should teach and delight. Shelley is satirizing Wordsworth's didactic harangues in his various prefaces, 1800–15.

[85]Philosopher Immanuel Kant (1724–1804) influenced Coleridge and Wordsworth; F. Born's Latin translation was published in Leipzig in 1796–98.

[86]Frenzy of words (Latin).

I looked on them nine several days,
    And then I saw that they were bad;
A friend, too, spoke in their dispraise,—   530
He never read them;—with amaze
    I found Sir William Drummond had.[87]

When the book came, the Devil sent
    It to "P. Verbovale,[88] Esquire,"
With a brief note of compliment,   535
By that night's Carlisle mail. It went,
    And set his soul on fire.

Fire, which *ex luce praebens fumum*,[89]
    Made him beyond the bottom see
Of truth's clear well—when I and you, Ma'am,   540
Go, as we shall do, *subter humum*,[90]
    We may know more than he.

Now Peter ran to seed in soul
    Into a walking paradox;
For he was neither part nor whole,   545
Nor good, nor bad—nor knave nor fool;
    —Among the woods and rocks

Furious he rode, where late he ran,
    Lashing and spurring his tame hobby;[91]
Turned to a formal puritan,   550
A solemn and unsexual man,—
    He half believed *White Obi*.[92]

---

[87]In *Academical Questions* (1805), Drummond criticized Kant.

[88]"Quasi, *Qui valet verba:—i.e.* all the words which have been, are, or may be expended by, for, against, with, or on him. A sufficient proof of the utility of this History. Peter's progenitor who selected this name seems to have possessed *a pure anticipated cognition* of the nature and modesty of this ornament of his posterity." [Shelley's note.]

[89]Makes smoke out of light. In *Ars Poetica* Horace famously praised the opening of Homer's *Odyssey* for not giving "flame first and then smoke, but from smoke to let light appear."

[90]Under the earth; die.

[91]Small horse, but also "hobby-horse" (preoccupation).

[92]Christianity (see p. 246, n. 7).

This steed in vision he would ride,
    High trotting over nine-inch bridges,
With Flibbertigibbet,[93] imp of pride,   555
Mocking and mowing[94] by his side—
A mad-brained goblin for a guide—
    Over corn-fields, gates, and hedges.

After these ghastly rides, he came
    Home to his heart, and found from thence   560
Much stolen of its accustomed flame;
His thoughts grew weak, drowsy, and lame
    Of their intelligence.

To Peter's view, all seemed one hue;
    He was no Whig, he was no Tory;   565
No Deist[95] and no Christian he;—
He got so subtle, that to be
    Nothing, was all his glory.

One single point in his belief
    From his organization sprung,   570
The heart-enrooted faith, the chief
Ear in his doctrines' blighted sheaf,
    That "Happiness is wrong";

So thought Calvin and Dominic;[96]
    So think their fierce successors, who   575
Even now would neither stint nor stick
Our flesh from off our bones to pick,
    If they might "do their do."

His morals thus were undermined:—
    The old Peter—the hard, old Potter—   580
Was born anew within his mind;

---

[93]A devilish imp named in *King Lear* (3.4.120).

[94]Grimacing.

[95]One who believes in God, but not the divinity of Jesus Christ. A Whig favors Parliamentary rule against monarchal absolutism; a Tory favors a strong monarchy.

[96]John Calvin (1509–64) and St. Dominic (1170–1221) both denounced earthly pleasures and enforced their beliefs by persecuting heretics.

He grew dull, harsh, sly, unrefined,
    As when he tramped beside the Otter.[97]

In the death hues of agony
    Lambently[98] flashing from a fish,   585
Now Peter felt amused to see
Shades like a rainbow's rise and flee,
    Mixed with a certain hungry wish.[99]

So in his Country's dying face
    He looked—and, lovely as she lay,   590
Seeking in vain his last embrace,
Wailing her own abandoned case,
    With hardened sneer he turned away:

And coolly to his own soul said;—
    "Do you not think that we might make   595
A poem on her when she's dead:—
Or, no—a thought is in my head—
    Her shroud for a new sheet I'll take:

My wife wants one.—Let who will bury
    This mangled corpse! And I and you,   600
My dearest Soul, will then make merry,

---

[97] "A famous river in the new Atlantis of the Dynastophylic Pantisocratists." [Shelley's note.] Coleridge, who praised the river Otter in a sonnet and joined with Southey in 1794 to plan a (never realized) utopian commune named *Pantisocracy* in Pennsylvania. "Dynastophylic" means "dynasty-loving."

[98] Glimmering on the surface.

[99] "See the description of the beautiful colours produced during the agonising death of a number of trout, in the fourth part of a long poem in blank verse, published within a few years. That poem contains curious evidence of the gradual hardening of a strong but circumscribed sensibility, of the perversion of a penetrating but panic stricken understanding. The Author might have derived a lesson which he had probably forgotten from these sweet and sublime verses:—

    This lesson, Shepherd, let us two divide,
    Taught both by what she shews and what conceals,
    Never to blend our pleasure or our pride
    With sorrow of the meanest thing that feels." [Shelley's note.]

The final lines of Wordsworth's *Hart-Leap Well*, in *Lyrical Ballads* (1800); "she" is Nature. The "long poem" is Wordsworth's *Excursion* (1814).

As the Prince Regent did with Sherry,[100]—"
    "Aye—and at last desert me too."

And so his Soul would not be gay,
    But moaned within him; like a fawn   605
Moaning within a cave, it lay
Wounded and wasting, day by day,
    Till all its life of life was gone.

As troubled skies stain waters clear,
    The storm in Peter's heart and mind   610
Now made his verses dark and queer:
They were the ghosts of what they were,
    Shaking dim grave-clothes in the wind.

For he now raved enormous folly,
    Of Baptisms, Sunday-schools, and Graves,   615
'Twould make George Colman[101] melancholy
To have heard him, like a male Molly,[102]
    Chanting those stupid staves.[103]

Yet the Reviews, who heaped abuse
    On Peter while he wrote for freedom,   620
So soon as in his song they spy
The folly which soothes tyranny,
    Praise him, for those who feed 'em.

"He was a man, too great to scan;—
    A planet lost in truth's keen rays:—   625
His virtue, awful and prodigious;—
He was the most sublime, religious,
    Pure-minded Poet of these days."

As soon as he read that, cried Peter,
    "Eureka! I have found the way   630
To make a better thing of metre

---

[100]The Prince of Wales, Prince Regent in 1819, abandoned his earlier Whig drinking companions, including playwright Richard Brinsley Sheridan, and took up with reactionary sycophants.

[101]George Colman, "the Younger" (1762–1836), author of light, bawdy farces.

[102]A homosexual.

[103]Stanzas.

Than e'er was made by living creature
    Up to this blessèd day."

Then Peter wrote odes to the Devil;—
    In one of which he meekly said: 635
"May Carnage and Slaughter,
Thy niece and thy daughter,[104]
May Rapine and Famine,
Thy gorge ever cramming,
    Glut thee with living and dead!   640

    May Death and Damnation,
    And Consternation,
Flit up from Hell with pure intent!
    Slash them at Manchester,[105]
    Glasgow, Leeds, and Chester;   645
Drench all with blood from Avon to Trent.

    Let thy body-guard yeomen
    Hew down babes and women,
And laugh with bold triumph till Heaven be rent!
    When Moloch[106] in Jewry   650
    Munched children with fury,
It was thou, Devil, dining with pure intent."[107]

PART SEVENTH
Double Damnation

The Devil now knew his proper cue.—
    Soon as he read the ode, he drove

[104]Cheering the British victory at Waterloo, Wordsworth wrote, "Almighty God! / . . . / . . . Carnage is thy daughter" (*Ode, 1815*). He changed these lines in 1845.

[105]Peterloo—as if Peter's inspiration, which he would export to other British cities.

[106]In Leviticus 18.21, children are burned as live sacrifices to the god Moloch. See also Milton, *PL* (2.43) and *On the Morning of Christ's Nativity*.

[107]"It is curious to observe how often extremes meet. Cobbett and Peter use the same language for a different purpose: Peter is indeed a sort of metrical Cobbett. Cobbett is however more mischievous than Peter, because he pollutes a holy and now unconquerable cause with the principles of legitimate murder; whilst the other only makes a bad one ridiculous and odious.

    "If either Peter or Cobbett should see this note, each will feel more indignation at being compared to the other than at any censure implied in the moral perversion laid to their charge." [Shelley's note.]

To his friend Lord MacMurderchouse's,[108]   655
A man of interest in both houses,
    And said:—"For money or for love,

Pray find some cure or sinecure;
    To feed from the superfluous taxes
A friend of ours—a poet—fewer   660
Have fluttered tamer to the lure
    Than he." His lordship stands and racks his

Stupid brains, while one might count
    As many beads as he had boroughs,[109]—
At length replies; from his mean front,   665
Like one who rubs out an account,
    Smoothing away the unmeaning furrows:

"It happens fortunately, dear Sir,
    I can. I hope I need require
No pledge from you, that he will stir   670
In our affairs;—like Oliver,[110]
    That he'll be worthy of his hire."

These words exchanged, the news sent off
    To Peter, home the Devil hied,[111]—
Took to his bed; he had no cough,   675
No doctor,—meat and drink enough,—
    Yet that same night he died.

The Devil's corpse was leaded down;[112]
    His decent heirs enjoyed his pelf,[113]

---

[108]William Lowther, 1st Earl of Lonsdale (1757–1844), who secured a minor government appointment for Wordsworth in 1813, but before then cheated Wordsworth and his siblings (chouse: cheat) out of money due them from the estate of their father, his employee.

[109]Parliamentary districts. Before reform, landlords such as Lowther controlled rural boroughs of a few hundred dependent subjects, while teeming cities such as Manchester had no representation at all—hence the Peterloo demonstration.

[110]Notorious government spy and *agent provocateur* W. J. Richards, known as "Oliver."

[111]Hurried.

[112]Weighted down with lead.

[113]Personal property, but suggesting stolen goods.

Mourning-coaches, many a one,   680
Followed his hearse along the town:—
    Where was the Devil himself?

When Peter heard of his promotion,
    His eyes grew like two stars for bliss:
There was a bow of sleek devotion   685
Engendering in his back; each motion
    Seemed a Lord's shoe to kiss.

He hired a house,[114] bought plate, and made
    A genteel drive up to his door,
With sifted gravel neatly laid,—   690
As if defying all who said,
    Peter was ever poor.

But a disease soon struck into
    The very life and soul of Peter—
He walked about—slept—had the hue   695
Of health upon his cheeks—and few
    Dug better—none a heartier eater.

And yet a strange and horrid curse
    Clung upon Peter, night and day;
Month after month the thing grew worse,   700
And deadlier than in this my verse
    I can find strength to say.

Peter was dull—he was at first
    Dull—O, so dull—so very dull!
Whether he talked, wrote, or rehearsed—   705
Still with this dulness was he cursed—
    Dull—beyond all conception—dull.[115]

No one could read his books—no mortal,
    But a few natural friends, would hear him;
The parson came not near his portal;   710

[114]When Wordsworth assumed his government job in 1813, he moved to a large house, Rydal Mount.

[115]Evoking Alexander Pope's *Dunciad*, Shelley consigns Peter to the company of dunces. Pope's poem concludes with a vision of universal darkness and chaos in which Truth has retreated to her cavern, Philosophy has abandoned humanity, Religion has hidden her light, and Morality has expired.

His state was like that of the immortal
    Described by Swift[116]—no man could bear him.

His sister, wife, and children yawned,
    With a long, slow, and drear ennui,
All human patience far beyond;   715
Their hopes of Heaven each would have pawned,
    Anywhere else to be.

But in his verse, and in his prose,
    The essence of his dulness was
Concentred and compressed so close,   720
'Twould have made Guatimozin doze
    On his red gridiron of brass.[117]

A printer's boy, folding those pages,
    Fell slumbrously upon one side;
Like those famed Seven who slept three ages.[118]   725
To wakeful frenzy's vigil-rages,
    As opiates, were the same applied.

Even the Reviewers who were hired
    To do the work of his reviewing,
With adamantine nerves, grew tired;—   730
Gaping and torpid they retired,
    To dream of what they should be doing.

And worse and worse, the drowsy curse
    Yawned in him, till it grew a pest—
A wide contagious atmosphere,   735
Creeping like cold through all things near;
    A power to infect and to infest.

His servant-maids and dogs grew dull;
    His kitten, late a sportive elf;
The woods and lakes, so beautiful,   740

---

[116]In *Gulliver's Travels* (1726, 1735) Jonathan Swift (later Dean of the English Church in Ireland) introduces the Struldbruggs, doomed to live forever (part 3, ch. 10).

[117]Montezuma's nephew and successor, Aztec leader Guatimozin, lost Mexico City to Cortez and was tortured on a brass grill.

[118]In *The Decline and Fall of the Roman Empire* (1776–88), Edward Gibbon describes three young Ephesian men who were sealed in a cave and slept for nearly 200 years (three lifetimes).

Of dim stupidity were full,
    All grew dull as Peter's self.

The earth under his feet—the springs,
    Which lived within it a quick life,
The air, the winds of many wings,   745
That fan it with new murmurings,
    Were dead to their harmonious strife.

The birds and beasts within the wood,
    The insects, and each creeping thing,
Were now a silent multitude;   750
Love's work was left unwrought—no brood
    Near Peter's house took wing.

And every neighbouring cottager
    Stupidly yawned upon the other:
No jackass brayed; no little cur   755
Cocked up his ears;—no man would stir
    To save a dying mother.

Yet all from that charmed district went
    But some half-idiot and half-knave,
Who rather than pay any rent,   760
Would live with marvellous content,
    Over his father's grave.

No bailiff dared within that space,
    For fear of the dull charm, to enter;
A man would bear upon his face,   765
For fifteen months in any case,
    The yawn of such a venture.

Seven[119] miles above—below—around—
    This pest of dulness holds its sway;
A ghastly life without a sound;   770
To Peter's soul the spell is bound—
    How should it ever pass away?

𝔉𝔦𝔫𝔦𝔰

[119]Seven: perhaps a double joke—the poem, which ends in un-creation, has seven parts, like the seven days of God's creation.

Adonais

Shelley wrote Adonais *in spring and early summer 1821, following the death in Rome (23 February) of John Keats, aged 25. Shelley met Keats in 1817 and admired his poetry: when Shelley drowned in 1822, a copy of Keats's 1820 poems was in his pocket. When in summer 1820 Shelley learned that Keats was ill, he invited him to visit in Italy; Keats went with his friend Joseph Severn but died before he could meet up with Shelley. Although Keats died of consumption (tuberculosis), a rumor attributed the cause (including "the rupture of a blood-vessel in the lungs," mentioned in the Preface) to the* Quarterly Review's *cruel attack (April 1818) on Keats's* Endymion. *Shelley's elegy for Keats becomes the occasion to protest the harm done by the conservative, politically motivated reviews of young talent, including Shelley.*

Shelley told John and Maria Gisborne that Adonais *was "a highly wrought piece of art, and perhaps better, in point of composition, than anything I have written"; he told his publisher, Charles Ollier, that it was "perhaps the least imperfect of my compositions." Shelley had it printed at Pisa so he could supervise the process, and he sent copies to Ollier with instructions for a British edition. When the poem sold poorly, Ollier simply sold Shelley's Italian copies and never printed a new edition, though the poem was quoted extensively in the British reviews.* The Literary Gazette *and* Blackwood's Edinburgh Magazine *attacked it savagely.*

In presenting Keats as a frail victim of malicious reviews (which was disastrous for Keats's reputation), Shelley implies more than his physical vulnerability: frail also means ethereal, not of this world—and therefore destined for vindication in eternity. Steeped in allusions to literature and mythology, as well as to contemporary poetry and reviewing, Shelley's poem is a comprehensive cultural, intellectual, and spiritual document that assumes an elite, educated audience. Shelley's intricately crafted Spenserian stanzas pay homage partly to Keats (who used the form in The Eve of St. Agnes, *1819) and partly to Byron (who used it in* Childe Harold's Pilgrimage, *1812–18). His immediate models for his pastoral elegy are two classical-era poems: the Greek poet Bion's lament (voiced by Aphrodite) for Adonis (part of which Shelley translated) and the dirge for Bion attributed to Bion's fellow poet, Moschus. The name "Adonais" alludes in part to Adonis, the beautiful youth loved by Venus. When Adonis was killed by a boar while hunting, Venus changed him into an anemone flower. Adonis is sometimes associated with Osiris because the festivals for both began in lamentations and concluded in joy, as if at a rebirth. The name further suggests the Hebrew word "Adonai" (Lord), to imply the divinity of this and all ideally inspired poets. Unlike most elegies,* Adonais *foresees neither consolation nor reconciliation on earth but embraces death as a transi-*

tion to Eternity—so much so that Mary Shelley and others thought that in the last part of the poem (and last stanza) Shelley is talking more about himself than Keats.

An Elegy on the Death of John Keats, Author of Endymion,[1] Hyperion, etc.

Ἀστὴρ πρὶν μὲν ἔλαμπένὶ ζωοῖσιν Ἐῷος
γῦν δὲ θανών λάμπεις Ἔσπερος ἐν φθιμένοις. —PLATO.[2]

PREFACE
Φάρμακον ἦλθε, Βίων, ποτὶ σὸν στόμα φάρμακον εἶδες.
πῶς τευ τοῖς χεύλεσσι ποτέραμε, κούκ ἐγλυκάνθη;
τίς δὲ βροτὸς τοσσοῦτον ἀνάμερος ἢ κεράοαι τοι,
ἢ δοῦναι λαλέοντι το φάρμακον; ἔκφυγεν ὦδάν.
        — MOSCHUS, EPITAPH. BION.[3]

It is my intention to subjoin to the London edition of this poem, a criticism upon the claims of its lamented object to be classed among the writers of the highest genius who have adorned our age. My known repugnance to the narrow principles of taste on which several of his earlier compositions were modelled proves at least that I am an impartial judge. I consider the fragment of *Hyperion*, as second to nothing that was ever produced by a writer of the same years.

John Keats died at Rome of a consumption, in his twenty-fourth year, on the—of—1821; and was buried in the romantic and lonely cemetery of the Protestants in that city, under the pyramid which is the tomb of Cestius, and the massy walls and towers, now mouldering and desolate, which formed the circuit of antient Rome. The cemetery is an open space among the ruins, covered in

[1]*Endymion* (1818) was harshly reviewed; Keats felt he had outgrown his poetic project about Hyperion, which concerned the Titan god doomed to be overthrown by Apollo. This unfinished poem appeared, despite Keats's objections, in the 1820 volume that Shelley had with him when he drowned.

[2]"Thou wert the morning star among the living, / Ere thy fair light had fled; / Now, having died, thou art as Hesperus, giving / New splendour to the dead"; epigram on Aster ("star") attributed to Homer (Shelley's translation). Hesperus is the evening star; the morning star is Venus.

[3]"Poison came to thy lips, Bion; poison didst thou eat. How could it come to such lips and not be sweetened? What human was so brutal as to mix the drug for thee, or give it to thee, who heard thy voice? He escapes my song." From Moschus, *Elegy for Bion*. The last sentence means "he is not named in my song."

winter with violets and daisies. It might make one in love with death, to think that one should be buried in so sweet a place.[4]

The genius of the lamented person to whose memory I have dedicated these unworthy verses, was not less delicate and fragile than it was beautiful; and where cankerworms abound, what wonder if its young flower was blighted in the bud? The savage criticism on his *Endymion*, which appeared in the *Quarterly Review*, produced the most violent effect on his susceptible mind; the agitation thus originated ended in the rupture of a blood-vessel in the lungs; a rapid consumption ensued, and the succeeding acknowledgements from more candid critics,[5] of the true greatness of his powers, were ineffectual to heal the wound thus wantonly inflicted.

It may be well said, that these wretched men know not what they do.[6] They scatter their insults, and their slanders, without heed as to whether the poisoned shaft lights on a heart made callous by many blows, or one, like Keats's composed of more penetrable stuff.[7] One of their associates is, to my knowledge, a most base and unprincipled calumniator.[8] As to *Endymion*, was it a poem, whatever might be its defects, to be treated contemptuously by those who had celebrated, with various degrees of complacency and panegyric, *Paris*, and *Woman*, and a *Syrian Tale*, and Mrs. Lefanu, and Mr. Barrett, and Mr. Howard Payne, and a long list of the illustrious obscure? Are these the men, who in their venal good nature, presumed to draw a parallel between the Reverend Mr. Milman and Lord Byron?[9] What gnat did they strain at here, after having

[4]In *Ode to a Nightingale* (1819) Keats writes of being "half in love with easeful Death" (l. 52). The Shelleys' son William was buried in this cemetery, and Shelley would lie there later.

[5]Among them, Francis Jeffrey in the *Edinburgh Review*.

[6]"Father, forgive them; for they know not what they do," says Jesus of his crucifixion (Luke 23.34).

[7]Hamlet wonders whether his mother's hasty remarriage after his father's death reflects a hard heart, or one made of "more penetrable stuff (*Hamlet* 3.4.35–36). When Byron was ridiculed by reviewers for his first efforts, he retaliated with a satire to show them that "they, too, are penetrable stuff" (*English Bards and Scotch Reviewers*); see *Adonais* 18.

[8]Poet Laureate Robert Southey castigated Shelley's poetry and ideas. In a draft, Shelley names Southey.

[9]Rev. George Croly's anonymous *Paris in 1815* and Eaton Stannard Barrett's *Woman* (1810), both reviewed favorably in the *Quarterly*; Henry Gally Knight's *A Syrian Tale* (1816); novelist Alicia Le Fanu; American dramatist John Howard Payne; Rev. Henry Hart Milman (author of dramatic plays like *Fazio*, 1815).

swallowed all those camels?[10] Against what woman taken in adultery, dares the foremost of these literary prostitutes to cast his opprobrious stone? Miserable man! you, one of the meanest, have wantonly defaced one of the noblest specimens of the workmanship of God. Nor shall it be your excuse, that, murderer as you are, you have spoken daggers, but used none.[11]

The circumstances of the closing scene of poor Keats's life were not made known to me until the Elegy was ready for the press. I am given to understand that the wound which his sensitive spirit had received from the criticism of *Endymion*, was exasperated by the bitter sense of unrequited benefits; the poor fellow seems to have been hooted from the stage of life, no less by those on whom he had wasted the promise of his genius, than those on whom he had lavished his fortune and his care. He was accompanied to Rome, and attended in his last illness by Mr. Severn, a young artist of the highest promise, who, I have been informed, "almost risked his own life, and sacrificed every prospect to unwearied attendance upon his dying friend." Had I known these circumstances before the completion of my poem, I should have been tempted to add my feeble tribute of applause to the more solid recompense which the virtuous man finds in the recollection of his own motives. Mr. Severn can dispense with a reward from "such stuff as dreams are made of."[12] His conduct is a golden augury of the success of his future career—may the unextinguished Spirit of his illustrious friend animate the creations of his pencil, and plead against Oblivion for his name!

Adonais

I

I weep for Adonais—he is dead!
O, weep for Adonais! though our tears
Thaw not the frost which binds so dear a head!
And thou, sad Hour,[13] selected from all years

---

[10]Jesus calls the scribes and Pharisees "blind guides, which strain at a gnat, and swallow a camel" (Matthew 23.24). For the woman taken in adultery, see John 8.3–11.

[11]"I will speak daggers but use none," Hamlet promises his mother (*Hamlet* 3.2.414).

[12]Prospero is describing life's fragility, and the fragility of his grand illusion (*The Tempest* 4.1.156–57).

[13]One of the Seasons goddesses.

To mourn our loss, rouse thy obscure compeers,
And teach them thine own sorrow, say: "With me
Died Adonais; till the Future dares
Forget the Past, his fate and fame shall be
An echo and a light unto eternity!"

II

Where wert thou, mighty Mother,[14] when he lay,
When thy Son lay, pierced by the shaft which flies
In darkness?[15] where was lorn Urania
When Adonais died? With veilèd eyes,
'Mid listening Echoes, in her Paradise
She sate, while one, with soft enamoured breath,
Rekindled all the fading melodies,
With which, like flowers that mock the corse[16] beneath,
He had adorned and hid the coming bulk of Death.

III

Oh, weep for Adonais—he is dead!
Wake, melancholy Mother, wake and weep!
Yet wherefore? Quench within their burning bed
Thy fiery tears, and let thy loud heart keep
Like his, a mute and uncomplaining sleep;
For he is gone, where all things wise and fair
Descend;—oh, dream not that the amorous Deep[17]
Will yet restore him to the vital air;
Death feeds on his mute voice, and laughs at our despair.

IV

Most musical of mourners, weep again!
Lament anew, Urania!—He[18] died,
Who was the Sire of an immortal strain,

[14]Urania is Milton's muse in *PL* (1.6, 7.1) Urania Venus is one of the names of Venus, who loved and mourned Adonis. The shaft is the boar tusk that killed him and an image of the hostile reviews that "killed" Keats.

[15]The review of *Endymion* was unsigned.

[16]Corpse.

[17]The eternal abyss.

[18]Milton, "the third among the sons of light" (l. 36) after Homer and Dante. Milton is a political as well as a poetic hero to Shelley and Byron.

Blind, old, and lonely, when his country's pride,
The priest, the slave, and the liberticide,[19]
Trampled and mocked with many a loathèd rite
Of lust and blood; he went, unterrified,
Into the gulf of death; but his clear Sprite
Yet reigns o'er earth; the third among the sons of light.

V

Most musical of mourners, weep anew!
Not all to that bright station dared to climb;
And happier they their happiness who knew,
Whose tapers yet burn through that night of time
In which suns perished; others more sublime,
Struck by the envious wrath of man or god,
Have sunk, extinct in their refulgent prime;
And some yet live, treading the thorny road,
Which leads, through toil and hate, to Fame's serene abode.

VI

But now, thy youngest, dearest one, has perished—
The nursling of thy widowhood, who grew,
Like a pale flower by some sad maiden cherished,
And fed with true-love tears, instead of dew;
Most musical of mourners, weep anew!
Thy extreme[20] hope, the loveliest and the last.
The bloom, whose petals nipped before they blew[21]
Died on the promise of the fruit, is waste;
The broken lily lies—the storm is overpast.

VII

To that high Capital,[22] where kingly Death
Keeps his pale court[23] in beauty and decay,
He came; and bought, with price of purest breath,
A grave among the eternal.—Come away!

[19]One who kills or destroys liberty; see "England in 1819" (p. 79).
[20]Last; final.
[21]Bloomed.
[22]Rome.
[23]The Protestant Cemetery.

Haste, while the vault of blue Italian day
Is yet his fitting charnel-roof! while still
He lies, as if in dewy sleep he lay;
Awake him not! surely he takes his fill
Of deep and liquid rest, forgetful of all ill.

VIII

He will awake no more, oh, never more!—
Within the twilight chamber spreads apace
The shadow of white Death, and at the door
Invisible Corruption waits to trace
His extreme way to her dim dwelling-place;
The eternal Hunger[24] sits, but pity and awe
Soothe her pale rage, nor dares she to deface
So fair a prey, till darkness, and the law
Of change, shall o'er his sleep the mortal curtain draw.

IX

Oh, weep for Adonais!—The quick Dreams,
The passion-wingèd Ministers of thought,
Who were his flocks, whom near the living streams
Of his young spirit he fed, and whom he taught
The love which was its music, wander not,—
Wander no more, from kindling brain to brain,
But droop there, whence they sprung; and mourn their lot
Round the cold heart, where, after their sweet pain,
They ne'er will gather strength, or find a home again.

X

And one[25] with trembling hands clasps his cold head,
And fans him with her moonlight wings, and cries;
"Our love, our hope, our sorrow, is not dead;
See, on the silken fringe of his faint eyes,
Like dew upon a sleeping flower, there lies
A tear some Dream has loosened from his brain."
Lost Angel of a ruined Paradise!
She knew not 'twas her own; as with no stain
She faded, like a cloud which had outwept its rain.

[24]Death as devourer.
[25]Of the Dreams.

XI

One from a lucid urn of starry dew
Washed his light limbs as if embalming[26] them;
Another clipped her profuse locks, and threw
The wreath upon him, like an anadem,[27]
Which frozen tears instead of pearls begem;
Another in her wilful grief would break
Her bow and wingèd reeds,[28] as if to stem
A greater loss with one which was more weak;
And dull the barbèd fire against his frozen cheek.

XII

Another Splendour on his mouth alit,[29]
That mouth, whence it was wont to draw the breath
Which gave it strength to pierce the guarded wit,
And pass into the panting heart beneath
With lightning and with music: the damp death
Quenched its caress upon his icy lips;
And, as a dying meteor stains a wreath
Of moonlight vapour, which the cold night clips,[30]
It flushed through his pale limbs, and passed to its eclipse.

XIII

And others came . . . Desires and Adorations,
Wingèd Persuasions and veiled Destinies,
Splendours, and Glooms, and glimmering Incarnations
Of hopes and fears, and twilight Phantasies;
And Sorrow, with her family of Sighs,
And Pleasure, blind with tears, led by the gleam
Of her own dying smile instead of eyes,
Came in slow pomp;—the moving pomp might seem
Like pageantry of mist on an autumnal stream.

[26]Not only funereal but soothing and honoring.
[27]Head-garland.
[28]Arrows.
[29]Keats's poetry.
[30]Embraces; cuts off; eclipses.

XIV

All he had loved, and moulded into thought,
From shape, and hue, and odour, and sweet sound,
Lamented Adonais. Morning sought
Her eastern watch-tower, and her hair unbound,
Wet with the tears which should adorn the ground,
Dimmed the aëreal eyes that kindle day;
Afar the melancholy thunder moaned,
Pale Ocean in unquiet slumber lay,
And the wild Winds flew round, sobbing in their dismay.

XV

Lost Echo sits amid the voiceless mountains,
And feeds her grief with his remembered lay,
And will no more reply to winds or fountains,
Or amorous birds perched on the young green spray,
Or herdsman's horn, or bell at closing day;
Since she can mimic not his lips, more dear
Than those for whose disdain she pined away
Into a shadow of all sounds:[31]—a drear
Murmur, between their songs, is all the woodmen hear.

XVI

Grief made the young Spring wild, and she threw down
Her kindling buds, as if she Autumn were,
Or they dead leaves; since her delight is flown,
For whom should she have waked the sullen year?
To Phoebus was not Hyacinth so dear[32]
Nor to himself Narcissus, as to both
Thou, Adonais: wan they stand and sere[33]
Amid the faint companions of their youth,
With dew all turned to tears; odour, to sighing ruth.[34]

---

[31]For rejecting Echo, Narcissus was cursed to fall in love with his own reflection; he pined to death and was transformed into a flower.

[32]Phoebus Apollo, god of the sun, loved Hyacinth, whom jealous Zyphyrus, god of the west wind, killed. Apollo turned Hyacinth's blood into a flower and placed his body among the constellations.

[33]Dry; withered.

[34](Is turned to) sighing distress.

XVII

Thy spirit's sister, the lorn nightingale[35]
Mourns not her mate with such melodious pain;
Not so the eagle, who like thee could scale
Heaven, and could nourish in the sun's domain
Her mighty youth with morning, doth complain,
Soaring and screaming round her empty nest,
As Albion[36] wails for thee: the curse of Cain[37]
Light on his head who pierced thy innocent breast,
And scared the angel soul that was its earthly guest!

XVIII

Ah, woe is me! Winter is come and gone,
But grief returns with the revolving year;
The airs and streams renew their joyous tone;
The ants, the bees, the swallows reappear;
Fresh leaves and flowers deck the dead Seasons' bier;[38]
The amorous birds now pair in every brake,[39]
And build their mossy homes in field and brere;[40]
And the green lizard, and the golden snake,
Like unimprisoned flames, out of their trance[41] awake.

XIX

Through wood and stream and field and hill and Ocean
A quickening life from the Earth's heart has burst
As it has ever done, with change and motion,
From the great morning of the world when first
God dawned on Chaos;[42] in its stream immersed,
The lamps[43] of Heaven flash with a softer light;
All baser things pant with life's sacred thirst;

[35]In Keats's *Ode to a Nightingale*, the nightingale sings from exquisite happiness, not the traditional pain and sorrow.

[36]Mythic name for England.

[37]The fratricide cursed by God (Genesis 4.10–15).

[38]Coffin platform.

[39]Thicket.

[40]Briar.

[41]Hibernation.

[42]The first state of Creation (Genesis 1.3–5).

[43]Stars.

Diffuse themselves; and spend in love's delight,
The beauty and the joy of their renewèd might.

XX

The leprous corpse, touched by this spirit tender,
Exhales itself in flowers of gentle breath;
Like incarnations of the stars, when splendour
Is changed to fragrance, they illumine death
And mock the merry worm that wakes beneath;
Nought we know, dies. Shall that alone which knows[44]
Be as a sword consumed before the sheath
By sightless[45] lightning?—the intense atom glows
A moment, then is quenched in a most cold repose.

XXI

Alas! that all we loved of him should be,
But for our grief, as if it had not been,
And grief itself be mortal! Woe is me!
Whence are we, and why are we? of what scene
The actors or spectators? Great and mean
Meet massed in death, who lends what life must borrow.
As long as skies are blue, and fields are green,
Evening must usher night, night urge the morrow,
Month follow month with woe, and year wake year to sorrow.

XXII

He will awake no more, oh, never more!
"Wake thou," cried Misery, "childless Mother, rise
Out of thy sleep, and slake,[46] in thy heart's core,
A wound more fierce than his, with tears and sighs."
And all the Dreams that watched Urania's eyes,
And all the Echoes whom their sister's[47] song
Had held in holy silence, cried: "Arise!"
Swift as a Thought by the snake Memory stung,
From her[48] ambrosial rest the fading Splendour sprung.

[44]The mind.
[45]Invisible; unseeing.
[46]Soothe.
[47]Echo's.
[48]Urnaia's.

XXIII

She rose like an autumnal Night, that springs
Out of the East, and follows wild and drear
The golden Day, which, on eternal wings,
Even as a ghost[49] abandoning a bier,
Had left the Earth a corpse. Sorrow and fear
So[50] struck, so roused, so rapped Urania;
So saddened round her like an atmosphere
Of stormy mist; so swept her on her way
Even to the mournful place where Adonais lay.

XXIV

Out of her secret Paradise she sped,
Through camps and cities rough with stone, and steel,
And human hearts, which to her aery tread
Yielding not, wounded the invisible
Palms[51] of her tender feet where'er they fell:
And barbèd tongues, and thoughts more sharp than they,
Rent the soft Form they never could repel,
Whose sacred blood, like the young tears of May,
Paved with eternal flowers that undeserving way.

XXV

In the death-chamber for a moment Death,
Shamed by the presence of that living Might,
Blushed to annihilation, and the breath
Revisited those[52] lips, and Life's pale light
Flashed through those limbs, so late[53] her dear delight.
"Leave me not wild and drear and comfortless,
As silent lightning leaves the starless night!
Leave me not!" cried Urania: her distress
Roused Death: Death rose and smiled, and met her vain caress.

[49]Spirit, soul.
[50]Thus; intensely.
[51]Soles.
[52]Adonais's.
[53]Recently, lately.

XXVI

Stay yet awhile! speak to me once again;
Kiss me, so long but as a kiss may live;
And in my heartless[54] breast and burning brain
That word, that kiss, shall all thoughts else survive,
With food of saddest memory kept alive,
Now thou art dead, as if it were a part
Of thee, my Adonais! I would give
All that I am to be as thou now art!
But I am chained to Time, and cannot thence depart!

XXVII

O gentle child, beautiful as thou wert,
Why didst thou leave the trodden paths of men
Too soon, and with weak hands though mighty heart
Dare the unpastured dragon in his den?[55]
Defenceless as thou wert, oh, where was then
Wisdom the mirrored shield,[56] or scorn the spear?
Or hadst thou waited the full cycle, when
Thy spirit should have filled its crescent[57] sphere,
The monsters of life's waste had fled from thee like deer.

XXVIII

The herded wolves, bold only to pursue;
The obscene ravens, clamorous o'er the dead;
The vultures to the conqueror's banner true
Who feed where Desolation first has fed,
And whose wings rain contagion;—how they fled,
When, like Apollo, from his golden bow
The Pythian of the age[58] one arrow sped
And smiled!—The spoilers tempt no second blow,
They fawn on the proud feet that spurn them lying low.

---

[54]Not unfeeling, but lovelorn.

[55]Hostile critics.

[56]In Greek myth, the gorgon Medusa's stare can turn men to stone. Perseus borrowed the shiny shield of Athena (Wisdom) and slew Medusa, whose image he saw reflected there.

[57]The moon's full phase.

[58]Byron skewers his critics as Apollo slew Python.

XXIX

The sun comes forth, and many reptiles spawn;
He sets, and each ephemeral[59] insect then
Is gathered into death without a dawn,
And the immortal stars awake again;
So is it in the world of living men:
A godlike mind soars forth, in its delight
Making earth bare and veiling heaven, and when
It sinks, the swarms that dimmed or shared its light
Leave to its kindred lamps[60] the spirit's awful night."

XXX

Thus ceased she: and the mountain shepherds came,[61]
Their garlands sere, their magic mantles rent;
The Pilgrim of Eternity,[62] whose fame
Over his living head like Heaven is bent,
An early but enduring monument,
Came, veiling all the lightnings of his song
In sorrow; from her wilds Ierne sent
The sweetest lyrist of her saddest wrong,
And Love taught Grief to fall like music from his tongue.[63]

XXXI

Midst others of less note, came one frail Form,[64]
A phantom among men; companionless
As the last cloud of an expiring storm
Whose thunder is its knell; he, as I guess,
Had gazed on Nature's naked loveliness,
Actaeon-like,[65] and now he fled astray
With feeble steps o'er the world's wilderness,
And his own thoughts, along that rugged way,
Pursued, like raging hounds, their father and their prey.

[59]Living for one day.

[60]Lamps: stars; awful: awe-inspiring.

[61]In elegies, consolation often begins with the dead's grieving peers' visit.

[62]Byron.

[63]Thomas Moore, Irish ("Ierne") author of popular and politically tuned *Irish Melodies* (1808–34).

[64]Shelley.

[65]In Greek mythology, hunter Actaeon was punished for seeing Diana bathing naked: turned into a stag, he was torn to pieces by his own hounds.

XXXII

A pardlike[66] Spirit beautiful and swift—
A Love in desolation masked;—a Power
Girt round with weakness;—it can scarce uplift
The weight of the superincumbent[67] hour;
It is a dying lamp, a falling shower,
A breaking billow;—even whilst we speak
Is it not broken? On the withering flower
The killing sun smiles brightly: on a cheek
The life can burn in blood, even while the heart may break.

XXXIII

His head was bound with pansies overblown,
And faded violets, white, and pied, and blue;
And a light spear topped with a cypress cone,
Round whose rude shaft dark ivy-tresses grew[68]
Yet dripping with the forest's noonday dew,
Vibrated, as the ever-beating heart
Shook the weak hand that grasped it; of that crew
He came the last, neglected and apart;
A herd-abandoned deer struck by the hunter's dart.

XXXIV

All stood aloof, and at his partial[69] moan
Smiled through their tears; well knew that gentle band
Who in another's fate now wept his own,
As in the accents of an unknown land
He sung new sorrow; sad Urania scanned
The Stranger's mien, and murmured: "Who art thou?"
He answered not, but with a sudden hand
Made bare his branded and ensanguined brow,
Which was like Cain's or Christ's[70]—oh! that it should be so!

[66]Leopard-like.

[67]Overhanging.

[68]The cypress cone symbolizes mourning, but the pine-cone-tipped *thyrsus* (staff) is associated with Dionysus, the god of feeling.

[69]Favoring one side or party.

[70]The reviews expressed outrage at Shelley's equation of these two sufferers: the first murderer and the savior of mankind—as well as at Shelley's presumption in comparing Cain's tortures to Christ's.

XXXV

What softer voice is hushed over the dead?
Athwart what brow is that dark mantle thrown?
What form leans sadly o'er the white death-bed,
In mockery of monumental stone,[71]
The heavy heart heaving without a moan?
If it be He,[72] who, gentlest of the wise,
Taught, soothed, loved, honoured the departed one,
Let me not vex, with inharmonious sighs,
The silence of that heart's accepted sacrifice.

XXXVI

Our Adonais has drunk poison—oh!
What deaf and viperous murderer could crown
Life's early cup with such a draught of woe?
The nameless worm[73] would now itself disown:
It felt, yet could escape, the magic tone
Whose prelude held all envy, hate, and wrong,
But what was howling in one breast alone,
Silent with expectation of the song,
Whose master's hand is cold, whose silver lyre unstrung.

XXXVII

Live thou, whose infamy is not thy fame!
Live! fear no heavier chastisement from me,
Thou noteless[74] blot on a remembered name!
But be thyself, and know thyself to be!
And ever at thy season be thou free
To spill the venom when thy fangs o'erflow:
Remorse and Self-contempt shall cling to thee;
Hot Shame shall burn upon thy secret brow,
And like a beaten hound tremble thou shalt—as now.

[71]Like a funerary sculpture, but mocking because not dead.

[72]Leigh Hunt, steadfast supporter of Keats, target of much conservative invective for championing liberal causes and castigating British monarchy.

[73]The *Quarterly*'s anonymous reviewer.

[74]Of no note; doomed to obscurity; anonymous.

XXXVIII

Nor let us weep that our delight is fled
Far from these carrion kites[75] that scream below;
He wakes or sleeps with the enduring dead;
Thou canst not soar where he is sitting now.[76]
Dust to the dust![77] but the pure spirit shall flow
Back to the burning fountain whence it came,
A portion of the Eternal, which must glow
Through time and change, unquenchably the same,
Whilst thy cold embers choke the sordid hearth of shame.[78]

XXXIX

Peace, peace! he is not dead, he doth not sleep—
He hath awakened from the dream of life—
'Tis we, who lost in stormy visions, keep
With phantoms an unprofitable strife,
And in mad trance, strike with our spirit's knife
Invulnerable nothings.—We decay
Like corpses in a charnel; fear and grief
Convulse us and consume us day by day,
And cold hopes swarm like worms within our living clay.

XL

He has outsoared the shadow of our night;
Envy and calumny and hate and pain,
And that unrest which men miscall delight,
Can touch him not and torture not again;
From the contagion of the world's slow stain
He is secure, and now can never mourn
A heart grown cold, a head grown gray in vain;
Nor, when the spirit's self has ceased to burn,
With sparkless ashes load an unlamented urn.

---

[75]Hawk-like predatory birds.

[76]Satan rebuked the angels Ithuriel and Zephon for failing to recognize in him the angel who once sat where they dared not soar (*PL* 4.828–29). "Wakes or sleeps" (l. 336) reflects Shelley's uncertainty about eternal life.

[77]Leave the body to the earth.

[78]Keats's immortality is in his poetry, and in his becoming "one with Nature" (l. 370) he achieves transcendence to Eternity.

XLI

He lives, he wakes—'tis Death is dead,[79] not he;
Mourn not for Adonais.—Thou young Dawn,
Turn all thy dew to splendour, for from thee
The spirit thou lamentest is not gone;
Ye caverns and ye forests, cease to moan!
Cease, ye faint flowers and fountains, and thou Air,
Which like a mourning veil thy scarf hadst thrown
O'er the abandoned Earth, now leave it bare
Even to the joyous stars which smile on its despair!

XLII

He is made one with Nature: there is heard
His voice in all her music, from the moan
Of thunder, to the song of night's sweet bird;[80]
He is a presence to be felt and known
In darkness and in light, from herb and stone,
Spreading itself where'er that Power may move
Which has withdrawn his being to its own;
Which wields the world with never-wearied love,
Sustains it from beneath, and kindles it above.

XLIII

He is a portion of the loveliness
Which once he made more lovely: he doth bear
His part, while the one Spirit's plastic[81] stress
Sweeps through the dull dense world, compelling there,
All new successions to the forms they wear;
Torturing th'unwilling dross that checks its flight
To its own likeness, as each mass may bear;
And bursting in its beauty and its might
From trees and beasts and men into the Heaven's light.

---

[79]Allusion to John Donne's *Holy Sonnet 6* ("Death be not proud," c. 1611): "And death shall be no more. Death thou shalt die" (l. 14).

[80]Keats's *Hyperion* (the fallen thunder god) and his *Ode to a Nightingale*.

[81]Pliant.

XLIV

The splendours of the firmament of time[82]
May be eclipsed, but are extinguished not;
Like stars to their appointed height they climb,
And death is a low mist which cannot blot
The brightness it may veil. When lofty thought
Lifts a young heart above its mortal lair,
And love and life contend in it, for what
Shall be its earthly doom, the dead live there
And move like winds of light on dark and stormy air.

XLV

The inheritors of unfulfilled renown[83]
Rose from their thrones, built beyond mortal thought,
Far in the Unapparent. Chatterton
Rose pale,—his solemn agony had not
Yet faded from him; Sidney, as he fought
And as he fell and as he lived and loved
Sublimely mild, a Spirit without spot,
Arose; and Lucan, by his death approved:
Oblivion as they rose shrank like a thing reproved.

XLVI

And many more, whose names on Earth are dark,
But whose transmitted effluence[84] cannot die
So long as fire outlives the parent spark,
Rose, robed in dazzling immortality.
"Thou art become as one of us," they cry,
"It was for thee yon kingless[85] sphere has long
Swung blind in unascended majesty,
Silent alone amid an Heaven of Song.
Assume thy wingèd throne, thou Vesper[86] of our throng!"

[82]Stars.

[83]Those who died before achieving the fame they deserved. The young genius Thomas Chatterton (1752–70) poisoned himself at 17; the heroic and famously unselfish Sir Philip Sidney (1554–86); one of Shelley's favorite Roman republican poets, Lucan (39–65), committed suicide.

[84]Outflowing light or power.

[85]Awaiting its king; or a world without kings (a republican Eternity).

[86]The evening star, Hesperus.

XLVII

Who mourns for Adonais? Oh, come forth,
Fond[87] wretch! and know thyself and him aright.
Clasp with thy panting soul the pendulous Earth;[88]
As from a centre, dart thy spirit's light
Beyond all worlds, until its spacious might
Satiate the void circumference: then shrink
Even to a point within our day and night;
And keep thy heart light lest it make thee sink
When hope has kindled hope, and lured thee to the brink.

XLVIII

Or go to Rome, which is the sepulchre,
Oh, not of him, but of our joy:[89] 'tis nought
That ages, empires, and religions there
Lie buried in the ravage they[90] have wrought;
For such as he can lend,—they borrow not
Glory from those who made the world their prey;
And he is gathered to the kings of thought
Who waged contention with their time's decay,
And of the past are all that cannot pass away.

XLIX

Go thou to Rome,—at once the Paradise,
The grave, the city, and the wilderness;
And where its wrecks like shattered mountains rise,
And flowering weeds, and fragrant copses dress
The bones of Desolation's nakedness
Pass, till the spirit of the spot shall lead
Thy footsteps to a slope of green access
Where, like an infant's smile, over the dead
A light of laughing flowers along the grass is spread;

---

[87]Foolish or dotingly unthinking.

[88]Suspended in space, as in *PL*: "The pendulous round Earth with balanc't Aire / In counterpoise" (4.1000–1001).

[89]The English cemetery at Rome, where Shelley's son William is buried, and where Keats is, too. Shelley will join them.

[90]Religious and civic leaders who "ravage" the mortal world, unlike "the kings of thought" (l. 430) whose lives and works are eternal and glorious.

L

And gray walls moulder round, on which dull Time
Feeds, like slow fire upon a hoary brand;[91]
And one keen pyramid[92] with wedge sublime,
Pavilioning the dust of him who planned
This refuge for his memory, doth stand
Like flame transformed to marble; and beneath,
A field is spread, on which a newer band
Have pitched in Heaven's smile their camp of death,[93]
Welcoming him we lose with scarce extinguished breath.

LI

Here pause: these graves are all too young as yet
To have outgrown the sorrow which consigned
Its charge to each; and if the seal is set,
Here, on one fountain of a mourning mind,[94]
Break it not thou! too surely shalt thou find
Thine own well full, if thou returnest home,
Of tears and gall. From the world's bitter wind[95]
Seek shelter in the shadow of the tomb.
What Adonais is, why fear we to become?

LII

The One remains, the many change and pass;
Heaven's light forever shines, Earth's shadows fly;[96]
Life, like a dome of many-coloured glass,
Stains[97] the white radiance of Eternity,
Until Death tramples it to fragments.[98]—Die,
If thou wouldst be with that which thou dost seek!
Follow where all is fled!—Rome's azure sky,

---

[91] Ash-covered ember.

[92] The tomb of the Roman tribune Caius Cestius in this cemetery.

[93] In Italian *campo santi* (sacred field) is the word for cemetery.

[94] Shelley's grief over his buried son.

[95] The evil air (mal-aria) that killed William Shelley.

[96] Flee.

[97] Colors, refracts, discolors, degrades.

[98] The atmosphere refracts the sun's "white" light into prismatic colors even as the Eternal One is diffused into "the many" mortal beings. Death restores unity.

Flowers, ruins, statues, music, words, are weak
The glory they transfuse with fitting truth to speak.

LIII

Why linger, why turn back, why shrink, my Heart?
Thy hopes are gone before:[99] from all things here
They have departed; thou shouldst now depart!
A light is passed from the revolving year,
And man, and woman; and what still is dear
Attracts to crush, repels to make thee wither.
The soft sky smiles,—the low wind whispers near:
'Tis Adonais calls! oh, hasten thither,
No more let Life divide what Death can join together.[100]

LIV

That Light whose smile kindles the Universe,
That Beauty in which all things work and move,
That Benediction which the eclipsing Curse
Of birth can quench not, that sustaining Love
Which through the web of being blindly wove
By man and beast and earth and air and sea,
Burns bright or dim, as each are mirrors of
The fire for which all thirst; now beams on me,
Consuming the last clouds of cold mortality.

LV

The breath whose might I have invoked in song
Descends on me; my spirit's bark is driven,
Far from the shore, far from the trembling throng
Whose sails were never to the tempest given;
The massy earth and spherèd skies are riven!
I am borne darkly, fearfully, afar;
Whilst, burning through the inmost veil of Heaven,
The soul of Adonais, like a star,[101]
Beacons from the abode where the Eternal are.

[99]Gone ahead; departed (like Shelley's hopes for happiness and fame).

[100]Ironic inversion of the wedding service's command, "What God has joined together let no man put asunder."

[101]Adonais's soul is a navigational star, beaconing (and beckoning) the poet toward Eternity. *Borne* puns on *born*—the rebirth into Eternity; "a star" echoes "Aster," Plato's beloved. Wordsworth figured Milton as a star ("thy soul was like a star"), and Keats used the star prominently in his sonnet "Bright Star."

Lines Written on Hearing the News of the Death of Napoleon

Written in summer 1821 and published with "Hellas." After Waterloo, Napoleon was exiled to the remote southern Atlantic island of St. Helena, where he died on 5 May 1821. Many of Shelley's friends admired Napoleon for destroying the feudal establishment in Spain, Italy, and Germany, but Shelley felt he had corrupted, then destroyed, the French Revolution's republican principles.

What! alive and so bold, O Earth?
    Art thou not overbold?
    What! leapest thou forth as of old
In the light of thy morning mirth,
The last of the flock of the starry fold?[1]   5
Ha! leapest thou forth as of old?
Are not the limbs still when the ghost is fled,
And canst thou move, Napoleon being dead?

How! is not thy quick heart cold?
    What spark is alive on thy hearth?   10
How! is not *his* death-knell knolled?[2]
    And livest *thou* still, Mother Earth?
Thou wert warming thy fingers old
O'er the embers covered and cold
Of that most fiery spirit, when it fled—   15
What, Mother, do you laugh now he is dead?

"Who has known me of old," replied Earth,
    "Or who has my story told?
    It is thou who art overbold."
And the lightning of scorn laughed forth   20
As she sung, "To my bosom I fold
All my sons when their knell is knolled,
And so with living motion all are fed,
And the quick spring like weeds out of the dead.

Still alive and still bold," shouted Earth,   25
    "I grow bolder and still more bold.

[1]The poem is a dialogue with Earth, reborn in her original form as the last-created planet (l. 5). Like *Prometheus Unbound* and "The Sensitive-Plant," the poem explores whether the death of any individual alters Nature's eternal condition. A common theme in the period is the individual's insignificance in relation to the universe; *cf.* "Ozymandias."
[2]Tolled.

The dead fill me ten thousandfold
Fuller of speed, and splendour, and mirth.
I was cloudy, and sullen, and cold,
Like a frozen chaos uprolled,   30
Till by the spirit of the mighty dead
My heart grew warm. I feed on whom I fed.[3]

Ay, alive and still bold," muttered Earth,
    "Napoleon's fierce spirit rolled,
        In terror and blood and gold,   35
A torrent of ruin to death from his birth.
Leave the millions who follow to mould
The metal before it be cold;
And weave into his shame, which like the dead
Shrouds me, the hopes that from his glory fled."[4]   40

from *A Defence of Poetry*
or, Remarks Suggested by an Essay Entitled "The Four Ages of Poetry"

In late 1820 Ollier's Literary Miscellany *published "The Four Ages of Poetry," an essay by Shelley's friend Thomas Love Peacock. Shelley read it in Italy in mid-February 1821 and by 20 March had sent the first part of his response to Charles Ollier, intending two more sections. But* Miscellany *failed after that one issue, and Shelley's essay remained unpublished until Mary Shelley published it in 1840, removing the most specific references to Peacock's* Four Ages. *Peacock's essay argues that the imaginative arts always decline in an age dominated by science and empiricism. He traces this decline through four "ages" of civilization (Iron, Golden, Silver, Brass), the last, a modern age so corrupt that it reverts to the barbarism of the Age of Iron, even as it imagines that it is reviving the Golden Age. Modern poetry is populated by egoists such as Wordsworth, fantasy-tale tellers such as Byron and Scott—all irrelevant in a world of scientific and industrial progress.*

Shelley argued for the durable power of art, especially poetry. His Defence *reflects his reading of Plato (especially* Ion *and* Symposium, *both of which he translated), Sidney's* Apology for Poetry *(1595), and Dr.*

[3]In consuming the dead she produced, Earth is fortified, drawing strength, warmth, and joy from "the mighty dead" who labored in life to help mankind.

[4]Napoleon disappointed Earth and mankind by abandoning liberty's cause ("hopes") for despotism.

Johnson's Rasselas, Prince of Abysinnia *(1759), along with a wide, eclectic reading across literature, criticism, history, philosophy, economics, and science. Shelley argues that poetry is a moral literature propelling its readers beyond self-interest into sympathy with others. Poetry joins humanity in its visionary ideals, its inspiration by ideal truths, and so renovates us by showing familiar realities in previously unapprehended ways. Shelley's essay combines a dense texture of literary references with striking metaphors drawn from the natural world. He likens the poet's mind to a fading ember as the poet moves from inspiration to composition in inadequate words. Even so, Shelley argues, poetry still has force in its advocacy of liberty—political, intellectual, visionary. Thus his famous last sentence, "Poets are the unacknowledged legislators of the World."*

According to one mode of regarding those two classes of mental action, which are called reason and imagination, the former may be considered as mind contemplating the relations borne by one thought to another, however produced; and the latter as mind acting upon those thoughts so as to colour them with its own light, and composing from them as from elements, other thoughts, each containing within itself the principle of its own integrity. The one is the τὸ ποιεῖν, or the principle of synthesis, and has for its object those forms which are common to universal nature and existence itself; the other is the λογιζειν,[1] or principle of analysis, and its action regards the relations of things, simply as relations; considering thoughts, not in their integral unity, but as the algebraical representations which conduct to certain general results. Reason is the enumeration of quantities already known; Imagination the perception of the value of those quantities, both separately and as a whole. Reason respects the differences, and Imagination the similitudes of things. Reason is to Imagination as the instrument to the agent, as the body to the spirit, as the shadow to the substance.

Poetry, in a general sense, may be defined to be "the expression of the Imagination": and poetry is connate[2] with the origin of man. Man is an instrument over which a series of external and internal impressions are driven, like the alternations of an ever-changing wind over an Æolian lyre,[3] which move it by their motion to ever-changing melody. But there is a principle within the human being, and perhaps within all sentient beings, which acts otherwise than in the lyre, and

---

[1]"Making" and "reasoning."

[2]Born with.

[3]Wind harp.

produces not melody alone, but harmony, by an internal adjustment of the sounds and motions thus excited to the impressions which excite them. It is as if the lyre could accommodate its chords to the motions of that which strikes them, in a determined proportion of sound; even as the musician can accommodate his voice to the sound of the lyre. A child at play by itself will express its delight by its voice and motions; and every inflexion of tone and gesture will bear exact relation to a corresponding antitype in the pleasurable impressions which awakened it; it will be the reflected image of that impression; and as the lyre trembles and sounds after the wind has died away, so the child seeks, by prolonging in its voice and motions the duration of the effect, to prolong also a consciousness of the cause. In relation to the objects which delight a child, these expressions are, what Poetry is to higher objects. The savage (for the savage is to ages what the child is to years) expresses the emotions produced in him by surrounding objects in a similar manner; and language and gesture, together with plastic[4] or pictorial imitation, become the image of the combined effect of those objects and his apprehension of them. Man in society, with all his passions and his pleasures, next becomes the object of the passions and pleasures of man; an additional class of emotions produces an augmented treasure of expressions; and language, gesture, and the imitative arts, become at once the representation and the medium, the pencil and the picture, the chisel and the statue, the chord and the harmony. The social sympathies, or those laws from which as from its elements society results, begin to develope themselves from the moment that two human beings coexist; the future is contained within the present as the plant within the seed; and equality, diversity, unity, contrast, mutual dependence become the principles alone capable of affording the motives according to which the will of a social being is determined to action, inasmuch as he is social; and constitute pleasure in sensation, virtue in sentiment, beauty in art, truth in reasoning, and love in the intercourse of kind. Hence men, even in the infancy of society, observe a certain order in their words and actions, distinct from that of the objects and the impressions represented by them, all expression being subject to the laws of that from which it proceeds. But let us dismiss those more general considerations which might involve an inquiry into the principles of society itself, and restrict our view to the manner in which the imagination is expressed upon its forms.

[4]Sculpture.

In the youth of the world, men dance and sing and imitate natural objects, observing in these actions, as in all others, a certain rhythm or order. And, although all men observe a similar, they observe not the same order, in the motions of the dance, in the melody of the song, in the combinations of language, in the series of their imitations of natural objects. For there is a certain order or rhythm belonging to each of these classes of mimetic[5] representation, from which the hearer and the spectator receive an intenser and purer pleasure than from any other: the sense of an approximation to this order has been called taste by modern writers. Every man in the infancy of art, observes an order which approximates more or less closely to that from which this highest delight results: but the diversity is not sufficiently marked, as that its gradations should be sensible, except in those instances where the predominance of this faculty of approximation to the beautiful (for so we may be permitted to name the relation between this highest pleasure and its cause) is very great. Those in whom it exists to excess are poets, in the most universal sense of the word; and the pleasure resulting from the manner in which they express the influence of society or nature upon their own minds, communicates itself to others, and gathers a sort of reduplication from that community. Their language is vitally metaphorical; that is, it marks the before unapprehended relations of things, and perpetuates their apprehension, until the words which represent them, become through time signs for portions or classes of thoughts instead of pictures of integral thoughts; [. . .] In the infancy of society every author is necessarily a poet, because language itself is poetry; and to be a poet is to apprehend the true and the beautiful, in a word the good which exists in the relation, subsisting, first between existence and perception, and secondly between perception and expression. [. . .]

But Poets, or those who imagine and express this indestructible order, are not only the authors of language and of music, of the dance and architecture and statuary and painting; they are the institutors of laws and the founders of civil society and the inventors of the arts of life and the teachers, who draw into a certain propinquity[6] with the beautiful and the true that partial apprehension of the agencies of the invisible world which is called religion. Hence all original religions are allegorical or susceptible of allegory, and like Janus[7] have a double

[5]Aristotle called *mimesis* (imitation) the basis of art (*Poetics*).
[6]Proximity.
[7]Roman god of beginnings and endings (cf. January).

face of false and true. Poets, according to the circumstances of the age and nation in which they appeared, were called in the earlier epochs of the world legislators or prophets:[8] a poet essentially comprises and unites both these characters. For he not only beholds intensely the present as it is, and discovers those laws according to which present things ought to be ordered, but he beholds the future in the present, and his thoughts are the germs of the flower and the fruit of latest time. Not that I assert poets to be prophets in the gross sense of the word, or that they can foretell the form as surely as they foreknow the spirit of events: such is the pretence of superstition, which would make poetry an attribute of prophecy, rather than prophecy an attribute of poetry. A Poet participates in the eternal, the infinite and the one; as far as relates to his conceptions, time and place and number are not. [. . .]

We have thus circumscribed the word Poetry within the limits of that art which is the most familiar and the most perfect expression of the faculty itself. [. . .] The distinction between poets and prose writers is a vulgar error. The distinction between philosophers and poets has been anticipated. Plato was essentially a poet—the truth and splendour of his imagery and the melody of his language is the most intense that it is possible to conceive. He rejected the measure of the epic, dramatic, and lyrical forms, because he sought to kindle a harmony in thoughts divested of shape and action, and he forbore to invent any regular plan of rhythm which would include, under determinate forms, the varied pauses of his style. Cicero[9] sought to imitate the cadence of his periods but with little success. Lord Bacon was a poet.[10] His language has a sweet and majestic rhythm, which satisfies the sense, no less than the almost superhuman wisdom of his philosophy satisfies the intellect; it is a strain which distends, and then bursts the circumference of the reader's mind, and pours itself forth together with it into the universal element with which it has perpetual sympathy. All the authors of revolutions in opinion are not only necessarily poets as they are inventors, nor even as their words unveil the permanent analogy of things by images which participate in the life of truth; but as their periods are harmonious and rhythmical and contain in themselves the elements of verse;

[8]In his *Defence of Poesie* (1595), Sidney translates *vates* (Roman for poets) as prophet; Shelley's term "legislator" refers to laws of human behavior.

[9]Roman statesman and orator, 1st c. BCE.

[10]"See the *Fillium Labyrinthi* and the *Essay on Death* particularly." [Shelley's note.] Bacon is best known as an essayist and scientist.

being the echo of the eternal music. Nor are those supreme poets, who have employed traditional forms of rhythm on account of the form and action of their subjects, less capable of perceiving and teaching the truth of things, than those who have omitted that form. Shakspeare, Dante and Milton (to confine ourselves to modern writers) are philosophers of the very loftiest power.

A Poem is the very image of life expressed in its eternal truth. There is this difference between a story and a poem, that a story is a catalogue of detached facts, which have no other connexion than time, place, circumstance, cause and effect; the other is the creation of actions according to the unchangeable forms of human nature, as existing in the mind of the creator, which is itself the image of all other minds.[11] The one is partial, and applies only to a definite period of time, and a certain combination of events which can never again recur; the other is universal, and contains within itself the germ of a relation to whatever motives or actions have place in the possible varieties of human nature. Time, which destroys the beauty and the use of the story of particular facts, stript of the poetry which should invest them, augments that of Poetry, and for ever developes new and wonderful applications of the eternal truth which it contains. Hence epitomes have been called the moths of just history; they eat out the poetry of it.[12] The story of particular facts is as a mirror which obscures and distorts that which should be beautiful: Poetry is a mirror which makes beautiful that which is distorted. [. . .]

Having determined what is poetry, and who are poets, let us proceed to estimate its effects upon society.

Poetry is ever accompanied with pleasure: all spirits upon which it falls, open themselves to receive the wisdom which is mingled with its delight. [. . .] A Poet is a nightingale who sits in darkness, and sings to cheer its own solitude with sweet sounds;[13] his auditors are as men entranced by the melody of an unseen musician, who feel that they are moved and softened, yet know not whence or why. The poems of Homer and his contemporaries were the delight of infant Greece; they were the elements of that social system which is the column upon which all succeeding civilisation has reposed. Homer embodied the ideal perfection of his age in human character; nor can we doubt that those who read his verses were awakened to an ambition

[11]A distinction made in Aristotle (*Poetics*).

[12]In *Advancement of Learning* Bacon called epitomes (mere summaries) "the moths of history" (3.2.4).

[13]See "To a Sky-Lark" (p. 228) and Keats's *Ode to a Nightingale*.

of becoming like to Achilles, Hector and Ulysses:[14] the truth and beauty of friendship, patriotism and persevering devotion to an object, were unveiled to the depths in these immortal creations: the sentiments of the auditors must have been refined and enlarged by a sympathy with such great and lovely impersonations, until from admiring they imitated, and from imitation they identified themselves with the objects of their admiration. Nor let it be objected, that these characters are remote from moral perfection, and that they can by no means to be considered as edifying patterns for general imitation. Every epoch under names more or less specious has deified its peculiar errors; Revenge is the naked Idol of the worship of a semi-barbarous age; and Self-deceit is the veiled Image of unknown evil before which luxury and satiety lie prostrate. But a poet considers the vices of his contemporaries as the temporary dress in which his creations must be arrayed, and which cover without concealing the eternal proportions of their beauty. An epic or dramatic personage is understood to wear them around his soul, as he may the antient armour or modern uniform around his body; whilst it is easy to conceive a dress more graceful than either. The beauty of the internal nature cannot be so far concealed by its accidental vesture, but that the spirit of its form shall communicate itself to the very disguise, and indicate the shape it hides from the manner in which it is worn. A majestic form and graceful motions will express themselves through the most barbarous and tasteless costume. [. . .]

The whole objection however of the immorality of poetry rests upon a misconception of the manner in which poetry acts to produce the moral improvement of man. Ethical science arranges the elements which poetry has created, and propounds schemes and proposes examples of civil and domestic life: nor is it for want of admirable doctrines that men hate, and despise, and censure, and deceive, and subjugate one another. But Poetry acts in another and diviner manner. It awakens and enlarges the mind itself by rendering it the receptacle of a thousand unapprehended combinations of thought. Poetry lifts the veil from the hidden beauty of the world, and makes familiar objects be as if they were not familiar; it reproduces all that it represents, and the impersonations clothed in its Elysian light[15] stand thence-forward in the minds of those who

---

[14]Heroes of Homer's Trojan war epic, *The Iliad*; Ulysses is hero of his *Odyssey*. As "the elements" of the Greek social system, Homer's poems embodied the exemplary values of Greek culture.

[15]The light of Eternity in the afterlife (Elysian Fields).

have once contemplated them, as memorials of that gentle and exalted content which extends itself over all thoughts and actions with which it coexists. The great secret of morals is Love; or a going out of our own nature, and an identification of ourselves with the beautiful which exists in thought, action, or person, not our own. A man, to be greatly good, must imagine intensely and comprehensively; he must put himself in the place of another and of many others; the pains and pleasures of his species must become his own. The great instrument of moral good is the imagination; and poetry administers to the effect by acting upon the cause. Poetry enlarges the circumference of the imagination by replenishing it with thoughts of ever new delight, which have the power of attracting and assimilating to their own nature all other thoughts, and which form new intervals and interstices whose void for ever craves fresh food. Poetry strengthens that faculty which is the organ of the moral nature of man, in the same manner as exercise strengthens a limb. [. . .] Our system of divesting the actor's face of a mask, on which the many expressions appropriated to his dramatic character might be moulded into one permanent and unchanging expression, is favourable only to a partial and inharmonious effect; it is fit for nothing but a monologue, where all the attention may be directed to some great master of ideal mimicry. The modern practice of blending comedy with tragedy, though liable to great abuse in point of practice, is undoubtedly an extension of the dramatic circle; but the comedy should be as in King Lear, universal, ideal and sublime.[16] [. . .]

—The Author of the Four Ages of Poetry has prudently omitted to dispute on the effect of the Drama upon life and manners. [. . .] The connexion of scenic exhibitions with the improvement or corruption of the manners of men, has been universally recognised: in other words, the presence or absence of poetry in its most perfect and universal form has been found to be connected with good and evil in conduct or habit. The corruption which has been imputed to the drama as an effect begins, when the poetry employed in its constitution ends: I appeal to the history of manners whether the periods of the growth of the one and the decline of the other have not corresponded with an exactness equal to any example of moral cause and effect.

The drama at Athens, or wheresoever else it may have approached to its perfection, coexisted with the moral and intellectual greatness of the age. The tragedies of the Athenian poets are as mir-

---

[16]Shakespeare's *King Lear* was unstageable in Shelley's day because of its mad king.

rors in which the spectator beholds himself, under a thin disguise of circumstance, stript of all but that ideal perfection and energy which every one feels to be the internal type of all that he loves, admires, and would become. The imagination is enlarged by a sympathy with pains and passions so mighty that they distend in their conception the capacity of that by which they are conceived; the good affections are strengthened by pity, indignation, terror and sorrow; and an exalted calm is prolonged from the satiety of this high exercise of them into the tumult of familiar life: even crime is disarmed of half its horror and all its contagion by being represented as the fatal consequence of the unfathomable agencies of nature; error is thus divested of its wilfulness; men can no longer cherish it as the creation of their choice. In a drama of the highest order there is little food for censure or hatred; it teaches rather self-knowledge and self-respect. Neither the eye nor the mind can see itself, unless reflected upon that which it resembles. The drama, so long as it continues to express poetry, is a prismatic and many-sided mirror, which collects the brightest rays of human nature and divides and reproduces them from the simplicity of these elementary forms, and touches them with majesty and beauty, and multiplies all that it reflects, and endows it with the power of propagating its like wherever it may fall. [. . .]

The drama being that form under which a greater number of modes of expression of poetry are susceptible of being combined than any other, the connexion of poetry and social good is more observable in the drama than in whatever other form: and it is indisputable that the highest perfection of human society has ever corresponded with the highest dramatic excellence; and that the corruption or the extinction of the drama in a nation where it has once flourished, is a mark of a corruption of manners, and an extinction of the energies which sustain the soul of social life. But, as Machiavelli[17] says of political institutions, that life may be preserved and renewed, if men should arise capable of bringing back the drama to its principles. And this is true with respect to poetry in its most extended sense: all language, institution and form, require not only to be produced but to be sustained: the office and character of a poet participates in the divine nature as regards providence, no less than as regards creation. [. . .]

---

[17]Politically pragmatic, often ruthless Florentine philosopher (1469–1527), famous for *The Prince*, also wrote comedies.

The same revolutions within a narrower sphere had place in antient Rome; but the actions and forms of its social life never seem to have been perfectly saturated with the poetical element. The Romans appear to have considered the Greeks as the selectest treasuries of the selectest forms of manners and of nature, and to have abstained from creating in measured language, sculpture, music or architecture, anything which might bear a particular relation to their own condition, whilst it should bear a general one to the universal constitution of the world. [. . . The] great writers of the Virgilian age saw man and nature in the mirror of Greece. The institutions also and the religion of Rome were less poetical than those of Greece, as the shadow is less vivid than the substance. Hence poetry in Rome, seemed to follow rather than accompany the perfection of political and domestic society. The true Poetry of Rome lived in its institutions; for whatever of beautiful, true and majestic they contained could have sprung only from the faculty which creates the order in which they consist. The life of Camillus, the death of Regulus; the expectation of the Senators, in their godlike state, of the victorious Gauls; the refusal of the Republic to make peace with Hannibal, after the battle of Cannæ,[18] were not the consequences of a refined calculation of the probable personal advantage to result from such a rhythm and order in the shows of life, to those who were at once the poets and the actors of these immortal dramas. The imagination beholding the beauty of this order, created it out of itself according to its own idea; the consequence was empire, and the reward ever-living fame. These things are not the less poetry, *quia carent vate sacro*.[19] They are the episodes of that cyclic poem written by Time upon the memories of men. The Past, like an inspired rhapsodist, fills the theatre of everlasting generations with their harmony.

At length the antient system of religion and manners had fulfilled the circle of its revolution. And the world would have fallen into utter anarchy and darkness, but that there were found poets among the authors of the Christian and Chivalric systems of manners and religion, who created forms of opinion and action never before conceived; which, copied into the imaginations of men, be-

---

[18]Roman soldier and statesman Camillus (c. 446–365 BCE); Roman general Regulus, captured and tortured to death in Carthage (c. 250 BCE); when the Gauls invaded Rome in 390 BCE, the senators sat so still that they were mistaken for statues. After Hannibal's armies conquered the village of Cannae (216 BCE), the Romans refused to surrender and eventually conquered Hannibal's Carthage.

[19]"Because they have no sacred bard" (Horace, *Odes* 9.28).

came as generals to the bewildered armies of their thoughts. It is foreign to the present purpose to touch upon the evil produced by these systems: except that we protest, on the ground of the principles already established, that no portion of it can be attributed to the poetry they contain.

It is probable that the poetry of Moses, Job, David, Solomon and Isaiah had produced a great effect upon the mind of Jesus and his disciples. The scattered fragments preserved to us by the biographers of this extraordinary person, are all instinct with the most vivid poetry. But his doctrines seem to have been quickly distorted. [. . .]

The poetry in the doctrines of Jesus Christ, and the mythology and institutions of the Celtic[20] conquerors of the Roman empire, outlived the darkness and the convulsions connected with their growth and victory, and blended themselves in a new fabric of manners and opinion. It is an error to impute the ignorance of the dark ages to the Christian doctrines or the predominance of the Celtic nations. Whatever of evil their agencies may have contained sprung from the extinction of the poetical principle, connected with the progress of despotism and superstition. Men, from causes too intricate to be here discussed, had become insensible and selfish: their own will had become feeble, and yet they were its slaves, and thence the slaves of the will of others: lust, fear, avarice, cruelty and fraud, characterised a race amongst whom no one was to be found capable of *creating* in form, language, or institution. The moral anomalies of such a state of society are not justly to be charged upon any class of events immediately connected with them, and those events are most entitled to our approbation which could dissolve it most expeditiously. It is unfortunate for those who cannot distinguish words from thoughts, that many of these anomalies have been incorporated into our popular religion. [. . .]

The incorporation of the Celtic nations with the exhausted population of the South, impressed upon it the figure of the poetry existing in their mythology and institutions. The result was a sum of the action and reaction of all the causes included in it; for it may be assumed as a maxim that no nation or religion can supersede any other without incorporating into itself a portion of that which it supersedes. The abolition of personal and domestic slavery, and the emancipation of women from a great part of the degrading restraints of antiquity were among the consequences of these events.

[20]Tribes of Northern Europe.

The abolition of personal slavery is the basis of the highest political hope that it can enter into the mind of man to conceive. The freedom of women produced the poetry of sexual love. Love became a religion, the idols of whose worship were ever present. It was as if the statues of Apollo and the Muses had been endowed with life and motion, and had walked forth among their worshippers; so that earth became peopled by the inhabitants of a diviner world. The familiar appearance and proceedings of life became wonderful and heavenly; and a paradise was created as out of the wrecks of Eden. And as this creation itself is poetry, so its creators were poets; and language was the instrument of their art. [. . .]

The poetry of Dante may be considered as the bridge thrown over the stream of time, which unites the modern and antient world. The distorted notions of invisible things which Dante and his rival Milton have idealised, are merely the mask and the mantle in which these great poets walk through eternity enveloped and disguised. It is a difficult question to determine how far they were conscious of the distinction which must have subsisted in their minds between their own creeds and that of the people. Dante at least appears to wish to mark the full extent of it by placing Riphæus, whom Virgil calls *justissimus unus*, in Paradise, and observing a most heretical caprice in his distribution of rewards and punishments.[21] And Milton's poem contains within itself a philosophical refutation of that system of which, by a strange and natural antithesis, it has been a chief popular support.[22] Nothing can exceed the energy and magnificence of the character of Satan as expressed in Paradise Lost. It is a mistake to suppose that he could ever have been intended for the popular personification of evil. Implacable hate, patient cunning, and a sleepless refinement of device to inflict the extremest anguish on an enemy, these things are evil; and although venial in a slave are not to be forgiven in a tyrant; although redeemed by much that ennobles his defeat in one subdued, are marked by all that dishonours his conquest in the victor. Milton's Devil as a moral being is as far superior to his God as one who perseveres in some purpose which he has conceived to be excellent in spite of adversity and torture, is to one who in the cold security of un-

[21]In the *Aeneid*, Aeneas calls Riphaeus the "most just" of the Trojans, whose death causes Aeneas to question the justice of the gods. In *Paradiso*, Dante places him in the Circle of the Just.

[22]Christianity; the antithesis is the magnificent character of Satan, which Shelley was not alone in finding superior—poetically, dramatically, morally, and politically—to Milton's tyrannical God.

doubted triumph inflicts the most horrible revenge upon his enemy, not from any mistaken notion of inducing him to repent of a perseverance in enmity, but with the alleged design of exasperating him to deserve new torments. Milton has so far violated the popular creed (if this shall be judged to be a violation) as to have alleged no superiority of moral virtue to his God over his Devil. And this bold neglect of a direct moral purpose is the most decisive proof of the supremacy of Milton's genius. He mingled as it were the elements of human nature, as colours upon a single pallet, and arranged them in the composition of his great picture according to the laws of epic truth, that is, according to the laws of that principle by which a series of actions of the external universe and of intelligent and ethical beings is calculated to excite the sympathy of succeeding generations of mankind. [. . .]

Homer was the first, and Dante the second epic poet: that is, the second poet, the series of whose creations bore a defined and intelligible relation to the knowledge, and sentiment, and religion, and political conditions of the age in which he lived, and of the ages which followed it, developing itself in correspondence with their development. [. . .] Milton was the third Epic Poet. For if the title of epic in its highest sense be refused to the Æneid, still less can it be conceded to the Orlando Furioso, the Gerusalemme Liberata, the Lusiad, or the Fairy Queen.[23] [. . .]

The age immediately succeeding to that of Dante, Petrarch, and Boccacio, was characterized by a revival of painting, sculpture, and architecture. Chaucer caught the sacred inspiration, and the superstructure of English literature is based upon the materials of Italian invention.

But let us not be betrayed from a defence into a critical history of Poetry and its influence on Society. Be it enough to have pointed out the effects of poets, in the large and true sense of the word, upon their own and all succeeding times and to revert to the partial instances cited as illustrations of an opinion the reverse of that attempted to be established in the Four Ages of Poetry.

But poets have been challenged to resign the civic crown to reasoners and mechanists[24] on another plea. It is admitted that the exercise of the imagination is most delightful, but it is alleged that that of reason is more useful. Let us examine, as the grounds of this

---

[23]The epics by Renaissance poets Ariosto, Tasso, Camoens, and Spenser.

[24]Contemporary Utilitarian philosophers for whom social usefulness—the greatest good for the greatest number—is the highest value.

distinction, what is here meant by Utility. Pleasure or good in a general sense, is that which the consciousness of a sensitive and intelligent being seeks, and in which when found it acquiesces. There are two kinds of pleasure, one durable, universal, and permanent; the other transitory and particular. Utility may either express the means of producing the former or the latter. In the former sense, whatever strengthens and purifies the affections, enlarges the imagination, and adds spirit to sense, is useful. But the meaning in which the Author of the Four Ages of Poetry seems to have employed the word utility is the narrower one of banishing the importunity of the wants of our animal nature, the surrounding men with security of life, the dispersing the grosser delusions of superstition, and the conciliating such a degree of mutual forbearance among men as may consist with the motives of personal advantage.

Undoubtedly the promoters of utility in this limited sense, have their appointed office in society. They follow the footsteps of poets, and copy the sketches of their creations into the book of common life. They make space, and give time. Their exertions are of the highest value so long as they confine their administration of the concerns of the inferior powers of our nature within the limits due to the superior ones. But while the sceptic destroys gross superstitions, let him spare to deface, as some of the French writers have defaced, the eternal truths charactered upon the imaginations of men. Whilst the mechanist abridges, and the political œconomist combines, labour, let them beware that their speculations, for want of correspondence with those first principles which belong to the imagination, do not tend, as they have in modern England, to exasperate[25] at once the extremes of luxury and want. They have exemplified the saying, "To him that hath, more shall be given; and from him that hath not, the little that he hath shall be taken away."[26] The rich have become richer, and the poor have become poorer; and the vessel of the state is driven between the Scylla and Charybdis[27] of anarchy and despotism. Such are the effects which must ever flow from an unmitigated exercise of the calculating faculty. [. . .]

The production and assurance of pleasure in this highest sense is true utility. Those who produce and preserve this pleasure are Poets or poetical philosophers.

[25]Intensify.

[26]"For he that hath, to him shall be given: and he that hath not, from him shall be taken even that which he hath." Echoing Mark 4.25, Shelley anticipates Marx's critique of economic inequality.

[27]The rocks and whirlpool that endangered ships in the narrow Strait of Messina.

The exertions of Locke, Hume, Gibbon, Voltaire, Rousseau,[28] and their disciples, in favour of oppressed and deluded humanity, are entitled to the gratitude of mankind. Yet it is easy to calculate the degree of moral and intellectual improvement which the world would have exhibited, had they never lived. A little more nonsense would have been talked for a century or two; and perhaps a few more men, women, and children, burnt as heretics. We might not at this moment have been congratulating each other on the abolition of the Inquisition in Spain.[29] But it exceeds all imagination to conceive what would have been the moral condition of the world if neither Dante, Petrarch, Boccaccio, Chaucer, Shakspeare, Calderon, Lord Bacon, nor Milton, had ever existed; if Raphael and Michael Angelo had never been born; if the Hebrew poetry had never been translated; if a revival of the study of Greek literature had never taken place; if no monuments of antient sculpture had been handed down to us; and if the poetry of the religion of the antient world had been extinguished together with its belief. The human mind could never, except by the intervention of these excitements, have been awakened to the invention of the grosser sciences,[30] and that application of analytical reasoning to the aberrations of society, which it is now attempted to exalt over the direct expression of the inventive and creative faculty itself.

We have more moral, political, and historical wisdom, than we know how to reduce into practice; we have more scientific and œconomical knowledge than can be accommodated to the just distribution of the produce which it multiplies. The poetry in these systems of thought, is concealed by the accumulation of facts and calculating processes. There is no want of knowledge respecting what is wisest and best in morals, government, and political œconomy, or at least what is wiser and better than what men now practise and endure. But we let *"I dare not* wait upon *I would,* like the poor cat i'

[28]"I follow the classification adopted by the author of the Four Ages of Poetry. But Rousseau was essentially a poet. The others, even Voltaire, were mere reasoners." [Shelley's note.] John Locke, British anti-authoritarian philosopher whose *Essay Concerning Human Understanding* (1690) discusses the limits of human capacity; David Hume, Scottish empirical philosopher, economist, historian, author of *A Treatise of Human Nature* (1739–40); Edward Gibbon, author of *History of the Decline and Fall of the Roman Empire* (1776–88); Voltaire (1694–1778), French Enlightenment playwright and philosopher.

[29]The Spanish Inquisition, instituted by the Catholic Church in 1480 to suppress heresy, was not abolished until 1820, following the Spanish Revolution.

[30]Physics and the natural sciences.

the adage."[31] We want the creative faculty to imagine that which we know; we want the generous impulse to act that which we imagine; we want the poetry of life: our calculations have outrun conception; we have eaten more than we can digest. The cultivation of those sciences which have enlarged the limits of the empire of man over the external world, has, for want of the poetical faculty, proportionally circumscribed those of the internal world; and man, having enslaved the elements, remains himself a slave. To what but a cultivation of the mechanical arts in a degree disproportioned to the presence of the creative faculty, which is the basis of all knowledge, is to be attributed the abuse of all invention for abridging and combining labour, to the exasperation of the inequality of mankind? From what other cause has it arisen that the discoveries which should have lightened, have added a weight to the curse imposed on Adam? Poetry, and the principle of Self, of which money is the visible incarnation, are the God and Mammon[32] of the world.

The functions of the poetical faculty are two-fold; by one it creates new materials of knowledge, and power, and pleasure; by the other it engenders in the mind a desire to reproduce and arrange them according to a certain rhythm and order, which may be called the beautiful and the good. The cultivation of poetry is never more to be desired than at periods when, from an excess of the selfish and calculating principle, the accumulation of the materials of external life exceed the quantity of the power of assimilating them to the internal laws of human nature. The body has then become too unwieldy for that which animates it.

Poetry is indeed something divine. It is at once the centre and circumference of knowledge; it is that which comprehends all science, and that to which all science must be referred. It is at the same time the root and blossom of all other systems of thought; it is that from which all spring, and that which adorns all; and that which, if blighted, denies the fruit and the seed, and withholds from the barren world the nourishment and the succession of the scions of the tree of life. It is the perfect and consummate surface and bloom of all things; it is as the odour and the colour of the rose to the texture of the elements which compose it, as the form and splendour of unfaded beauty to the secrets of anatomy and corruption. What were Virtue, Love, Patriotism, Friendship, etc.—what were the scenery

[31]Lady Macbeth is chiding Macbeth for cowardice (1.7.44–45).

[32]Worldly possessions; "Ye cannot serve God and Mammon," says Jesus (Matthew 6.24).

of this beautiful Universe which we inhabit— what were our consolations on this side of the grave—and what were our aspirations beyond it—if Poetry did not ascend to bring light and fire from those eternal regions where the owl-winged faculty of calculation dare not ever soar? Poetry is not like reasoning, a power to be exerted according to the determination of the will. A man cannot say, "I will compose poetry." The greatest poet even cannot say it; for the mind in creation is as a fading coal which some invisible influence, like an inconstant wind, awakens to transitory brightness: this power arises from within, like the colour of a flower which fades and changes as it is developed, and the conscious portions of our natures are unprophetic either of its approach or its departure. Could this influence be durable in its original purity and force, it is impossible to predict the greatness of the results; but when composition begins, inspiration is already on the decline, and the most glorious poetry that has ever been communicated to the world is probably a feeble shadow of the original conception of the poet. I appeal to the greatest Poets of the present day, whether it is not an error to assert that the finest passages of poetry are produced by labour and study. The toil and the delay recommended by critics can be justly interpreted to mean no more than a careful observation of the inspired moments, and an artificial connexion of the spaces between their suggestions by the intertexture of conventional expressions; a necessity only imposed by the limitedness of the poetical faculty itself. For Milton conceived the Paradise Lost as a whole before he executed it in portions. We have his own authority also for the Muse having "dictated" to him the "unpremeditated song,"[33] and let this be an answer to those who would allege the fifty-six various readings of the first line of the Orlando Furioso. Compositions so produced are to poetry what mosaic is to painting. This instinct and intuition of the poetical faculty is still more observable in the plastic and pictorial arts: a great statue or picture grows under the power of the artist as a child in the mother's womb, and the very mind which directs the hands in formation is incapable of accounting to itself for the origin, the gradations, or the media of the process.

Poetry is the record of the best and happiest moments of the happiest and best minds. We are aware of evanescent[34] visitations of

---

[33]Milton's description of *PL* (9.21–24); see also "To a Sky-Lark" (p. 228).

[34]Impermanent, transitory.

thought and feeling sometimes associated with place or person, sometimes regarding our own mind alone, and always arising unforeseen and departing unbidden, but elevating and delightful beyond all expression: so that even in the desire and the regret they leave, there cannot but be pleasure, participating as it does in the nature of its object. It is as it were the interpenetration of a diviner nature through our own; but its footsteps are like those of a wind over a sea, which the morning calm erases, and whose traces remain only as on the wrinkled sand which paves it. These and corresponding conditions of being are experienced principally by those of the most delicate sensibility and the most enlarged imagination; and the state of mind produced by them is at war with every base desire. The enthusiasm of virtue, love, patriotism, and friendship, is essentially linked with these emotions; and whilst they last, self appears as what it is, an atom to a Universe. Poets are not only subject to these experiences as spirits of the most refined organisation, but they can colour all that they combine with the evanescent hues of this etherial[35] world; a word, a trait in the representation of a scene or a passion, will touch the enchanted chord, and reanimate, in those who have ever experienced those emotions, the sleeping, the cold, the buried image of the past. Poetry thus makes immortal all that is best and most beautiful in the world; it arrests the vanishing apparitions which haunt the interlunations[36] of life, and veiling them, or in language or in form, sends them forth among mankind, bearing sweet news of kindred joy to those with whom their sisters abide—abide, because there is no portal of expression from the caverns of the spirit which they inhabit into the universe of things.[37] Poetry redeems from decay the visitations of the divinity in man.

Poetry turns all things to loveliness; it exalts the beauty of that which is most beautiful, and it adds beauty to that which is most deformed; it marries exultation and horror, grief and pleasure, eternity and change; it subdues to union under its light yoke all irreconcilable things. It transmutes all that it touches, and every form moving within the radiance of its presence is changed by wondrous sympathy to an incarnation of the spirit which it breathes: its secret alchemy turns to potable gold the poisonous waters which flow from death through life; it strips the veil of familiarity from the world, and lays bare the naked and sleeping beauty which is the spirit of its forms.

[35]Heavenly.

[36]The dark phase between the old and new moons.

[37]Cf. the opening lines of "Mont Blanc."

All things exist as they are perceived; at least in relation to the percipient.[38] "The mind is its own place, and of itself can make a heaven of hell, a hell of heaven."[39] But poetry defeats the curse which binds us to be subjected to the accident of surrounding impressions. And whether it spreads its own figured curtain, or withdraws life's dark veil from before the scene of things, it equally creates for us a being within our being. It makes us the inhabitants of a world to which the familiar world is a chaos. It reproduces the common universe of which we are portions and percipients, and it purges from our inward sight the film of familiarity which obscures from us the wonder of our being. It compels us to feel that which we perceive, and to imagine that which we know. It creates anew the universe, after it has been annihilated in our minds by the recurrence of impressions blunted by reiteration. It justifies the bold and true word of Tasso—*Non merita nome di creatore, se non Iddio ed il Poeta.*[40]

A Poet, as he is the author to others of the highest wisdom, pleasure, virtue and glory, so he ought personally to be the happiest, the best, the wisest, and the most illustrious of men. As to his glory, let Time be challenged to declare whether the fame of any other institutor of human life be comparable to that of a poet. That he is the wisest, the happiest, and the best, inasmuch as he is a poet, is equally incontrovertible: the greatest poets have been men of the most spotless virtue, of the most consummate prudence, and, if we would look into the interior of their lives, the most fortunate of men: and the exceptions, as they regard those who possessed the poetic faculty in a high yet inferior degree, will be found on consideration to confirm rather than destroy the rule. [. . .]

Poetry, as has been said, differs in this respect from logic, that it is not subject to the controul of the active powers of the mind, and that its birth and recurrence have no necessary connexion with the consciousness or will. It is presumptuous to determine that these are the necessary conditions of all mental causation, when mental effects are experienced insusceptible of being referred to them. The frequent recurrence of the poetical power, it is obvious to suppose, may produce in the mind a habit of order and harmony correlative

---

[38]British empiricist philosopher George Berkeley (1685–1753) stated, "*esse est percipi*" (to be is to be perceived).

[39]Satan speaking in Hell (*PL* 1.254–55)—though Shelley either revises or misremembers Milton's "in itself."

[40]"No one deserves the name of Creator but God and the Poet," quoted in Italian in Serassi's *Life of Torquato Tasso* (1785).

with its own nature and with its effects upon other minds. But in the intervals of inspiration, and they may be frequent without being durable, a poet becomes a man, and is abandoned to the sudden reflux of the influences under which others habitually live. But as he is more delicately organised than other men, and sensible to pain and pleasure, both his own and that of others, in a degree unknown to them, he will avoid the one and pursue the other with an ardour proportioned to this difference. And he renders himself obnoxious to calumny, when he neglects to observe the circumstances under which these objects of universal pursuit and flight have disguised themselves in one another's garments.

But there is nothing necessarily evil in this error, and thus cruelty, envy, revenge, avarice, and the passions purely evil, have never formed any portion of the popular imputations on the lives of poets. [. . .]

The first part of these remarks has related to Poetry in its elements and principles; and it has been shown, as well as the narrow limits assigned them would permit, that what is called Poetry, in a restricted sense, has a common source with all other forms of order and of beauty according to which the materials of human life are susceptible of being arranged, and which is Poetry in an universal sense.

The second part[41] will have for its object an application of these principles to the present state of the cultivation of Poetry, and a defence of the attempt to idealize the modern forms of manners and opinions, and compel them into a subordination to the imaginative and creative faculty. For the literature of England, an energetic development of which has ever preceded or accompanied a great and free development of the national will, has arisen as it were from a new birth. In spite of the low-thoughted envy which would undervalue contemporary merit, our own will be a memorable age in intellectual achievements, and we live among such philosophers and poets as surpass beyond comparison any who have appeared since the last national struggle for civil and religious liberty. The most unfailing herald, companion, and follower of the awakening of a great people to work a beneficial change in opinion or institution, is Poetry. At such periods there is an accumulation of the power of communicating and receiving intense and impassioned conceptions respecting man and nature. The persons in whom this power resides, may often, as far as regards many portions of their nature, have little apparent correspondence with that spirit of good of which they are the ministers. But even whilst they

---

[41]No second part survives; perhaps Shelley wanted a public response before proceeding.

deny and abjure, they are yet compelled to serve, the Power which is seated on the throne of their own soul. It is impossible to read the compositions of the most celebrated writers of the present day without being startled with the electric life which burns within their words. They measure the circumference and sound the depths of human nature with a comprehensive and all-penetrating spirit, and they are themselves perhaps the most sincerely astonished at its manifestations, for it is less their spirit than the spirit of the age. Poets are the hierophants[42] of an unapprehended inspiration, the mirrors of the gigantic shadows which futurity casts upon the present, the words which express what they understand not, the trumpets which sing to battle and feel not what they inspire: the influence which is moved not, but moves. Poets are the unacknowledged legislators of the World.[43]

~~~

Thomas Love Peacock

> *Shelley's* Defence of Poetry *is far more famous than the essay that inspired it. "The Four Ages of Poetry" is a satire of modern poetry that also makes some serious points about the place of poetry—and art—in the modern world. The son of a modest family, Peacock (1785–1866) was already embarked on a career as a writer when he met Shelley in 1812. He is best known for his satirical novel* Nightmare Abbey *(1817), in which many contemporary writers appear. In 1818, Peacock went to work for the powerful East India Company, where his supervisor was utilitarian philosopher James Mill. In a utilitarian spirit, Peacock proposes that modern poets are self-infatuated dabblers with little to contribute to human welfare.*

from The Four Ages of Poetry

POETRY, like the world, may be said to have four ages, but in a different order: the first age of poetry being the age of iron; the second, of gold; the third, of silver; and the fourth, of brass.

The first, or iron age of poetry, is that in which rude bards celebrate in rough numbers the exploits of ruder chiefs, in days when

---

[42]Interpreters of secret or unconscious knowledge.

[43]In Samuel Johnson's *Rasselas*, the prince's tutor, Imlac, observes that a poet should write "as the interpreter of nature, and the legislator of mankind" (ch. 10). Shelley had first drafted this final section in 1819 to conclude the first chapter of his political treatise, *A Philosophical View of Reform*, where he wrote not just "poets" but "poets and philosophers."

every man is a warrior, and when the great practical maxim of every form of society, "to keep what we have and to catch what we can," is not yet disguised under names of justice and forms of law, but is the naked motto of the naked sword, which is the only judge and jury in every question of *meum* and *tuum*.[1] In these days, the only three trades flourishing (besides that of priest which flourishes always) are those of king, thief, and beggar: the beggar being for the most part a king deject, and the thief a king expectant. [. . .] The successful warrior becomes a chief; the successful chief becomes a king: his next want is an organ to disseminate the fame of his achievements and the extent of his possessions; and this organ he finds in a bard, who is always ready to celebrate the strength of his arm, being first duly inspired by that of his liquor. This is the origin of poetry, which, like all other trades, takes its rise in the demand for the commodity, and flourishes in proportion to the extent of the market.

This is the first stage of poetry before the invention of written letters. [. . .] Poets are as yet the only historians and chroniclers of their time. [. . .]

The golden age of poetry finds its materials in the age of iron. This age begins when poetry begins to be retrospective; when something like a more extended system of civil polity is established; when personal strength and courage avail less to the aggrandizing of their possessor and to the making and marring of kings and kingdoms, and are checked by organized bodies, social institutions, and hereditary successions. Men also live more in the light of truth and within the interchange of observation; and thus perceive that the agency of gods and genii is not so frequent among themselves as, to judge from the songs and legends of the past time, it was among their ancestors. [. . . Poetry] still exists without rivals in any other department of literature; and even the arts, painting and sculpture certainly, and music probably, are comparatively rude and imperfect. [. . .] It is cultivated by the greatest intellects of the age, and listened to by all the rest. This is the age of Homer, the golden age of poetry. Poetry has now attained [. . .] the point which it cannot pass: genius therefore seeks new forms for the treatment of the same subjects: [. . .]

Then comes the silver age, or the poetry of civilized life. This poetry is of two kinds, imitative and original. The imitative consists in recasting, and giving an exquisite polish to, the poetry of the age of gold; [. . .] the original is chiefly comic, didactic, or satiric; [. . .]

[1]Mine and yours.

The poetry of this age is characterized by an exquisite and fastidious selection of words, and a laboured and somewhat monotonous harmony of expression: but its monotony consists in this, that experience having exhausted all the varieties of modulation, the civilized poetry selects the most beautiful, and prefers the repetition of these to ranging through the variety of all. [. . .]

This state of poetry is however a step towards its extinction. Feeling and passion are best painted in, and roused by, ornamental and figurative language; but the reason and the understanding are best addressed in the simplest and most unvarnished phrase. Pure reason and dispassionate truth would be perfectly ridiculous in verse. [. . .]

Thus the empire of thought is withdrawn from poetry, as the empire of facts had been before. [T]he poet of the age of iron celebrates the achievements of his contemporaries; the poet of the age of gold celebrates the heroes of the age of iron; the poet of the age of silver re-casts the poems of the age of gold. [. . .]

It is now evident that poetry must either cease to be cultivated, or strike into a new path. The poets of the age of gold have been imitated and repeated till no new imitation will attract notice: the limited range of ethical and didactic poetry is exhausted: the associations of daily life in an advanced state of society are of very dry, methodical, unpoetical matters-of-fact: but there is always a multitude of listless idlers, yawning for amusement, and gaping for novelty: and the poet makes it his glory to be foremost among their purveyors.

Then comes the age of brass, which, by rejecting the polish and the learning of the age of silver, and taking a retrograde stride to the barbarisms and erude traditions of the age of iron, professes to return to nature and revive the age of gold. This is the second childhood of poetry [, which features] a verbose and minutely-detailed description of thoughts, passions, actions, persons, and things, in [a] loose rambling style of verse. [. . .]

The iron age of classical poetry may be called the bardic; the golden, the Homeric; the silver, the Virgilian; and the brass, the Nonnic.[2]

Modern poetry has also its four ages: but "it wears its rue with a difference."[3] [. . .]

[From the poetry of medieval Europe], dispersed in the rhymes of minstrels and the songs of the troubadours, arose the golden age,

[2]Egyptian-born Greek poet Nonnus (4th c.) wrote *Dionysiaca*, an epic of the god Dionysus.

[3]Ophelia, telling Gertrude that their sorrows are very different (*Hamlet* 4.5.183).

in which the scattered materials were harmonized and blended about the time of the revival of learning; but with this peculiar difference, that Greek and Roman literature pervaded all the poetry of the golden age of modern poetry, and hence resulted a heterogeneous compound of all ages and nations in one picture; an infinite licence, which gave to the poet the free range of the whole field of imagination and memory. This was carried very far by Ariosto,[4] but farthest of all by Shakespeare and his contemporaries. [. . .]

The greatest of English poets, Milton, may be said to stand alone between the ages of gold and silver, combining the excellencies of both; for with all the energy, and power, and freshness of the first, he united all the studied and elaborate magnificence of the second.

The silver age succeeded; beginning with Dryden,[5] coming to perfection with Pope, and ending with Goldsmith, Collins, and Gray. [. . .]

The silver age was the reign of authority; but authority now began to be shaken, not only in poetry but in the whole sphere of its dominion. [. . .] To some such perversion of intellect we owe that egregious confraternity of rhymesters, known by the name of the Lake Poets;[6] who certainly did receive and communicate to the world some of the most extraordinary poetical impressions that ever were heard of, and ripened into models of public virtue, too splendid to need illustration. They wrote verses on a new principle; saw rocks and rivers in a new light; and remaining studiously ignorant of history, society, and human nature, cultivated the phantasy only at the expence of the memory and the reason; and contrived, though they had retreated from the world for the express purpose of seeing nature as she was, to see her only as she was not, converting the land they lived in into a sort of fairy-land, which they peopled with mysticisms and chimaeras. This gave what is called a new tone to poetry, and conjured up a herd of desperate imitators, who have brought the age of brass prematurely to its dotage.

The descriptive poetry of the present day has been called by its cultivators a return to nature. Nothing is more impertinent than this pretension. Poetry cannot travel out of the regions of its birth, the uncultivated lands of semi-civilized men. [. . .] While the historian and the philosopher are advancing in, and accelerating, the progress of knowledge, the poet is wallowing in the rubbish of de-

[4]Italian Renaissance poet, author of the epic *Orlando Furioso* (1516).
[5]Dryden is the great 17th-c. poet, following Milton; the others span the 18th c.
[6]Southey, Wordsworth, and Coleridge.

parted ignorance, and raking up the ashes of dead savages to find gewgaws and rattles for the grown babies of the age. Mr. Scott digs up the poachers and cattle-stealers of the ancient border. Lord Byron cruizes for thieves and pirates on the shores of the Morea and among the Greek Islands. Mr. Southey wades through ponderous volumes of travels and old chronicles, from which he carefully selects all that is false, useless, and absurd, as being essentially poetical; and when he has a commonplace book full of monstrosities, strings them into an epic. Mr. Wordsworth picks up village legends from old women and sextons; and Mr. Coleridge, to the valuable information acquired from similar sources, superadds the dreams of crazy theologians and the mysticisms of German metaphysics [. . . .]

Now when we consider [. . .] that the great and permanent interests of human society become more and more the main spring of intellectual pursuit; that in proportion as they become so, the subordinacy of the ornamental to the useful will be more and more seen and acknowledged; and that therefore the progress of useful art and science, and of moral and political knowledge, will continue more and more to withdraw attention from frivolous and unconducive, to solid and conducive studies: that therefore the poetical audience will not only continually diminish in the proportion of its number to that of the rest of the reading public, but will also sink lower and lower in the comparison of intellectual acquirement: when we consider that the poet must still please his audience, and must therefore continue to sink to their level, while the rest of the community is rising above it: we may easily conceive that the day is not distant, when the degraded state of every species of poetry will be as generally recognized as that of dramatic poetry has long been: and this not from any decrease either of intellectual power, or intellectual acquisition, but because intellectual power and intellectual acquisition have turned themselves into other and better channels, and have abandoned the cultivation and the fate of poetry to the degenerate fry of modern rhymesters, and their olympic judges, the magazine critics, who continue to debate and promulgate oracles about poetry, as if it were still what it was in the Homeric age, the all-in-all of intellectual progression, and as if there were no such things in existence as mathematicians, astronomers, chemists, moralists, metaphysicians, historians, politicians, and political economists, who have built into the upper air of intelligence a pyramid, from the summit of which they see the modern Parnassus far beneath them, and, knowing how small a place it occupies in the comprehensive-

ness of their prospect, smile at the little ambition and the circumscribed perceptions with which the drivellers and mountebanks
upon it are contending for the poetical palm and the critical chair.

～

Sonnet to Byron

*This sonnet was probably written after Byron's arrival at Pisa, 1 No-
vember 1821. Lines 1–7 were first published by Thomas Medwin in*
The Shelley Papers *(1832); lines 1–9 and 12–14 in his* Life of Shelley
*(1847). The poem was revised and completed by William Michael
Rossetti, who published it in his* Complete Poetical Works of Percy
Bysshe Shelley *(1870).*

[I am afraid these verses will not please you, but]
If I esteemed you less, Envy would kill
Pleasure, and leave to Wonder and Despair
The ministration of the thoughts that fill
The mind which, like a worm whose life may share
A portion of the unapproachable,   5
Marks your creations rise as fast and fair
As perfect worlds at the Creator's will.[1]

But such is my regard that nor your power
To soar above the heights where others [climb],
Nor fame, that shadow of the unborn hour   10
Cast from the envious future on the time,
Move one regret for his unhonoured name
Who dares these words:—the worm beneath the sod
May lift itself in homage of the God.

---

[1]In the manuscript draft, just after this line, Shelley wrote, "presenting itself before
the gilded throne" (Byron's commercial success); he later canceled those words.

Late Lyrics

These are private communications in poetry, never intended for publication. In January 1821, while living in Pisa, the Shelleys met Edward and Jane Williams, who became close friends. A retired army officer, Edward shared Shelley's love of boating, and Jane began teaching Shelley Spanish. In May both couples moved some seven miles from Pisa, where Shelley and Edward enjoyed boating on the Serchio River. By 1822, increasingly estranged from Mary, Shelley found in Jane an ideal soulmate and the inspiration for numerous lyric poems that he sent her in the spring. He had already sent Edward a poem ("The Serpent Is Shut Out from Paradise") detailing his distress. In March he wrote a poem to accompany a guitar he purchased for Jane. At the end of April the couples moved to Lerici, on the Gulf of Spezia, where they shared a house. There Shelley wrote more lyrics to Jane, sailed with Edward, and began writing "The Triumph of Life," which was unfinished and largely unrevised when he and Williams drowned in a storm on 8 July.

The Serpent Is Shut Out from Paradise[1]

[Shelley sent the poem to Williams with this note:

Looking over the portfolio in which my friend[2] used to keep his verses, & in which those I sent you the other day were found,—I have lit upon these; which as they are too dismal for <u>me</u> to keep I send them to you.

If any one of the stanzas should please you, you may read them to Jane, but to no one else,—and yet on second thought I had rather you would not.]

[1]Shelley's friends (especially Byron) called Shelley "the snake."
[2]Edward.

The serpent is shut out from Paradise.
　　The wounded deer must seek the herb no more
　　　　In which its heart-cure lies:
　　The widowed dove must cease to haunt a bower
Like that from which its mate with feigned sighs　　　　　5
　　　　Fled in the April hour.
I too must seldom seek again
Near happy friends a mitigated pain.

Of hatred I am proud,—with scorn content;
　　Indifference, that once hurt me, now is grown　　　　10
　　　　Itself indifferent;
　　But, not to speak of love, pity alone
Can break a spirit already more than bent.
　　　　The miserable one
Turns the mind's poison into food,—　　　　　　　　15
Its medicine is tears,—its evil good.

Therefore, if now I see you seldomer,
　　Dear friends, dear <u>friend</u>! know that I only fly
　　　　Your looks, because they stir
　　Griefs that should sleep, and hopes that cannot die:　　20
The very comfort that they minister
　　　　I scarce can bear, yet I,
(So deeply is the arrow gone)
Should quickly perish if it were withdrawn.

When I return to my cold home, you ask　　　　　　25
　　Why I am not as I have ever been.
　　　　<u>You</u> spoil me for the task
　　Of acting a forced part in life's dull scene,—
Of wearing on my brow the idle mask
　　　　Of author, great or mean,　　　　　　　　30
In the world's carnival. I sought
Peace thus, and but in you I found it not.

Full half an hour, to-day, I tried my lot
　　With various flowers, and every one still said,
　　　　"She loves me—loves me not."　　　　　　35
　　And if this meant a vision long since fled—
If it meant fortune, fame, or peace of thought—
　　　　If it meant,— (but I dread

To speak what you may know too well)
Still there was truth in the sad oracle.   40

The crane o'er seas and forests seeks her home;
   No bird so wild but has its quiet nest,
      When it no more would roam;
   The sleepless billows on the ocean's breast
Break like a bursting heart, and die in foam,   45
      And thus at length find rest:
Doubtless there is a place of peace
Where MY weak heart and all its throbs will cease.

I asked her,[3] yesterday, if she believed
   That I had resolution. One who <u>had</u>   50
      Would ne'er have thus relieved
   His heart with words,—but what his judgement bade
Would do, and leave the scorner unrelieved.
      These verses are too sad
To send to you, but that I know,   55
Happy yourself, you feel another's woe.

To Jane. The Invitation[1]

Best and brightest, come away—
Fairer far than this fair day,
Which, like thee to those in sorrow,
Comes to bid a sweet good-morrow
To the rough ear just awake   5
In its cradle on the brake.[2]—
The brightest hour of unborn spring,
Through the winter wandering,
Found, it seems, the halycon[3] morn

[3]Mary Shelley.

---

[1]Published in *1824* with the following poem as *The Pine Forest of the Cascine, near Pisa*; in *1839* Mary Shelley separated them and gave them their present titles. Note the light, song-like tetrameter couplets.

[2]Thicket, clump of brush.

[3]Calm, undisturbed (the word derives from a Greek myth in which bereft lovers enjoy a brief interval together).

To hoar February born.   10
Bending from Heaven, in azure mirth,
It kissed the forehead of the earth,
And smiled upon the silent sea,
And bade the frozen streams be free,
And waked to music all their fountains,   15
And breathed upon the frozen mountains,
And like a prophetess of May
Strewed flowers upon the barren way,
Making the wintry world appear
Like one on whom thou smilest, dear.   20

Away, away from men and towns,
To the wild wood and the downs,
To the silent wilderness
Where the soul need not repress
Its music lest it should not find   25
An echo in another's mind,
While the touch of Nature's art
Harmonizes heart to heart.—
I leave this notice on my door
For each accustomed visitor—   30
"I am gone into the fields
To take what this sweet hour yields.
Reflection, you may come to-morrow,
Sit by the fireside with Sorrow—
You with the unpaid bill, Despair,   35
You, tiresome verse-reciter, Care,
I will pay you in the grave,
Death will listen to your stave[4]—
Expectation too, be off!
To-day is for itself enough—   40
Hope, in pity mock not woe
With smiles, nor follow where I go;
Long having lived on thy sweet food,
At length I find one moment's good
After long pain—with all your love   45
This you never told me of."

[4]Stanza.

Radiant Sister of the day,
Awake, arise, and come away
To the wild woods and the plains,
And the pools where winter-rains   50
Image all their roof of leaves,
Where the pine its garland weaves
Of sapless green and ivy dun[5]
Round stems that never kiss the Sun—
Where the lawns and pastures be,   55
And the sand hills of the sea—
Where the melting hoar-frost wets
The daisy-star that never sets,
And wind-flowers, and violets
Which yet join not scent to hue   60
Crown the pale year weak and new
When the night is left behind
In the deep east dun and blind
And the blue noon is over us,
And the multitudinous   65
Billows murmur at our feet,
Where the earth and ocean meet,
And all things seem only one
In the universal Sun.—

To Jane: the Recollection

Feb. 2, 1822

Now the last day of many days,
All beautiful and bright as thou,
The loveliest and the last, is dead,
Rise, Memory, and write its praise!
Up to thy wonted[1] work! come, trace   5
The epitaph of glory fled,—
For now the Earth has changed its face,
A frown is on the Heaven's brow.

[5]Dull.

———

[1]Customary, with a pun on "wanted" (desired).

I

We wandered to the pine forest
    That skirts the ocean foam,   10
The lightest wind was in its nest,
    The Tempest in its home;
The whispering waves were half asleep,
    The clouds were gone to play,
And on the bosom of the deep   15
    The smile of Heaven lay;
It seemed as if the hour were one
    Sent from beyond the skies,
Which scattered from above the sun
    A light of Paradise.   20

II

We paused amid the pines that stood
    The giants of the waste,
Tortured by storms to shapes as rude
    As serpents interlaced,
And soothed by every azure breath,   25
    That under Heaven is blown,
To harmonies and hues beneath,
    As tender as its own;
Now all the tree-tops lay asleep,
    Like green waves on the sea,   30
As still as in the silent deep
    The Ocean woods may be.

III

How calm it was! the silence there
    By such a chain was bound
That even the busy woodpecker   35
    Made stiller by her sound
The inviolable quietness;
    The breath of peace we drew
With its soft motion made not less
    The calm that round us grew.—   40
There seemed from the remotest seat
    Of the white mountain-waste,
To the soft flower beneath our feet,

A magic circle traced,
A spirit interfused around,   45
    A thrilling, silent life:
To momentary peace it bound
    Our mortal nature's strife;—
And still I felt the centre of
    The magic circle there   50
Was <u>one</u> fair form that filled with love
    The lifeless atmosphere.

IV

We paused beside the pools that lie
    Under the forest bough,—
Each seemed as 'twere a little sky   55
    Gulfed in a world below;
A firmament of purple light
    Which in the dark earth lay
More boundless than the depth of night,
    And purer than the day—   60
In which the lovely forests grew
    As in the upper air,
More perfect, both in shape and hue,
    Than any spreading there.
There lay the glade and neighbouring lawn,   65
    And through the dark green wood
The white sun twinkling like the dawn
    Out of a speckled cloud.
Sweet views, which in our world above
    Can never well be seen,   70
Were imaged by the water's love
    Of that fair forest green;
And all was interfused beneath
    With an Elysian[2] glow,
An atmosphere without a breath,   75
    A softer day below—
Like one beloved, the scene had lent
    To the dark water's breast,
Its every leaf and lineament
    With more than truth expressed;

[2]Elysian Fields; eternal home of the happy dead (Greek myth).

Until an envious wind crept by,   80
    Like an unwelcome thought
Which from the mind's too faithful eye
    Blots one dear image out.—
Though thou art ever fair and kind
    The forests ever green,   85
Less oft is peace in S——'s mind
    Than calm in waters seen.

With a Guitar, to Jane[1]

[In a note to Jane, Shelley wrote, "If this melancholy old song suits any of your tunes, or any that humour of the moment may dictate, you are welcome to it. Do not say it is mine to any one, even if you think so; indeed, it is from the torn leaf of a book out of date. . . "]

Ariel to Miranda:—Take
This slave of Music,[2] for the sake
Of him who is the slave of thee,
And teach it all the harmony
In which thou canst, and only thou,   5
Make the delighted spirit glow,
Till joy denies itself again,
And, too intense, is turned to pain;
For by permission and command
Of thine own Prince Ferdinand,   10
Poor Ariel sends this silent token
Of more than ever can be spoken;
Your guardian spirit, Ariel, who,
From life to life, must still pursue
Your happiness;—for thus alone   15
Can Ariel ever find his own.
From Prospero's enchanted cell,

[1]First published in *The Athenaeum*, 20 October 1832. The characters are from Shakespeare's *The Tempest*; Jane is Miranda (Prospero's daughter), Shelley is the spirit Ariel, Edward is Miranda's lover Ferdinand. The song-like tetrameter couplets hint that Shelley intended Jane to sing with the guitar.

[2]The guitar.

As the mighty verses tell,
To the throne of Naples, he
Lit you o'er the trackless sea,   20
Flitting on, your prow before,
Like a living meteor.
When you die, the silent Moon,
In her interlunar³ swoon,
Is not sadder in her cell   25
Than deserted Ariel.
When you live again on earth,
Like an unseen star of birth,⁴
Ariel guides you o'er the sea
Of life from your nativity.   30
Many changes have been run
Since Ferdinand and you begun
Your course of love, and Ariel still
Has tracked your steps, and served your will;
Now, in humbler, happier lot,   35
This is all remembered not;
And now, alas! the poor sprite is
Imprisoned, for some fault of his,
In a body like a grave;—
From you he only dares to crave,   40
For his service and his sorrow,
A smile today, a song tomorrow.

The artist who this idol⁵ wrought,
To echo all harmonious thought,
Felled a tree, while on the steep   45
The woods were in their winter sleep,
Rocked in that repose divine
On the wind-swept Apennine;⁶
And dreaming, some of Autumn past,
And some of Spring approaching fast,   50
And some of April buds and showers,
And some of songs in July bowers,

³Dark phase between the old and new moons.
⁴Astrology says that one's life is influenced by the natal star.
⁵The guitar, made of wood ("tree," l. 45).
⁶Italian peak.

And all of love; and so this tree,—
O that such our death may be!—
Died in sleep, and felt no pain,   55
To live in happier form again:
From which, beneath Heaven's fairest star,
The artist wrought this loved Guitar,
And taught it justly to reply,
To all who question skilfully,   60
In language gentle as thine own;
Whispering in enamoured tone
Sweet oracles of woods and dells,
And summer winds in sylvan cells;
For it had learned all harmonies   65
Of the plains and of the skies,
Of the forests and the mountains,
And the many-voiced fountains;
The clearest echoes of the hills,
The softest notes of falling rills,   70
The melodies of birds and bees,
The murmuring of summer seas,
And pattering rain, and breathing dew,
And airs of evening; and it knew
That seldom-heard mysterious sound,   75
Which, driven on its diurnal[7] round,
As it floats through boundless day,
Our world enkindles on its way.—
All this it knows, but will not tell
To those who cannot question well   80
The Spirit that inhabits it;
It talks according to the wit
Of its companions; and no more
Is heard than has been felt before,
By those who tempt it to betray   85
These secrets of an elder day:
But, sweetly as its answers will
Flatter hands of perfect skill,
It keeps its highest, holiest tone
For our beloved Jane alone.   90

[7]Daily.

To Jane: 'The Keen Stars Were Twinkling'[1]

[Shelley gave this poem to Jane with a note: "I sate down to write some words for an ariette which might be profane—but it was in vain to struggle with the ruling spirit, who compelled me to speak of things sacred to yours & Wilhelmeister's[2] indulgence—I commit them to your secrecy and your mercy & will try & do better another time."]

> The keen stars were twinkling,
> And the fair moon was rising among them,
> >> Dear Jane![3]
> > The guitar was tinkling,
> But the notes were not sweet till you sung them   5
> >> Again.—
> > As the moon's soft splendour
> O'er the faint cold starlight of Heaven
> >> Is thrown,
> > So your voice most tender   10
> To the strings without soul had then given
> >> Its own.
>
> > The stars will awaken,
> Though the moon sleep a full hour later,
> >> To-night;   15
> > No leaf will be shaken
> Whilst the dews of your melody scatter
> >> Delight.
> > Though the sound overpowers,
> Sing again, with your dear voice revealing   20
> >> A tone
> > Of some world far from ours,
> Where music and moonlight and feeling
> >> Are one.

---

[1]Published (incomplete) in *The Athenaeum* (17 November 1832) as "An Ariette for Music. To a Lady singing to her Accompaniment on the Guitar." Published as "To —" in *1839*. An ariette is a light song.

[2]A pun on Williams's name and Goethe's 1795 novel, *Wilhelm Meister's Apprenticeship*.

[3]In *1839*, Mary Shelley substituted "****" for Jane's name (she was still living).

Lines Written in the Bay of Lerici[1]

She left me at the silent time
When the moon had ceased to climb
The azure path of Heaven's steep,
And like an albatross[2] asleep,
Balanced on her wings of light,   5
Hovered in the purple night,
Ere she sought her ocean nest
In the chambers of the West.
She left me, and I stayed alone
Thinking over every tone   10
Which, though silent to the ear,
The enchanted heart could hear,
Like notes which die when born, but still
Haunt the echoes of the hill;
And feeling ever—oh, too much!—   15
The soft vibration of her touch,
As if her gentle hand, even now,
Lightly trembled on my brow;
And thus, although she absent were,
Memory gave me all of her   20
That even Fancy dares to claim:—
Her presence had made weak and tame
All passions, and I lived alone
In the time which is our own;
The past and future were forgot,   25
As they had been, and would be, not.
But soon, the guardian angel gone,
The daemon[3] reassumed his throne
In my faint heart. I dare not speak
My thoughts, but thus disturbed and weak   30
I sat and saw the vessels glide
Over the ocean bright and wide,
Like spirit-winged chariots sent
O'er some serenest element

[1]Possibly Shelley's final lyric, perhaps incomplete, composed c. 24 June 1822. First published in *Macmillan's Magazine*, 1862.

[2]The albatross was believed to sleep in the air.

[3]Inner malevolent spirit.

For ministrations strange and far;   35
As if to some Elysian[4] star
Sailed for drink to medicine[5]
Such sweet and bitter pain as mine.
And the wind that winged their flight
From the land came fresh and light,   40
And the scent of winged flowers,
And the coolness of the hours
Of dew, and sweet warmth left by day,
Were scattered o'er the twinkling bay.
And the fisher with his lamp   45
And spear about the low rocks damp
Crept, and struck the fish which came
To worship the delusive flame.[6]
Too happy they, whose pleasure sought
Extinguishes all sense and thought   50
Of the regret that pleasure [   ][7]
Destroying life alone, not peace!

The Triumph of Life

> *"The Triumph of Life" was unfinished when Shelley died in July 1822. It is a dream vision of intense longing and desire, rendered in the intricate, cascading* terza rima *that Shelley admired in Dante's* Divine Comedy *and Petrarch's* Trionfi *(a poetic sequence progressing from mortal to eternal, divine love), with a sensation of being never-ending, each stanza containing the seed of the next one.*
>
> *One puzzle is announced by Shelley's title: what is the triumph? Does "Life" mean mortal life, or eternal life? Traditionally, a "triumph" is a victory parade by a conquering hero, displaying the spoils and prisoners of conquest. Did Shelley intend to embrace the gloomy view that Rousseau describes, or did he plan to repudiate it as error? Perhaps the poem was to be a debate like* Alastor *and "Julian and Maddalo," with the reader left to weigh the arguments.*

[4]Elysian Fields, home of the happy dead (Greek myth).
[5]Medicate.
[6]Fish can be attracted to light.
[7]The line is missing a final word (to rhyme with "peace").

Swift as a spirit hastening to his task
    Of glory and of good, the Sun sprang forth
Rejoicing in his splendour, and the mask

    Of darkness fell from the awakened Earth.
The smokeless altars of the mountain snows   5
    Flamed above crimson clouds, and at the birth

Of light, the Ocean's orison[1] arose
    To which the birds tempered their matin[2] lay,
All flowers in field or forest which unclose

    Their trembling eyelids to the kiss of day,   10
Swinging their censers in the element,
    With orient incense lit by the new ray

Burned slow and inconsumably, and sent
    Their odorous sighs up to the smiling air,
And in succession due, did Continent,   15

    Isle, Ocean, and all things that in them wear
The form and character of mortal mould
    Rise as the Sun their father rose, to bear

Their portion of the toil which he of old
    Took as his own and then imposed on them;   20
But I, whom thoughts which must remain untold

    Had kept as wakeful as the stars that gem
The cone of night,[3] now they were laid asleep,
    Stretched my faint limbs beneath the hoary stem

Which an old chestnut flung athwart the steep   25
    Of a green Apennine:[4] before me fled
The night; behind me rose the day; the Deep

[1]Prayer.
[2]Early morning song.
[3]Earth's shadow.
[4]Italian mountains.

Was at my feet, and Heaven above my head
When a strange trance over my fancy grew
    Which was not slumber, for the shade it spread 30

Was so transparent that the scene came through
    As clear as when a veil of light is drawn
O'er evening hills they glimmer; and I knew

    That I had felt the freshness of that dawn,
Bathed in the same cold dew my brow and hair 35
    And sate as thus upon that slope of lawn

Under the self same bough, and heard as there
    The birds, the fountains and the Ocean hold
Sweet talk in music through the enamoured air.
    And then a Vision on my brain was rolled. . . . 40

        As in that trance of wondrous thought I lay
This was the tenour of my waking dream.
    Methought I sate beside a public way

Thick strewn with summer dust, and a great stream
    Of people there was hurrying to and fro 45
Numerous as gnats upon the evening gleam,

    All hastening onward, yet none seemed to know
Whither he went, or whence he came, or why
    He made one of the multitude, yet so

Was borne amid the crowd as through the sky 50
    One of the million leaves of summer's bier.[5]—
Old age and youth, manhood and infancy,

    Mixed in one mighty torrent did appear,
Some flying from the thing they feared and some
    Seeking the object of another's fear, 55

---

[5]A common comparison of the dead to fallen leaves; cf. "Ode to the West Wind" (ll. 2–5).

And others as with steps towards the tomb
      Pored on the trodden worms that crawled beneath,
And others mournfully within the gloom

      Of their own shadow walked, and called it death . . .
And some fled from it as it were a ghost,   60
      Half fainting in the affliction of vain breath.

But more with motions which each other crost
      Pursued or shunned the shadows the clouds threw
Or birds within the noonday ether lost,

      Upon that path where flowers never grew;   65
And weary with vain toil and faint for thirst
      Heard not the fountains whose melodious dew

Out of their mossy cells forever burst
      Nor felt the breeze which from the forest told
Of grassy paths, and wood lawns interspersed   70

      With overarching elms and caverns cold,
And violet banks where sweet dreams brood, but they
      Pursued their serious folly as of old . . . .

And as I gazed methought that in the way
      The throng grew wilder, as the woods of June   75
When the South wind shakes the extinguished day.—

      And a cold glare, intenser than the noon
But icy cold, obscured with [   ]⁶ light
      The Sun as he the stars. Like⁷ the young moon

When on the sunlit limits of the night   80
      Her white shell trembles amid crimson air
And whilst the sleeping tempest gathers might

---

⁶Left blank in manuscript; indicated thus hereafter.

⁷An extended simile, the tenor of which appears at l. 87. The old moon with the new moon in her arms, signaling an impending storm, appears in Coleridge's "Dejection: An Ode" (1802; republished 1817).

Doth, as a herald of its coming, bear
The ghost of her dead Mother, whose dim form
    Bends in dark ether from her infant's chair,[8]   85

So came a chariot on the silent storm
    Of its own rushing splendour, and a Shape
So sate within as one whom years deform

    Beneath a dusky hood and double cape
Crouching within the shadow of a tomb,   90
    And o'er what seemed the head, a cloud like crape,[9]

Was bent a dun and faint etherial gloom
    Tempering the light; upon the chariot's beam
A Janus[10]-visaged Shadow did assume

    The guidance of that wonder-winged team.   95
The Shapes which drew it in thick lightnings
    Were lost: I heard alone on the air's soft stream

The music of their ever moving wings.
    All the four faces of that charioteer
Had their eyes banded[11] . . . little profit brings   100

    Speed in the van[12] and blindness in the rear,
Nor then avail the beams that quench the Sun
    Or that his banded eyes could pierce the sphere

Of all that is, has been, or will be done.—
    So ill was the car guided, but it past   105
With solemn speed majestically on . . .

    The crowd gave way, and I arose aghast,
Or seemed to rise, so mighty was the trance,
    And saw like clouds upon the thunder blast

[8]New moon's crescent.
[9]Black crepe-silk, worn for mourning.
[10]Two-faced Roman god associated with beginnings and/or endings.
[11]Blindfolded.
[12]Front position.

The million with fierce song and maniac dance   110
      Raging around; such seemed the jubilee
As when to greet some conqueror's advance

      Imperial Rome poured forth her living sea
From senate house and prison and theatre
      When Freedom left those who upon the free   115

Had bound a yoke which soon they stooped to bear.[13]
      Nor wanted[14] here the true similitude
Of a triumphal pageant, for where'er

      The chariot rolled a captive multitude
Was driven; all those who had grown old in power   120
      Or misery,—all who have their age subdued,[15]

By action or by suffering, and whose hour
      Was drained to its last sand in weal or woe,
So that the trunk survived both fruit and flower;

      All those whose fame or infamy must grow   125
Till the great winter[16] lay the form and name
      Of their own earth with them forever low,

All but the sacred few[17] who could not tame
      Their spirits to the Conqueror, but as soon
As they had touched the world with living flame   130

      Fled back like eagles to their native noon,
Or those who put aside the diadem
      Of earthly thrones or gems, till the last one

Were there; for they of Athens and Jerusalem
      Were neither mid the mighty captives seen   135
Nor mid the ribald crowd that followed them

---

[13]The celebrants of Roman triumph would soon lose their own freedom under Roman imperialism.

[14]Was missing.

[15]Have subdued others in their own age.

[16]Eternal death.

[17]Visionary reformers including, implicitly, Shelley.

Or fled before . . . . Swift, fierce and obscene
The wild dance maddens in the van, and those
    Who lead it, fleet as shadows on the green,

Outspeed the chariot and without repose   140
    Mix with each other in tempestuous measure
To savage music . . . . Wilder as it grows,

    They, tortured by the agonizing pleasure,
Convulsed and on the rapid whirlwinds spun
    Of that fierce spirit, whose unholy leisure   145

Was soothed by mischief since the world begun,
    Throw back their heads and loose their streaming hair,
And in their dance round her who dims the Sun

    Maidens and youths fling their wild arms in air
As their feet twinkle; they recede, and now   150
    Bending within each other's atmosphere

Kindle invisibly; and as they glow
    Like moths by light attracted and repelled,
Oft to new bright destruction come and go.

    Till like two clouds into one vale impelled   155
That shake the mountains when their lightnings mingle
    And die in rain,—the fiery band which held

Their natures, snaps . . . ere the shock cease to tingle
    One falls and then another in the path
Senseless, nor is the desolation single,   160

    Yet ere I can say *where* the chariot hath
Past over them; nor other trace I find
    But as of foam after the Ocean's wrath

Is spent upon the desert shore.—Behind,
    Old men, and women foully disarrayed   165
Shake their grey hair in the insulting wind,

    Limp in the dance and strain, with limbs decayed,
To reach the car of light which leaves them still
    Farther behind and deeper in the shade.

But not the less with impotence of will   170
      They wheel, though ghastly shadows interpose
Round them and round each other, and fulfill

      Their work and to the dust whence they arose
Sink and corruption veils them as they lie
      And frost in these performs what fire in those.[18]   175

Struck to the heart by this sad pageantry,
      Half to myself I said, "And what is this?
Whose shape is that within the car? and why"—

      I would have added—"is all here amiss?"
But a voice answered . . . "Life" . . . I turned and knew   180
      (O Heaven have mercy on such wretchedness!)

That what I thought was an old root which grew
      To strange distortion out of the hill side
Was indeed one of that deluded crew,

      And that the grass which methought hung so wide   185
And white, was but his thin discoloured hair,
      And that the holes it vainly sought to hide

Were or had been eyes.—"If thou canst forbear
      To join the dance, which I had well forborne,"
Said the grim Feature,[19] of my thought aware,   190

      "I will now tell that which to this deep scorn
Led me and my companions, and relate
      The progress of the pageant since the morn.

If thirst of knowledge doth not thus abate,
      Follow it even to the night, but I   195
Am weary" . . . Then like one who with the weight

      Of his own words is staggered, wearily
He paused, and ere he could resume, I cried,
      "First who art thou?" . . . "Before thy memory

---

[18]Performed in those.

[19]Shape or form; Milton's Death is as a "grim Feature" (*PL* 10.279).

I feared, loved, hated, suffered, did, and died,   200
    And if the spark with which Heaven lit my spirit
Earth had with purer nutriment supplied

    Corruption would not now thus much inherit
Of what was once Rousseau[20]—nor this disguise
    Stain that within which still disdains to wear it.—   205

If I have been extinguished, yet there rise
    A thousand beacons from the spark I bore."—
"And who are those chained to the car?" "The Wise,

    The great, the unforgotten: they who wore
Mitres and helms and crowns, or wreathes of light,[21]   210
    Signs of thought's empire over thought; their lore

Taught them not this—to know themselves; their might
    Could not repress the mutiny within,
And for the morn of truth they feigned, deep night

    Caught them ere evening." "Who is he with chin   215
Upon his breast and hands crost on his chain?"
    "The Child of a fierce hour; he sought to win

The world, and lost all it did contain
    Of greatness, in its hope destroyed; and more
Of fame and peace than Virtue's self can gain   220

    Without the opportunity which bore
Him on its eagle's pinion to the peak
    From which a thousand climbers have before

---

[20]Jean-Jacques Rousseau (1712–78), philosophical idealist whose writings provided the foundation of the French Revolution, which led first to civil war and terror, then to Napoleonic tyranny; author of *Julie, ou la Nouvelle Heloise*, a novel of erotic passion and an implicit polemic against restraint (Rousseau abandoned his several illegitimate offspring to orphanages), and of *Émile, ou l'Education*—a program of liberal inquiry in harmony with nature, but also of "natural" subjection of women, much criticized by Mary Shelley's mother, Mary Wollstonecraft, in *A Vindication of the Rights of Woman* (1792).

[21]Mitres: Cardinals' hats; wreathes of light: saints' haloes. Shelley sees saints as mere institutionalized icons of a repressive religion.

Fall'n as Napoleon fell."—I felt my cheek
　　　　Alter to see the great form pass away　　　　225
Whose grasp had left the giant world so weak

　　　　That every pigmy[22] kicked it as it lay—
And much I grieved to think how power and will
　　　　In opposition rule our mortal day—

And why God made irreconcilable　　　　230
　　　　Good and the means of good; and for despair
I half disdained mine eye's desire to fill

　　　　With the spent vision of the times that were
And scarce have ceased to be . . . "Dost thou behold,"
　　　　Said then my guide, "those spoilers spoiled, Voltaire,　　235

Frederic, and Kant, Catherine, and Leopold,
　　　　Chained hoary anarch, demagogue and sage[23]
Whose name the fresh world thinks already old—

　　　　For in the battle Life and they did wage
She[24] remained conqueror—I was overcome　　　　240
　　　　By my own heart alone, which neither age

Nor tears nor infamy nor now the tomb
　　　　Could temper to its object."—"Let them pass"—
I cried—"the world and its mysterious doom

　　　　Is not so much more glorious than it was　　　　245
That I desire to worship those who drew
　　　　New figures on its false and fragile glass

As the old faded."—"Figures ever new
　　　　Rise on the bubble, paint them how you may;
We have but thrown, as those before us threw,　　　　250

[22]The monarchs overthrown by Napoleon returned with a vengeance after Waterloo.

[23]Shelley has no admiration for Voltaire and the contemporary "enlightened despots" (Frederick "the Great" of Prussia, Catherine "the Great" of Russia, Leopold Grand Duke of Tuscany) or even philosopher Immanuel Kant, whose philosophical idealism turned away from political concerns.

[24]Life.

Our shadows on it as it past away.
But mark, how chained to the triumphal chair
　　The mighty phantoms of an elder day—

All that is mortal of great Plato there
　　Expiates the joy and woe his master knew not;[25]　　255
That star that ruled his doom was far too fair—

　　And Life, where long that flower of Heaven grew not,
Conquered the heart by love which gold or pain
　　Or age or sloth or slavery could subdue not—

And near [　　] walk the [　　　] twain,　　260
　　The tutor and his pupil,[26] whom Dominion
Followed as tame as vulture in a chain.—

　　The world was darkened beneath either pinion
Of him whom from the flock of conquerors
　　Fame singled as her thunderbearing minion;　　265

The other long outlived both woes and wars,
　　Throned in new thoughts of men, and still had kept
The jealous keys of truth's eternal doors

　　If Bacon's spirit [　　]27 had not leapt
Like lightning out of darkness; he compelled　　270
　　The Proteus shape of Nature's[28] as it slept

To wake and to unbar the caves that held
　　The treasure of the secrets of its reign—
See the great bards of old who inly quelled

　　The passions which they sung, as by their strain[29]　　275
May well be known: their living melody
　　Tempers its own contagion to the vein

[25]Unlike the sexually restrained Socrates, Plato loved the boy Aster (Greek for "star"), composing for him the epigram quoted in the epigraph to *Adonais*.

[26]Aristotle and Alexander (the Great).

[27]Bacon's science was inductive, a swerve from the Aristotelian tradition of deductive reasoning.

[28]"Nature's spirit"; Proteus: sea god who alters his shape to elude capture.

[29]Song; the strain of their disciplined emotions.

Of those who are infected with it—I
     Have suffered[30] what I wrote, or viler pain!—

————

And so my words were seeds of misery—   280
     Even as the deeds of others."[31]—"Not[32] as theirs,"
I said—he pointed to a company

     In which I recognized amid the heirs
Of Caesar's crime from him to Constantine,[33]
     The Anarchs[34] old whose force and murderous snares   285

Had founded many a sceptre bearing line
     And spread the plague of blood and gold abroad,[35]
And Gregory and John and men divine[36]

     Who rose like shadows between Man and god
Till that eclipse, still hanging under Heaven,   290
     Was worshipped by the world o'er which they strode

For the true Sun it quenched.[37]—"Their power was given
     But to destroy," replied the leader—"I
Am one of those who have created, even

     If it be but a world of agony."—   295
"Whence camest thou and whither goest thou?
     How did thy course begin," I said, "and why?

Mine eyes are sick of this perpetual flow
     Of people, and my heart of one sad thought.—
Speak."—"Whence I came, partly I seem to know,   300

[30]Suffered the experience or consequences of.

[31]Rousseau's works had a corrupting influence.

[32]Your deeds are not as bad.

[33]First Christian emperor of Rome, founder of the Holy Roman Empire.

[34]Tyrants.

[35]The Crusades.

[36]Church fathers.

[37]The eclipse of Christ's philosophy by popes, emperors, and theologians, involves the pun of eclipsed Son in eclipsed Sun.

And how and by what paths I have been brought
To this dread pass, methinks even thou mayst guess;
    Why this should be my mind can compass not;

Whither the conqueror hurries me still less.
    But follow thou, and from spectator turn   305
Actor or victim in this wretchedness,

    And what thou wouldst be taught I then may learn
From thee.—Now listen[38] . . . In the April prime
    When all the forest tops began to burn

With kindling green, touched by the azure clime   310
    Of the young year, I found myself asleep
Under a mountain which from unknown time

    Had yawned into a cavern high and deep,
And from it came a gentle rivulet
    Whose water like clear air in its calm sweep   315

Bent the soft grass and kept for ever wet
    The stems of the sweet flowers, and filled the grove
With sound which all who hear must needs forget

    All pleasure and all pain, all hate and love,
Which they had known before that hour of rest: 320
    A sleeping mother then would dream not of

The only child who died upon her breast
    At eventide, a king would mourn no more
The crown of which his brow was dispossest

    When the sun lingered o'er the Ocean floor   325
To gild his rival's new prosperity.—
    Thou wouldst forget thus vainly to deplore

Ills, which if ills, can find no cure from thee,
    The thought of which no other sleep will quell
Nor other music blot from memory—   330

---

[38]Rousseau's narrative of his dream-vision recapitulates the poet-narrator's dream in which he appears. The dream-within-a-dream mirroring bodes an infinite regression that has its counterpart in the potentially unending *terza rima*.

So sweet and deep is the oblivious spell.[39]—
Whether my life had been before that sleep
    The Heaven which I imagine, or a Hell

Like this harsh world in which I wake to weep,
    I know not. I arose and for a space   335
The scene of woods and waters seemed to keep,

    Though it was now broad day, a gentle trace
Of light diviner than the common Sun
    Sheds on the common Earth, but all the place

Was filled with many sounds woven into one   340
    Oblivious melody, confusing sense
Amid the gliding waves and shadows dun;

    And as I looked the bright omnipresence
Of morning through the orient cavern[40] flowed,
    And the Sun's image radiantly intense   345

Burned on the waters of the well that glowed
    Like gold, and threaded all the forest maze
With winding paths of emerald fire—there stood

    Amid the sun, as he amid the blaze
Of his own glory, on the vibrating   350
    Floor of the fountain, paved with flashing rays,

A shape all light, which with one hand did fling
    Dew on the earth, as if she were the Dawn
Whose invisible rain forever seemed to sing

    A silver music on the mossy lawn,   355
And still before her on the dusky grass
    Iris her many coloured scarf had drawn.—

---

[39]Producing forgetfulness.

[40]The eastern sky, images as a dome-like cavern.

In her right hand she bore a chrystal glass
    Mantling with bright Nepenthe;[41]—the fierce splendour
Fell from her as she moved under the mass   360

    Of the deep cavern, and with palms[42] so tender
Their tread broke not the mirror of its billow,
    Glided along the river, and did bend her

Head under the dark boughs, till like a willow
    Her fair hair swept the bosom of the stream   365
That whispered with delight to be their pillow.—

    As one enamoured is upborne in dream
O'er lily-paven lakes mid silver mist
    To wondrous music, so this shape might seem

Partly to tread the waves with feet which kist   370
    The dancing foam, partly to glide along
The airs that roughened the moist amethyst,

    Or the slant morning beams that fell among
The trees, or the soft shadows of the trees;
    And her feet ever to the ceaseless song   375

Of leaves and winds and waves and birds and bees
    And falling drops moved in a measure new
Yet sweet, as on the summer evening breeze

    Up from the lake a shape of golden dew
Between two rocks, athwart the rising moon,   380
    Dances in the wind, where eagle never flew.—

And still her feet, no less than the sweet tune
    To which they moved, seemed as they moved, to blot
The thoughts of him who gazed on them, and soon

---

[41]Greek for "no pain"—a drug to wipe out all memory of pain, anger, and sorrow. The woman with the transforming goblet may be a divine angel or may recall Circe, whose drug enchants Ulysses' sailors, turning them into beasts.

[42]Foot soles.

All that was seemed as if it had been not,   385
As if the gazer's mind was strewn beneath
  Her feet like embers, and she, thought by thought,

Trampled its fires into the dust of death,
  As Day upon the threshold of the east
Treads out the lamps of night,[43] until the breath   390

  Of darkness reillumines even the least
Of heaven's living eyes—like day she came,
  Making the night a dream; and ere she ceased

To move, as one between desire and shame
  Suspended, I said—'If, as it doth seem,   395
Thou comest from the realm without a name,

  Into this valley of perpetual dream,
Shew whence I came, and where I am, and why—
  Pass not away upon the passing stream.'

'Arise and quench thy thirst,' was her reply,   400
  And as a shut lily, stricken by the wand
Of dewy morning's vital alchemy,[44]

  I rose; and, bending at her sweet command,
Touched with faint lips the cup she raised,
  And suddenly my brain became as sand   405

Where the first wave had more than half erased
  The track of deer on desert Labrador,
Whilst the fierce wolf from which they fled amazed

  Leaves his stamp visibly upon the shore
Until the second bursts—so on my sight   410
  Burst a new Vision never seen before.—

---

[43]The sun obliterates starlight.

[44]Alchemy is the science, still pursued in the 18th c. by no less a student than Isaac Newton, of discovering how to turn base metals into gold.

And the fair shape waned in the coming light
       As veil by veil the silent splendour drops
From Lucifer,[45] amid the chrysolite[46]

       Of sunrise ere it strike the mountain tops—   415
And as the presence of that fairest planet[47]
       Although unseen is felt by one who hopes

That his day's path may end as he began it
       In that star's smile, whose light is like the scent
Of a jonquil when evening breezes fan it,   420

       Or the soft note in which his dear lament
The Brescian shepherd breathes,[48] or the caress
       That turned his weary slumber to content.—

So knew I in that light's severe excess
       The presence of that shape which on the stream   425
Moved, as I moved along the wilderness,

       More dimly than a day appearing dream,
The ghost of a forgotten form of sleep
       A light from Heaven whose half extinguished beam

Through the sick day in which we wake to weep   430
       Glimmers, forever sought, forever lost.—
So did that shape its obscure tenour keep

       Beside my path, as silent as a ghost;
But the new Vision, and its cold bright car,
       With savage music, stunning music, crost   435

The forest, and as if from some dread war
       Triumphantly returning, the loud million
Fiercely extolled the fortune of her star.—

[45]Lucifer: alternative name for Venus as morning and evening star, and Satan's name before he fell from Heaven.

[46]Pale yellow-green mineral.

[47]Lucifer/Venus, again.

[48]"The favorite song, 'Stanco di pascolar le peccorelle,' is a Brescian national air." [Mary Shelley's note.]

A moving arch of victory the vermilion
And green and azure plumes of Iris had   440
    Built high over her wind-winged pavilion,[49]

And underneath aetherial glory clad
    The wilderness, and far before her flew
The tempest of the splendour which forbade

    Shadow to fall from leaf or stone;—the crew   445
Seemed in that light like atomies[50] that dance
    Within a sunbeam.—Some upon the new

Embroidery of flowers that did enhance
    The grassy vesture of the desert, played,
Forgetful of the chariot's swift advance;   450

    Others stood gazing till within the shade
Of the great mountain its light left them dim.—
    Others outspeeded it, and others made

Circles around it like the clouds that swim
    Round the high moon in a bright sea of air,   455
And more did follow, with exulting hymn,

    The chariot and the captives fettered there,
But all like bubbles on an eddying flood
    Fell into the same track at last and were

Borne onward.—I among the multitude   460
    Was swept; me sweetest flowers delayed not long,
Me not the shadow nor the solitude,

    Me not the falling stream's Lethean[51] song,
Me, not the phantom of that early form
    Which moved upon its motion,—but among   465

---

[49]The rainbow forms a triumphal arch over the path taken by Life's car.
[50]Atoms of dust.
[51]The underworld river Lethe's water produces forgetfulness of life on earth.

The thickest billows of the living storm
    I plunged, and bared my bosom to the clime
Of that cold light, whose airs too soon deform.—

    Before the chariot had begun to climb
The opposing steep of that mysterious dell,   470
    Behold a wonder worthy of the rhyme

Of him[52] whom from the lowest depths of Hell
    Through every Paradise and through all glory
Love led serene, and who returned to tell

    In words of hate and awe the wondrous story   475
How all things are transfigured, except Love;
    For deaf as is a sea which wrath makes hoary

The world can hear not the sweet notes that move
    The sphere whose light is melody to lovers—
A wonder worthy of his rhyme—the grove   480

    Grew dense with shadows to its inmost covers,
The earth was grey with phantoms, and the air
    Was peopled with dim forms, as when there hovers

A flock of vampire-bats before the glare
    Of the tropic sun, bring ere evening   485
Strange night upon some Indian isle,—thus were

    Phantoms diffused around, and some did fling
Shadows of shadows, yet unlike themselves,
    Behind them, some like eaglets on the wing

Were lost in the white blaze, others like elves   490
    Danced in a thousand unimagined shapes
Upon the sunny streams and grassy shelves;

    And others sate chattering like restless apes
On vulgar paws and voluble like fire.
    Some made a cradle of the ermined capes   495

---

[52]Dante, the famous poet of *terza rima*, the rhyme of *The Divine Comedy*, to which
Shelley alludes.

Of kingly mantles, some upon the tiar[53]
    Of pontiffs sate like vultures, others played
Within the crown which girt with empire

    A baby's or an idiot's brow, and made
Their nests in it; the old anatomies[54]   500
    Sate hatching their base broods under the shade

Of demon wings, and laughed from their dead eyes
    To reassume the delegated power
Arrayed in which these worms did monarchize

    Who make this earth their charnel.[55]—Others more   505
Humble, like falcons sate upon the fist
    Of common men, and round their heads did soar,

Or like small gnats and flies, as thick as mist
    On evening marshes, thronged about the brow
Of lawyer, statesman, priest and theorist,   510

    And others like discoloured flakes of snow
On fairest bosoms and the sunniest hair
    Fell, and were melted by the youthful glow

Which they extinguished; for like tears, they were
    A veil to those from whose faint lids they rained   515
In drops of sorrow.— I became aware

    Of whence those forms proceeded which thus stained
The track in which we moved; after brief space
    From every form the beauty slowly waned,

From every firmest limb and fairest face   520
    The strength and freshness fell like dust, and left
The action and the shape without the grace

---

[53]Papal crown.
[54]Skeletons.
[55]Charnel house, mortuary chapel, or burial place.

Of life; the marble brow of youth was cleft
With care, and in the eyes where once hope shone
    Desire like a lioness bereft   525

Of its last cub, glared ere it died; each one
    Of that great crowd sent forth incessantly
These shadows, numerous as the dead leaves blown

    In Autumn evening from a poplar tree—
Each, like himself and like each other were,   530
    At first, but soon distorted, seemed to be

Obscure clouds moulded by the casual air;
    And of this stuff the car's creative ray
Wrought all the busy phantoms that were there

    As the sun shapes the clouds—thus, on the way   535
Mask after mask fell from the countenance
    And form of all, and long before the day

Was old, the joy which waked like Heaven's glance
    The sleepers in the oblivious valley, died,
And some grew weary of the ghastly dance   540

    And fell, as I have fallen by the way side,
Those soonest from whose forms most shadows past
    And least of strength and beauty did abide.—"

"Then, what is Life?" I said . . . the cripple cast
    His eye upon the car which now had rolled   545
Onward, as if that look must be the last,

    And answered . . . . "Happy those for whom the fold
Of

⁓ Contemporary Reviews of Shelley's Writing

In Shelley's lifetime, reviewing was polemical—part of cultural warfare—politically motivated and often personally vicious. There were periodicals from all parties. Thomas Wooler's *Black Dwarf* was anti-government and radically pro-reform; John and Leigh Hunt's liberal *Examiner* was less defiant in stance; the *New Monthly Magazine* and the older *Quarterly Review* were staunchly Tory, anti-Jacobin, and anti-Napoleon. *Blackwood's Edinburgh Magazine* wielded class snobbery against middle-class poets such as Keats and Hunt, "Cockney" upstarts.

Shelley was sometimes called "Cockney" for his association with Hunt and was always attacked for his unorthodox religious views, including his atheism, and for his views on social institutions (such as marriage). Recognizing his talents, critics wanted to disarm his influence. Some reviewers attacked him as a bad poet so they could dismiss his opinions and morals. Others called his writing difficult and obscure. Yet even some of the most negative reviews can concede Shelley's strengths as writer and thinker. Romantic-era reviews were typically unsigned, to convey the sense of corporate judgment, rather than one reviewer's opinion. The reviews often included long passages from the works, not included here.

from *Blackwood's Edinburgh Magazine*

Founded in 1817 as a Tory alternative to the powerful Whig journal, The Edinburgh Review, *the politically conservative* Blackwood's *published widely in poetry, fiction, and essays and attacked, often satirically, liberal and reformist writers. In October 1817 it began the arti-*

cles on "*the Cockney School of Poetry*" targeting Leigh Hunt, Keats, and, eventually, Shelley. This unsigned review may be by J. G. Lockhart, who despised Shelley's political and moral beliefs but appreciated him as a poet, or perhaps by John Wilson and W. S. Lockhart.

7 (September 1820): 679–87. [review of PU *and Other Poems*]

Whatever may be the difference of men's opinions concerning the measure of Mr. Shelley's poetical power, there is one point in regard to which all must be agreed, and that is his Audacity. [. . .]

It would be highly absurd to deny, that this gentleman has manifested very extraordinary powers of language and imagination in his treatment of the allegory, however grossly and miserably he may have tried to pervert its purpose and meaning. But of this more anon. In the meantime, what can be more deserving of reprobation than the course which he is allowing his intellect to take, and that too at the very time when he ought to be laying the foundations of a lasting and honourable name. There is no occasion for going round about the bush to hint what the poet himself so unblushingly and sinfully blazoned forth in every part of his production. With him, it is quite evident that the Jupiter whose downfall has been predicted by Prometheus, means nothing more than Religion in general, that is, every human system of religious belief; and that, with the fall of this, he considers it perfectly necessary (as indeed we also believe, though with far different feelings) that every system of human government also should give way and perish. The patience of the contemplative spirit in Prometheus is to be followed by the daring of the active Demogorgon, at whose touch all "old thrones" are at once and for ever to be cast down into the dust. It appears too plainly, from the luscious pictures with which his play terminates, that Mr. Shelley looks forward to an unusual relaxation of all moral *rules*—or rather, indeed, to the extinction of all moral feelings, except that of a certain mysterious indefinable *kindliness*, as the natural and necessary result of the overthrow of all civil government and religious belief. It appears, still more wonderfully, that he contemplates this state of things as the ideal SUMMUM BONUM.[1] In short it is quite impossible that there should exist a more pestiferous mixture of blasphemy, sedition, and sensuality,

[1]Highest good.

than is visible in the whole structure and strain of this poem—which, nevertheless, and notwithstanding all the detestation its principles excite, must and will be considered by all that read it attentively, as abounding in poetical beauties of the highest order—as presenting many specimens not easily to be surpassed, of the moral sublime of eloquence—as overflowing with pathos, and most magnificent in description. Where can be found a spectacle more worthy of sorrow than such a man performing and glorying in the performance of such things? His evil ambition,—from all he has yet written, but most of all, from what he has last and best written, his *Prometheus*,—appears to be no other, than that of obtaining the highest place among those poets,—enemies, not friends, of their species,—who, as a great and virtuous poet has well said (putting evil consequence close after evil cause),

Profane the God-given strength, and *mar the lofty line.*[2] [. . .]

[. . .] But the truth of the matter is this, and it is impossible to conceal it were we willing to do so, that Mr. Shelley is destined to leave a great name behind him, and that we, as lovers of true genius, are most anxious that this name should ultimately be pure as well as great.

[. . .] Let us hope that Percy Bysshe Shelley is not destined to leave behind him, like [Voltaire], a name for ever detestable to the truly FREE and the truly WISE. He talks in his preface about MILTON, as a "Republican," and a "bold inquirer into Morals and religion." Could any thing make us despise Mr. Shelley's understanding, it would be such an instance of voluntary blindness as this! Let us hope, that ere long a lamp of genuine truth may be kindled within his "bright mind"; and that he may walk in its light the path of the true demigods of English genius, having, like them, learned to "fear God and honour the king."[3]

from *The London Magazine and Monthly Critical and Dramatic Review* 2

This review of PU and Other Poems *is probably by the editor of* The London Magazine, *John Scott, who despised politically influenced reviewing.*

---

[2]Walter Scott, *Marmion: A Tale of Flodden Field* (1808), Introduction, l. 283.

[3]"Honour all men. Love the brotherhood. Fear God. Honour the king." 1 Peter 2.17.

(September and October 1820): 306–08, 382–91.

[September, pp. 306–09]
[. . .] Of *Prometheus Unbound*, the principal poem in this beautiful collection, we profess to give no account. It must be reserved for our second series, as it requires more than ordinary attention. The minor pieces are stamped throughout with all the vigorous peculiarities of the writer's mind, and are everywhere strongly impregnated with the alchymical properties of genius. But what we principally admire in them is their strong and healthy freshness, and the tone of interest that they elicit. They possess the fever and flush of poetry; the fragrant perfume and sunshine of a summer's morning, with its genial and kindly benevolence. It is impossible to peruse them without admiring the peculiar property of the author's mind, which can doff in an instant the cumbersome garments of metaphysical speculations, and throw itself naked as it were into the arms of nature and humanity. The beautiful and singularly original poem of "The Cloud" will evince proofs of our opinion, and show the extreme force and freshness with which the writer can impregnate his poetry.

[October, pp. 382–91]
This is one of the most stupendous of those works which the daring and vigorous spirit of modern poetry and thought has created. We despair of conveying to our readers, either by analysis or description, any idea of its gigantic outlines, or of its innumerable sweetnesses. It is a vast wilderness of beauty, which at first seems stretching out on all sides into infinitude, yet the boundaries of which are all cast by the poet; in which the wildest paths have a certain and noble direction; and the strangest shapes which haunt its recesses, voices of gentleness and of wisdom. It presents us with the oldest forms of Greek mythology, informed with the spirit of fresh enthusiasm and of youngest hope; and mingles with these the creatures of a new mythology, in which earth, and the hosts of heaven, spirits of time and of eternity, are embodied and vivified, to unite in the rapturous celebration of the reign of Love over the universe.

This work is not, as the title would lead us to anticipate, a mere attempt to imitate the old tragedy of the Greeks. [. . .] But the subject is so treated, that we lose sight of persons in principles, and soon feel that all the splendid machinery around us is but the shadow of things unseen, the outward panoply of bright expectations and theories, which appear to the author's mind instinct with eternal and eternally progressive blessings. The fate of Prometheus probably suggested, even to the heroic bard by whom it was celebrated in older time, the temporary predominance of brute force over intellect; the oppression of right by might; and the final deliverance of the spirit of humanity from the iron grasp of its foes. But, in so far as we can judge from the mighty fragment which time has spared,[1] he was contented with exhibiting the visible picture of the magnanimous victim, and with representing his deliverance, by means of Hercules, as a mere personal event, having no symbolical meaning. In Mr. Shelley's piece, the deliverance of Prometheus, which is attended by the dethroning of Jupiter, is scarcely other than a symbol of the peaceful triumph of goodness over power; of the subjection of might to right; and the restoration of love to the full exercise of its benign and all-penetrating sympathies. To represent vividly and poetically this vast moral change, is, we conceive, the design of this drama, with all its inward depths of mystical gloom, its pregnant clouds of imagination, its spiry eminences of icy splendour, and its fair regions overspread by a light "which never was by sea or land,"[2] which consecrates and harmonizes all things.

To the ultimate prospect exhibited by that philosophical system which Mr. Shelley's piece embodies, we have no objection. There is nothing pernicious in the belief that, even on earth, man is destined to attain a high degree of happiness and of virtue. The greatest and wisest have ever trusted with the most confiding faith to that nature, with whose best qualities they were so richly gifted. They have felt that in man were undeveloped capabilities of excellence; stores of greatness, suffered to lie hidden beneath basest lumber; sealed up fountains, whence a brighter day might loosen streams of fresh and ever-living joys. In the worst and most degraded minds, vestiges of goodness are not wanting; some old recollections of early virtue; some feeling of wild generosity or unconquerable love; some divine instinct; some fragments of lofty principle; some unextinguishable longings after nobleness and peace, indicate that there is good in man which can never yield to the storms of passion or the decays of time. On these divine instances of pure and holy virtue; on history; on science; on imagination; on the essences of love and hope; we may safely rest, in the expectation that a softer and tenderer light will ultimately dawn on our species. We further agree with Mr. Shelley, that Revenge is not the weapon with

[1] Aeschylus's *Prometheus Bound.*
[2] Echoing Wordsworth's *Elegiac Stanzas* on Peele Castle, l. 15 (i.e., "the consecration, and the Poet's dream," l. 16).

which men should oppose the erring and the guilty. He only speaks in accordance with every wise writer on legislation, when he deprecates the infliction of one vibration of unnecessary pain on the most criminal. He only echoes the feeling of every genuine Christian, when he contends for looking with deep-thoughted pity on the vicious, or regarding them tenderly as the unfortunate, and for striving "not to be overcome of evil, but to overcome evil with good."[3] He only coincides with every friend of his species, when he deplores the obstacles which individuals and systems have too often opposed to human progress. But when he would attempt to realize in an instant his glorious visions; when he would treat men as though they are now the fit inhabitants of an earthly paradise; when he would cast down all restraint and authority as enormous evils; and would leave mankind to the guidance of passions yet unsubdued, and of desires yet unregulated, we must protest against his wishes, as tending fearfully to retard the good which he would precipitate. Happy, indeed, will be that time, of which our great philosophical poet, Wordsworth, speaks, when love shall be an "unclouded light, and joy its own security."[4] But we shall not hasten this glorious era by destroying those forms and dignities of the social state, which are essential to the restraint of the worst passions, and serviceable to the nurture of the kindliest affections. The stream of human energy is gathering strength; but it would only be scattered in vain, were we rashly to destroy the boundaries which now confine it in its deep channel; and it can only be impeded by the impatient attempt to strike the shores with its agitated waters.

Although there are some things in Mr. Shelley's philosophy against which we feel it a duty thus to protest, we must not suffer our difference of opinion to make us insensible to his genius. As a poem, the work before us is replete with clear, pure, and majestical imagery, accompanied by a harmony as rich and various as that of the loftiest of our English poets.

from *The Quarterly Review* 26

Founded in 1809, the Quarterly *was a fiercely conservative supporter of the aristocracy, the monarchy, and the Anglican Church, and its publishers targeted writers, especially from the lower classes, whose*

[3]Romans 12.21.

[4]Wordsworth, *Ode to Duty* (1807), ll. 18–19.

politics were objectionable—but even gentry such as Shelley were vulnerable. In April 1818 the Quarterly *published the notorious and supposedly fatal attack on Keats's* Endymion.

(October 1821): 168–80 [review of *PU and Other Poems*]

A great lawyer of the present day is said to boast of practising three different modes of writing: one which any body can read; another which only himself can read; and a third, which neither he nor any body else can read. So Mr. Shelley may plume himself upon writing in three different styles: one which can be generally understood; another which can be understood only by the author; and a third which is absolutely and intrinsically unintelligible. Whatever his command may be of the first and second of these styles, this volume is a most satisfactory testimonial of his proficiency in the last.

If we might venture to express a general opinion of what far surpasses our comprehension, we should compare the poems contained in this volume to the visions of gay colours mingled with darkness, which often in childhood, when we shut our eyes, seem to revolve at an immense distance around us. In Mr. Shelley's poetry all is brilliance, vacuity, and confusion. We are dazzled by the multitude of words which sound as if they denoted something very grand or splendid: fragments of images pass in crowds before us; but when the procession has gone by, and the tumult of it is over, not a trace of it remains upon the memory. The mind, fatigued and perplexed, is mortified by the consciousness that its labour has not been rewarded by the acquisition of a single distinct conception; the ear, too, is dissatisfied: for the rhythm of the verse is often harsh and unmusical; and both the ear and the understanding are disgusted by new and uncouth words, and by the awkward, and intricate construction of the sentences.

The predominating characteristic of Mr. Shelley's poetry, however, is its frequent and total want of meaning. [. . .]

The want of meaning in Mr. Shelley's poetry takes different shapes. Sometimes it is impossible to attach any signification to his words; sometimes they hover on the verge between meaning and no meaning, so that a meaning may be obscurely conjectured by the reader, though none is expressed by the writer; and sometimes they convey ideas, which, taken separately, are sufficiently clear, but, when connected, are altogether incongruous. [. . .]

It may seem strange that such a volume should find readers, and still more strange that it should meet with admirers. We are ourselves surprized by the phenomenon: nothing similar to it occurred to us, till we recollected the numerous congregations which the incoherencies of an itinerant Methodist preacher attract. These preachers, without any connected train of thought, and without attempting to reason, or to attach any definite meaning to the terms which they use, pour out a deluge of sonorous words that relate to sacred objects and devout feelings. These words, connected as they are with all that is most venerable in the eyes of man, excite a multitude of pious associations in the hearer, and produce in him a species of mental intoxication. [. . .] In the same way, poetry like that of Mr. Shelley presents every where glittering constellations of words, which taken separately have a meaning, and either communicate some activity to the imagination, or dazzle it by their brilliance. [. . .] The reader is conscious that his mind is raised from a state of stagnation, and he is willing to believe, that he is astounded and bewildered, not by the absurdity, but by the originality and sublimity of the author.

It appears to us much more surprizing, that any man of education should write such poetry as that of *Prometheus Unbound*, than, that when written, it should find admirers. [. . .] Mr. Shelley tells us, that he imitates the Greek tragic poets: can he be so blinded by self-love, as not to be aware that his productions have not one feature of likeness to what have been deemed classical works, in any country or in any age?

[. . .] The proofs of Mr. Shelley's genius, which his admirers allege, are the very exaggeration, copiousness of verbiage, and incoherence of ideas which we complain of as intolerable. [. . .] The want of meaning is called sublimity, absurdity becomes venerable under the name of originality, the jumble of metaphor is the richness of imagination, and even the rough, clumsy, confused structure of the style, with not unfrequent violations of the rules of grammar, is, forsooth, the sign and effect of a bold overflowing genius, that disdains to walk in common trammels. [. . .]

But great as are Mr. Shelley's sins against sense and taste, would that we had nothing more to complain of! Unfortunately, to his long list of demerits he has added the most flagrant offences against morality and religion. We should abstain from quoting instances, were it not that we think his language too gross and too disgusting to be dangerous to any but those who are corrupted beyond the hope of amendment. [. . .]

[. . . It] is a praiseworthy precaution in an author, to temper irreligion and sedition with nonsense, so that he may avail himself, if need be, of the plea of lunacy before the tribunals of his country. [. . .] But what is to be said of a man, who, like Mr. Shelley, wantonly and unnecessarily goes out of his way, not to reason against, but to revile Christianity and its author? Let him adduce his arguments against our religion, and we shall tell him where to find them answered: but let him not presume to insult the world, and to profane the language in which he writes, by rhyming invectives against a faith of which he knows nothing but the name.

The real cause of his aversion to Christianity is easily discovered. Christianity is the great prop of the social order of the civilized world; this social order is the object of Mr. Shelley's hatred; and, therefore, the pillar must be demolished, that the building may tumble down.

[. . .] Mr. Shelley says, that his intentions are pure. Pure! They be so in his vocabulary; for, (to say nothing of his having unfortunately mistaken nonsense for poetry, and blasphemy for an imperious duty,) vice and irreligion, and the subversion of society are, according to his system, pure and holy things; Christianity, and moral virtue, and social order, are alone impure. But we care not about his intentions, or by what epithet he may choose to characterize them, so long as his works exhale contagious mischief. On his own principles he must admit, that, in exposing to the public what we believe to be the character and tendency of his writings, we discharge a sacred duty. He professes to write in order to reform the world. The essence of the proposed reformation is the destruction of religion and government. Such a reformation is not to our taste; and he must, therefore, applaud us for scrutinizing the merits of works which are intended to promote so detestable a purpose. Of Mr. Shelley himself we know nothing, and desire to know nothing. Be his private qualities what they may, his poems (and it is only with his poems that we have any concern) are at war with reason, with taste, with virtue, in short, with all that dignifies man, or that man reveres.

from *The Literary Gazette and Journal of Belles Lettres* 255

> *Founded in 1817 for a popular readership, the weekly* Gazette *sponsored biased reviews that could make or break a reputation; this review of* Adonais *may be by the editor, William Jerdan.*

(December 8, 1821): 772–3

We have already given some of our columns to this writer's merits, and we will not now repeat our convictions of his incurable absurdity. On the last occasion of our alluding to him,[1] we were compelled to notice his horrid licentiousness and profaneness, his fearful offences to all the maxims that honorable minds are in the habit of respecting, and his plain defiance of Christianity. On the present occasion we are not met by so continued and regular a determination of insult, though there are atrocities to be found in the poem quite enough to make us caution our readers against its pages. "Adonais" is an elegy after *the manner of Moschus*, on a foolish young man, who, after writing some volumes of very weak, and, in the greater part, of very indecent poetry, died some time since of a consumption: the breaking down of an infirm constitution having, in all probability, been accelerated by the discarding his neck cloth, a practice of the cockney poets,[2] who look upon it as essential to genius, inasmuch as neither Michael Angelo, Raphael or Tasso are supposed to have worn those antispiritual incumbrances. [. . .]

[. . . Quotes as "a passage of memorable and ferocious blasphemy" lines 304-06: "He . . . with a sudden hand / Made bare his branded and ensanguined brow, / Which was like Cain's or Christ's"]

What can be said to the wretched person capable of this daring profanation. The name of the first murderer—the accurst of God—brought into the same aspect image with that of the Saviour of the World! We are scarcely satisfied that even to quote such passages may not be criminal. The subject is too repulsive for us to proceed even in expressing our disgust for the general folly that makes the Poem as miserable in point of authorship, as in point of principle. We know that among a certain class this outrage and this inanity meet with some attempt at palliation, under the idea that frenzy holds the pen. That any man who insults the common order of society, and denies the being of God, is essentially mad we never doubted. But for the madness, that retains enough of rationality to be wilfully mischievous, we can have no more lenity than for the appetites of a wild beast. The poetry of the work is *contemptible*— a mere collection of bloated words heaped on each other without

---

[1]Review of *Queen Mab*, published on 19 May 1821.

[2]The contemptuous term launched by *Blackwood's Edinburgh Magazine* in 1817 for Leigh Hunt and his circle, including Keats, Hazlitt, and Shelley.

order, harmony, or meaning; the refuse of a schoolboy's common-place book, full of the vulgarisms of pastoral poetry, yellow gems and blue stars, bright Phoebus and rosy-fingered Aurora; and of this stuff is Keats's wretched Elegy compiled. [. . .]

It is so far a fortunate thing that this piece of impious and utter absurdity can have little circulation in Britain. [. . .] Solemn as the subject is, (for in truth we must grieve for the early death of any youth of literary ambition,) it is hardly possible to help laughing at the mock solemnity with which Shelley charges the *Quarterly Review* for having murdered his friend with—a critique! If criticism killed the disciples of that school, Shelley would not have been alive to write an Elegy on another. [. . .]

Further Reading

Cultural, Intellectual, and Literary Contexts

Behrendt, Stephen C. *Royal Mourning and Regency Culture: Elegies and Memorials of Princess Charlotte*. Macmillan/St. Martin's, 1997.

Butler, Marilyn. *Romantics, Rebels and Reactionaries: English Literature and Its Background 1760–1830*. Oxford UP, 1981.

Chandler, James. *England in 1819: The Politics of Literary Culture and the Case of Romantic Historicism*. U of Chicago P, 1998.

Colley, Linda. *Britons: Forging the Nation, 1707–1837*. Yale UP, 1992.

Cox, Jeffrey N. *Poetry and Politics in the Cockney School: Keats, Shelley, Hunt and Their Circle*. Cambridge UP, 1998.

Curran, Stuart. *Poetic Form and British Romanticism*. Oxford UP, 1986.

Gaull, Marilyn. *English Romanticism: The Human Context*. W. W. Norton, 1988.

Low, Donald A. *That Sunny Dome: A Portrait of Regency Britain*. Dent, 1977.

McCalman, Iain. *Radical Underworld: Prophets, Revolutionaries and Pornographers in London, 1795–1840*. Cambridge UP, 1988.

Mee, Jon. *Romanticism, Enthusiasm, and Regulation: Poetics and the Policing of Culture in the Romantic Period*. Oxford UP, 2003.

Morton, Timothy, ed. *The Cambridge Companion to Percy Bysshe Shelley*. Cambridge UP, 2006.

Newlyn, Lucy. *Reading, Writing and Romanticism: The Anxiety of Reception*. Oxford UP, 2000.

Oerlemans, Onno. *Romanticism and the Materiality of Nature*. U of Toronto P, 2002.

Parker, Mark. *Literary Magazines and British Romanticism.* Cambridge UP, 2000.

Siskin, Clifford. *The Historicity of Romantic Discourse.* Oxford UP, 1988.

St. Clair, William. *The Reading Nation in the Romantic Period.* Cambridge UP, 2004.

Wolfson, Susan J. "Editorial Privilege: Mary Shelley and Percy Shelley's Audiences." In *The Other Mary Shelley: Beyond Frankenstein,* eds. Audrey A. Fisch, Anne K. Mellor, and Esther H. Schor. Oxford UP, 1993, 17–38.

———. *Formal Charges: The Shaping of Poetry in British Romanticism.* Stanford UP, 1997.

Wolfson, Susan J., and Peter Manning, eds. *The Longman Anthology of British Literature.* Volume 2a, *The Romantics and Their Contemporaries.* Longman, 2006.

Wood, Marcus. *Radical Satire and Print Culture 1790–1822.* Clarendon P, 1994.

Woodring, Carl. *Politics in English Romantic Poetry.* Harvard UP, 1970.

Percy Bysshe Shelley: Life and Work

Major Editions

Behrendt, Stephen C., ed. *Zastrozzi and St. Irvyne.* Broadview P, 2002.

Everest, Kelvin, gen. ed., and G. M. Matthews, ed. *The Poems of Shelley* (Longman Annotated English Poets series). Vol. 1 (1989), vol. 2 (2000); 3 vols. projected.

Forman, Harry Buxton, ed. *Percy Bysshe Shelley: Prose Works.* Reeves and Turner, 1876.

———. *The Poetical Works of Percy Bysshe Shelley.* 4 vols. Reeves and Turner, 1876.

Ingpen, Roger, and Walter E. Peck. *The Complete Works of Percy Bysshe Shelley.* 10 vols. Ernest Benn, 1926–30.

Murray, E. B., ed. *The Prose Works of Percy Bysshe Shelley.* Clarendon P, 1993.

Reiman, Donald H., and Neil Fraistat, eds. *Shelley's Poetry and Prose.* 2nd ed. W. W. Norton, 2002.

———, eds. *The Complete Poetry of Percy Bysshe Shelley.* Johns Hopkins UP. Vol. 1 (2000), vol. 2 (2004); 7 vols. projected.

Reiman, Donald H., and Sharon B. Powers, eds. *Shelley's Poetry and Prose*. W. W. Norton, 1977.

Shelley, Mary W., ed. *Posthumous Poems of Percy Bysshe Shelley*. John and Henry L. Hunt, 1824.

———. *The Poetical Works of Percy Bysshe Shelley*. 4 vols. Edward Moxon, 1839.

———. *Essays, Letters from Abroad, Translations and Fragments*. 2 vols. Edward Moxon, 1840.

Biographical Studies

Bieri, James. *Percy Bysshe Shelley: A Biography*. 2 vols. U of Delaware P, 2004–5.

Cameron, Kenneth Neill. *The Young Shelley: Genesis of a Radical*. Macmillan, 1950.

———. *Shelley: The Golden Years*. Harvard UP, 1974.

Holmes, Richard. *Shelley: The Pursuit*. Weidenfeld and Nicholson, 1974.

Reiman, Donald H. *Percy Bysshe Shelley*. Twayne/G. K. Hall, 1990.

St. Clair, William. *The Godwins and the Shelleys: The Biography of a Family*. Johns Hopkins UP, 1991.

White, Newman Ivey. *Shelley*. 2 vols. Alfred A. Knopf, 1940.

Wroe, Ann. *Being Shelley: The Poet's Search for Himself*. Pantheon, 2007.

Scholarly and Critical Studies

Behrendt, Stephen C. *Shelley and His Audiences*. U of Nebraska P, 1989.

Bennett, Betty T., and Stuart Curran, eds. *Shelley: Poet and Legislator of the World*. Johns Hopkins UP, 1996.

Clark, Timothy. *Embodying Revolution: The Figure of the Poet in Shelley*. Oxford UP, 1989.

Cronin, Richard. *Shelley's Poetic Thoughts*. St. Martin's, 1981.

Curran, Stuart. *Shelley's Annus Mirabilis: The Maturing of an Epic Vision*. Huntington Library, 1975.

Dawson, P. M. S. *The Unacknowledged Legislator: Shelley and Politics*. Clarendon Press, 1980.

Duff, David. *Romance and Revolution: Shelley and the Politics of a Genre*. Cambridge UP, 1994.

Ferber, Michael. *The Poetry of Shelley*. Penguin, 1993.

Hoagwood, Terence Alan. *Skepticism and Ideology: Shelley's Political Prose and Its Philosophical Context from Bacon to Marx*. U of Iowa P, 1988.

Hogle, Jerrold. *Shelley's Process: Radical Transference and the Development of His Major Works*. Oxford UP, 1988.

Hughes, Daniel. "Kindling and Dwindling: The Poetic Process in Shelley." *Keats-Shelley Journal* 13 (1964): 13–28.

Jones, Steven E. *Shelley's Satire: Violence, Exhortation, and Authority*. Northern Illinois UP, 1994.

Keach, William. *Shelley's Style*. Methuen, 1984.

Morton, Timothy. *Shelley and the Revolution in Taste: The Body and the Natural World*. Cambridge UP, 1994.

Roberts, Hugh. *Shelley and the Chaos of History: A New Politics of Poetry*. Pennsylvania State UP, 1997.

Robinson, Charles E. *Shelley and Byron: The Snake and Eagle Wreathed in Fight*. Johns Hopkins UP, 1976.

Ruston, Sharon. *Shelley and Vitality*. Palgrave Macmillan, 2005.

Scrivener, Michael Henry. *Radical Shelley: The Philosophical Anarchism and Utopian Thought of Percy Bysshe Shelley*. Princeton UP, 1982.

Sperry, Stuart. *Shelley's Major Verse: The Narrative and Dramatic Poetry*. Harvard UP, 1988.

Wasserman, Earl R. *Shelley: A Critical Reading*. Johns Hopkins UP, 1971.

Webb, Timothy. *Shelley: A Voice Not Understood*. Humanities P, 1977.

Weisman, Karen A. *Imageless Truth: Shelley's Poetic Fictions*. U of Pennsylvania P, 1994.

Wheatley, Kim. *Shelley and His Readers: Beyond Paranoid Politics*. U of Missouri P, 1999.

White, Newman Ivey. *The Unextinguished Hearth: Shelley and His Contemporary Critics*. Duke UP, 1938.

Wolfson, Susan J. "Keats Enters History: Autopsy, *Adonais*, and the Fame of Keats." In *Keats and History*, ed. Nicholas Roe. Cambridge UP, 1995, 17–45.